Boom, Bust, and Beyond

New Perspectives on the 1720 Stock Market Bubble

Edited by
Stefano Condorelli and Daniel Menning

DE GRUYTER
OLDENBOURG

ISBN 978-3-11-059056-2
e-ISBN (PDF) 978-3-11-059213-9
e-ISBN (EPUB) 978-3-11-059071-5

Library of Congress Control Number: 2019938927

Bibliographic information published by the Deutsche Nationalbibliothek
The Deutsche Nationalbibliothek lists this publication in the Deutsche Nationalbibliografie; detailed bibliographic data are available on the Internet at http://dnb.dnb.de.

Cover image: "If you want to escape poverty, then come and buy stock," Der Europäische Niemand 17 (1720). (Courtesy of Universitätsbibliothek Regensburg)
Printing and binding: CPI books GmbH, Leck

www.degruyter.com

Acknowledgements

Many of the chapters in this volume originate from the conference "Boom, Bust and Beyond: New Perspectives on the 1719 – 20 stock Euphoria" which was held at the University of Tübingen in April 2018. Funding for the conference as well as this book was provided by the German Research Foundation (DFG) via the Collaborative Research Center 923 "Threatened Orders – Societies under Stress", project E04 – "After the stock market crash of 1720 – threat diagnosis and crises' management in Paris and London" as well. For his part, Stefano Condorelli's research was funded by the Swiss National Science Foundation. We would like to thank these institutions for their generous support. Also, we would like to express our gratitude to the authors of this volume. It is thanks to them that this book is published in advance of the tercentennial, and we hope its findings will have an influence on the debates to come well beyond the year 2020.

In addition, we are grateful to Renate Dürr (Tübingen), who was a co-organizer of the conference. Kristin Condotta Lee (New Orleans) and Lena Moser (Tübingen) helped with the proof-reading, and Julietta Fricke (Tübingen) took care of the footnotes. Finally, we would like to thank Eve Rosenhaft who discovered the cover image and permitted us to use it.

Tübingen/Naples, March 2019

https://doi.org/10.1515/9783110592139-001

Table of Contents

III. Understanding Speculation – Micro to Macro

Stefano Condorelli, Daniel Menning

Boom, Bust and Beyond – An Introduction

"I will be going to Pasewalk and Stettin and Prussia for fourteen days next Tuesday to see how matters stand there," wrote King Frederick William I of Prussia to Prince Leopold of Anhalt-Dessau in the summer of 1723. "Had I not decided upon it I would certainly not do it, because these are dependences of a different world and their returns I consider to be another Mississippi."[1] With this analogy between parts of his realm and the region along the *Mississippi River*, the king must have immediately conjured up in the mind of Prince Leopold images of the French stock market speculation and crash a few years earlier. The prodigious rise and fall of the Mississippi Bubble astonished Europe between 1719 and 1720. A myriad of newspaper articles and letters had disseminated news about the masses of stockjobbers feverishly trading Mississippi shares in the narrow Parisian *rue Quincampoix* all over the continent.[2] Equating his provinces with Louisiana, did Frederick William thus mean that he considered Pomerania and East Prussia – like the Parisian shares after the crash – as ultimately worthless promises of immense riches?

As Frederick William crossed his provinces in person in 1723, he truly may have believed that he had expended immense riches on a province that was worthless. Pomerania and, to a lesser degree, East Prussia had been hard hit by the Great Northern War (1700 – 1721), and both had been devastated by the Great Plague (1709 – 1711). In the early 1720s they were still partially depopulated. In addition, the Pomeranian provincial capital of Stettin had been besieged twice during the war and had experienced significant destruction from bombardment. Yet, there was most likely a good degree of irony in the king's original statement. Just three years earlier, in 1720, the Prussian king had bought those parts of Pomerania that he was now about to cross, paying two million thalers. This sum constituted roughly 50 % of the Prussian state budget in 1714 and was, therefore, an enormous amount of money for a country still mostly relying on an agricultural

The first part of the introduction was written together by Daniel Menning and Stefano Condorelli; the second part (starting with "New perspectives on the 1720 bubbles") by Daniel Menning.

1 Frederick William I to Prince Leopold, Potsdam 5.7.1723, in *Die Briefe König Friedrich Wilhelms I. an den Fürsten Leopold zu Anhalt-Dessau*, ed. Otto Krauske (Berlin: Paul Parey, 1905), 227.
2 See Stefano Condorelli, "La presse étrangère et le Système de Law (1716 – 20)," in '*Gagnons sans savoir comment': Représentations du Système de Law du XVIIIe à nos jours*, ed. Florence Magnot-Ogilvy (Rennes: Presses Universitaires de Rennes, 2017), 183 – 206.

https://doi.org/10.1515/9783110592139-002

economy.[3] In addition, Pomerania's and East Prussia's potential for grain production was well known and a number of good harvests had been made in Prussia's eastern provinces in the early 1720s. Also, upon the king's invitation, Huguenots had settled in the province over the previous years. The country may not have looked terribly promising; yet, the expectations of riches to be derived from these provinces were much more probable than those built on the Mississippi, at least in the early 1720s.[4]

Leaving aside the uncertain precision of the analogy, what may seem surprising, perhaps, is the apparent casualness of the reference to the Mississippi itself. The king was clearly relying on Prince Leopold to grasp at once the reference and potential irony. Yet, it is well known that eighteenth-century royalties – like people in general – were avid readers of news, in particular international ones.[5] Moreover, the Mississippi Bubble had indeed been a gigantic event. Be that as it may, the fact that the king did chose that example three years after the crash, suggests a lasting permeation of Prussian court thinking by the 1720 stock market speculation.[6]

Frederick William, however, had not only been a passive observer of the bubble. There is evidence that he also actively participated in the stock market and, what is more – given the immoral reputation that short trading had at the time – that he did so by betting on falling prices. In another letter to Prince Leopold in October 1720, the king stated: "The English shares are declining well-behavedly, the Dutch are also doing poorly, but I am profiting from it. Hope to double my capital."[7] We do not know how the king exactly managed his share trading, yet it makes sense to think that he operated through nominees, possibly via Prussian diplomats in London or bankers in Amsterdam. Anyhow, Frederick William most likely was not the only Prussian investor, though definite evidence is hard to come by. Already in March 1720, the Prussian ambassador in London

3 Adolph Friedrich Riedel, *Der brandenburgisch-preußische Staatshaushalt in den beiden letzten Jahrhunderten* (Berlin: Ernst & Korn, 1866), 53–54.

4 Hans Branig, *Geschichte Pommerns. Teil II: Von 1648 bis zum Ende des 18. Jahrhunderts* (Cologne: Böhlau, 2000), 73–92. Only a year after his letter complaining about the worthlessness of his provinces, Frederick William I was full of praise about the economic progress in Pomerania.

5 See for instance Andrew Pettegree, *The Invention of News: How the World Came to Know About Itself* (New Haven: Yale University Press, 2014).

6 For the German press the same has been shown by Eve Rosenhaft, "'All That Glitters is not Gold, but …': German Responses to the Financial Bubbles of 1720," in *Money in the German-Speaking Lands*, ed. Mary Lindemann and Jared Poley (Oxford and Providence: Berghahn, 2017), 74–95.

7 Frederick William I to Prince Leopold, Potsdam 17.10.1720, in *Briefe*, ed. Krauske, 172.

reported that Field Marshal Count Alexander Dohna-Schlobitten might sell his annuities and buy stocks.[8] Later data on share ownership in the South Sea Company in 1723 – the best available – reveals that 44 investors resided in Berlin.[9] It seems quite likely that some, if not most, of them were drawn into these investments during 1720.

Needless to say, the king also paid close attention to the political implications of the financial events. His correspondence with diplomats in Paris and London shows that they were trying to assess the extent to which these unfolding events possibly were altering the balance of power in Europe. Would John Law succeed in shrinking the French sovereign debt? Would the South Sea Company achieve a similar goal in Britain? Could a new war result from the momentary weaknesses of France and Britain, caused by their respective stock market crashes? In that respect, the Prussian government was no exception. We find throughout Europe – both in the diplomatic correspondence and the press – the same questions and the same attention to the political repercussions of the bubbles.

Prussia really stood out, however, in that it appears to be (together with Poland) the only large European country in 1720 without a single project for a joint-stock company. Research thus far in the archives has given no result, and although it is possible that some scheme may be discovered some day, it is nonetheless clear that Prussia largely shunned the stock euphoria – and the rush for state financial innovations that came with it – which swept so intensely over the rest of the continent around 1720.

There were two reasons that may partially explain this apparent disinterest. First, Prussia was the only European power not seriously in debt after the conclusion of the War of the Spanish Succession and the Great Northern War. Therefore, a debt-for-equity swap – which was central to the Système de Law in Paris and to the South Sea Company scheme in London – was unnecessary in Berlin.[10] Second, rather than chartering a new company, Frederick William was then on the lookout to sell the company he already had. This was the Brandenburg-African Company that had been created by his father in 1682. The firm was bankrupt, and what is more the king also realized that competing with Britain and the Unit-

8 Johann von Wallenrodt to Frederick William I, London 22.3./2.4.1720, in Geheimes Staatsarchiv Preußischer Kulturbesitz (GSTAPK), I. HA, Rep. 11, Nr. 1908, 39.

9 The South Sea Company transfer ledgers for 1720 are missing. Peter G.M. Dickson, *The Financial Revolution in England: A Study in the Development of Public Credit, 1688–1756* (London: MacMillan, 1967), 316.

10 As the best introduction to Prussian history see Christopher Clark, *Iron Kingdom: The Rise and Downfall of Prussia 1600–1947* (London: Penguin Books, 2007), 85–94.

ed Provinces in trade would create a constant source of potential frictions with these powers.[11] Therefore, in a sort of interesting parallel with his short-selling of the English and Dutch equity markets, Frederick William took advantage of the 1720 stock euphoria to get rid of those African forts that belonged to the Brandenburg enterprise. The English Royal African Company was interested in buying them as was a joint-stock firm newly created in the German city of Emden.[12] Ultimately, however, the forts were sold to the Dutch West India Company in 1721.[13]

The Prussian king has been, hitherto, an unknown actor in the 1720 bubble. And yet, he is exemplary in two ways. First, he highlights how the events were still in the memory of people who lived at quite a distance from the main actions. Second, he demonstrates that there was a political dimension to the bubble that extended beyond Anglo-French competition. The king's October 1720 letter to Prince Leopold is likewise remarkable for a number of reasons. First of all, that letter represents the only evidence we have so far of a monarch personally stockjobbing the market. This is a finding that says a lot about the diffusion of financial expertise around 1720 as well as about cultural change. To put Frederick William's speculation in perspective, let us consider that Samuel Johnson's *A Dictionary of the English Language* in 1755 still defined the *stockjobber* as "a low wretch who gets money by buying and selling shares in the funds." It is all the more interesting to find a monarch-speculator precisely in a country, Prussia, that does not have the reputation of being a frontrunner in early-eighteenth century financial innovation. What is more, the letter is one of the very few direct evidences of a 1720 "counterminer" (to use the contemporary Dutch term), that is to say a short-seller. Most sources on the subject are indirect, such as newspapers fulminating against these individuals, judicial documents attesting that they could be imprisoned when caught, or a playing card showing a "Jew" accused of short-selling being thrown into a pond by an angry mob.[14]

---

11 Victor Ring, *Asiatische Handlungscompagnien Friedrichs des Großen: Ein Beitrag zur Geschichte des preußischen Seehandels und Aktienwesens* (Berlin: Carl Heymanns Verlag, 1890), 5–29.

12 "Oprichting van verscheiden Handelschappen binnen en buiten Europa, die hier in Embden, door een Compagnie von Commerci, kann gedrevem worden, tot goeden provit van deselve, en seer vordeelig voor onse Stad en Land wegens de verscheiden Manufacturen die deshalven hier konde opgerichtet worden en deselve met reel minder Onkosten kunnen uitvoeren als de Hollanders", undated, in Niedersächsisches Landesarchiv Aurich, Rep. 4, B IVe, Nr. 179, 53–58.

13 Richard Schück, *Brandenburg-Preußens Kolonial-Politik unter dem Großen Kurfürsten und seinen Nachfolgern (1647–1721)* (Leipzig: Grunow, 1889), 1:286–312.

14 See for instance *The London Journal*, 24.9.1720; Bibliotheque Nationale de France, Bibliotheque de l'Arsenal, Bastille, ms 10657, f. 173. For the playing card see the nine of spades in the 1720 Bubble playing cards, Harvard, Kress collection.

The Historiography of the 1720 Bubbles

We have placed Prussia and its king at the very beginning of our book precisely to emphasize how much there is still to be discovered about the 1720 events, in spite of the enormous collective work that already has been done. Each new generation of scholars brought its new questions and perspectives, and the literature is now so vast and diverse that it would be impossible to give a comprehensive account of it in even a dozen pages. It is nonetheless possible – without pretending to be exhaustive – to outline some of the main strands of research. First of all, there are classical works of the single national equity booms, such as the ones by Émile Levasseur, William R. Scott, John Carswell, Peter G.M. Dickson, or Edgar Faure.[15] These have introduced cohorts of academics to the field and paved the way for subsequent historiographical developments.

A second important strand – which involved mostly financial economists – has focused on the question of the rationality or irrationality of the 1720 bubbles. There has been an intense debate, providing significant insights but also raising a number of critiques.[16] Critiques have underlined, for example, that some of

15 Émile Levasseur, *Recherches historiques sur le Système de Law* (Paris: Guillaumin, 1854); William R. Scott, *The Constitution and Finance of English, Scottish, and Irish Joint-stock Companies to 1720*, 3 vols. (Cambridge: Cambridge University Press, 1912); John Carswell, *The South Sea Bubble* (London: Cresset Press, 1960; rev. ed. Washington, DC: Alan Sutton, 1993); Dickson, *The Financial Revolution*; Edgar Faure, *La banqueroute de Law, 17 juillet 1720* (Paris: Gallimard, 1977). See also Herbert Lüthy, *La banque protestante en France de la révocation de l'Edit de Nantes à la Révolution*, vol. 1 (Paris: S.E.V.P.E.N., 1959); Antoin E. Murphy, *John Law: Economic Theorist and Policy-maker* (Oxford: Clarendon Press, 1997); Julian Hoppit, "The Myths of the South Sea Bubble," *Transactions of the Royal Historical Society 12* (2002): 141–165. For the 1720 Dutch bubble, see in particular G. Van Rijn, *De Aktiehandel in 1720 te Rotterdam en de Maatschappij van Assurantie, Discontering en Beleening dezer Stad* (Rotterdam, 1899); Frederikus P. Groeneveld, *De economische crisis van het jaar 1720* (Amsterdam: Universiteit van Amsterdam, 1949); C.H. Slechte, "De Maatschappij van Assurantie, Disonteering en Beleening der stad Rotterdam van 1720, bekeken naar haar produktiefactoren over de periode 1720–1874," *Rotterdams Jaarboekje* 7 (1970): 252–310; C.H. Slechte, *Een Noodlottig Jaar voor veel Zotte en Wijze: De Rotterdamse Windhandel van 1720* (The Hague: Martinus Nijhoff, 1982); Oscar Gelderblom and Joost Jonker, "Mirroring Different Follies: The Character of the 1720 Bubble in the Dutch Republic," in *The Great Mirror of Folly: Finance, Culture, and the Crash of 1720*, ed. William N. Goetzmann et al. (New Haven: Yale University Press, 2013), 121–139. For the Hamburg bubble: Caesar Amsinck, "Die Ersten Hamburgischen Assecuranz-Compagnien und der Actienhandel im Jahre 1720," *Zeitschrift des Vereins für Hamburgische Geschichte* 9 (1894): 465–494.

16 See in particular Charles P. Kindleberger, *Manias, Panics and Crashes: A History of Financial Crises* (London: MacMillan Press, 1978); Larry Neal, *The Rise of Financial Capitalism: International Capital Markets in the Age of Reason* (Cambridge and New York: Cambridge University Press, 1990); Richard Dale, *The First Crash: Lessons from the South Sea Bubble* (Princeton: Princeton

these works, as they tried to prove or disprove one particular economic theory, were losing sight of the historical context and that they made questionable presuppositions about secular continuity in matters of economic behavior, such as greed and rationality.[17] On the other hand, it is noteworthy that the genealogy of the question about the rationality or irrationality of the bubbles can be traced back to 1720, namely to contemporary debates about the over- or undervaluation of the *Compagnie des Indes* and South Sea Company's shares.[18]

A third, very broadly defined, line of research has undertaken to review these traditional narratives through new perspectives and, often, also by drawing on new archival sources. To name but a few of these new interpretations, there have been investigations into the importance of networks of investors, the role played by women within equity markets, the trajectory of individual actors (such as company directors or specific stockjobbers), the relative magnitudes of the bubbles, and – at the other end of the spectrum – the social, cultural, and philosophical frameworks of the bubble.[19] In an inverted standpoint,

University Press, 2004); Peter Temin and Hans-Joachim Voth, "Riding the South Sea Bubble," *American Economic Review* 94 (2004): 1654–1668; Gary S. Shea, "Financial Market Analysis Can Go Mad (in the Search for Irrational Behaviour During the South Sea Bubble)," *Economic History Review* 60 (2007): 742–765; François R. Velde, "Was John Law's System a Bubble? The Mississippi Bubble Revisited," in *The Origins and Development of Financial Markets and Institutions: From the Seventeenth Century to the Present*, ed. Jeremy Attack and Larry Neal (Cambridge and New York: Cambridge University Press, 2009), 99–120; Helen J. Paul, *The South Sea Bubble: An Economic History of Its Origins and Consequences* (London and New York: Routledge, 2011); Rik G.P. Frehen, William N. Goetzmann, and K. Geert Rouwenhorst, "New Evidence on the First Financial Bubble," *Journal of Financial Economics* 108 (2013): 585–607. All the above-mentioned works focus in some way on the rationality vs. irrationality question. Yet, it is important to note that many of them have a larger scope and investigate other aspects of the 1720 events.

17 William Deringer, "For What It's Worth: Historical Financial Bubbles and the Boundaries of Economic Rationality," *ISIS* 106 (2015): 646–656; Koji Yamamoto, "Beyond Rational vs Irrational Bubbles: James Brydges the First Duke of Chandos During the South Sea Bubble," in *Le crisi finanziarie: Gestione, implicazioni sociali e conseguenze nell'età preindustriale*. Selezione di ricerche, ed. Giampiero Nigro (Firenze: Firenze University Press, 2016), 327–357

18 See for instance the pamphlet attributed to John Law, *A Full and Impartial Account of the Company of Mississippi, Otherwise called the French East-India Company Projected and Settled by Mister Law* (London, 1720); [Archibald Hutcheson], *Some Seasonable Considerations for those who are desirous, by Subscription or Purchase, to Become Proprietors of South-Sea stock* (London, 1720).

19 This is indeed a very broad category. Among the most recent works (and not mentioning many studies that would deserve to be): P. Hoffman, G. Postel-Vinay, and J. Rosenthal, *Des marchés sans prix: Une économie politique du crédit à Paris, 1660–1870* (Paris: Ed. de l'Ecole des hautes études en sciences sociales, 2001); Larry Neal and Stephen Quinn, "Networks of Information, Markets, and Institutions in the Rise of London as a Financial Centre, 1660–1720,"

other works have studied the events of 1720 as part of broader developments, especially as accelerators of economic, political, and cultural change. To give just a few examples, the impact of the bubble recently has been examined in relation to the progress of political arithmetic, the notion of "self-organization", and the evolution of literary ideas.[20]

All these aforementioned studies, it must be acknowledged, mostly focus on France, Britain, and – to a much lesser degree – the United Provinces. By contrast, a fifth historiographical strand has investigated what we may broadly

Financial History Review 8 (2001): 7–26; Anne Laurence, "Lady Betty Hastings, Her Half-Sisters, and the South Sea Bubble: Family Fortunes and Strategies," *Women's History Review* 15 (2006): 533–540; Anne Laurence, "Women Investors, 'That Nasty South Sea Affair' and the Rage to Speculate in Early Eighteenth-Century England," *Accounting, Business and Financial History* 16 (2006): 245–264; Anne Laurence, "Women, Banks and the Securities Market in Early Eighteenth-Century England," in *Women and Their Money 1700–1950: Essays on Women and Finance*, ed. Anne Laurence, Josephine Maltby, and Janette Rutterford (London and New York: Routledge, 2009), 46–58; Carl Wennerlind, *Casualties of Credit: The English Financial Revolution*, 1620–1720 (Cambridge, Mass.: Harvard University Press, 2011); Richard Kleer, "'The Folly of Particulars': The Political Economy of the South Sea Bubble," *Financial History Review* 19 (2012): 175–197; Larry Neal, *'I Am Not Master of Events': The Speculations of John Law and Lord Londonderry in the Mississippi and South Sea Bubbles* (New Haven: Yale University Press, 2012); Richard Kleer, "Riding a Wave: The Company's Role in the South Sea Bubble," *Economic History Review* 68 (2015): 264–285; Amy Froide, *Silent Partners: Women as Public Investors During Britain's Financial Revolution*, 1690–1750 (Oxford: Oxford University Press, 2017); Stefano Condorelli, "Price Momentum and the 1719–20 Bubbles: A Method to Compare and Interpret Booms and Crashes in Asset Markets," *MPRA Papers* (2018); Andrew Odlyzko, "Newton's Financial Misadventures in the South Sea Bubble," Working Paper (2018); Arnaud Orain, *La politique du merveilleux: Une autre histoire du Système de Law (1695–1795)* (Paris: Fayard, 2018);

20 Catherine Ingrassia, *Authorship, Commerce, and Gender in Early Eighteenth-Century England: A Culture of Paper Credit* (Cambridge: Cambridge University Press, 1998); Silke Stratmann, *Myths of Speculation: The South Sea Bubble and 18th-Century English Literature* (Munich: Wilhelm Fink, 2000); Rebecca Spang, "The Ghost of Law: Speculating on Money, Memory and Mississippi in the French Constituent Assembly," *Historical Reflections* 31 (2005): 3–25; Judy Hayden, "Of Windmills and Bubbles: Harlequin Faustus on the Eighteenth-Century State," *Huntington Library Quarterly* 77 (2014): 1–16; Julia V. Douthwaite, "How Bad Economic Memories Are Made: John Law's System in *Les lettres persanes*, *Manon Lescaut*, and 'The Great Mirror of Folly'," *L'Esprit Créateur* 55 (2015): 43–58; Jonathan Sheehan and Dror Wahrman, *Invisible Hands: Self-Organization and the Eighteenth Century* (Chicago: The University of Chicago Press, 2015); John Shovlin, "Jealousy of Credit: John Law's 'System' and the Geopolitics of Financial Revolution," *Journal of Modern History* 88 (2016): 275–305; William Deringer, *Calculated Values: Finance, Politics, and the Quantitative Age* (Cambridge: Cambridge University Press, 2018). Also, numerous articles in William N. Goetzmann et al., ed., *The Great Mirror of Folly: Finance, Culture, and the Crash of 1720* (New Haven: Yale University Press, 2013); Magnot-Ogilvy, ed., *'Gagnons sans savoir comment'*.

call the pan-European dimension of the bubble. This strand has been gaining momentum in recent years, with studies ranging from the micro-historical (the creation of a bank in Kassel in 1721) to the pan-European level.[21] The Prussian example at the beginning of this introduction fits obviously into this last line of research.

New Perspectives on the 1720 Bubbles

This volume does not engage with one of these strands of research in particular. Rather, the chapters that follow contribute to all groups mentioned above, trying to integrate novel aspects into the narrative and searching for innovative perspectives on the 1720 stock market bubble at-large. What emerges are building blocks for a new history of the first European stock market bubble.

Starting this introduction with the the king of Prussia emphasizes one such point that this volume makes: London, Paris and the United Provinces were not the only places intimately connected to the stock market bubble during the boom, the bust and their aftermath. Instead, actors all over Europe and in

---

21 André.-E. Sayous, "L'affaire de Law et les Genevois," *Revue d'Histoire Suisse* 17 (1937): 310–340; Charles H. Wilson, *Anglo-Dutch Commerce and Finance in the Eighteenth Century* (Cambridge: Cambridge University Press, 1941); E. Schubert, *The Ties That Bound: Eighteenth Century Market Behavior in Foreign Exchange, International Goods, and Financial Assets*, unpublished Ph.D. dissertation (Urbana-Champaign, 1986). Among the most recent studies that have focused on the periphery of the bubble: Stefan Altorfer, "Bulle oder Bär? Der bernische Staat und die 'South Sea Bubble' von 1720," in *Globalisierung – Chancen und Risiken: Die Schweiz in der Weltwirtschaft 18–20. Jahrhundert*, ed. Hans-Jörg Gilomen, Margrit Müller, and Béatrice Veyrassat (Zürich: Chronos, 2003), 61–86; Nikolaus Linder, "'Diess Jahr hat das grosse Unglück so allerorten in Franckreich, Engelland, Holland, Genf um sich gegriffen ...': Zu den Gründen für den Bankrott der ersten Berner Bank 1720," in Globalisierung, ed. Gilomen et al.; Nikolaus Linder, Die Berner Bankenkrise von 1720 und das Recht: Eine Studie zur Rechts-, Banken- und Finanzgeschichte der Alten Schweiz (Zürich: Chronos, 2004); Patrick Walsh, "The Bubble on the Periphery: Scotland and the South Sea Bubble," *Scottish Historical Review* 91 (2012): 106–124; Rik G.P. Frehen, William N. Goetzmann, and K. Geert Rouwenhorst, "Finance in the Great Mirror of Folly," in *The Great Mirror*, ed. Goetzmann et al.; Stefano Condorelli, *The 1719–20 Stock Euphoria: A Pan-European Perspective, MPRA Papers* (2014); Patrick Walsh, *The South Sea Bubble and Ireland: Money, Banking and Investment, 1690–1721* (Woodbridge: The Boydell Press, 2014); Eve Rosenhaft, "'All That Glitters Is Not Gold, But...': German Responses to the Financial Bubbles of 1720," in *Money in the German-Speaking Lands*, ed. Mary Lindemann and Jared Poley (Oxford and Providence: Berghahn, 2017), 74–95; Stefano Condorelli and Daniel Menning, "Wirtschaftspolitik in Zeiten der europäischen Börseneuphorie: Die Gründung der Leyh- und Commercien-Compagnie und die Reform der Tuchproduktion in Hessen-Kassel 1721," *Hessisches Jahrbuch für Landesgeschichte* 68 (2018): 99–114.

many of its transoceanic dependencies felt themselves and, indeed, were linked to the speculative fever: as politicians or merchants, as investors or speculators, as projectors and/or as members of a cultural community in which the Mississippi and the South Sea became *lieux de mémoire*. Building on the results of research into this wider geographical outreach of the events, we do not, however, only consider 1720 in a broader geographical scope for curiosity's sake. Instead, we seek larger causal logics to the events and, thereby, try to grasp the different meanings of the 1720 bubble within the eighteenth century and beyond. Therefore, the first part of this volume will engage with the geographical frame within which the 1720 European bubble needs to be understood.

The second part looks at the established or traditional narratives more closely. Scholars lately have been reexamining primary sources and by reinterpreting or recontextualizing them, as well as by connecting them to recent revisions of early eighteenth century history, they question and rethink the older narratives, especially with regard to the South Sea Bubble.[22] After almost three centuries and confronted with huge amounts of research, this certainly is not an easy task. Yet, it is one that seems quite rewarding. It appears that most primary sources about the events in 1720 and the roguish behavior of the South Sea Company directors were heavily influenced (unsurprisingly) by political and economic motives and not by an effort to get at the heart of the matter. Untangling these distortions reveals different narratives and causal logics of the London events. In addition, newly discovered sources reopen older debates, suggesting different conclusions. Taken together, the chapters forming this part of the book question the validity of traditional accounts and their explanations of events in and around 1720, some of which are at the heart of the rational/irrational debate.

Finally, the third part of this volume aims at understanding the very concept of speculation, from a micro to a macro perspective. The temporal scope of these chapters differs from the short term, encompassing a few weeks in 1719–20, to the long term, overarching the eighteenth century. Some contributors are interested in the conceptualizations as well as the cultural explanations of the phenomenon of speculation. Others study individual investors' decision-making processes in minute detail. Contributors to this section pay attention to the research about the rationality/irrationality of the South Sea and Mississippi bubbles. Yet, they do not limit their study to this binary code but, rather, search for more complex explanations. At the same time, these chapters embed speculation socially and culturally, thus connecting their findings to other ongoing re-

22 For a recent revision of the history of the Mississippi Bubble see Orain, *La politique du merveilleux*.

search. They provide important clues about people's behavior in the stock market more generally, while also showing that men and women in 1720 struggled to make sense of the ways speculators acted. The authors thus highlight how contemporaries started to develop new explanations that would help understand the frantic share trading, on both an individual and collective level. Their chapters not only provide evidence as to the ways in which contemporaries and later generations interpreted events post-bubble but also how their explanations shifted during the bubble itself.

Overall, we believe that these three parts will help in reinterpreting the 1720 stock market bubble in fundamental ways.

The Chapters

The first part of the book, *Broadening the Geographical Frame*, takes the reader to different parts of Europe and beyond in the period between roughly 1700 and the mid-1720s. It starts with Peter Ericsson's and Patrik Winton's investigation of the circulation of ideas that underpinned the bubble. That John Law's treatise *Money and Trade Considered with a Proposal for Supplying the Nation with Money* (1705) circulated widely in Europe, was translated by 1720 and was republished repeatedly over the remainder of the century – making it one of the 80 economic bestsellers in the early modern period – is a well-known fact.[23] Yet, what has been less studied is the impact that the Scottish financier's ideas had on other countries' policies.[24] In their chapter, Ericsson and Winton show that Swedish officials paid close attention to fiscal reforms, especially in France but also in Britain, during the War of the Spanish Succession and that they also were aware of Law's ideas. Swedish interest stemmed from the fact that the kingdom under Charles XII struggled to raise enough money to keep fighting the Northern War. Since Swedish elites were unwilling to engage in novel ways of financing, Charles XII hired Baron Georg Heinrich von Görtz, a German, to implement a new system that focused on monetizing the Swedish economy through the introduction of bonds and token copper coins. While there are many parallels to the French experiments under Law, Görtz's work preceded the Scotsman's. This chronology testifies to a European discourse on fiscal reform, in which John Law was

23 Erik S. Reinert et al., *80 Economic Bestsellers before 1850: A Fresh Look at the History of Economic Thought*, Research Paper (2017).

24 For one example, see Karl-Heinz Schmidt, "Geldwirtschaft, Banken und Finanzen," in *Im Auftrag der Krone: Friedrich Karl von Hardenberg und das Leben in Hannover um 1750*, ed. Wilken von Bothmer and Marcus Köhler (Rostock: Hinstorff, 2011), 93–99.

very visible but not singular. The Swedish reforms mostly have escaped notice beyond the country's own historiography so far, because they did not end in a bubble in 1720. Instead, the experiments were folded during a constitutional rearrangement after the death of Charles XII in late 1718, as traditional elites reacquired political control and brought in a conservative monetary policy again.

Moving from the dissemination of financial ideas throughout Europe prior to 1719 – 20 to the bubble year itself, the dialogue between Stefano Condorelli and Daniel Menning also highlights the circulation of economic concepts across Europe. They debate the pan-European thinking about corporations and the flotation of new joint-stock companies, which were connected to the waves of speculation in Paris, London and the United Provinces. What is clear from the evidence is that the bursting of bubbles in one place did not stop the thinking about company promotion in others. Thus, at first sight, surprisingly, the crashes in Paris and London did not discourage projectors and governments elsewhere in Europe. The authors suggest that, to understand this behavior, first, one needs to take seriously the connection that contemporaries saw between the idea of the joint-stock company and its potential for economic development. Second, international money flows in 1720 allowed more remote places to try to attract international investment capital that might stimulate local joint-stocks. Finally, authorities also tried to devise company charters that would allow them to reap the benefits of economic development while, at the same time, prohibiting speculation or preventing it as far as possible from entering their countries by other means.

These debates between promoters and governments were, however, no straightforward matter, as Eve Rosenhaft shows in her microstudy of company promotion in the German principality of Braunschweig-Wolfenbüttel between 1718 and 1723. Proposals for economic improvement, in this case, were sent from competing London projectors to local German officials. While one British group promoted a linen production in the German territory and signed articles of association in 1720, a different projector already received approval for a lottery scheme in 1718 and, in the summer of 1720, applied for a charter to add a joint-stock bank to the gambling enterprise. Detailed analysis of the linen company investors shows their involvement in the trade of this commodity in Britain, making it look like they were not investing for the sake of London paper speculation but because of business prospects. The bank, in contrast, looks much more like a fraudulent proposal. While Braunschweig officials originally were interested in both projects, informing themselves and trying to learn about the organizational form of the joint-stock company, they were scared by the London stock market crash in the fall of 1720 as well as its politico-economic aftermath, and they ultimately rejected the bank proposal. Doubts about the linen company also grew, though it did operate facilities in Braunschweig until running out of money in 1721. Overall, the behavior of the German principality's government testifies to the interest in economic advancement that was an important prerequisite for the European dimension of the bubble. In addition, it unveils the complications that arose from translating business concepts and transferring them from centers of European economic development to more remote countries.

Traditional scholarship also quite regularly emphasizes that the bubbles were all about speculation but not about the companies' trade itself nor the regions they targeted.[25] Malick W. Ghachem newly questions this position by showing how closely John Law integrated the *Compagnie des Indes* into the workings of the early eighteenth-century slave trade and colonial system. The conglomerate that the Scottish financier formed was well placed to benefit from enslaving people in Africa and exploiting their labor in the western hemisphere. At the same time, Ghachem shows, the Caribbean – and more especially Saint-Domingue – was not unaffected by the events in Paris. As French merchants paid Caribbean planters with paper money from the *Banque Royale* in 1720, they transferred depreciating claims to the latter and thereby created economic difficulties on the islands. Colonists also were quite embittered about the *Compagnie des Indes* in the years that followed the bubble. Anger now focused on the monopoly rights of the corporation for importing slaves, which it exercised effectively for some time. As a revenge against this "unjust" monopoly, the colonists called for free trade and boycotted French manufactures. This stunt proved successful, and commerce was reopened after the *Compagnie des Indes* accepted its economic defeat. In turn, a free trade in slaves also set in motion the spectacular rise of the Saint-Domingue plantation economy.

The second part of the book, *Engaging with Traditional Narratives*, revisits a number of key themes that belong to longstanding histories, especially of the South Sea Bubble. Richard A. Kleer returns to the rationale behind the South Sea Company's debt conversion scheme in 1720. Yet, his story differs significantly from previous ones. Kleer shows that, while the South Sea directors publicly claimed that the Company was to profit from the conversion by means of 'surplus' stock, they really targeted the regular specie flow from state coffers that a government debt administrator could count on. Controlling this, the South Sea Company would be well placed to dislodge the Bank of England from its key position in national finance. Once this happened, the specie flow would allow the South Sea Company to perform lucrative banking functions. This was the profit that the directors expected from the whole scheme. Meanwhile,

---

25 For France, this recently has been voiced again by Shovlin, "Jealousy of Credit."

considering the £7.7 million gift the company was to pay to the government, the state stood to profit from a de facto reduced interest rate on the national debt. This, however, was hard to sell to current state creditors, who would suffer from the reduction. For this reason, the idea of a 'surplus' stock was born, intended to convince investors with insufficient financial knowledge that converting their holdings would be a good idea. The explanation, while surprising at first, is consistent with surviving evidence of the directors' behavior in the stock market itself. Since they did not expect to profit from any 'surplus' stock, they also did not try to drive up the share price artificially. Rather, whenever they entered the market, the directors attempted to stabilize the value of Company shares each time it showed signs of weakness. This was necessary, because the South Sea directors needed to keep investors happy and state creditors willing to become share owners. In the long run, however, things got out of hand and it was impossible to avert the crash.

Whereas Kleer focuses on the economic rationale, Abigail Swingen reintroduces politics. Ideological debates about the financial revolution and the nature of credit as well as the partisan origins of the South Sea Company in 1711 have been investigated thoroughly. Disputes about the 1720 scheme as well as the post-bubble discussion about the causes of the crash, however, usually have been studied in terms of their economic precision.[26] Swingen shows that this ignores the fact that there was still no political consensus about the financial revolution in the early 1720s. Instead, arguments about the South Sea scheme and the bursting of the bubble were very much couched in partisan terms of the acceptance and repudiation of the public debt, which had evolved since the 1690s. Frequently, opinions that voiced doubt as to the national debt were associated with attempting to destroy the constitution and supporting a Jacobite revolution. Robert Walpole, who usually appears as the man who saved Britain from catastrophe after the bursting of the South Sea Bubble, emerges from the chapter not only as an adroit politician of finance but also as someone who utilized these ideological debates to his personal advantage – clear up to the Atterbury Plot of 1722.

Daniel Menning looks at yet another aspect of the traditional narrative, namely the economic effects of the bursting of the South Sea Bubble. Over the last few decades, the impact of this event on the overall British economy has

---

26 See, for example, the debate about Archibald Hutcheson's analysis of the South Sea scheme between Richard Dale, *The First Crash*, 82–90; Helen J. Paul, *Archibald Hutcheson's Reputation as an Economic Thinker: His Pamphlets, the National Debt and the South Sea Bubble*, Research Paper (Southampton, 2009). For more economic readings also Deringer, "For What It's Worth," 646–650.

been seen as negligible. Menning counters these arguments with a microstudy of the British Baltic Sea trade. Using the Sound Toll Registers, an exceptionally rich source on (merchant) ship traffic through the Danish-Swedish Sound, allows for a close analysis of London business with this eastern trading arena. The data shows that traffic between London and the countries bordering the Baltic Sea was quite lively in early 1720 but slowed down in late summer, as speculation in London reached its climax and as contemporaries complained about a disregard for normal business. The post-bubble year saw a significant decline in the British capital's Baltic Sea trade by roughly 50 percent. Detailed analysis reveals that the first half of the year was very sluggish, and trade only picked up again during the summer. Thus, there are significant indications of post-bubble economic dislocation. Turning from the trade itself to the terms of trade, Menning suggests that the decline may, in part, be attributable to the structure of the British commercial exchange with the Baltic. As English merchants had a negative balance of trade with Sweden and Russia in particular, money had to be transferred for payment of goods. With ready cash scarce after the bubble's bursting, importers did not want to send additional specie east, causing the decline of London's Baltic Sea trade. In contrast, Dutch commercial intercourse with the same area went on unperturbed in 1721 – but merchants in the United Provinces had the advantage of a positive balance of trade.

That the South Sea Bubble was not the only financial scandal of the first half of the eighteenth-century is something that has not yet received much attention in bubble historiography. As Amy M. Froide shows, the measures taken by Parliament to deal with the South Sea Bubble not only had been used before, but the same procedures also were applied afterwards to the Charitable Corporation Scandal of 1732. What is more, the memory of the 1720 events informed subsequent discussions about financial mismanagement. Participants to the debate lasting from 1732 to 1734 were eager to draw parallels between the South Sea Bubble and the Charitable Corporation, particularly in blaming directors for what happened, emphasizing the 'suffering' of investors, accentuating losses and fraud, asking the government and Parliament to step in and help, and describing the public benefits of the South Sea Company and Charitable Corporation. The purpose of connecting the events in 1732 to those a dozen years earlier was, however, clearly meant to secure contemporary financial assistance and political regulation – not to provide a precise comparison between them.

The chapters in the final part of this book, *Understanding Speculation – Micro to Macro*, study the events in 1720 from the perspective of contemporary investors. Furthermore, it looks at their ideas about the workings of the economy and at the reinterpretations of the bubbles by later generations. Marlene Kessler explores the exceptionally rich letters of one investor, which illuminate his trading in Paris in late 1719 and early 1720. Inquiring into Jean Vercour's comprehension of the stock market's functioning and his fictional expectations of the short-term future, she discovers crucial differences over time. Though Vercour, as a bill trader from Liege, was not wholly unprepared for the paper speculation in Paris, he had trouble understanding the dynamics of price development in November and early December of 1719. Because he could not explain to himself what was going on and he expected a fall in prices, Vercour decided to get into the market and out again quickly, after making a healthy profit. He was successful to this end, although he later decided to re-enter *rue Quincompaix* in late December and stayed in until February. This time, however, he had a different understanding of the workings of the stock market. He now paid much closer attention to John Law, who began influencing share prices again around Christmas. Understanding the Scotman's actions now seemed crucial to success in speculation. Thus, the expectations stimulated by Law had become much more important for Vercour during his second excursion into Mississippi shares. Understanding investors' short-term expectations of future development thus helps to create a more nuanced image of investment in 1719–20.

Dror Wahrman's chapter considers speculation from a more abstract point of view. He asks how contemporaries' perceived causality and how they attempted to explain what looked to them like a speculative frenzy in which the relationship between cause and effect had dissolved. Minor events seemed to cause major price fluctuations and finally the crash. Trying to reestablish causal logics after the bubble, divine intervention was one option. Another way of making sense of what had occurred was to claim that a few people (i.e. the directors) had been pulling strings in the background, rigging the market and artificially stimulating demand in shares. In contrast to these more traditional approaches, however, Wahrman suggests one can also discern a new mode of thinking about human behavior. Not yet clearly defined, but with important implications for the future, writers began applying ideas of self-organization that eventually would developed into Adam Smith's concept of the invisible hand. Some thus claimed that although individual actions did not always make sense and order appeared to be absent in speculation, it was in fact still present on a higher level.

The next chapter by Anne L. Murphy starts out with analyses concerning the dot-com and 2008 crash, in which critics found too much testosterone in financial markets and have blamed the predominance of men in investment banks for the resulting instability. Looking back at female investment in 1720, an opposite narrative emerges. Women already were active investors by the second decade of the eighteenth century, and some made money during the bubble while others lost – thus, the story of female investment appears to be a complex one. In contemporary print culture, however, it was not. Female participation in the market was envisioned almost exclusively negatively. There were two elements that critics connected to female involvement. First, by gaining from share speculation, newly rich women appeared to overturn social order. Second, feminine character traits and the feminization of male speculators were held responsible for the instability of the financial market – an idea that already had been connected to the fickleness of "Lady Credit" by the early eighteenth century. Conversely, for critics of female involvement, male mastery of the market would allow for a return to normality in the post-bubble period. Murphy concludes that female gendering in 1720 helped to ignore more general problems connected to financial markets, by blaming a single factor – i. e. gender – for the speculative excesses. Gendering market behavior thus provided and still provides fodder for moral critics, but it does little to explain the actual events, whether in 1720 or 2008.

A long-term, eighteenth-century perspective is taken by Jean-Yves Grenier, who studies political economists' search for order in the formation of stock market prices. He focuses on encounters with and the resolution of four major problems since the 1670s. First, normally in markets, if the price of a good rose, demand declined. However, in the share market the opposite appeared to be the case – increasing prices stimulated demand and falling ones quelled it. Thus, the workings of financial exchanges appeared disorderly. Yet, political economists of the time concluded differently, by assuming that the seeming chaos in price formation simply resulted from the constant arrival and interpretation of news. Second, the relationship between goods and prices in the stock market, at times, looked like it was out of "just" proportion. This meant that values were established without "just causes". Some authors tried to explain the price swings by pointing to the influence of anticipations on future earnings, rather than events themselves, thereby saving justice. Third, writers knew the concept of fundamental value and also perceived deviations of share prices from it – again, a problem if one believed in fair prices. One way of explaining this was that private, not public, information concerning the future development of a company was the most trustworthy. Such information was, of course and by definition, not available to everyone. Therefore, investors' estimates as to the value of shares differed substantially. But, by extension, this also meant that prices could not reflect fundamental values. Fourth, if, thus, fundamental value could not explain price formation in the stock market, early modern thinkers concluded, then values must be established by self-referentiality. As a result, the mechanisms of the stock market were not inexplicable to political economists in the eighteenth century. Instead, they could be integrated into their thinking.

Finally, Christine Zabel cautions us about simply applying the label 'speculation' to the 1720 events. While modern understandings of the term perfectly describe the bubbles for us, contemporaries would not have understood our usage.

As Zabel shows, people in the early eighteenth century used words such as 'bubble', 'système', 'windhandel', 'agiotage' or 'stockjobbing' to describe what they witnessed. These alluded to the airy nature of projects and also to the excessive self-interest at play. The label of 'speculation' only was attached to the events during the late eighteenth century as French revolutionaries gazed backwards. Their new terminology was built on the redefinition of the term 'speculation' during the 1750s, when French political economists began redefining self-interest as a positive trait for the overall welfare. In the 1780s, this conception was mathematized, and 'speculation' turned into a weighing of probabilities. The positive connotation was taken up in 1789, when the French National Assembly struggled with continuing to pay interest on the life-annuities the former government had sold. Only a few years later, however, these life-annuities and their origins in mathematic 'speculation' were reinterpreted as egoistic inventions by selfish bankers with detrimental effects to the public good. 'Speculation' thus became synonymous with 'agiotage' – an immoral way of making money. This development was carried forward into debates about revolutionary paper money. Its opponents feared that the *assignats* would have the same consequences as John Law's experiment with the non-metallic currency had, namely that they would result in morally-condemnable self-interested 'speculation' and in political disaster. Supporters of paper money, in contrast, embraced Law's legacy. They complained that the Scotsman had not been radical enough, since he failed in getting rid of annuities completely. As a result, according to supporters of paper money, self-interested speculative bankers were able to fleece the public for the next 70 years. As a more general outcome of the debate, the arguments, whether brought forward by supporters or opponents of the *assignats*, made it possible to use the concept of 'speculation' when talking about the 1720 events.

Future Research

Drawing on the contributions of this book, there are a number of objectives for future research that will help to rewrite the history of the 1720 bubbles and to redefine their place within eighteenth century history.

Re-reading sources: Richard Kleer's reinterpretation of the share trading activities of the South Sea Company directors opens up the question as to whether we need to review other transactions performed by the managers of the Company during 1720. The accounts held with the Sword Blade Bank that Carswell repeatedly cites as evidence of improper dealings[27] come to mind or the books listing the directors' possessions and transactions in 1720–21, which were drawn up after the bubbles deflation.[28] Adding to the doubts that Kleer raises about the traditional account of directors' behavior, we have Abigail Swingen's argument that the politicized nature of many sources produced during and after the bubble may not have received sufficient attention yet. Though it seems doubtful that we can completely untangle a precise account of 'what exactly happened' from the primary material, paying more attention to how ideologies informed the depiction of contemporary events may open up new avenues to understanding the South Sea Bubble's political legacy. To put it more bluntly: though many researchers have relied on the Report of the Committee of Secrecy investigating the South Sea Bubble in early 1721, the participants of this inquiry may only have been marginally interested in leaving behind a correct account of the events for posterity – and mostly in influencing current political struggles in London. Also relating to political aims, the Committee report has to be read, using the hints provided by Dror Wahrman, as an attempt to establish a narrative of the bubble year that followed contemporary rules of cause and effect.

New sources: Many traditional narratives have relied on a very circumscribed set of primary evidence – mostly official documents and company records. As Murphy, Kessler, Menning, and Wahrman demonstrate, there is much that can be gained for the history of the South Sea and Mississippi bubbles by uncovering previously unused archival records and thoroughly reading the abundant pamphlet literature. Yet again, the difficulty that researchers constantly will face with regard to this and the previous point is disentangling from the sources what actually happened as compared to how people tried to make sense of what they witnessed with their sometimes limited knowledge of finance and their conceptualizations of the workings of the economy.

Temporal scope: Using the example of Braunschweig-Wolfenbüttel, Rosenhaft shows that the dramatic bubbles in Paris and London were the climax of a much longer search for means of economic improvement that began earlier or was most likely constantly present at a local level. This finding is well in line with Stefano Condorelli's research at the level of the European continent, which showed early signs of corporation euphoria from 1714 onwards[29] and which also connects to his and Menning's discussion of company promotion across Europe between 1719 and 1721. Looking beyond the bubble year, Grenier

27 Carswell, *South Sea Bubble*, chs. 7 and 8.
28 The reference also available in Carswell, *South Sea Bubble*, 221–222.
29 Condorelli, *The 1719–20 Stock Euphoria.*

demonstrates that understanding the workings of the stock market was a problem that political economists thought about both before and long after 1720. In addition, Froide provides hints of earlier resolutions of financial scandals that politicians could build upon after the South Sea Bubble burst. Furthermore, she tempts us to think about the ways in which the South Sea Bubble as an argument continued to inform debates as well as the precise impact this memory had on eighteenth-century financial markets. This is in line with Zabel's research on the complex and regionally specific memorialization of the events and the purposes to which such reminiscences were put in France. Interestingly, and in a similar light, when Adam Smith wrote about the organizational form of the joint-stock company in the late 1770s, he did not worry about speculation. In his *Wealth of Nations* he stated: "The explication of them [the stock-jobbing projects of 1720] would be foreign to the present subject."[30] Although the South Sea and Mississippi bubbles have at times been seen in their cultural context, more research into the long-term impact will help to more clearly define the place of the 1720 bubble within eighteenth century history at large. In size, the bubble was certainly a one-off event, but beyond that, it appears to have been very much a child of its times as well as something that influenced critical thinking for generations.

Geographical frames: The chapter by Ericsson and Winton on Swedish fiscal policies encourages further comparative research. Almost all European powers labored under enormous amounts of debt from the War of the Spanish Succession and the Great Northern War. While the forward-moving ideas in finance were most evident in France and Britain, these countries were part of a larger discourse on fiscal reform across Europe. As a means to uncover alternative, failed or even never-tried paths of fiscal retrenchment, a closer look at other countries could be valuable. Similar conclusions are reached in the discussion between Condorelli and Menning about joint-stock promotion during the bubble period and in Rosenhaft's analysis of the Braunschweig bubble companies. There was and remains a European dimension to economic policies, which testifies to the intertwining of governments, promoters and investors. The history of the bubble should, therefore, be written as an entangled one. From this vantage point different speeds of economic development could come into sight and thereby historians may tackle the problem of the origins of the European economic divergence in the later eighteenth century. Finally, Ghachem's paper encourages us to look even beyond the continent and to search for the global dimensions of the bubble

30 Adam Smith, *An Inquiry into the Nature and Causes of the Wealth of Nations* (1776; London: Penguin, 1999), 333.

period. Even though it would have been difficult for those living abroad to speculate, even less so to do it successfully, the effects of the joint-stock boom were felt far away from the centers of the events.

Our volume ultimately argues that there is still scope for further research, with the promise to surpass traditional narratives that now have been told for almost 300 years.

I. Broadening the Geographical Frame

Peter Ericsson, Patrik Winton

The Rise and Fall of a New Credit System. Transnational Financial Experiments and Domestic Power Struggles in Sweden, 1710–1720

This chapter deals with a little known episode in Swedish and European history: the huge expansion of liquidity and the establishment of a new credit system under the absolute regime of Charles XII and the subsequent default committed by the new parliamentary regime that came to power after the king's death. These developments were part of a larger trend of financial innovations introduced in many European states, which among other things led up to the Mississippi and the South Sea Bubbles. The Swedish case, like the ones of Denmark and Austria, has received little attention from historians. As a result, scholarly narratives of this crucial period in the financial history of Europe have been imprinted by the proceedings in Britain and France. This has led to a focus on spectacular financial bubbles, while broader questions concerning the diffusion, reception and implementation of ideas and practices of financial innovations have been less prominent.

Ideas on how governments should tackle increasing fiscal pressure, stemming from the growth of armies and navies and protracted inter-state conflicts, were transnational in character. Governments gathered information about competing states and the fiscal and financial reforms they initiated. Some of these ideas were adopted, while others were discarded. However, arguments and ideas did not travel by themselves. There had to be specific reasons to seek new ways of tackling administrative problems. In other words, a receptive political context was crucial to the diffusion and the outcome of reform projects.[1] By examining the Swedish case more closely, we will shed light on how the recep-

---

1 E.g. Sophus A. Reinert, *Translating Empire: Emulation and the Origins of Political Economy* (Cambridge, Mass.: Harvard University Press, 2011), 1–10; Thomas Leng, "Epistemology: Expertise and Knowledge in the World of Commerce," in *Mercantilism Reimagined: Political Economy in Early Modern Britain and Its Empire*, ed. Philip J. Stern and Carl Wennerlind (Oxford: Oxford University Press, 2013), 97–116, here 108–113; Keith Tribe, "Concluding Remarks," in *Cameralism in Practice: State Administration and Economy in Early Modern Europe*, ed. Marten Seppel and Keith Tribe (Woodbridge: Boydell Press, 2017), 263–268, here 264–266.

https://doi.org/10.1515/9783110592139-003

tion and adaptation of financial innovations ultimately was a question of political power.

By 1715, Charles XII and the Swedish state were in deep trouble. The Great Northern War had raged for fifteen years. After the loss of two field armies, at Poltava in 1709 and at Tönningen in 1713, and with Finland and the Baltic possessions occupied by Russian forces, the war was being fought with mainly domestic resources against virtually all of the states in eastern and northern Europe. For over five years, the king had resided in the Ottoman Empire, where he fled after the defeat at Poltava in the hope of forging an alliance against Russia. In the meantime, the Council in Stockholm discretely had been suing for peace through English mediation. On his return, Charles thwarted the resistance against his policies, and the war effort was resumed with renewed vigor. Up until the death of the king, these efforts were largely efficacious.[2]

In order to accomplish his military aims, Charles XII had to reform war finance completely. Traditional forms of finance – such as direct and indirect taxes, loans from the Bank of Sweden, subsidies from foreign governments, floating debts of unpaid salaries and government deliveries, and living off enemy territory – were no longer sufficient.[3] Instead, credit had to provide the basis for continued warfare. As in the case of France and John Law, the catalyst for the new financial policies was an outsider. Baron Georg Heinrich von Görtz, *Geheimerat* of Holstein-Gottorp, became the confident of the king and the new system that emerged has traditionally been associated with his name in Swedish historiography.[4] Yet, for the larger part of the period, Görtz either was away on diplomatic missions or held prisoner in the Dutch Republic. Thus, although he would have drawn up the guidelines for the system (and like John Law, he called it his *system*), the actual implementations were carried out by officials, or indeed, by the king himself. Görtz was important, even instrumental, to the new financial system. The outcome, however, was not the product of a single mind.

2 Jerker Rosén, *Det engelska anbudet om fredsmedling 1713: En studie i politisk propaganda* (Lund: Gleerup, 1946); Walter Ahlström, *Arvid Horn och Karl XII 1710–1713* (Lund: Blom, 1959); Ragnhild M. Hatton, *Charles XII of Sweden* (London: Weidenfeld and Nicolson, 1968), 309–380.

3 For a summary of traditional forms of war finance, see Jan Lindegren, "The Swedish 'Military State' 1560–1720," *Scandinavian Journal of History* 10 (1985): 305–336, here 316–336; Jan Glete, "The Swedish Fiscal-Military State in Transition and Decline, 1650–1815," in *War, State and Development: Fiscal-Military States in the Eighteenth Century*, ed. Rafael Torres Sánchez (Pamplona: Ediciones Universidad de Navarra, 2007), 87–108.

4 E.g. Gösta Lindeberg, *Svensk ekonomisk politik under den Görtzka perioden* (Lund: Gleerup, 1941); Sten Carlsson and Jerker Rosén, *Svensk historia: Tiden före 1718* (Stockholm: Svenska bokförlaget, 1962), 559.

Instead, it was the result of a combination of innovative thinking; assessments of other states' experiences; and, not least, trial and error.

Transnational Fiscal Experiences and Swedish Discussions

There are numerous indications that Swedish officials were well aware of a variety of fiscal and financial practices deployed by other European states. In particular, there was an interest in French developments. In 1695, the French government launched the *capitation*, a head tax paid by all subjects, with the exception of the clergy. The population was divided into classes, which paid between 1 and 2,000 *livres* according to their status.[5] In this way, the government established a precedent wherein those who could best afford it paid the most. Such measures were well in line with an established discourse at the *riksdag*, Sweden's legislative assembly of estates, when extraordinary taxation was negotiated.[6]

More radical was the establishment of the *dixième* in October 1710. This was a tax on income generated by property. As such, it disregarded social status and privileges, individual as well as corporate, hereditary as well as purchased. All property owners were regarded as equals, only differentiated by how much money they earned. Moreover, the tax overtly targeted the wealthy. In this way, it went against the ideology of a corporate society based on privileges that the regime of Louis XIV had made its outmost to preserve.[7]

The *dixième* had several features in common with the Swedish *contribution*, which was issued in 1713, 1715 and 1716.[8] Nevertheless, the *contribution* targeted

---

5 Gary B. McCollim, *Louis XIV's Assault on Privilege: Nicolas Desmaretz and the Tax on Wealth* (Rochester: Rochester University Press, 2012), 37–44; Guy Rowlands, *The Financial Decline of a Great Power: War, Influence, and Money in Louis XIV's France* (Oxford: Oxford University Press, 2012), 63.

6 Peter Ericsson, "Corporative Privileges Undermined: The Meaning of Extra-Ordinary Taxation in Sweden in the 17th and 18th Centuries," in *Fiscal Systems in the European Economy from the 13th to the 18th Centuries*, ed. Simonetta Cavaciocchi (Firenze: Firenze University Press, 2008), 757–769, here 760–767. At the meetings of the estates in the 1680s and 1690s, the estates had waived their right to approve or reject new taxation. The estates also committed themselves to take responsibility for any loans raised by the king during wartime, Sven Grauers, *Sveriges Riksdag: Den svenska riksdagen under den karolinska tiden* (Stockholm: Sveriges Riksdag, 1932), 4:106–119.

7 Marcel Marion, *Les impôts directs sous l'Ancien Régime principalement au 18:e siècle* (Paris: Cornély, 1910), 269; McCollim, *Louis XIV's Assault*, 1–2; Rowlands, *The Financial Decline*, 64.

8 Previous research has found the precursor to this method of taxation in German and in particular Austrian cameralist thinking. In particular Daniel Almqvist, "Feifs finansiella reformer

not only the income from property, but property itself. The explicit purpose was to raise resources in such a way that the heaviest burden would fall on the wealthiest. At public meetings attended by all taxpayers in a neighborhood, without regard for privileges or social standing, everyone assessed the value of their property. Property owners paid two percent on their possessions, with some qualifications. Most notably, the farmsteads of freeholding peasants were not included in the assessment. The *contribution* was intended to replace all other extraordinary levies.[9] A reasonable assumption is that in both Sweden and France the architects behind the taxes tried to find new sources of revenue, which were only available in the wealthier part of the population. In England, the government of William III also initiated a number of measures to collect more revenue from the land tax by targeting large landowners.[10]

Swedish officials also considered French financial practices, particularly the issuing of *billets de monnaie*. This paper money started to circulate when French authorities re-stamped coins in the autumn of 1701. In reality, this meant yet another debasement of the currency. Because of a limited capacity at the mints, receipts for the coins turned in for re-stamping began to be accepted as legal tender. These receipts almost immediately became interest bearing instruments of credit. Their numbers were initially modest, but military setbacks necessitated ever-larger emissions without any connection to metallic assets. In 1707, the government accepted them as tax payments but only to a quarter of the amount due. This did not strengthen their credit, despite further efforts to increase their value. In 1710, the government deemed that they could no longer uphold the situation,

och Wilhelm von Schröders 'Fürstliche Schatz- und Rent-Cammer'," *Karolinska förbundets årsbok* (1922): 233–253, but also Åsa Karlsson, *Den jämlike undersåten: Karl XII:s förmögenhetsbeskattning 1713* (Uppsala: Acta Universitatis Upsaliensis, 1994), point to the fact that Casten Feif, the most influential of Charles XII's officials at the time when the tax ordinance was prepared, twice mentions Austrian cameralist Wilhelm von Schröder's book 'Fürstliche Schatz- und Rent-Cammer' in his correspondence. However, on both occasions Feif emphasized that he did *not* have access to the book in question. Casten Feif to Nicodemus Tessin, 30.5.1712 and 22.6.1713, in *Handlingar ur v. Brinkmanska archivet på Trolle-Ljungby I*, ed. Gustav Andersson (Örebro: Lindh, 1859), 155, 170; Almqvist, "Feifs finansiella reformer," 246–247; Karlsson, *Den jämlike undersåten*, 57–78, esp. 61.

9 *Publication och Förordning på hwad sätt Contributionerne efter en billig jämlikhet skola utgiöras til undersåtarnes lindring*, 4.6.1713; Karlsson, *Den jämlike undersåten*, 100–101.

10 Peter G.M. Dickson, *The Financial Revolution in England: A Study in the Development of Public Credit 1688–1756* (London: Macmillan, 1967), 24; Patrick K. O'Brien, "The Political Economy of British Taxation, 1660–1815," *Economic History Review* 41 (1988): 1–32, here 19; Rowlands, *The Financial Decline*, 63.

and the receipts were withdrawn from circulation and the holders were given annuities in exchange for the bills.[11]

These experiences were not lost on Swedish financial policymakers. In November 1710, the king wrote a letter to the Royal Council in Stockholm, in which he asked them to consider the introduction of lottery bonds and notes of credit as new ways to raise money. He did not provide any further details on how to organize such projects, but the letter demonstrates that Charles and his advisors, residing in the Ottoman Empire at the time, were aware of the existence of similar fiscal arrangements in other countries. The councilors in Stockholm claimed that the subjects of the king had no resources left to lend and that the government's coffers were empty. According to them, it was therefore extremely difficult to finance the equipping of naval squadrons and the deployment of regiments in Germany, while at the same time defending the realm itself. Charles was used to such arguments. His response was to urge the councilors to pursue his policies more diligently and to seek new ways to mobilize resources.[12]

The councilors, too, were knowledgeable about fiscal innovations in other states, as became evident in their discussions on the king's demands. Gustaf Cronhielm had heard that the king of France liquidated his bills only after great damages to the economy. Carl Gustaf Frölich agreed and pointed out that such bills had also been harmful in other countries. Fabian Wrede thought that it would be very difficult to implement such projects, since both paper bills and lottery bills would require a large fund as collateral. Such resources were available in England and the Dutch Republic, he claimed, but in Sweden, the Crown and its subjects were poorer. Although other councilors stressed the necessity to find new resources, most of them agreed with Wrede that the biggest obstacle for the implementation of the king's suggestions was the problem of creating a sufficiently large collateral fund.[13]

The councilors did not deny the king's request outright. Instead, they passed it on to the directors of the Bank of Sweden. The Bank operated with a guarantee from the Estates, which also elected its directors. It provided credit to the govern-

---

11 Richard Bonney, "France and the First European Paper Money Experiment," *French History* 15 (2001): 254–272, here 255–257; Rowlands, *The Financial Decline*, 108–127; Joël Félix, "The Most Difficult Financial Matter That Has Ever Presented Itself: Paper Money and the Financing of Warfare under Louis XIV," *Financial History Review* 25 (2018): 43–70, here 53–66.

12 Swedish National Archives (SNA), Det odelade kansliet, Rådsprotokoll, vol. 103a, 11.4.1711.

13 SNA, Det odelade kansliet, Rådsprotokoll, vol. 103a, 11. and 13.4.1711. One of the lotteries the councillors referred to was probably the Million Adventure lottery in England; see Anne L. Murphy, *The Origins of English Financial Markets: Investment and Speculation before the South Sea Bubble* (Cambridge: Cambridge University Press, 2009), 34.

ment, especially during wartime; but after 1709, the directors were becoming hesitant as they worried that the state would not be able to supply the necessary collateral, nor to maintain interest payments.[14]

As to the king's proposal, the Bank drafted a long and detailed answer, discussed and signed by the directors and a committee of representatives from the nobility, the clergy and the burghers. It stressed a number of both empirical and theoretical circumstances and problems associated with the introduction of paper money, especially if the Bank would be the issuer. They supported most of their arguments by citing previous Swedish experiences with credit notes issued by the Stockholm Banco in the early 1660s. They pointed out that the number of notes in circulation had increased to the point that the Bank could no longer honor them, despite efforts from the Bank and from the political leadership to strengthen its credit. The government therefore had removed these notes from circulation at great costs for the state. When the Bank of Sweden was founded in 1668, the authorities – very much in response to the failure of Stockholm Banco and in an attempt to regain the population's trust in banking institutions – decided on a statute banning the new bank from issuing paper notes. The statute was reiterated in 1675, 1681 and 1700, which would make it very difficult for the Bank, but also implicitly for the king, to revoke that promise. Moreover, a revocation would hurt the depositors' trust in the Bank, the representatives argued, and all efforts to maintain the Bank's credit in a challenging situation would be futile.[15]

The representatives of the Bank also used foreign cases to prove that it was very problematic to maintain the credit of paper notes. First, they referred to the English re-coinage of 1696 when the government issued exchequer bills that later fell 22–24 percent in value.[16] Then, they turned to France, where they pointed out that the holders of paper bills sold them at a 75 percent discount. Furthermore, if the Swedish government resorted to the French solution when paying the salaries of civil servants and military officers, these individuals would

14 Sven Brisman, *Sveriges Riksbank: Bankens tillkomst och verksamhet 1668–1918. Den Palmstruchska banken och Riksens Ständers Bank under den karolinska tiden* (Stockholm: Norstedts, 1918), 81–220.

15 SNA, Sveriges riksbank, Bankofullmäktiges renskrivna protokoll, vol. 26, 19.4.1711; SNA, Skrivelser till Kungl. Maj:t, Bankofullmäktige, vol. 584, 8.6.1711. On Stockholm Banco and the credit notes, see Brisman, *Sveriges Riksbank*, 54–80.

16 SNA, Skrivelser till Kungl. Maj:t, Bankofullmäktige, vol. 584, 8.6.1711. The accuracy of this information is noteworthy, as this number is very close to the report that Charles Montague, Chancellor of the Exchequer, provided to the Secretary at War, William Blathwait, in July 1696, Dickson, *The Financial Revolution*, 366–367.

have to accept significant discounts when using their notes. In order to stress this point, two transcripts of letters from persons residing in France were included. In the first letter, an anonymous Swedish nobleman active at court argued that he had to trade his paper bills at a 75 percent loss in order to get access to acceptable money. In the second letter, dated April 1711, an unnamed merchant in Lyon stated that the *billets de monnaie* had lost 65 percent of their nominal value while the *billets de subsistence* had declined by 70 percent.[17] In order to avoid such upheaval, the representatives from the Bank concluded that it would not be in the interest of the Bank, the king, or the subjects of the realm to introduce similar notes of credit in Sweden. The representatives sent the reply to the Council, which agreed with the conclusion.[18] Charles was not pleased with the reply. He pointed out that other countries with similar problems could maintain their credit, re-stamp the coins or introduce paper money. He thought it strange that no such initiatives were taken in Sweden.[19]

The actions in Stockholm among the leading government officials show that they were hesitant and faultfinding when considering financial innovations. While they were clearly knowledgeable about the financial developments in both England and France, they did not view these as opportunities to find new resources. Instead, they interpreted the innovations as a threat to the existing financial order, which the king's father, Charles XI, and his advisors had established in the 1680s and 1690s. Some councilors had spent their whole careers creating fiscal structures, inspired by cameralism, which emphasized order and the proper assigning of specific revenues to specific expenditure.[20] Paper money would overturn such structures. Although not clearly stated, councilors like Wrede thought that the king should balance government accounts by increasing government revenue or by resorting to traditional borrowing and, if necessary, by reducing expenditure. They did not want him to resort to financial innovation.

Charles responded to this circumspect resistance by launching administrative reforms and depriving the Council of any real power. Instead, an outsider, Görtz, who very timely had sought out the king and offered his services, became the most powerful man in the realm beneath the throne. Both in writing and especially through personal consultations in 1715 and 1716, Görtz, in all likelihood,

---

17 SNA, Skrivelser till Kungl. Maj:t, Bankofullmäktige, vol. 584, 8.6.1711.

18 SNA, Det odelade kansliet, Rådsprotokoll, vol. 103a, 13.6.1711.

19 Casten Feif to Nicodemus Tessin, 17.7.1713, in *Handlingar ur v. Brinkmanska archivet*, 175.

20 Stellan Dahlgren, "Ekonomisk politik och teori under Karl XI:s regering," *Karolinska förbundets årsbok* (1998): 47–104; Marten Seppel, "Introduction: Cameralism in Practice," in *Cameralism in Practice: State Administration and Economy in Early Modern Europe*, ed. Marten Seppel and Keith Tribe (Woodbridge: Boydell Press, 2017), 1–16, here 4–11.

presented diplomatic, economic and fiscal ideas that were well in line with those considered by Charles. The king's confidence in Görtz led to his placement at the head of a new government agency, *upphandlingsdeputationen,* through which all government expenditure was eventually channeled.[21] Undoubtedly, Görtz functioned as a type of medium between the Swedish and international contexts, since he was knowledgeable about both the theoretical and practical aspects of the financial innovations that other governments had implemented in Europe.[22]

In a memorandum written to the king early in 1716, Görtz brought up the French experiences and argued for the benefits of the introduction of token coins. He referred to them as a sort of credit and compared them to the *billets de monnaie.* He rhetorically asked, how one could be so presumptuous as to hope to do better than such a wise and experienced Council as the French one, under such a sensible king as Louis XIV and in a country where there was so much money and consequently so much more credit? Yet, Görtz claimed, such arguments did not strike at the matter itself but, rather, at its execution.[23] According to him, the French had made two mistakes:

> That these token coins, billets or jettons, were not proportioned, first, against a fund, by which they could later be redeemed, and, second, to the circulating money, but they immediately flooded the entire [state] budget, so that their credit was immediately stifled, and therefore all ready money was driven out of commerce and probably out of the country.[24]

By considering these two errors, Görtz argued, the solution to the problem presented itself.[25]

---

21 Sven Grauers, "De politiska relationerna mellan Arvid Bernhard Horn och Georg Heinrich von Görtz åren 1707–1719," *Karolinska förbundets årsbok* (1963): 159–208, here 193–197; Sven Grauers, "Georg Heinrich von Görtz" in *Svenskt biografiskt lexikon* (Stockholm: Norstedts, 1967–1969), 17:171–172.

22 Cf. Tribe, "Concluding Remarks," 264.

23 Des Baron von Goerz ausführliches Gutachten, wie dem damahligen betrübten Zustand in Schweden aufgeholfen werden könne? Dem König Carl XII 1716, in Friedrich Carl von Moser, *Rettung der Ehre und Unschuld, des weiland Königl. Schwedischen Staats-Ministers und herzogl. Schleswig-Hollsteinischen Geheimen-Raths und Ober-Hof-Marschalls Georg Heinrichs, Freyherrn von Schlitz, genannt von Goerz, aus des Königs Carl des XII. des schwedischen Senats, der schwedischen Herrn und Männer, Original- und andern Urkunden, erwiesen. Mit XXX Beylagen* (1776), Beylage No. 1, 389–392.

24 Goerz in Moser, *Rettung der Ehre und Unschuld,* 390. Translated by the authors.

25 Goerz in Moser, *Rettung der Ehre und Unschuld,* 389–392.

Görtz's System and the Token Money

In 1705, John Law published *Money and trade considered with a proposal for supplying the nation with money* in order to suggest ways to improve the Scottish economy. Law's ideas circulated around the need to increase liquidity, ideas which Görtz shared. The two men were in personal contact with each other. Görtz twice travelled to Paris, in August 1716 and in January and February 1717, and, on both occasions, they met in person.[26] They also corresponded with each other. Görtz's primary concern at the time was to gain diplomatic support and to secure the consignation of French subsidies for Swedish warfare, but he was also inspired by John Law's financial ideas and abilities.[27] In a letter to an associate in January 1718, Görtz even argued that if Law would lose his position in France, he would try to persuade him to offer his services to the Swedish king.[28] Although there is no evidence that the two men discussed financial issues in detail, the connections between Law and Görtz underscore that we cannot examine developments in France and Sweden as parallel cases with no contact between them. Instead, there were concrete transfers of knowledge, which created correlations between some of the measures advocated by Law and key parts of the system that Görtz introduced in Sweden.

In France, authorities used augmentations of coin values several times during the final years of Louis XIV's regime, but the Swedish state did not resort to manipulating the metal content of its coins until 1715, after 15 years of intensive warfare.[29] Thus, the values of the unwieldy copper plates as well as that of the copper coins were upgraded. As the amount of liquidity was boosted in the following years, they were devaluated back to their original value in December 1717. At the same time, the silver coins, *caroliner*, were banned as means of payment. Such measures included complex re-stamping of the coinage, with the intentions of ultimately withdrawing metal coins from circulation and replacing them with other forms of legal tender. In order to secure the metal currency for the Crown, favorable terms for the payment of taxes with the discontinued coins, or for their

26 Claude J. Nordmann, *La crise du nord au début du XVIIIe siècle* (Paris: Librairie générale de droit et de jurisprudence, 1956), 67–68, 75, 90.

27 SNA, Görtzska samlingen, vol. E3790, Letter from Görtz to Law, 20.8.1717; Theodor Westrin, "Frih. Georg von Görtz' bref ur fängelset i Arnhem 1717," *Historisk Tidskrift* (1898): 89–134, here 113; Nordmann, *La crise du nord*, 63–90.

28 SNA, Görtzska samlingen, vol. E3791, Letter from Görtz to Poniatowsky, 6.1.1718.

29 On the French measures, see Rowlands, *The Financial Decline*, 101–103, 124–126.

exchange, were offered.[30] Replacing metal currency with other forms of legal tender was not unique to Sweden. In France, Law deployed similar measures. Indeed, after his fall from power, there were perceptions in the highest echelons of the state that Law was not only a good friend of Görtz's but also that he was inspired by his example to withdraw French gold and silver coins from circulation.[31] The differences in economic and political contexts, however, resulted in variations in their exploits.

Manipulation of the currency was not a central feature of Görtz's system. Instead, its most important component was the release of government bonds. Formally, these were issued by a government agency, *kontributionsränteriet*, which was overseen by the estates. The bonds were set in high denominations, from 100 to 10,000 daler silver coins (*dsm.*). Their duration was relatively short and it varied between different bond issues. They yielded an annual interest of 6 percent, and holders could sell them on a secondary market. The government used all property in the Swedish realm as collateral, and it allocated half of the *contribution* to interest payments. Moreover, the government secured the repayment of the capital by building up a fund paid for by yet another extraordinary tax, *upphandlingsavgiften*. Investors could buy the bonds with cash and – later on – token coins, precious metals or international bills of exchange.[32]

Originally, the bonds were primarily intended to circulate on an international market, especially among a rather limited circuit of Dutch investors. The bonds were therefore initially denominated in an internationally viable currency, the *Reichsthaler*, in order to bring an influx of currency to the realm. With the aim of promoting the bonds as well as conducting unofficial diplomacy, Görtz set out on a journey to Amsterdam in the early summer of 1716. He managed to close a deal, in which a group of investors set up a new company, François Peterman & Co. The investors committed themselves to bring the equivalent of 2 million *riksdaler* in gold and silver to Sweden in exchange for a monopoly on the minting of that bullion. Furthermore, they would receive the bonds at a very favorable

30 E.g. *Kongl. Maj:ts Nådigste Förordning om förhöjningen På de härtils slagne Koppar-Plåtar och Koppar-skilliemynt*, Stockholm 17.5.1715; *Kongl. Maj:ts Nådigste Påbud om Förhöjningen af Carolinernes wärde. Påbud*, Stockholm 23.1.1716; *Kongl. Maj:ts Nådige Placat, Om Koppar-Myntetz Devalverande*, Lund 5.12.1717; *Kongl. Maj:ts nådige Förordning om Carolinernas Uphäfwande /Och Silfwer-Skillie-Myntets förhöjande*, Lund 20.12.1717; *Kongl. Maj:ts ytterligare Förordning om det Gamla Silwermyntets Uphäfwande*, Lund 7.3.1718.

31 Archives Nationales, Paris, K 885, pièce 1, 'Mémoire personnel aux sieurs Pâris sur les affaires générales où ils furent employés', f. 86–87. We are very grateful to Stefano Condorelli for drawing our attention to this source.

32 *Publication angående Uphandlings Wercket som på en wiss Fond eller Grund är inrättat*, Stockholm 29.12.1715; Lindeberg, *Svensk ekonomisk politik*, 81–85.

exchange rate. They also were granted free trade with the Swedish realm. Producers of export commodities, in particular iron, would have to deliver their goods at designated warehouses where authorities would pay them with bills, which would circulate as legal tender. Members of the consortium behind Peterman & Co. then would buy the goods from said warehouses, thereby bringing in even more currency to Sweden, while bypassing the merchants of the Swedish staple towns. However, this elaborate plan was abandoned when Dutch authorities arrested Görtz on a British initiative, following his contacts with Jacobites. The political developments, combined with uncertainties brought on by privateering and naval blockades, caused the investors to withdraw.[33]

The plans to raise a consolidated public debt through a private company, which at the same time was involved in trade, is obviously similar to the South Sea Company in England and to the Mississippi Company in France. Since Sweden did not have any colonies, the company focused on trade between Sweden itself and the Dutch Republic. As in England and France, the core operation was the management of the public debt. But an important difference was that Sweden was still engaged in large-scale warfare, and thus the primary intention was to advance new resources for military spending, whereas in the two western European states the objective was to fund huge floating debts that already had been accrued.[34]

Early in 1716, and parallel to the efforts to consolidate Peterman & Co., there were attempts to establish a domestic private company staffed with wealthy merchants who were to be entrusted with the task of putting more bonds into circulation. These bonds, now denominated in dsm., were offered for sale to the public. They also were used to pay for government expenditure, in effect military contracts, and the company promised to redeem any drafts on the state. However, there seems to have been little interest for this arrangement among the merchant community in Sweden, despite offers to buy bonds at very beneficial rates. Instead, a bureau – the aforementioned *upphandlingsdeputationen* – was formed and staffed by a small number of officials under the single leadership of Görtz. Through this bureau, virtually all state revenue and expenditure flowed. Thus, it became the hub of the entire Swedish administration. This fact predictably gave rise to widespread resentment among overlooked officials.[35]

---

33 Per Sörensen, "Karl XII:s utrikespolitik efter hemkomsten från Turkiet," in *Karl XII: Till 200-årsdagen av hans död*, ed. Samuel E. Bring (Stockholm: Norstedts, 1918), 413 – 472, here 430 – 437; Lindeberg, *Svensk ekonomisk politik*, 122 – 135, 139 – 140.

34 Lindeberg, *Svensk ekonomisk politik*, 107 – 108.

35 Lindeberg, *Svensk ekonomisk politik*, 88 – 105.

Again, the Swedish solution exhibited similarities with the organizational structure of Law's system in France. A small organization under the undisputed leadership of an outsider, who relied entirely on the confidence of the king (or the regent), was able to absorb the financial and the economic policy of the realm.[36] In doing so, both Görtz and Law challenged the interests of the established elites.

However, the Swedish government bonds were a disappointment. Their sales were slow, but, since they were the basis for the entire system, it was imperative that they circulated. Therefore, they were not only used to pay military contractors but also to consolidate old floating debts and even to compensate for forced loans. Because of these emissions, the build-up of funds intended for the redemption of these bonds could not keep pace with their dispersal. In the end, bonds were issued to a total value of 2.5 million dsm. The government also issued so-called salary notes to civil servants and military officers in 1715 as a substitute for ready cash. As such, they were denominated in uneven sums. The salary notes yielded 6 percent interest and, like the bonds, they could be traded on a secondary market. Projected as a temporary measure, with a total value of 1.2 million dsm., they still freed a considerable amount of the ordinary revenues for other purposes.[37] In an international comparison, the salary notes were not unlike the French *billets de monnaie*.

As it turned out, bonds and salary notes were insufficient to fund the war effort. Instead, token coins would make up the bulk of the increased liquidity. The king ordered the stamping of token money in 1715, and the first ordinance on the introduction of the token coins was dated 8 March 1716. These were to be accepted to their full denomination of 1 dsm. in all transactions in the realm, including tax payments. The exception was for half of the *contribution* and the *upphandlingsavgift*, which had been set aside to service the interest of the bonds and which would have to be paid in specie. Holders of token coins could also exchange them for bonds or ready cash, but only in Stockholm.[38] The coins were very light; their copper content was low; and they were not backed by bullion. They actually constituted a form of symbolic currency, not un-

36 In a letter to Law, Görtz stressed that Charles XII had absolute trust in him. SNA, Görtzska samlingen, vol. E3790, Letter from Görtz to Law, 20.8.1717. See also Lindeberg, *Svensk ekonomisk politik*, 93–94.

37 Jonatan Julén, *Om Sveriges statsskuld 1718 och betalningen av densamma* (Gothenburg: Göteborgs Kungl. vetenskaps- och vitterhets-samhälle, 1916), 27; Lindeberg, *Svensk ekonomisk politik*, 108–109; Jan Lindegren, "Krig och skuld: Den svenska statsskuldens historia ca. 1600–1800," *Kungl. Vetenskapssamhällets i Uppsala Årsbok* (2007–2008): 81–110, here 97.

38 *Kongl. Maj:ts Öpne Påbud Angående De Myntetekn [...]*, 8.3.1716, Årstrycket.

like paper money. In fact, paper bills were initially issued in conjunction with them, but they never came close to the volumes of the coins. Thus, the value of the token money ultimately depended on people's confidence in it.[39]

Görtz initially was hesitant about their introduction.[40] In the aforementioned memorandum that he wrote to the king on the subject, he managed at least theoretically to integrate them into his system. Drawing on the experience of the *billets de monnaie*, he claimed that the key to a successful launch of token money was to maintain government credit. In order to achieve this, the token coins would have to be released in proportion to the total amount of circulating liquidity; a fund would have to be assigned for their redemption; and holders should be able to profit from exchanging them into bonds. In this way, the bonds themselves would form part of the collateral offered for the token coins. Görtz stressed the importance of deducing the amount of token money that could be released. He arrived at a proportion of 1 : 3, relative the value of circulating legal tender. After a brief calculation of the number of coins in circulation, how much foreign currency could flow into the realm, and the value of the realm's exports, he concluded that a projected 2 million dsm. in token coins safely could be issued.[41] Although the relentless demands from continued warfare soon outpaced Görtz's calculations, he did not attempt to restrict the increasing volumes.

The token coins were issued in a succession of editions, each one with a different stamp and a different name. One edition would circulate for a limited period and then be exchanged for a new one. After their redemption, the old editions were re-launched at values of 1 or 2 *öre* (there were 32 öre to 1 dsm.), thus taking advantage of coins already manufactured to remedy the constant shortage of small change. The first edition (*Kronan*) was released in the spring of 1716 and amounted to little more than 2 million dsm, while the second edition (*Publica Fide*), issued in October 1716, amounted to 3.8 million. In April 1717, the largest single edition (*Wett och Vapen*) of 9 million dsm. was released. In January 1718, the next edition (*Flink och färdig*) of 7.4 million dsm. was issued. In June of the same year, a succession of editions (*Jupiter, Saturnus, Phoebus, Mars* and *Merkurius*) emerged in circulation, the first four of them amounted to 3 million each and the final one to 6 million. Together these editions totaled a staggering 18 million dsm.[42] At each consecutive exchange, an ever-larger amount was released, in particular during 1718. In the end, an unprecedented amount

39 Julén, *Om Sveriges statsskuld*, 23–27; Jan Lindegren, "Krig och skuld," 97.

40 Daniel Almqvist, "Om de karolinska mynttecknens ursprung," *Karolinska förbundets årsbok* (1936): 187–213, here 194–204.

41 Goerz in Moser, *Rettung der Ehre und Unschuld*, 397–404.

42 Julén, *Om Sveriges statsskuld*, 90.

of at least 21.5 million dsm. of token money was circulated. It has been estimated that this was equivalent to the accumulated volume of copper coins issued during the previous 90 years.[43]

By vastly increasing the amount of liquidity in circulation, an effect was achieved that John Law advocated in his *Money and trade considered*, namely setting people to work in exchange for cash payments.[44] The Norwegian campaign of 1718 relied on the participation of large number of peasants performing transport services for the military. As tens of thousands of peasants were commissioned and paid in token coins,[45] the relationship between state and subjects, king and peasants became increasingly monetized. Concurrently, because of military demand and the increasing availability of resources, both internal and external merchants provided grain and other foodstuffs to the army and navy.[46] Thus, traders from Amsterdam, Hamburg, Hull and Lübeck as well as Gothenburg and Stockholm participated in and drew benefits from the strengthening of the Swedish state's credit. For Görtz, it was important that both foreign merchants and local peasants were integrated into his financial system. The foreign merchants' participation in the system was primarily driven by their interest in Swedish bar iron, which they received in exchange for importing foodstuffs. It seems that many transactions were carried out in Swedish currency, which meant that foreign merchants had to handle token coins. Not everyone was pleased by this, but the merchants accepted such an arrangement as long as it was possible for them to sell the Swedish bar iron in international markets at a profit.[47]

43 Eli F. Heckscher, *Sveriges Ekonomiska Historia från Gustav Vasa: Första delen. Före frihetstiden* (Stockholm: Bonniers, 1936), 2:634; Jan Lindegren, "From Ystad to Frederikshald: Charles XII and the Great Northern War 1716–1718," in *Perspektiver på Den store nordiske krig 1700–1721: 300 år etter Carl XIIs fall*, ed. Knut Arstad (Oslo: Forsvarsmuseet, 2018).

44 John Law, *Money and Trade Considered, with a Proposal for Supplying the Nation with Money* (Edinburgh, 1705), 13–15; Antoin E. Murphy, *John Law: Economic Theorist and Policy-maker* (Oxford: Clarendon Press, 1997), 78–79.

45 Jan Lindegren, "Karl XII.," in *Kungar och krigare: Tre essäer om Karl X Gustav, Karl XI och Karl XII* (Stockholm: Atlantis, 1992), 197–206; Lindegren, "From Ystad to Frederikshald."

46 Gothenburg Regional Archives (GRA), Göteborgs rådhusrätt och magistrat före 1900, Notarii publici protokoll, vol. 6, 10.2., 8.3., 14–15.3., 19.3., 21.3., 21.4., 20–21.5., 31.5.1718; SNA, Görtzska samlingen, vol. E3807, Letters 9.6. and 16.6. 1718; Erik Lindberg, "The Swedish Salt Market During the Great Northern War," *Scandinavian Economic History Review* 57 (2009): 191–206, here 199–201.

47 For examples of bills between merchants, see GRA, Göteborgs rådhusrätt och magistrat före 1900, Notarii publici protokoll, vol. 6, 16.7. and 8.8.1718. See also Archiv der Hansestadt Lübeck, Altes Senatsarchiv, Externa Suecica, vol. 516, Magistrate in Lübeck to Johann Wolter, 21.10.1719, Gerhard Breyer to Magistrate in Lübeck, 19.3.1720. For examples of foreign merchants owning

Although the token coins made the Norwegian campaign possible, there was one ambition that was not fulfilled. With all probability, Görtz and the king had hoped that the coins would be used to a greater degree by the public to make investments in bonds.[48] If this had occurred, the circulating stock of money would have been reduced; the risk of inflation would have diminished; and a funded long-term debt would have been accumulated, which would have been much easier to handle than huge amounts of token cash. Neither Görtz nor the king had initially planned to increase the circulating liquidity by, as it turned out, more than ten times. However, the bulk of the increase was not dictated by monetary considerations but by escalating military requirements, especially in the year 1718.

Dismantling the System

With the death of Charles XII on 30 November 1718, the new financial system ended. The General Staff suspended the campaign in Norway and sent the army back to their recruitment districts, without any preparation for their sustenance. The new leadership immediately arrested Görtz. As a foreigner and a royal favorite he made a very convenient scapegoat for all the unpopular actions of the previous regime. After a hasty mock trial, in what can only be described as a politically motivated juridical murder, Görtz was executed on 19 February 1719. Meanwhile, since the succession to the throne was undecided, the late king's sister Ulrica Eleonora had to renounce royal absolutism as a condition for her ascension. When the *riksdag* gathered in Stockholm in January 1719, a new constitution was adopted that gave the *riksdag* power over fiscal and foreign policy.[49]

The Estates agreed to wind down the former regime's war policy and to reduce the role of the monarchy. But there was no concord on the question of what to do with the financial system. At the same time, the interpretation of and the reaction to the new political situation by people outside the halls of power affected the political leadership's policy options and especially the value of the

token coins, see SNA, Riksens ständers kontor, Kammarkontoret, Nummerlistor över 14-öres försäkringssedlar, vol. 1787, City of Gothenburg.

48 *Publication angående Uphandlings Wercket som på en wiss Fond eller Grund är inrättat*, Stockholm 29.12.1715.

49 Lennart Thanner, *Revolutionen i Sverige efter Karl XII:s död: Den inrepolitiska maktkampen under tidigare delen av Ulrika Eleonora d.y:s regering* (Uppsala, Diss. 1953); Werner Buchholz, *Staat und Ständegesellschaft in Schweden zur Zeit des Überganges vom Absolutismus zum Ständeparlamentarismus 1718–1720* (Stockholm: Acta Universitatis Stockholmiensis, 1979).

token coins. The changes-in-power created uncertainty about the previous regime's commitments, which in turn affected people's actions. On 11 December 1718, the new regime sent out a proclamation, which clarified that the token coins should remain in use and that they should be accepted in all types of transactions without any premium. The proclamation also pointed out that the government would replace token coins with money that had a clear value in relation to copper and silver.[50] Since the proclamation did not specify a time or the terms for this change, it rather increased uncertainty. Thus, reports started to come in to the authorities that people refused to deal with token coins or demanded much higher prices of customers paying with the currency. In Gothenburg, for instance, notaries reported in January 1719 that the value of token coins had depreciated by 50 percent.[51]

In the ensuing political debates many noblemen and clergymen stressed the need to withdraw the token coins from circulation as quickly as possible. The brothers Pehr and Conrad Ribbing were vocal proponents of such a course of action. As leading officials and noble landowners, they had been opposed to the administrative and financial reforms initiated by Görtz and the late king, and they had taken an active part in the commission against Görtz.[52] According to Conrad Ribbing, it was severely deleterious for a realm to have false and incorrect coins in circulation. It led to the loss of credit, increases in prices, a deteriorating exchange rate and the exodus of capital. Moreover, peasants, who owned many token coins, preferred to consume their assets rather than to sell their produce. Neither would they perform any work in exchange for payments, Ribbing claimed. He also stressed that the enormous size of the debt and the lack of specie assets made it necessary to drastically reduce the value of the token coins.[53]

This criticism, which manifests an intellectual link to the 1711 reply from the bank's representatives regarding the introduction of notes of credit, clearly focused on the need to return to a fiscal situation which promoted economic and social order and the hierarchy that went with it. The upheavals to both social relations and the workings of the state, which Ribbing thought the expansion of

---

50 *Placat Angående Myntetekns och Ständernes Mindre Zedlars owägerlige emottagande til des annat redbart Mynt blifwer anskaffat.* Stockholm 11.12.1718.

51 SNA, Det odelade kansliet, Rådsprotokoll, vol. 127, 11.12.1718; GRA, Göteborgs rådhusrätt och magistrat före 1900, Notarii publici protokoll, vol. 7, 23.7.1724.

52 Björn Asker, "Pehr Ribbing," *Svenskt biografiskt lexikon* (Stockholm: Norstedts, 1998–2000), 30:123.

53 SNA, Sekreta utskottets protokoll 1719, vol. R2384, 5.3.1719. See also SNA, Det odelade kansliet, Rådsprotokoll, vol. 128, 23.4.1719.

liquidity created, had to end quickly, even if it meant a drastic reduction in the state's capacity to wage war.

Several actors, especially with ties to international trade and to the iron-works sector, but also to the previous regime, questioned Ribbing's arguments by stressing the negative consequences of even a partial default. Casten Feif, for instance, a former advisor to Charles XII and owner of a sulphur-works, agreed to withdraw the coins from circulation, but he stressed that it had to be executed very cautiously in order to ensure that the less wealthy population would not lose their livelihood. He also emphasized the importance of maintaining the state's credit, since credit made it possible for the government to have a larger expenditure at hand than provided by its revenue. It was therefore necessary to ensure the exchange of the token coins at their nominal value and to avoid the indignity of a public bankruptcy.[54]

Another critic was the noble civil servant Daniel Niklas von Höpken, who had worked with Görtz in *upphandlingsdeputationen.* He argued that it would be impossible to force people to accept the token coins once they lost their credit. Since many foreign merchants had transformed their goods into token money, the state risked to lose its credit not only domestically but also abroad. He agreed with Conrad Ribbing that it was necessary to withdraw the token coins from circulation and that it was not possible to exchange all of them for specie coins in 1719. Yet, the solution was not to default on the token coins. Instead, they should be exchanged for government bonds yielding 1.5 percent annual interest. After the realm had negotiated a peace settlement, reductions in military spending and the long-term lease of government estates would create a fund that could be used to liquidate the bonds. Such a process would uphold the government's credit and prevent a default that would ruin many of its subjects.[55] Later, Höpken suggested that the realm should create a fund by negotiating a loan in the Dutch Republic, mortgaging the tax revenues from the province of Gotland as collateral.[56]

Höpken was also deeply involved in attempts in 1719 and 1720 to create a Swedish East India Company. The background to this plan was a visit to Charles XII in 1718 by representatives from the pirates in Madagascar, who wished to seek safety in an international state system increasingly hostile to privateering. The pirates offered to provide the Swedish king with ships and other resources in exchange for protection. The plan promised to strengthen the Swedish naval ca-

54 SNA, Sekreta utskottets protokoll 1719, vol. R2384, 8.4.1719.
55 SNA, Det odelade kansliet, Rådsprotokoll, vol. 127, 17.2.1719.
56 SNA, Sekreta utskottets protokoll 1719, vol. R2384, 26.5.1719.

pacity and to establish a Swedish colony in the Indian Ocean with access to the slave trade.[57] Moreover, it also entailed the formation of commercial links with Asia. Both the king and Görtz viewed the plans favorably, and they sent government officials to establish direct contact with the pirates. After the king's death, the new regime renewed the offer of protection and recognition, but its plans became more focused on trade as hostilities with Denmark ceased. Thus, the Swedish government chartered a company with the purpose of establishing trade between Sweden and Asia. The company depended on foreign capital and the expertise provided by the pirates, but its formation encountered financial problems after the collapse of the South Sea and Mississippi bubbles. Nevertheless, with the help of government resources, ships were equipped and sailed toward the Indian Ocean, but the expedition failed.[58] A more successful East India Company was eventually formed in 1731, with Höpken as an investor but without the ties to pirates in Madagascar.[59] In the discussions about the formation of the company in 1719 and 1720, Höpken stressed that the company would be beneficial for the state by strengthening toll revenues and by reducing the cost of importing colonial goods. No one in the deliberations, however, suggested that the government could use the company to convert or reduce the government's debt.[60]

The arguments and actions of Feif and Höpken show that there were political attempts not to salvage the token coins but to uphold a state dependent on credit. Such attempts included protecting the interests of all holders of government debt against the traditional elite. Höpken especially attempted to continue the policies of the former regime, by emphasizing the need to create new resour-

---

57 On the role of Madagascar in international trade, see Virginia B. Platt, "The East India Company and the Madagascar Slave Trade," *William and Mary Quarterly* 26 (1969): 548–577.

58 SNA, Det odelade kansliet, Rådsprotokoll, vol. 128, 21.4.1719, vol. 136, 25.5., 15.6., 20.6.1721; SNA, Riksarkivets ämnessamlingar, Handel och sjöfart, vol. 192a, Underdånigst Berättelse and instructions to Otto Klinckowström and Carl Gustaf Mandel, 8.8.1720; SNA, Riksarkivets ämnessamlingar, Handel och sjöfart, vol. 52, D.N. von Höpken's plan for a East India Company in 1720; C.K.S. Sprinchorn, "Madagaskar och dess sjöröfvare i Karl XII:s historia," *Karolinska förbundets årsbok* (1921): 241–276; Finn Bergstrand, "Då Madagaskar skulle bli svenskt – och England katolskt," *Karolinska förbundets årsbok* (1997): 28–42.

59 SNA, Svea Hovrätt, Adliga bouppteckningar, EIXB:17, 26.1.1742, Probate inventory after D.N. von Höpken; Leos Müller, "The Swedish East India Trade and International Markets: Re-Exports of Teas, 1731–1813," *Scandinavian Economic History Review* 51 (2003): 28–44, here 31–32.

60 SNA, Riksarkivets ämnessamlingar, Handel och sjöfart, vol. 52, D.N. von Höpken's plan for a East India Company in 1720; SNA, Det odelade kansliet, Rådsprotokoll, vol. 132, 11.5.1720, vol. 133, 2.8.1720; SNA, Skrivelser till Kungl. Maj:t, Kommerskollegium till Kungl. Maj:t, vol. 26, 23.7.1720.

ces that could strengthen the realm's credit and that would fortify the ties between the state and the international mercantile community. By doing so, he did not just follow in the footsteps of Görtz, but he also adhered to John Law's ideas and policies.

Another group, which collectively owned most of the token coins, and which staunchly opposed any default on them, was the peasantry. They emphasized that they had always considered the coins valid and that they could not afford to lose anything on them. They argued that as they had accepted the coins at their nominal value, they would return them at their nominal value. The peasants also stressed that they only had token coins for the payment of their taxes and that, if the other estates agreed to a default, they would not sign the decision.[61]

Despite the opposition from the peasantry and from representatives of trade and manufacturing interests, the *riksdag* decided to default on the token coins. Thus, the arguments presented by several noblemen and clergymen about the necessity to remove an unreliable currency prevailed. The decision was a victory for the established elite, which had seen the war policy and the new fiscal system as a threat to their interests. For them, dismantling royal absolutism, and the fiscal and financial policies, were two sides of the same coin. Concurrently, the groups involved in the expansion of the credit system and those who benefitted from it, lost political influence. The peasantry, who had strengthened their relative position because of the regime's need for the resources that they could deliver, especially lost out politically and economically when the new regime was established.

The default in April 1719 entailed a 50 percent cut in the value of the token coins, but the estates did not target the salary notes or the government bonds. Consequently, during a few weeks in June, more than 200,000 transactions were conducted, in which token coins with a total value of more than 20 million dsm. were removed from circulation. In their place, the government gave the owners so-called "insurance notes", with a formal denomination of 14/32 of the value of the token coins turned in. After eight days, the token coins were returned to their holders, now going as small change with a denomination of 2/32 of their original value. The insurance notes were only redeemable as payment for a new customs duty, but owners could sell them on a secondary market. Yet,

61 SNA, Sekreta utskottets protokoll 1719, vol. R2384, 9.4., 16.4., 29.5.1719.

their market value remained very low for nearly a decade. The market for the insurance notes existed into the 1760s.[62]

There are parallels, but also differences, between the collapse and liquidation of Görtz's and John Law's financial systems. In Sweden, the system was ultimately contingent upon the support of and trust in an absolutist king. On his death, there were severe doubts if the new regime would honor his commitments which reduced confidence in the token coins. Once they started to fall, they could not be saved. In France, the system did not fail because the political regime was brought down. Instead, Law's attempts to control liquidity by reducing the face value of the bank notes led to a fall in people's trust in the system. As in Sweden, it became impossible to regain confidence once it had been lost. In Sweden, a majority at the *riksdag* targeted the groups with the most widely distributed share of the debt in a partial default meant to reduce liquidity. In France, the government tried to protect the smallholders, as claimants received new perpetual annuities in exchange for their assets stemming from Law's system. Larger creditors, meanwhile, had to accept reductions when their claims were exchanged into annuities. Later, the regime organized a series of deflationary measures in order to come to terms with rising prices. The process of recognizing, categorizing and transforming claims also occurred in Sweden, but only for a series of specific claims excluded from the default. Like in France, holders of claims could trade their assets on a secondary market, which existed for decades. Finally, both processes were a way for mostly traditional elites to regain control and to offset the economic, political and social upheavals created by the financial innovations introduced in the 1710s.[63]

Conclusion

In order to continue the Great Northern War, Charles XII and his advisors had to find new ways of mobilizing resources. Although he did not face constitutional constraints when introducing new taxes, the king was clearly aware that it was

---

62 SNA, Riksens ständers kontor, Nummerlistor över 14-öres försäkringssedlar, vol. 1775–1795 Stockholm City Archives, Klara kyrkoarkiv, Kyrkoräkenskaper, Huvudbok 1719 and 1725, vol. 40 and 46; SNA, Riksens ständers kontor, Kammarkontorer, Licentmemorialböcker, 1764, vol. 520.

63 Karl Åmark, *Sveriges statsfinanser 1719–1809* (Stockholm: Norstedts, 1961), 675–712; François R. Velde, "French Public Finance between 1683 and 1726," in *Government Debts and Financial Markets in Europe*, ed. Fausto Piola Caselli (London: Pickering & Chatto, 2008), 135–165, here 151–156.

not sufficient to rely on established means of war finance. Financial innovations, which would increase liquidity and strengthen the realm's credit both internally and externally, had become necessary. Charles and his advisors were therefore receptive to new ideas, and the French experiences during the War of the Spanish Succession especially offered valuable examples.

Leading circles in Sweden shared an awareness of these financial innovations, but not everyone in the political elite shared the king's ambitions. Opponents used cameralist arguments on the need to maintain fiscal order in combination with complaints about a lack of government resources. For the king, it became apparent that he could rely neither on the established organization nor on his leading officials to implement new measures. Instead, he had to turn to an outsider, as many early modern rulers had done before him, and to build new government structures alongside financial innovation. Thus, when Charles XII and Georg Heinrich von Görtz met and designed a new system, it was a result of this critical juncture between a receptive political context and ideas about financial innovation. Görtz, clearly inspired by John Law and knowledgeable about financial practices in Britain, France and the Dutch Republic, was an important medium in the transmission of knowledge.

Beside political support, the system relied on the creation of new financial instruments and the monetization of local resources as well as on increasing flows of money and goods both within Sweden and between Sweden and markets in Germany and the Dutch Republic. Thus, it became necessary to integrate and make the largest section of the population, the peasantry, economically involved in the system, at the same time as the Crown strengthened its ties with merchants in Amsterdam, Hamburg and Lübeck. The working of the system relied on the combination of and the interaction between the local and the international in order to strengthen the credit of the state. Consequently, various privileges and traditional ways of allocating government resources succumbed to the interests of the credit state. Like in France under John Law, it became necessary to draw larger sections of society into the system. Although this process did not develop into a financial bubble in Sweden, ideas about increasing the volume of transactions and activity in the economy through monetization were the same as in France.

Some financial novelties were introduced in Sweden shortly before they were initiated in France. This is not to say that Görtz and his Swedish system inspired John Law. Rather, it is a testimony to the fact that financial ideas were shared and circulated among a group of European financial innovators. The implementation of such ideas was driven by the combination of financial emergency and political receptiveness.

The Swedish system ended with the king's death. The new rulers mostly belonged to the traditional elite, who had lost out both economically and socially during the 1710s. As they came to dominate the *riksdag* in the spring of 1719, they were able to end the financial innovations in an attempt to return to the fiscal and social order that existed before the war. It was therefore politics rather than a financial speculative bubble that ultimately sealed the fate of the financial innovations in Sweden.

Yet, the credit state did not end with Görtz's system. The Bank of Sweden was operational, and the financial instruments and claims created during the Great Northern War circulated for several decades after the war ended. In other words, the market for government-issued financial instruments expanded during the eighteenth century. The system launched by Görtz and Charles XII contributed to the growth of that market through a huge addition of instruments, and, even if the new parliamentary regime reduced the liquidity and if many lost a lot of money when the system was dismantled, more people than before participated in financial transactions. Thus, the system successfully broadened and deepened the market, a process that continued long after the system itself was gone.

Stefano Condorelli, Daniel Menning

Chartering Companies. A Dialogue about the Timeline and the Actors of the Pan-European 1720 Stock Euphoria

Stefano Condorelli: Academic work is by definition a collective enterprise, a continuous and sedimented dialogue with colleagues, some alive, the others only living and speaking through their works. This collective dialogue, this constant intellectual exchange, remains mostly in the shadows. Of course, we continually quote other scholars in our works, but we generally do that for functional, strategic reasons: to give evidence supporting our arguments, or on the contrary to highlight the originality, the singularity of our approach ("they say, I say").[1] True, most publications contain acknowledgments. Yet, these are rarely very developed; they are most often simple lists of names rather than a form of dialogue. Nothing should be read as criticism here; it is simply a matter of fact that all academics know perfectly well. The largest part of the exchanges we have with our colleagues, living or dead, does not appear in our publications; like a kind of iceberg, most of it stays under the surface. This is the reason why we thought it would be interesting to write this chapter in the form of a dialogue. The dialogue with its ancient tradition as an embryonic form of plurality. And I must add that, on my side, the idea also stems from the conversations I have with my sister, the artist Céline Condorelli, who has co-written a book on this very subject.[2]

Daniel Menning: In our case, the dialogical form is also particularly appropriate, because we have been discussing the 1720 financial bubble for more than four years now. We each began our own research on the subject in a completely separate way. Independently, we both thought that it would be interesting to study this event from a broader perspective, that is to say, beyond the traditional focus on the Paris–London–Amsterdam triangle. When we first met in 2014, we discovered that our research was partly overlapping and partly complementary. We had mostly used different primary sources, and we were developing different arguments, and precisely for this reason we thought it would be interesting to start

1 To quote the famous book by Gerald Graff and Cathy Birkenstein, *'They Say/I Say': The Moves That Matter in Academic Writing* (New York: W.W. Norton, 2006).
2 Céline Condorelli, *The Company She Keeps* (London: Book Works, 2014).

https://doi.org/10.1515/9783110592139-004

working in parallel, sharing ideas and archival findings. Our collaboration led to this book and to the conference that preceded it in Tübingen.

The Timeline

M: One of the most salient and interesting features of the 1719–20 bubble is certainly its asynchronous character: stock markets inflating one after another across Europe. The French Mississippi Bubble gathered momentum in the spring of 1719, peaked in late December, and collapsed in May 1720; the London market started its dramatic rise in February 1720, reached its apex in August, and crashed in September; in Amsterdam, shares (in fact, mostly those of the West India Company) spiked in the spring and summer of 1720, and the bubble burst in September.[3] There was also short-lived speculation in Hamburg in July which the city council quickly suppressed.[4]

C: Interestingly, there was also a second, smaller, Dutch boom in October–November 1720, with, for instance, a company such as the Middelburg Assurance reaching a peak in its share price on 4 November.[5] The same month saw the bubble that I "discovered," namely that of the Lorraine Company.[6] Voltaire writes that he skipped his "souper" to rush to Nancy in order to "take shares" in the subscription.[7] It is not clear to what extent we should believe him when he boasts that he "trebled his capital." What we know for sure though – because the *Gazette d'Amsterdam* published the prices – is that Lorraine shares increased by 40 percent in a couple of weeks.

---

3 For comprehensive price data, see the *FGR 1720 price database* by Rik G.P. Frehen, William N. Goetzmann and K. Geert Rouwenhorst. For more information on the database see https://som.yale.edu/faculty-research/our-centers-initiatives/international-center-finance/data/historical-southseabubble, last visit 24.8.2018. For the calculation of the London and Amsterdam Indexes, see Stefano Condorelli, *Price Momentum and the 1719–20 Bubbles: A Method to Compare and Interpret Booms and Crashes in Asset Markets, MPRA Paper* (2018).

4 Caesar Amsinck, "Die ersten hamburgischen Assecuranz-Compagnien und der Actienhandel im Jahre 1720," *Zeitschrift des Vereins für Hamburgische Geschichte* 9 (1894): 465–494.

5 Frehen, Goetzmann and Rouwenhorst, *Price Database*.

6 Stefano Condorelli, *The 1719–20 Stock Euphoria: A Pan-European Perspective, MPRA Paper* (2014).

7 François Marie Arouet de Voltaire, *Pièces inédites de Voltaire, imprimées d'après les manuscrits originaux*, ed. Jean Cornelle Jacobsen (Paris, 1820), 213–217. The book mentions 1729, yet it is clear that the event took place in 1720. On the subject, see André Courbet, "Voltaire en Lorraine: Les séjours de 1720 et 1735," *Cahiers Voltaire* 13 (2014): 51–68.

M: As you have shown in your research paper, together with the bubbles themselves, there was a pan-European boom in joint-stock schemes.[8] Many projects were simply aborted; others successfully gave birth to a company though without triggering a wave of speculation (for instance the Austrian Oriental Company launched in 1719, which carried on its business for over a decade).[9] Anyhow, the point I want to raise here is that the wave of new undertakings subsided but did not dry up despite the successive 1720 stock market crashes. In April 1721, the landgrave of Hessen-Kassel chartered a *Kommerzbank* whose equities were effectively sold in the early summer;[10] in the second half of 1721, the Irish parliament was still debating proposals for a joint-stock bank in Dublin; other 1721 projects were being considered or implemented in the Austrian Netherlands, Braunschweig, Genoa, Hannover, Naples, Piedmont, Portugal, Russia, Sicily, Spain, and Switzerland.[11]

C: Clearly, the successive 1720 stock market crashes in Paris, London and Amsterdam had not entirely undermined the appeal of the joint-stock form. This may seem paradoxical, not only in our eyes, but also in the eyes of contemporaries. To give just one example among many, a Dutch newspaper, writing about a new scheme for an Ostend Company in January 1721, commented: "should we dare to trust [this new undertaking] after what has happened in France and in the neighboring countries?"[12]

M: So, the question is why contemporaries kept promoting companies and buying shares in spite of not only the sequence of crashes, but also of the reports about the apparent catastrophic economic and political dislocation in Paris and London. Surely, this was not done out of ignorance.

---

8 Condorelli, *Stock Euphoria.*

9 Josef Dullinger, "Die Handelskompagnien Österreichs nach dem Oriente und nach Ostindien in der ersten Hälfte des 18. Jahrhunderts," *Zeitschrift für Social- und Wirthschaftsgeschichte* 7 (1900): 44–83; Franz Martin Mayer, *Die Anfänge des Handels und der Industrie in Österreich und die orientalische Compagnie* (Innsbruck: Verlag der Wagner'schen Universitätsbuchhandlung, 1882).

10 Concerning this firm, which was still in operation in the nineteenth century, see Stefano Condorelli and Daniel Menning, "Wirtschaftspolitik im Zeichen der europäischen Börseneuphorie: Die Gründung der Leyh- und Commercien-Compagnie und die Reform der Tuchproduktion in Hessen-Kassel 1721," *Hessisches Jahrbuch für Landesgeschichte* 68 (2018): 99–114.

11 Condorelli, *Stock Euphoria.*

12 *Lettres Historiques*, January 1721, 113.

C: There is overwhelming evidence that financial information circulated widely throughout Europe, in particular via the press. A fundamental fact which has received little attention so far is that English and Dutch newspapers were not the only ones to give detailed financial news. The *Corriere di Vienna*, *Gazette de Berne*, *Gaceta de Madrid*, or *Avvisi di Napoli*, to name a few, regularly informed their readers of the latest financial developments, including the Paris, London, and Amsterdam stock market booms, and (sometimes) quoted share prices.[13]

M: You are of course right, and the same can be said for German newspapers. Eve Rosenhaft has shown the interest in the Paris events in central Europe.[14] Thus, by June 1720, people all over the continent were well aware of the failure of John Law.[15] With the crash in London in September, there was further compelling evidence that the bursting of speculative bubbles was a very likely occurrence, and that it did not depend on the nature of the political regime or other such factors (as some contemporaries had been thinking).[16] Thus, people – and more especially governments – were certainly aware of the potential dangers of speculation that could follow upon the heels of the chartering of joint-stock companies in their country. However, we have to keep in mind that the different actors, of course, did not face the same risks, and did not have the same motivations.

C: There is plenty of evidence that 1720 investors (at least the most experienced and sophisticated ones) often saw the succession of booms as an opportunity. Many of them thought that there was a profitable – albeit arduous – game that could be played, namely "riding" one bubble after the other.[17] The letters of the Duke of Chandos offer many examples of that game. Writing to Richard Cantillon in August 1720, he declared, for instance: "I believe buying up subscriptions as soon as they come out & selling them at a reasonable profit is the surest way for getting [a profit], for all subscrip[tions] rise upon their

13 Condorelli, *Stock Euphoria*.

14 Eve Rosenhaft, "'All That Glitters is not Gold, but …': German Responses to the Financial Bubbles of 1720," in *Money in the German-Speaking Lands*, ed. Mary Lindemann and Jared Poley (Oxford and Providence: Berghahn, 2017), 74–95.

15 Stefano Condorelli, "La presse étrangère et le Système de Law (1716–1720)," in '*Gagnons sans savoir comment*': *Représentations du Système de Law du XVIIIe à nos jours*, ed. Florence Magnot-Ogilvy (Rennes: Presses universitaires de Rennes, 2017), 183–206, here 198–200.

16 See for example Thomas Gordon, *Considerations Offered upon the Approaching Peace and upon the Importance of Gibraltar to the British Empire* (London, 1720), 28–29.

17 The classic example of an actor that successfully managed to ride a 1720 bubble is Hoare's Bank: see Peter Temin and Hans-Joachim Voth, "Riding the South Sea Bubble," *American Economic Review* 94 (2004): 1654–1668.

being first taken, though sometimes it lasts not long."[18] But this strategy was of course only potentially profitable for investors, whereas governments, in case of a market crash, would have to face the economic, social, and political consequences.

M: Both the French and British governments vacillated following the Mississippi and South Sea crashes. In France, John Law was exiled, narrowly escaping imprisonment and possibly death; in London, one minister, John Aislabie, was taken to the Tower, and Robert Walpole rose to power. It is noteworthy that foreign diplomats in London were unsure whether there might be another revolution with a potential return of the Stuarts. For instance, the Austrian resident reported in late October of 1720 that he had "experienced revolutions, invasions and rebellions [in Britain], but never seen the credit of this rich nation decreased to such a degree and witnessed the nation itself in such a general perplexion and calamity."[19] One would think that knowledge of the potential danger would have dissuaded governments from authorizing the promotion of further companies. Yet, it did not!

The Role of Governments and Emulation

C: The role of governments, of course, was central because it was not possible at the time to create a joint-stock company without some form of official approval – only in Britain, the situation was somewhat more ambiguous.[20] The state, therefore, played a key role all over Europe in the 1720 joint-stock boom. Yet, the complex dynamics between rulers, projectors, and all the other financial actors differed significantly from one country to another.

M: Regarding governments, I think we need to consider two different aspects. The multiple threats of share speculation (to which we will return later) and the promise of the joint-stock form. Throughout Europe, there was a great hope that the benefits offered by corporations would create opportunities for economic profit and development. In the Dutch Republic, for instance, the

---

18 Huntington Library, Stowe 57, 17, f. 163, 25.8.1720.

19 Johann Philipp Hoffmann to Charles IV, London 25.10.1720, in Österreichisches Staatsarchiv, Haus-, Hof- und Staatsarchiv, England, Korrespondenz, Karton 60, 24.

20 For a discussion of the unincorporated joint-stock company, see in particular Ron Harris, *Industrializing English Law: Entrepreneurship and Business Organization, 1720–1844* (Cambridge: Cambridge University Press, 2000), 137–167.

1720 joint-stock enterprises were frequently promoted by municipal and regional elites who tried to rejuvenate the economy of their respective hometowns or provinces. These authorities expected those companies, with extensive business interests in trade, manufacturing and finance, to spur the growth of the local economy.[21]

C: A similar perspective on economic policy can be found throughout Europe. For instance, in Venice where the senate favored the creation of a joint-stock company in 1720, on the grounds that it would contribute to the development and improvement of manufactures, increase tax entries, expand employment, and thus offer "a relief to the poor"[22] or in Russia, where Peter the Great projected a Persia Trading Company (and invited John Law to manage it) with the intent of developing trade and manufactures, and of colonizing the Caspian area.[23]

M: For me, a key concept to the understanding of governmental responses to speculation and company promotion seems to come from early modern political economy, and has been studied in depth by Sophus Reinert. "Emulation," according to him, was a basic mode of policy in the eighteenth century. It was "a noble alternative to 'envy' broadly signifying the desire to imitate and improve on superiors."[24] Governments across Europe constantly watched each other's measures, and evaluated their respective achievements and the adaptability of an opponent's actions to the conditions in their own territory. "[S]uccessful policies were invariably emulated and countervailed by competitors, an agonistic process further complicated by the fact that an emulatee inevitably changed the conditions for its success in the very process of forging ahead."[25] Even unsuccessful measures could be emulated, as sometimes small changes could make a policy work for one state that had failed elsewhere. Thus, "emulation," in con-

---

21 Oscar Gelderblom and Joost Jonker, "Mirroring Different Follies: The Character of the 1720 Bubble in the Dutch Republic," in *The Great Mirror of Folly: Finance, Culture and the Crash of 1720*, ed. William N. Goetzmann et al. (New Haven: Yale University Press, 2013), 121–139.

22 Archivio di Stato di Venezia, V Savi, scritture dei deputati al commercio 213, c. 27–30.

23 Document published in S.M. Troickij, "Le Système de John Law et ses continuateurs russes," in *La Russie et l'Europe*, xvie–xxe *siècles*, ed. Fernand Braudel et al. (Paris: S.E.V.P.E.N., 1970), 31–69, here 65–67.

24 Sophus A. Reinert, *Translating Empire: Emulation and the Origins of Political Economy* (Cambridge, Mass.: Harvard University Press, 2011), 2.

25 Sophus Reinert, "Rivalry: Greatness in Early Modern Political Economy," in *Mercantilism Reimagined: Political Economy in Early Modern Britain and Its Empire*, ed. Philip J. Stern and Carl Wennerlind (Oxford: Oxford University Press, 2013), 384–370, here 358.

trast to "imitation," focuses on adaptation and improvement instead of mere copying. This was exactly what authorities around 1720 were attempting.

C: The idea of adaptation rather than mere copying is indeed crucial. Yet, it seems to me that the notion of emulation makes particular sense among actors which are more or less equals, more or less in competition: France, Britain, Austria, etc. I am not sure that it provides a good description of the whole 1720 situation, where minor and even minuscule players (for instance the city of Emden) were inspired by what the big players were doing. Of course, we could say that there were several layers or clusters of emulation: among the major powers (France, Britain, the United Provinces, etc.), the Italian states (Venice, Genoa, etc.), the German principalities (Hessen, Braunschweig, etc.), the Dutch cities, etc. There was, in particular, a specific emulation between Portugal and Spain, with Portuguese diplomats in Madrid reporting to their government about any hint of a possible Spanish joint-stock project, and vice versa for the Spanish diplomats in Lisbon. On the other hand, I see "emulation" as mostly describing the intentions of governments. If we look instead at the projects of companies, with their strategic and technical aspects (corporate strategy, corporate governance, provisions regarding foreign investors, etc.) I would say that the actors were in fact imitating, copying, adapting. To take one example, the business model inaugurated by John Law in France – namely a firm made up of both a bank and a trading company – was imitated and adapted by many other joint-stock projects in the Austrian Netherlands, Braunschweig, Hannover, Lorraine, Piedmont, Portugal, Russia, and Spain.

M: My preference for "emulation" stems from the fact that beyond a government trying to improve the economic circumstances as a goal in itself, companies were frequently considered to be or portrayed as being part of a game in which one corporation's profit would be at the expense of some other place – as is especially evident with the marine insurance promotions in London, Rotterdam, and Hamburg. Each of the companies in these cities was emphasizing its ability to attract customers from outside the country/city at the expense of competitors, thereby drawing money into the local economy and thus making it more powerful.[26] Such economic competition was the side effect of political quarreling

---

26 Barry Supple, *The Royal Exchange Assurance: A History of British Insurance 1720–1970* (Cambridge: Cambridge University Press, 1970), 15–16; Sabine Go, *Marine Insurance in the Netherlands 1600–1780: A Comparative Institutional Approach* (Amsterdam: Amsterdam University Press, 2009), 216; *Unvorgreifliche Gedancken, das Assecurans-Wesen, hauptsächlich aber die in Hamburg auffgerichtete Assecurans-Compagnie betreffend* (Hamburg, 1720).

which between the larger states regularly erupted into warfare in the seventeenth and eighteenth centuries. Therefore, I think that the idea of emulation is fairly broad, and I prefer it because it is a concept contemporaries used. In addition it connects the bubbles to larger problems of eighteenth-century political economy.

C: I fully agree with you that it is fundamental to contextualize the 1720 bubble if we want to truly understand it, and from this perspective, the notion of emulation – which the contemporaries would have understood well – is indeed very useful. By contrast, in a paper under preparation, I am trying to analyze the 1720 joint-stock boom by drawing on a field of studies – policy innovation and diffusion – wholly unfamiliar to the eighteenth century.[27] Yet, I would argue that this field nonetheless offers a useful framework to examine the 1720 events. This is obviously not the place to detail the model, but let us just consider one of the mechanisms explaining diffusion, that is to say, competition among actors. The literature on the topic distinguishes two main factors of competition between governments: *spillover-induced* and *location-choice*.[28] Both factors played a role around 1720. Put simply, *spillover-induced* competition means that if a government adopts a new policy, this is going to affect the probability that a competitor will also adopt it. This element was very strong in 1720, as many schemes were targeted at improving state finance (debt restructuring, monetary financing, increasing revenues). There is plenty of evidence that contemporaries thought that these innovations could potentially affect the balance of power in Europe. This motive explains a great deal of the 1720 dynamic between France and Britain. It is well-know that the British cabinet began to discuss a plan for the conversion of the National Debt with the South Sea Company in the fall of 1719, precisely because at the time it appeared that John Law had managed, with a similar operation, to drastically reduce the weight of the French sovereign debt.[29] *Location-choice*, in our case, concerned the competition for international trade and capital flows.

27 See for instance J.L. Walker, "The Diffusion of Innovations Among the American States," *American Political Science Review* 63 (1969): 880 – 899.

28 For an overview see F.S. Berry and W.D. Berry, "Innovation and Diffusion: Models in Policy Research," in *Theories of the Policy Process*, ed. C.M. Weible and P.A. Sabatier, 3rd ed. (Boulder: Westview Press, 2014), 312 – 313.

29 John Carswell, *The South Sea Bubble* (London: Cresset Press, 1960), 99 – 101; Peter G.M. Dickson, *The Financial Revolution in England: A Study in the Development of Public Credit, 1688 – 1756* (London: MacMillan, 1967), 91 – 95.

International Flows of Capital

M: Competition for capital flows was certainly a key driving force of the successive company promotions. Circulating money had major implications for smaller cities and territories. Any successful company promotion was of course dependent on investment resources – which may not have been available locally. In 1720, governments throughout Europe discovered, or were told by company promoters, that international capital had become more accommodating and that the local supply was not the only pool of money where one could fish for subscriptions. There appears to have been a growing awareness that investment capital and speculative bubble-riding money travelled around Europe to those locations where new companies had been proposed or where they had been floated.

C: As a general framework, we have to keep in mind that capital was (paradoxically) not necessarily always a rare resource in early modern Europe.[30] Having said that, the years 1719–1721 clearly represented a new step in the international circulation of capital. Nothing is more emblematic than the huge influx of investors coming to Paris in the fall of 1719. The whole of Europe was stunned by the vivid descriptions of this mass of people (around two hundred thousand, according to contemporary reports), arriving from the provinces or from abroad, to buy shares of the Mississippi Company, and to trade in the rue Quincampoix.[31] Beyond anecdotal evidence, Larry Neal in particular has demonstrated – through the analysis of exchange rates – the importance of movements of capital between Paris, London, Amsterdam, and Hamburg.[32]

M: But the fact that investors shifted funds between the European (trading) capitals such as Paris, Amsterdam, London, and Hamburg may at first sight not have been a hopeful sign for authorities and promoters in cities of lesser economic and financial importance. Yet, things appear to have changed precisely around late 1719. Up until then, in a number of European cities, investment capital proved to be either scarce or not forthcoming, because the projects did not seem tempting enough. This lack of capital was at first a problem for anyone try-

---

30 See in particular Simon Kuznets, "Capital Formation in Modern Economic Growth (and Some Implications for the Past)," in *Proceedings of the Third International Conference of Economic History* (Paris: Mouton, 1968), 3:15–33; Fernand Braudel, *Civilisation matérielle et capitalisme, XV*e*–XVIII*e *siècle* (Paris: Armand Colin, 1979), 2:282–290.

31 Condorelli, "La presse," 192. See also Marlene Kessler's chapter in this volume.

32 Larry Neal, *The Rise of Financial Capitalism: International Capital Markets in the Age of Reason* (Cambridge and New York: Cambridge University Press, 1990), 62–80.

ing to emulate the successful French and earlier British company promotions. For example, in the first half of 1719, Emperor Charles VI chartered a trading firm to initiate a commodity exchange between Austria and the Ottoman Empire, one of the first new companies of the joint-stock boom. It was to profit from trade concessions Charles' negotiators had wrestled from the Ottomans in the peace treaty of Passarowitz the year before. Though according to Franz Martin Mayer the shares of the concern were advertised internationally, neither Viennese nor the intended Dutch or Italian merchants bought them to any larger degree. Only 75 shares (of a provisionally not specified number) sold by the end of the year – a marked failure from the point of view of the Habsburg government. In late 1719 and early 1720, another attempt at finding subscribers was made. Though the maximum number of shares was still not specified, the original sales price of 1,000 Rhenish guilders was only valid for six months. Afterwards, the market was to determine the price. But still, money was not forthcoming. The example shows that a company in a minor European trading center was not yet able to attract international speculative capital. Investors seem neither to have expected a successful Austrian Oriental Company, nor, given the unspecified number of shares of the company, an imminent Viennese stock market bubble.[33]

C: The case of Vienna is an interesting counter-example. By contrast, (although none of the schemes actually took off there) capital poured into Portugal in the spring and summer of 1720, in the expectation of a possible "Brazil Bubble." These capital flows left, in August, a huge "signature" in the Lisbon exchange rate on London and Amsterdam. There is also evidence of English speculators traveling to Portugal "to try their fortune" in the expected share price boom.[34]

M: I recently came across interesting additional pieces of evidence supporting your findings about the Portuguese "boom." According to the gazette *Europäische Fama*, 480,000 cruzados (about £64,000) were shipped from Falmouth to Lisbon in late August 1720, at a time when the London stock market was scrambling for liquidity.[35] Furthermore, the British consul in Lisbon, Thomas Burnett, wrote to a friend back in England that he was harassed by would-be investors:

---

33 Mayer, *Anfänge des Handels*, 75–79; Dullinger, "Handelskompagnien Österreichs," 47–48.
34 Condorelli, *Stock Euphoria*, 17 and figures 8 and 9. Eric Schubert, *The Ties That Bound: Eighteenth Century Market Behavior in Foreign Exchange, International Goods, and Financial Assets*, unpublished Ph.D. dissertation (Urbana-Champaign, 1986), 155, was the first to spot the spike in the Lisbon exchange rate in the summer 1720 and connect this finding to the Brazil Bubble.
35 *Europäische Fama* 238 (1720): 848.

> You can scarce imagine the vast Number of People that have wrote to me to put into the Brasil Stock for them. Some who never saw me, write to me that upon all occasions they have spoke very handsomely of me; others that I may remember to have seen them when I lived in the Temple: Another that he had a vast esteem for my Father and had read some of my Writings with great pleasure. Nay, which I never was honoured with before, I have some few Letters from Ladys of the first Quality to serve them on this Occasion. And all this upon the meer Report of a Stock, that never has yet come to a real Digestion.[36]

C: A comparable situation happened in Spain. There too, no joint-stock scheme got off the ground, and yet, the "meer report of a stock" (to quote Thomas Burnett) resulted in massive inflows of capital in the summer and again in the autumn of 1720. As in Portugal, these inflows left an unmistakable "signature" in the Cadiz exchange rate.[37] There were also significant capital flows – especially from France – coming to Nancy in November 1720, intended for investment in the Lorraine Company. To give a last example, there is evidence that English investors (and possibly other foreigners) had bought shares in an "Oriental Company" formed in Russia between 1720 and 1721. The firm was under the patronage of prince Menshikov (a close friend of Peter the Great) and had been designed to take advantage of the expected favorable outcome of the Lev Izmailov embassy that had been sent to Beijing in 1719 to negotiate a Sino-Russian trade agreement. Yet, negotiations failed in late 1721, resulting in the demise of the company.[38]

M: These money flows also apply to the German North Sea city of Emden, where a trading and manufacturing company was floated between September and November 1720. What is interesting is the register of the major shareholders that is extant in the regional archive. The document gives the name and place of residence of those who were eligible to vote for directorial positions. Overall, the list covers almost 70 percent of the owners of the 10,000 total shares.[39] One thing is immediately evident: large investments from Emdeners hardly existed.

---

36 Thomas Burnett to George Duckett, Lisbon 12.10.1720, in *The Letters of Thomas Burnett to George Duckett 1712–1722*, ed. David Nichol Smith (Oxford: Roxburghe Club, 1914), 171.

37 Condorelli, *Stock Euphoria*, 16–17 and figures 8 and 9.

38 For the sources and the exchange rates graph Condorelli, *Stock Euphoria*, 16–17, 65–66, 71, and figures 8 and 9. About the 1719–21 Sino-Russian negotiations: M.I. Sladkovskii, *History of Economic Relations Between Russia and China: From Modernization to Maoism* (New Brunswick: Transaction Publishers, 1966).

39 Register der Mans Personen die Eligibel syn tot Directeurs en Hooftparticipanten Van de Compagnie van Commerci, Navigatie etc. binnen de Stadt EMBDEN, Emden 18.11.1720, in Niedersächsisches Landesarchiv Aurich, Rep. 4, B IVe, Nr. 179, 47.

Only 55 shares or .55 percent were held by major investors living in the city, including the 25 shares owned by the promoter Elias Geraud, who was in fact a Huguenot recently arrived from Hamburg. Outside Emden, six major shareholders came from Germany (with a total of 90 shares), five from London (125 shares), two from Bruges (50 shares), against 309 large investors that came from the Dutch Republic and subscribed for 6,592 shares. Of these Dutch investors, a majority resided in Rotterdam (96 with 2,057 shares) and Amsterdam (186 with 3,965 shares).

C: There is, therefore, plenty of evidence that capital did not only flow inside the Paris–London–Amsterdam triangle; it circulated across the continent, from Portugal to Russia. What is more, the scene was not dominated by the largest players: the Lorraine and Emden cases demonstrate that even small and minuscule ventures managed to attract large numbers of foreign investors. This is not to say that 1720 investors were indiscriminately buying any stock in any country. The case of the Viennese Company – which was still looking for shareholders more than one year after its initial flotation – is an obvious example in this respect.

Taming Speculation, Safeguarding Against a Crash

M: Returning to the issue of speculation which we raised before, this was clearly something that worried many governments throughout Europe, even more so after the bursting of the Paris and London bubbles. Yet, on the other hand, contemporaries saw a number of ways to limit stock-jobbing. Moreover, there were dynamics which *de facto* kept it outside of particular countries or cities. Back to the Emden case, and considering the list of investors, one thing is striking, though we cannot be sure that the city council had anticipated this before authorizing the company. The geographical distribution of share-ownership seems to carry with it implications for stock trading. As the speculation with company shares would require seller and buyer to find each other, that task could be accomplished most easily in places where the number of share owners was reasonably large – this was more the case in Rotterdam and Amsterdam than in Emden itself. Therefore, if speculation with the shares were to occur, leading to a bubble that might burst, this would most likely happen not in the east Frisian town, but in the Dutch trading centers. In such a situation, attracting foreign investments into a joint-stock company had a twofold advantage: It helped overcome local constraints of investment capital and was, at the same time, a means of protecting oneself from the danger of establishing a share market within one's own city limits.

Very much in accordance with this line of reasoning was a rule in Hannover, where British projectors were pursuing charters for one manufacturing and one trading company. Lists of prospective investors almost exclusively include people from London. Thus, as in the Emden case, the risk of a share trade in the Electorate itself may not have been very large. Until the early fall, the Hanoverian government seems to have been unconcerned about speculation anyway. The charter for the manufacturing company from early July 1720 – thus, before the crash in London – explicitly allowed subscriptions to take place in Hannover.[40] Yet, discussing the trading company in early fall, for the first time, an article was inserted into the draft charter that prohibited stock subscriptions in the Electorate. It was elaborated over the following weeks, finally taking shape in the middle of November, when the charter stated:

> It is up to the company and its British members how they want to collect the necessary capital for the establishment at Harburg between themselves. [...] As far as our German subjects are concerned, no transfer of company capital or so called actions [into their possession ...] shall take place without our special consent [...]. Also, nowhere in our German territories shall subscriptions take place in which some of our German subjects may be concerned directly or indirectly.[41]

Thus, a simple clause in a charter seemed to be capable of providing additional protection from the dangers of importing speculation. It appeared possible to legally keep the share ownership and, thereby, speculative trading, out of the country.

C: We find many provisions to curb speculation in the projects and charters of other companies. One Spanish scheme of the end of 1720 stipulated, for instance, that share transfers could only take place through public notaries – a provision obviously intended to slow down the pace of trading.[42] In Ireland, while the parliament was debating a charter for a bank in the fall of 1721, it considered prohibiting transfers of stocks not registered in the company's book as a way "to

---

40 The most comprehensive account of the Harburg Company so far is A.J.G. Cummings, "The Harburgh Company and Its Lottery 1716–1723," in *Business in the Age of Reason*, ed. R.P.T. Davenport-Hines (London: Routledge, 1987), 1–18. It suffers, however, from a lack of sources on the company's early history. The account here is based on: Landesarchiv Hannover (LAH), Dep. 113, Nr. 22.

41 Draft of a charter, no place, 15.11.1720, in LAH, Dep. 113, Nr. 22, unfol., 73–75.

42 Archivo Historico Nacional de Madrid, Estado leg. 3188, n. 415, 34.

prevent stock jobbing."[43] Even more drastically, it seems that the Portuguese government was thinking, in the spring of 1721, about shares that could not be transferred at all.[44] Although we do not have all the details, there is some evidence that the project for a Swiss Trading Company of June 1721 established a similar rule.[45]

M: Another method was to transform, to a certain extent, the very nature of the shares. We find this, for example, in the charter of the Hessen-Kassel Bank. The company – projected by a Genevan banker who had actively participated in the Mississippi Bubble – received its charter in April 1721 and was one of the last successful flotations of the boom period. The stock carried a guaranteed annual interest of 5 percent, instead of a dividend connected to the yearly profits of the bank. Thus, the share resembled some modern-day bonds. Yet, the shareholders would also receive an additional revenue if the bank made a profit above 5 percent. Therefore, this was really a hybrid between a bond and share. Furthermore, the Hessen-Kassel shares would be sold at the original subscription price of 100 guilders as long as there were some of the 5,000 shares left in the possession of the bank. This was intended to preclude the successive mark-ups that had propelled the South Sea Company speculation, and it would serve to dampen the trade in shares as long as there were still any for sale by the bank itself. Finally, and what is most noteworthy, those willing to sell their shares, could do so to the company at all times, and it would take them back at the original price. Thereby, the bank intended to protect possible investors from losses due to a decline in the market share price.[46]

C: Of course, one might say that these safeguards against speculation and against a possible crash are not surprising given that all the above charters were drafted after the autumn of 1720, that is to say, following the triple crash in Paris, London, and Amsterdam. Yet, besides the timing of the charters, we have to keep in mind that there was a fundamental distinction, in early modern times, between illegitimate and legitimate forms of commerce. In the first half of the eighteenth century, there was still a strong discredit – whose origins went

43 Michael Ryder, "The Bank of Ireland, 1721: Land, Credit and Dependency," *Historical Journal* 25 (1982): 557–582, here 563.

44 Thomas Burnett to George Duckett, Lisbon 1.3.1721 N.S., in *Letters of Thomas Burnett*, 172.

45 *Lettres Historiques*, June 1721, 622.

46 "Fürstliches Privilegium welches der Leyh- und Commercien-Compagnie zu Etablierung eines Lombards in der Residentz-Stadt Cassel ertheilt worden," Schmalkalden 19.4.1721, in *Sammlung Fürstlich-Hessischer Landes-Ordnungen und Ausschreiben* (Kassel, 1777), 3:853–856.

back very far in time – attached to many financial activities, in particular to stock-jobbing and other forms of speculation. In the minds of many contemporaries, these were hardly distinguishable from usury or fraud, and they remained in any case marked by the indignity that was associated with lucre. What is interesting, however, is that mentalities were evolving: and nothing was really clear-cut. The Hamburg case is particularly interesting in this respect.

M: Yes, the Hamburg council prohibited share *trading* in the city just a few days after two insurance companies had been floated by their promoters in July 1720. Yet the projectors still continued with getting their businesses started. Interestingly, they argued that the prohibition did not affect the companies themselves, as the city mandate only referred to speculation with shares. They even thanked the council for halting speculation, and were thereby clearly drawing a line between company promotion and share trading. However, the city council followed up on the first prohibition by also outlawing the companies themselves a few days later. Nonetheless, the projectors were still hopeful, and presented a new plan for an insurance firm in October, this time with precise rules prohibiting speculation.[47] Unfortunately, the exact terms are no longer known, but they may have been along the lines of James Swift's suggestion for preventing the "Pernitious Practice of Stock-jobbing to the ruine of the Publick" in Irleand.[48] In September 1720, he had proposed that nobody should be allowed to sell the shares of a proposed Irish bank for more than 125 percent of the paid-up capital, thereby leaving only a small margin for speculative gains. Any transfers for prices higher than stipulated would be rendered void, and the share owner was to be dispossessed.

C: Thus, contemporaries attempted different experiments to curb equity trading and/or protect investors from a market crash. Some of these experiments concerned stock transfers, others the very nature of the shares, in the sense that they were made less speculative. The general idea was to find a way to get the economic advantages of the joint-stock form without the nuisance (as the contemporaries perceived it) of a speculative secondary market for stocks. Yet, the joint-stock form itself carried with it another problem of a different nature. Throughout the continent, we see that many governments – together with mercantile vested interests – were afraid that the new companies might be a sort

---

47 Amsinck, "Die ersten hamburgischen Assecuranz-Compagnien."
48 Mr. Swift about a Bank, [fall 1720], quoted in John Busteed, "Irish Private Banks," *Journal of the Cork Historical and Archaeological Society* 53 (1948): 32–38, here 37.

of Trojan horse: a vehicle allowing foreigners to take control of their local economy.

Ownership and Control

M: It is true that the practice of ensuring that shares were only held by investors from foreign countries carried with it one major difficulty: The government authorizing the company had to make sure that the business would be run to the advantage of the community rather than to its detriment. They certainly perceived a risk of foreigners sucking the wealth out of the body politic. But once again, there appeared to be solutions to this problem, in particular through specific provisions introduced in the charters. We find such, for example, in the United Provinces. As Oscar Gelderblom and Joost Jonker noted: "The corporate governance structure of nearly all [Dutch] projects demonstrated that local elites meant to retain a firm grip."[49] We may also look at the proposal by English businessmen for a bank in Braunschweig-Wolfenbüttel, a landlocked German territory. The projectors tried to anticipate the doubts of the ducal government. To counter any suspicion about the intentions of the English investors, the application for a charter reserved half the directorships for members of the territory's administration.[50] With this institutionalized influence, the civil servants would have been able to steer the company's business in the interest of their sovereign.

C: Portugal was another country where the question of foreign investors was a crucial issue. The Portuguese king and ministers were in favor of creating of a joint-stock company. Yet, they faced a dilemma. They believed that "New Christians" (descendants of Jewish families which had been forced to convert in the fifteenth century, and which were generally suspected of crypto-Judaism)[51] were the only Portuguese that would be able to invest substantial sums in the venture, but the "New Christians" requested safeguards from the Inquisition in order to do so.[52] Since the Inquisition did not seem ready to grant such safe-

49 Gelderblom and Jonker, "Mirroring Different Follies," 131.

50 Entwurf des Inhalts der fürstl. Verbriefung über die Anrichtung einer Banc in Braunschweig, undated, in Niedersächsisches Landesarchiv Wolfenbüttel, 4 Alt 5, Nr. 358, unfol.

51 On the complex question of Portuguese New Christians see in particular António José Saraiva, *The Marrano Factory: The Portuguese Inquisition and Its New Christians 1536–1765* (Leiden: Brill, 2011).

52 The question of safeguards for the New Christians had already been an important issue at the time of the flotation of the Portuguese India Company (1628) and the Portuguese Brazil Com-

guards, the alternative was to open the company widely to foreign capital. However, this could lead the company to "fall into the hands of foreigners," which the government opposed.[53] The matter was discussed for months by the government, with various projectors proposing different solutions. For instance, one scheme from late 1720 explicitly stipulated that the board of directors would be partially reserved for foreigners: a provision which was almost unique in the corporate charters of the time.[54] Yet, to make sure that the management of the company would stay in Portuguese hands, foreigners were only allotted 7 out of 21 directorships. Moreover, – in a spirit of reciprocity – these foreign directors would have to declare that Portuguese were allowed to vote in the companies of their own countries.

The End of the Joint-stock Euphoria

M: One remaining question is why the joint-stock euphoria abated. Had the euphoria ceased in the wake of the crash in Paris, London, or Amsterdam, the answer would have been quite simple. However, as we have seen, this was precisely not the case: the promotion of new companies continued (albeit at a slower pace) throughout 1720, and there was even a small equity boom in Lorraine in November, that is to say, two months after the collapse of the Amsterdam bubble. One aspect that has been connected to the end of the joint-stock boom, namely the Bubble Act of June 1720 in Britain, can of course only have been responsible for developments in that country.[55] And it only had limited success there, anyway, as shares could still be sold on the basis of patents, as in the case of the Royal Mines Company of Jamaica, which offered its stock to subscribers two

---

pany (1649): Charles Ralph Boxer, "Padre António Vierira, S.J. and the Institution of the Brazil Company in 1649," *Hispanic American Historical Review* 29 (1949): 474–497; A.R. Disney, "The First Portuguese India Company, 1628–33," *Economic History Review* 30 (1977): 242–258; Leonor Freire Costa, "Merchant Groups in the 17th-Century Brazilian Sugar Trade: Reappraising Old Topics with New Research Insights," *e-Journal of Portuguese History* 2 (2004): 1–11.

53 The whole matter is explained in a long account that a British diplomat sent to London: The National Archives, SP 89/28, 124.

54 "Projecto de uma nova Companhia de Commercio," in Biblioteca Nacional de Portugal, Colecção Pombalina, cod. 495, n. 23. I am grateful to Leonor Costa for advising me to consult this document.

55 See for this also Rik G.P. Frehen, William N. Goetzmann, and K. Geert Rouwenhorst, "New Evidence on the First Financial Bubble," *Journal of Financial Economics* 108 (2013): 585–607, here 605.

months after the Act's passage, and many existing companies could still sell further shares.[56] Nevertheless, it at least had a dampening effect.

C: Among the many factors that certainly contributed to subdue the pan-European stock euphoria, one of the most important was in all likelihood the scope for speculation. Around the fall of 1720, there was indeed a noticeable change in the rules governing the flotation of new companies. Before that date, namely during the central phase of the joint-stock boom (from the summer of 1719 to the summer of 1720), most new firms facilitated the marketing of their shares in a way that was *de facto* also fostering speculation. In particular, investors were often allowed to use leverage, that is to say, they had to pay upfront only a fraction of the full share price. For example, the September 1719 stock issue of the French Indies Company was, at first, payable in ten monthly instalments. However, in October 1719, John Law decided that these instalments would be due every quarter instead of every month. The *Nouveau Mercure* (a journal controlled by Law himself) explained with candor that this very "delay" had boosted the share price, and "attracted [to Paris] a prodigious quantity of foreigners & provincials" eager to participate in the *agiotage* of the rue Quincampoix.[57] Likewise, most English and Dutch companies floated around that time required minimal initial payments, sometimes as small as one percent of the nominal share price, and sometimes even less than that.[58] The *Daily Post* of 11 June 1720 advertised, for instance, a company asking its shareholders "no greater call the first year than 20s per 100 L stock [i. e. 1 percent], by four quarterly payments." These conditions, so favorable to investors and speculators, starkly contrasted with the terms these were offered afterwards. As we have noted above, in the last third of 1720 and throughout 1721, corporate schemes, far from favoring speculation, were generally striving to limit or even entirely suppress it.

M: Some later companies were also transforming the idea of the joint-stock in a direction that could hardly have pleased investors. For example, as we have seen above, by restricting potential capital gains, or even prohibiting share transfers. These regulations and restrictions were precisely undermining two great benefits of share ownership: capital gains and liquidity. Not all the schemes of late 1720 and 1721 were so drastic, of course, yet there was an overall tendency towards

56 C.E.L., "Royal Mines Company, 1720," *Gentleman's Magazine* 38 (1852): 137–139.
57 *Nouveau Mercure*, January 1720, 148–149. About these instalments see the chapter by Marlene Kessler.
58 Gelderblom and Jonker, "Mirroring Different Follies," 125.

more stringent rules compared to the pre-crash period. Would this not have contributed to curbing the stock euphoria?

C: In other words, we might say that even if the Paris, London, and Amsterdam stock market crashes did not directly cause the joint-stock boom to abate, they nonetheless indirectly participated in bridling it, since they triggered a backlash against stock-jobbing.

M: The three stock market crashes had, indirectly, a further adverse impact since (as we discussed above) they had a negative influence on money flows throughout Europe. The 1721 Hessen-Kassel Bank appears to have been a victim of these worsened conditions. Although it advertised its shares in Dutch newspapers, no international money seems to have been subscribed. Instead, the project relied on local supplies of capital, and a large part of the shares remained unsold. While we do not have the names of all buyers, there is evidence that most of the shares went to local investors within the principality, especially to government servants and Huguenot businessmen. In addition, a large chunk of 300 shares was acquired by Landgrave Charles X himself, and to an unknown extent by his daughter Wilhelmine-Charlotte.[59] More generally, it is telling that a number of contemporary companies switched from selling shares to vending lottery tickets to raise capital for their business in 1721, for instance the York Buildings Company in London, or the Viennese Oriental Company.[60] Shares were sometimes only the consolation price in these very different games of hazard.

Conclusion: The Joint-stock Boom in a Long-term Perspective

C: What is interesting, is that although the tide of new companies drastically subsided after the end of the stock euphoria, it did not dry up completely over the following years.[61] The Ostend Company received its charter in December 1722;[62]

59 *Gazette d'Amsterdam*, 16.5.1721; Subscribers' list, Schmalkalden 19.4.1721, in Stadtarchiv Kassel, S3, Nr. 171, 21–22.

60 A.J.G. Cummings, *The York Buildings Company: A Case Study in Eighteenth-Century Corporation Mismanagement*, unpublished Ph.D. dissertation (Strathclyde, 1980), 110–115; Dullinger, "Handelskompagnien Österreichs," 52–58.

61 However, this was not the case everywhere. Frehen, Goetzmann and Rowenhorst, "New Evidence," 606, underline that, after 1720, there were no significant equity issuance in the United Provinces until the nineteenth century.

the Corsico Company was established in Portugal in 1723, with the purpose of exporting slaves to Brazil;[63] the same year, the Chelsea Waterworks Company was floated in London;[64] a new Trading Company was launched in Lorraine in 1724.[65] Across Europe, there was an average of around one new joint-stock firm per year until the 1750s, when the numbers started to progressively grow again.

M: Evidently, governments and investors were still interested in the economic potential of joint-stock firms. Yet, it is noteworthy that – beside the question of the crashes themselves – the companies floated in 1719–20 were not proving to be particularly successful. To give a few examples, the two English marine insurances firms were far less successful than expected,[66] Richard Steele's Fish-Pool Company was unable to survive the competition of London's independent fishermen,[67] whereas other enterprises, such as the Royal Mines Company in Jamaica, went down in scandal. As it happens, the firm did not find any precious metals in the island, and in addition its director lost most of the firm's capital after having invested it in South Sea shares.[68]

C: The fate of most 1720 enterprises floated outside Britain was not anymore brilliant. The Milanese Casa di San Giuseppe closed its doors in 1722; the Lorraine Company was liquidated the same year; the Venetian Trade Company survived until the 1730s, yet it only operated on a small scale.[69] By contrast, the marine insurance firm Stad Rotterdam operated until the end of the twentieth century. However, far from initial expectations (and similar in that to its English counter-

62 *Lettres patentes* [...] *à la Compagnie générale à établir dans les Pays-Bas Autrichiens pour le commerce & la navigation aux Indes* (Gand, 1723).
63 Ernst Puning, "Transnationality and the Brazilian Slave Trade: The Case of the Corisco Company (1715–1730)," in *La Guinée Équatoriale aux Archives Nationales (XVIIIe – Début XXe Siècles)*, ed. Valérie Wulf (Paris: L'Harmattan, 2015), 61–90, here 80–81; National Archives, SP 89/31, f. 25, December 1723.
64 London Metropolitan Archives, ACC 2558/CH/1/1.
65 *Recueil des edits, ordonnances, declarations* [...] *du règne de Léopold I* (Nancy, 1734), 3:31.
66 Christopher Kingston, "Marine Insurance in Britain and America, 1720–1844," *Journal of Economic History* 67 (2007): 379–409; A.H. John, "The London Assurance Company and the Marine Insurance Market of the Eighteenth Century," *Economica* 25 (1958): 126–141. See now also Michael Aldous and Stefano Condorelli, "An Incomplete Revolution: Gorporate Governance Challenges of the London Assurance Company and the Limitations of the Joint Stock Form 1720–1725" forthcoming in *Enterprise & Society.*
67 See for this my forthcoming book.
68 C.E.L., "Royal Mines."
69 Condorelli, *Stock Euphoria.*

parts), by 1722 it had already given up the ambition of gaining a sizeable share of the Dutch market.[70]

On the other hand, the immense 1720 joint-stock boom itself is quite surprising when we consider that – with a few great exceptions, such as the English and Dutch East India Companies – most joint-stocks chartered prior to 1719 had not been particularly successful either.[71] The Dutch West India Company, the English Royal African Company, or the French *Compagnie des Indes Orientales* are prominent examples, together with the Brandenburg African Company that we mentioned in the introduction of this volume. The many notices in Savary des Brûlons' *Dictionnaire universel de commerce* show that contemporaries were fully aware of the difficulties of most of these pre-1719 firms.[72] Another important author of the time, Geronymo de Ustariz, underlined the "miscarriage" of many companies, noting in particular "the ruin of above 30 companies formed in France at several times, in different provinces, and upon various plans."[73]

M: There are, however, a number of factors that help explain why people in 1719–20 reevaluated the potential for joint-stocks, and suddenly saw them in a new positive light. On the one hand, John Law's Mississippi Company had for a while seemed tremendously successful. On the other hand, both in London and the United Provinces, projectors were exploring new potentialities of the joint-stock form. In particular, they were attempting to apply it to many new businesses, often hoping to capitalize from economies of scale. Besides, – and this was important given the contemporary debate about the evils of corporate monopolies[74] – these projectors claimed that they would not need monopoly privileges (contrary to most joint-stock companies of the past).[75]

---

70 Go, *Marine Insurance in the Netherlands*, 218–222.

71 The scholarship on the subject is immense. To give only one reference see Niels Steensgaard, "The Companies as a Specific Institution in the History of European Expansion," in *Companies and Trade: Essays on Overseas Trading Companies During the Ancien Régime*, ed. Leonard Blussé and Femme Gaastra (Leiden: Leiden University Press, 1981), 245–264.

72 Jaques Savary des Brûlons, *Dictionnaire universel de commerce* (Paris, 1723).

73 Geronymo de Ustariz, *The Theory and Practice of Commerce and Maritime Affairs* (Dublin, 1752), 117–118. The book was first edited in 1724 in French. A remark about the Ostend Company having just been floated indicates that the manuscript was written around 1723.

74 As recent introductions to the debate see Steve Pincus, "Rethinking Mercantilism: Political Economy, the British Empire, and the Atlantic World in the Seventeenth and Eighteenth Centuries," *William & Mary Quarterly* 69 (2012): 3–34; Perry Gauci, "Introduction," in *Regulating the British Economy 1660–1850*, ed. Perry Gauci (Oxford: Oxford University Press, 2011), 1–23.

75 See e.g. the complex discussions about a possible monopoly of the new marine insurance companies. Supple, *Royal Exchange Assurance*, 20–42; *The Special Report from the Committee*

C: In spite of the intense experimentation of the period 1719–1721 – and beside the specific question of speculation – there were a number of unsolved corporate problems that prevented most joint-stock companies of the time to live up to their full potential (or, to put it more accurately, to the full potential that their promoters had in mind). This was especially the case outside oceanic trade, particularly the East India one. One important issue concerned capital which was – given the contemporary economic structures – often either too small or too important (that is to say, too important to provide an adequate return for shareholders). Another fundamental question concerned the management of the firms, in particular what we call today the principal-agent problem. Adam Smith had obviously not been the first to underline the issue.[76] Geronymo de Ustariz, to quote him again, specifically attributed the failure of most joint-stock firms, first, to inadequate capital and, second, to the fact that "the directors, agents, and other dependants [sic] [of these firms] abused the trust reposed in them."[77]

M: These problems, and others like insider trading, would of course endure at least into the twentieth century. But as this chapter has hopefully shown, looking at the joint-stock company and share market speculation in its formative age is quite a revealing undertaking. The corporation was something that people experimented with in 1720, keen to use its potential, but wary of its perceived evils.

Appointed to Inquire into and Examine the Several Subscriptions for Fisheries, Insurances, Annuities for Lives, and all other Projects Carried on by Subscription, in and about the Cities of London and Westminster; and to Inquire into all Undertakings for Purchasing Joint-Stocks, or Obsolete Charters (London, 1720).

76 Adam Smith, *An Inquiry into the Nature and Causes of the Wealth of Nations* (1776; London: Penguin, 1999), 2:330.

77 Geronymo de Ustariz, "The Theory and Practice," 118.

Eve Rosenhaft

Linen and Lotteries: The Anatomy of an English Bubble Company in Germany

In the spring of 1718, administrators in the northwest German principality of Braunschweig were invited to consider two projects which promised to open up new financial and commercial horizons. One was a scheme for a manufacturing and trading company, and the other was a lottery, which rapidly developed into a proposal for a joint-stock bank. Both projects originated in England, and their proposers were implicated in various ways in the operations of London joint-stock enterprises, including the South Sea Company. I characterize them, not uncontroversially, as bubble companies, in the sense that their existence, and the seriousness with which they were taken in Braunschweig, reflected the search for new outlets for capital, the curiosity about the technology of joint-stock operations and the market in stocks and shares (*Actienhandel* in German), and the enthusiasm for new projects that characterized the boom around 1720.[1] This is irrespective of whether either of the projects described here was fraudulent; the lottery-and-bank project clearly was, while the partners in the

Elements of this study have been presented at seminars and conferences in Bern, London and Tübingen, and at annual meetings of the German History Society, the British Society for Eighteenth-Century Studies and the Social History Society. I am grateful to the participants in those meetings and to the editors of the present volume for their comments and suggestions. The research for the study was supported by a fellowship from the Herzog-August Bibliothek, Wolfenbüttel in 2013, and I acknowledge the continuing support of the HAB staff as well as the Director and staff of the Niedersächsisches Landesarchiv Wolfenbüttel. The writing of the chapter was completed during a period of residence at Sogang University, Seoul, as Humanities Korea+ Visiting Research Professor at the Critical Global Studies Institute. That work was supported the National Research Foundation of Korea Grant funded by the Korean Government (NRF-2017S1 A6 A3 A01079727).

1 Contemporary economists use the term 'bubble company' to denote an enterprise which is deliberately overvalued for the purposes of stimulating speculative trading. In the context of 1720, 'bubble', though generally used in a satirical or pejorative sense, covered the imaginative and projecting character of the new enterprises without necessarily implying that they were fraudulent. Rik Frehen, William N. Goetzmann, and K. Geert Rouwenhorst similarly argue that new companies offering opportunities for investment in a range of projects (they emphasise colonial trade and insurance) were an integral part of the boom and point out that the Bubble Act of 1720 led English investors, in particular, to seek new ways of deploying their capital abroad: "Finance in the Great Mirror of Folly," in *The Great Mirror of Folly: Finance, Culture and the Crash of 1720*, ed. William N. Goetzmann et al. (New Haven and London: Yale University Press, 2013), 63–87.

https://doi.org/10.1515/9783110592139-005

manufacturing and trading company gave every appearance of intending to see material returns on their investment.

Stefano Condorelli pointed out in 2015 that the financial and psychological overspill from the bubbles in Paris and London left its traces all over continental Europe; his survey of joint-stock enterprises with an "effective and open secondary market in shares" created in the wake of the boom identifies 78 such enterprises – banks, insurances, manufacturing and trading companies – in 23 political units outside of Britain, France and the United Netherlands – extending from Sweden to Sicily and from Russia to Portugal. He also argues that we should not see in this phenomenon evidence for the globalization of folly or fraud. I share his premise that "actors' intentions are no less significant than their achievements" – even failures (as most of these enterprises were) are interesting and, on inspection, may appear as serious experiments in exploiting the possibilities of innovation – exuberant, to be sure, but rational too.[2]

One of Condorelli's key findings is expressed in his identification of a "two-speed Europe" – two-speed in terms not only of non-synchronous industrial and commercial development but also of knowledge of financial technologies and the capacity of legal and political structures to accommodate new practices. The Braunschweig episode provides an excellent example of a "two-speed Europe", but it particularly allows us to observe the gears at work. In the exchanges between English and German actors over questions of process and principle that accompanied the initiation, implementation and collapse of the two projects, it is possible (to use another metaphor) to identify blockages in the flows of both knowledge and trust of the kind that are central to the transfer of technology (including new financial practices). The nature of the Braunschweig case and of the sources it generated thus invite a micro-historical approach to the global crisis of 1720. If, as Emma Rothschild argued in 1998, "a 'microhistory' of economic transformation [...] can [...] be seen as a source of opportunity for economic history", then "transformations" that were uneven, asynchronous or less than transformative call at least as urgently for close reading.[3]

---

2 Stefano Condorelli, *The 1719–20 Stock Euphoria: A Pan-European Perspective, MPRA Paper* (2014).

3 Emma Rothschild, "An Alarming Commercial Crisis in Eighteenth-Century Angoulême: Sentiments in Economic History," *Economic History Review* 51 (1998): 268–293, here 286. Rothschild cites Carlo Ginzburg and Carlo Poni's foundational text of 1979, published in English as "The Name and the Game: Unequal Exchange and the Historiographic Marketplace," in *Microhistory and the Lost Peoples of Europe*, ed. Edward Muir and Guido Ruggiero (Baltimore and London: Johns Hopkins University Press, 1991), 1–10.

The textual evidence for German responses to 1720 – periodical and pamphlet literature and ephemera of various kinds – provides evidence of a patchwork of knowingness and innocence, traditionalism and willingness to experiment, which shows us that Germans of the early eighteenth century were no less open-minded and adventurous in their view of the globalizing world than other Europeans. By the same token, though, they opened themselves to catastrophic disappointment. For at least three generations after the crash, 'Mississippi' would be a metaphor for flawed and foolish projects in the German lands and *Actienhandel* formally defined as a fraudulent activity.[4] The record of these particular bubble projects exposes how the mental machinery of that combination of enthusiasm for modernity and vulnerability of imagination operated in the conjuncture of 1720.

At the same time, the sources in this case allow us unusual access to material aspects of the 1720 conjuncture. In particular, it is possible to follow the movements of key actors, the ways in which they were networked, and their possible interests and motivations. In spite of what we know about the rapid circulation of print information and ideas, particularly in the boom years,[5] it is clear that individuals were crucially important to the transfer of information, and particularly of practical knowledge, across political borders as well as between town and country and the different regions within them. This is the case not least because physical travel to and presence in key spaces was so often essential to taking advantage of market opportunities, as visualized in images not only of the Rue Quincampoix and Exchange Alley or of the Café Quincampoix in Amsterdam but also (if less frequently) of rural roads crowded with hopeful investors travelling to Paris (see image 1).

The significance of international actors, even for what appear to be extremely local events, is made clear in recent work on the projects for a linen manufacture and joint-stock bank in the principality of Hessen-Kassel – projects that were roughly contemporaneous with the Braunschweig ones. There, the initiative for a new project came from a civil servant posted in the Netherlands, acting in awareness both of his employer's ambitions for economic improvement and of the variety of commercial and financial practices developing in the Atlantic

4 Eve Rosenhaft, "'All That Glitters Is Not Gold, But…': German Responses to the Financial Bubbles of 1720," in *Money in the German-Speaking Lands*, ed. Mary Lindemann and Jared Poley (Oxford and Providence: Berghahn, 2017), 74–95.

5 Cf. Arnaud Orain and Laurent Thézé, "Publicité, contre-publicité et représentations économiques du Système de Law: Le motif alchimique dans les poésies et chansons de la Régence," in *'Gagnons sans savoir comment' : Représentations du Système de Law du XVIIIe à nos jours*, ed. Florence Magnot-Ogilvy (Rennes: Presses Universitaires de Rennes, 2017), 129–148.

Image 1: "If you want to escape poverty, then come and buy stock," *Der Europäische Niemand* 17 (1720). (Courtesy of Universitätsbibliothek Regensburg)

economies. In the principality itself, the project was taken forward by specialists actively recruited from the Netherlands and France.[6] The Braunschweig case displays some similarities to that of Hessen-Kassel, but the geographic range of its cast of characters is more limited. The investors, speculators and projectors were mainly English, the courtiers and civil servants mainly German; and there is a stronger element of initiative (British) and response (German) in the events – though a key role fell to "cross-cultural brokers" moving physically as well as imaginatively between England and Germany.[7] This reflects the fact that the actors in this story were operating within the particular and relatively new "transfer zone" created by the personal union of Britain and Hanover in 1714.[8] One consequence of this connection was that members of the Hanoverian elite, themselves often in motion (along with King George I) between the two capitals, were drawn into the stock market. Information and opinion about the bubbles also circulated through the correspondence of German princesses in London and Paris. Elisabeth Charlotte of Orléans, mother of the French regent responsible for the Mississippi scheme, was the first cousin of George I and had grown up at the Hanoverian court, and among her confidantes were the Princess of Wales Caroline of Brandenburg-Ansbach (who held South Sea stock) and Caroline's lady-in-waiting Johanna Sophia of Schaumburg-Lippe.[9] The courts of Hanover and Braunschweig were linked by shared membership in the Guelph dynasty and by geography: the two residences were a day's ride apart.

Varied as the motives of all these actors certainly were, their actions had a very material object. The vicissitudes of the attempt to establish an English manufacturing and export business in a relatively underdeveloped German region remind us of the ways in which the desire for material goods and the

---

6 Stefano Condorelli and Daniel Menning, "Wirtschaftspolitik im Zeichen der europäischen Börseneuphorie: Die Gründung der Leyh- und Commercien-Compagnie und die Reform der Tuchproduktion in Hessen-Kassel 1721," *Hessisches Jahrbuch für Landesgeschichte* 68 (2018): 99–114.

7 Cf. Philip Curtin, *Cross-Cultural Trade in World History* (Cambridge: Cambridge University Press, 1984).

8 Cf. Michael Schaich, "Sprache. Kommunikation. Netzwerke: Kulturtransfers in der Personalunion," in *Als die Royals aus Hannover kamen: Hannovers Herrscher auf Englands Thron 1714–1837. Ausstellungskatalog*, ed. Katja Lembke (Dresden: Sandstein, 2014), 80–91; Arnd Reitemeier, ed., *Kommunikation und Kulturtransfer im Zeitalter der Personalunion zwischen Großbritannien und Hannover: 'To prove that Hanover and England are not entirely synonymous'* (Göttingen: Universitätsverlag, 2014).

9 Rosenhaft, "'All That Glitters'," 76; Eve Rosenhaft, "Women and Financial Knowledge in Eighteenth-Century Germany," in *Women and Their Money: Essays on Women and Finance 1700–1950*, ed. Anne Laurence, Josephine Maltby, and Janette Rutterford (London: Routledge, 2008), 59–72.

real world of trade persisted in the background of financial experiments, even if these are remembered chiefly for their immaterial character. They also show how the consequences of the boom and its aftermath reached into many corners of Europe and touched people at all levels of society.

New Projects: Thomas Pindar and Company

In March 1718, a certain Johann Gerhard Hopmann wrote from London to August Wilhelm, Duke of Braunschweig-Wolfenbüttel, sending him a proposal for the establishment of a new linen manufacture in the city of Braunschweig. The aim, as he stated it, was to stimulate the economy of the city and territory, by making possible the production of high-quality bleached linen for export to England. The establishment would be in the hands of a company patented by the Duke but made up of experienced English merchants. As an incentive for them to invest, these entrepreneurs would be granted the privilege of importing English goods and selling them locally and abroad without being charged duty. Any loss to the ducal treasury would be made up by the increase in general production and income, "so that not only can work and bread be provided for the mass of your poor subjects but much money can flow into the city and the territory and the commerce, trade and business that are currently depressed can be re-established and made to flourish again". The situation that Hopmann was addressing was that the residents of the territory, who relied on home spinning for their livelihoods, produced such poor-quality yarn that the fabric made from it could not attract good prices. By contrast, the Dutch were producing fine bleached linen for sale to England, though they were doing so by importing and processing cloth produced in the German lands. With proper management, Hopmann argued, it would be possible to produce both good yarn and fine linen in Braunschweig using local flax and the skills of local spinners and weavers. Moreover, he identified plenty of space in the city to lay out bleaching yards.[10]

By the summer of 1718, Hopmann was already on the hunt for London investors. At this point, he wrote, he was only looking for "perhaps 5 or 7" "wealthy merchants", but he had already raised a capital of 60,000 Reichsthaler (the contemporary equivalent of £13,500). Meanwhile, he asked his correspondent in Braunschweig to keep the plan a secret, in view of the fact that the English Par-

10 Project einer zu Braunschweig zu etablirenden Leine-Manufactur [...], in Niedersächsisches Landesarchiv Wolfenbüttel (NLA WO), 4 Alt 5 Nr. 358, 2–5.

liament was committed to protecting domestic linen manufacture.[11] The privy councilors in Braunschweig immediately began to explore the feasibility of the plan, and, in late July 1718, the Duke approved the outline proposal.[12] During the next two years, Hopmann continued to seek investors, but it was only in May 1720 that he was able to report success. The records of the ducal court in Wolfenbüttel include two copies of the articles of association signed on 9 May by Hopmann and 23 others. The English original, on parchment, was probably delivered by two Londoners who visited Braunschweig in June to meet Johann Friedrich Faber, the Duke's appointed negotiator; a German translation appears to have reached Wolfenbüttel before that.[13] The signatories declared that they had formed a "copartnership" for the purpose of linen manufacture "and for the baking and refining of sugar and a free comerce and dealing in all sorts of English commodityes"; the wares they named were tin, cloth of all sorts (excepting druggets, serges and other thin stuffs) and "such brown or muscovado sugar in the manner it comes from the Indies packt up in casks". As the articles noted, there were some specifics that remained to be negotiated with the Duke. He, for example, wanted to levy an excise both on the linen and on the confectionery manufactured by the company (there is no sign that the sugar refinery was ever developed); but, significantly, the parties explicitly agreed that duties on confectionery could be reduced if competition from well-established Hamburg producers threatened the success of the new enterprise. Both the range of duty-free goods and the number of years for which the privilege should be granted were (and would remain) points of contention. It was to discuss these points that the two delegates travelled to Braunschweig.

Trading under the name of Thomas Pindar and Company, the 24 partners were committed to raising a capital sum of £24,000 by each paying in £1,000. Ten percent of this was to be reserved to cover the cost of appointing factors and other employees to get the practical work underway in Braunschweig; the rest was to be divided into 25 shares, of which Hopmann would receive two. Shares could not be disposed of without the agreement of all "proprietors".[14] While the partners were awaiting the final go-ahead for production, the company's capital was invested in South Sea stock – a point that would prove impor-

---

11 Hopmann to Geheimer Rat, 2.7.1718, in NLA WO, 4 Alt 5 Nr. 358, 18–21. It is not clear which of the privy councillors this was.

12 Actum in der [...] Ratsstube Wolfenbüttel, 27.7.1718, in NLA WO, 4 Alt 5 Nr. 358.

13 Articles of Association, in NLA WO, 4 Alt 5 Nr. 358, 49–56 (German), 65 (English); English partners to Duke August Wilhelm, 23.6.1720, in NLA WO, 4 Alt 5 Nr. 358, 62. The two were Edward Morgan and Henry Grutzman. English spellings are original.

14 Thomas Pindar to Duke August Wilhelm, 2.4.1722, in NLA WO, 2 Alt 6546, 67–68.

tant in the future development of the project but also tells us something about its background.

Although English and German parties to the next two years' negotiations and correspondence consistently used the term company/*Compagnie* when referring to this new enterprise (and I follow them in this usage), in a formal or legal sense, it was a partnership. 'Share' had well-established vernacular and commercial uses that predated the issue of paper stock, and the prohibition on alienating shares is characteristic of partnership arrangements. There is no evidence that at that point the shares in the company were intended to be traded. Similarly, in the articles, the founding capital is called "joint stock", but this term was long current in partnership agreements and need not represent a commitment to the 'joint-stock form'.[15] There remains some ambiguity, however. This is particularly true of the use of the term "proprietors" to designate the partners. "[P]roprietor" was one of the standard designations for stockholders in businesses like the East India and South Sea Companies, and it features rarely, if at all, in contemporary texts on partnerships. Granted the fluidity of terminology characteristic of the period, then, the resonances of the company's copartnership terms with the lexis of the new financial technology are hard to overlook.

The best way to parse this ambiguity, which is also present in the German translation, may be to consider the timing of these projects. Hopmann's proposal (and indeed the lottery-and-bank scheme discussed below) is among the very earliest of the projects recorded by Condorelli, predating even the Mississippi scheme by a year. This is a reminder of the organic character of the conjuncture, which climaxed in the Paris and London bubbles but began with the proliferation of low-level and local entrepreneurial projects across Europe. These projects often responded to local impulses and circumstances, but, at the same time, they developed within transterritorial networks of communication and emulation and were conditioned by global events (like the War of the Spanish Succession), which had consequences for all European polities, though of different kinds and dimensions. At the same time, it appears that Hopmann's first proposal – whatever the original impulse – came too early to be attractive to many investors and that Thomas Pindar and Company was a product of the Bubble. The South Sea Act authorizing the Company's debt-for-equity scheme was promulgated on 7 April 1720. By 9 May, when the articles of association were signed, the trade in South Sea stock was accelerating and prices were beginning to rise. Ten days earlier, the Parliamentary Committee that was considering what would come to be

15 See, for example, the model articles of association in Jacob Giles, *Lex Mercatoria: Or the Merchant's Companion* (London, 1718), 297–340.

called the Bubble Act reported about the London bubble companies after three months' deliberation. That act, which received royal assent on 11 June, prohibited the raising of transferable stock by any company without a charter from the Crown. The practical consequence of the Bubble Act, it has been argued, was not to dampen entrepreneurial energies but to divert them into the creation of unincorporated shareholding partnerships.[16] Thomas Pindar and Company looks very much like one of those, and consideration of the personalities of its partners reinforces the impression that it was changes in business conditions precipitated by the South Sea project that gave Hopmann the opportunity to realize his plan.

Projectors and Investors

The articles of association for the new company were signed by Johann Gerhard Hopmann, as well as by 23 London investors. The London signatories styled themselves as follows:

Fisher Tench, Baronet, London
Thomas Pindar, London, Esq.
William Plomer, London, Linnendraper
Edward Clive, London, Gent.
Oswald Hoskyns, London, Merchant
Thomas Watts, London, Gent.
Henry Symonds, London, Linnendraper
Thomas Burgess, London, Merchant
William Doyle, London, Merchant
Cornelius Noortwyck, London, Merchant
William Oaker, London, Esq
John Martin, London, Esq.
Henry Grutzman, London, Merchant
William Nicholls, London, Merchant
Lewis Yonge, London, Linnendraper
Robert Smith, London, Merchant
William Stewart, London, Linnendraper
Walter Tredway, London, Merchant
Edward Morgan, London, Merchant
Henrich Marshall, London, Grocer
John Higden, London, Linnendraper
Henry Trollop, London, Linnendraper
Walter Bagnall, London, Esq.

What do we make of this list? How were these men mobilized and how can we assess their motivations, taking into account the context of the Bubble years? The key figure and leading cultural broker here was Johann Gerhard Hopmann, aka John Gerrard Hopman, and he was fit for the role not least by a degree of

16 Mark Freeman, Robin Pearson, and James Taylor, "Law, Politics and the Governance of English and Scottish Joint-stock Companies, 1600–1850," *Business History* 55 (2013): 633–649, here 637. I am grateful to Robin Pearson for personal advice on the vagaries of commercial terminology. Cf. Ron Harris, *Industrializing English Law: Entrepreneurship and Business Organization, 1720–1844* (Cambridge: Cambridge University Press, 2000), 137–167, on unincorporated companies.

cultural hybridity. In the German sources, Hopmann appears as a typical eighteenth-century civil servant, dependent on multiple commissions, hustling for income and preferment, and at the mercy of his lord. When he drafted his plan in 1718, he held a minor position in the diplomatic service (*Legationssekretär*), and, by mid-1721, he had been promoted twice to become August Wilhelm's *Resident* – or ambassador – in London. He was simultaneously *Resident* for Holstein and also, at various times, for Mecklenburg and the Hanse cities.[17] The English sources reveal him as a member of the loose community of transplanted Germans who had made themselves Englishmen to all intents and purposes.[18] In London, he moved in both mercantile and diplomatic circles. He was also adept in 'English' financial practices, through which he networked in various ways with some of the other Braunschweig partners. In June 1720, a month after the articles of association were signed, for example, Hopmann, Thomas Pindar and Henry Grutzman were involved in a complicated series of transactions involving the sale of £2,400 worth of South Sea subscriptions on Hopmann's account.[19] In 1721, when Hopmann married Rachel Rebow, the 16-year-old granddaughter of Colchester MP Isaac Rebow (a business associate of Fisher Tench),[20] the marriage contract stipulated that £1,000 of South Sea stock should be included in Rachel's marriage settlement; and subsequent renegotiations of trustee arrangements similarly involved new purchases of stocks and annuities.[21] In short, Hopmann was a man on the make in London and had learned to take advantage of the opportunities provided by the stock market.

The presence of Henry Grutzman's name among the signatories points to the mediating role of Anglo-German mercantile networks in this story. Grutzman was a German merchant, who had arrived from Riga in 1718 and been naturalized in 1719.[22] Cornelius Noortwyck, whose merchant activities included selling trade goods to the Royal African Company, was of Dutch origin and, in 1722, a near

17 Record of Hopmann's appointment November 1719, in NLA WO, 1 Alt 6 Nr. 85, 1–10; Reports of his diplomatic engagements in the London press, January 1720 to April 1721.

18 Cf. Margrit Schulte Beerbühl, *The Forgotten Majority: German Merchants in London, Naturalization, and Global Trade 1660–1815* (New York and Oxford: Berghahn, 2007).

19 See the records of subsequent litigation in The National Archives (TNA), C 11/50/7, C 11/1747/29, C 11/54/8.

20 They appear as co-defendants in lawsuits in TNA, C 11/2205/1 (1719), C 11/1417/7 (1720) – in 1719 as co-directors of the Society of Royal Mines and Mineral and Battery Works of City of London.

21 Litigation in TNA, C 11/570/16.

22 TNA, C 11/844/41; *The Benefits and Advantages Gained by the Late Septennial Parliament[...]* (London, n.d.), 10.

neighbor of Henry Grutzman.[23] Thomas Burgess traded in colonial goods, including tea and tobacco; his bookkeeper was a naturalized German, and he had dealings with a number of German merchants.[24] Letters in the Braunschweig files indicate that Burgess was conversant in German himself. Two additional men who do not figure in the list of partners but who played a key role in the enterprise were the factors whom the company hired to set up the business in Braunschweig: Johann Potgiesser and August(us) Rosenhagen. There is evidence to suggest that Potgiesser was hired in London and known to at least some of the company men. In 1720, he had completed five years' training with the merchant partners Henry Voguell (originally from Bremen) and Florian Göbel (a naturalized German). Voguell also was associated with Cornelius Noortwyck, acting with him as co-attorney for the daughter of a fellow merchant in 1727.[25]

The fact that the partners included six linen drapers is a pointer to the specific commercial context which probably informed their investments. Linen was, in the words of Negley Harte, "the most important manufactured import into pre-industrial England".[26] Hopmann's early letters referred specifically both to the demand for high-quality linen, a trade then dominated by Dutch suppliers, and to the protectionist policies that the British government was beginning to implement in the hope of fostering the domestic linen industry. As a consequence of high prices incurred by duties and other problems of supply, wholesale merchants already were withdrawing from the import of linen, and retailers increasingly were importing directly from the continent for both the domestic market and re-export.[27] In 1730, John Higden and his son were named among those linen drapers directly importing from Amsterdam, as was the firm Clavering & Trollop, which may well refer to Henry Trollop.[28] The sensitivity of this

23 Noortwyck's will in TNA, PROB 11/619/234; Land Tax records for Broad Street Ward, in London Metropolitan Archives; Wm. Hagar to the Directors of the East India Company, 18.10.1722, in TNA, T 70/24 Royal African Company letterbooks.

24 Litigation in TNA, C 11/2369/10, C 11/2572/21, E 134/1Geo2/East17.

25 *Daily Courant*, no. 8075, 28.8.1727. On Voguell and Göbel, see also Schulte Beerbühl, *Forgotten Majority*, 121, n. 56.

26 N.B. Harte, "The Rise of Protection and the English Linen Trade, 1690–1790," in *Textile History and Economic History*, ed. Negley B. Harte and Kenneth G. Ponting (Manchester: Manchester University Press, 1973), 75–112, here 75.

27 I am grateful to Professor David Ormrod for pointing me to this aspect of the background to the case.

28 Charles Wilson, *Anglo-Dutch Commerce and Finance in the Eighteenth Century* (Cambridge: Cambridge University Press, 1941), 54; David Ormrod, *The Rise of Commercial Empires: England and the Netherlands in the Age of Mercantilism, 1650–1770* (Cambridge: Cambridge University Press, 2003), 174–175.

group of tradesmen to restraints on the market is illustrated by Henry Trollop's advertisement of October 1722, in which he offered for sale a shipment of printed calicoes "to be sold to such as shall want to make up Furniture before Christmas next, when the Act [prohibiting the import of printed cotton] is to take place".[29]

The notion of manufacturing and processing their own linen in Germany for duty-free import at home thus might well have attracted linen drapers to invest. It seems likely, indeed, that Hopmann came up with his scheme after conversations with London acquaintances in the textile trade and that the initial capital he cited in his 1718 letter came from that commercial quarter. Another retailer with an interest in the commodities to be traded by the new company was Henrich (Henry) Marshall, who as a "grocer" would have sold imported spices and other imported consumables including sugar, tea and coffee. And (as detailed below) Cornelius Noortwyck was but one of several partners in Thomas Pindar and Company who had links to the transatlantic slave economy, a significant importer of German linens as trade goods and for use on American plantations.[30]

In many respects, the company members represent a mixed bag of commercial and broadly political actors, but, irrespective of their occupations, nearly all of them were party to, and indeed networked through, involvement in joint-stock enterprises which included notorious English bubble companies. Sir Fisher Tench was an MP and a director of both the South Sea Company and the Royal African Company. He owned a plantation in Virginia as well as extensive rural landholdings in England, and, on his death in 1736, he also left substantial investments in stock and securities of various kinds to his heirs.[31] Thomas Pindar, who gave his name to the company, was an Atlantic merchant who had been Deputy Governor of the Royal African Company and a successful lobbyist on its behalf between 1703 and 1710.[32] Thomas Watts was another director of the Royal African Company and, along with Pindar, Hoskyns and Tench, was also a member of another innovative project of the early eighteenth century, the Amicable Assurance Society. Hoskyns was a trustee with Watts, Smith and others of the London Assurance Company. Hoskyns and Watts also partnered in other enter-

29 *Post Boy*, no. 5184, 11.–13.10.1722.

30 Anka Steffen and Klaus Weber, "Spinning and Weaving for the Slave Trade: Proto-Industry in Eighteenth-Century Silesia," in *Slavery Hinterland: Transatlantic Slavery and Continental Europe, 1680–1850*, ed. Felix Brahm and Eve Rosenhaft (Woodbridge: Boydell & Brewer, 2016), 87–108.

31 William A. Pettigrew, *Freedom's Debt: The Royal African Company and the Politics of the Atlantic Slave Trade, 1675–1752* (Chapel Hill: Omohundro Institute of Early American History and Culture and University of North Carolina Press, 2013), 46, 76; Tench's will in TNA, PROB 11/680/174.

32 Pettigrew, *Freedom's Debt*, 130–139.

prises, including property-holding in South Carolina. Edward Clive was their lawyer.[33] Walter Bagnall was an enrolled Freeman in the Royal African Company, which normally signaled an intention to engage in the slave trade. In 1721, when the directors of the South Sea Company were facing prosecution, he stood bail for Co-Director Robert Surman.[34] The spirit with which these investors went into Hopmann's new company is perhaps best reflected in the fact that Pindar, Watts, Symonds, Burgess, Trollop, Martin, Morgan, Voguell and Smith were each and all (in various combinations) involved in one or more London joint-stock companies which were either created or proposed between 1718 and 1720 or changed their purposes in those years; some of those companies also deployed lotteries to raise capital and attract investors. They included the York Buildings Company, a scheme for joint-stock maritime insurance, and the Mines Royal, Mineral and Battery Works.[35] Trollop and Symonds held stock in the Hollow Sword Company, which, in spite of its name, was the South Sea Company's bank.[36]

Of the partners in Thomas Pindar and Company, then, none was poor – William Plomer left an estate of over £15,000 and made generous bequests to the dissenting churches[37] – and some had a direct material interest in the commercial and industrial aspects of the plan, as retailers or as merchants. Many belonged to international networks involved in maritime trade, including the slave trade, and they operated at one of the nodal points where Germans and Englishmen met to talk about business. And, within this mixed bag, gentlemen, retailers and merchants were linked by a shared enthusiasm for new joint-stock enterprises.

Clearly, the excitements, promises and risks of the South Sea as a field of commercial expansion were present in the background to the Braunschweig company project and at least served to reinforce the connections among the partners, if they were not the original basis of their association. If, in the summer of

---

33 *A List of the Members of the Corporation of the Amicable Society for a Perpetual Assurance Office* [...] (London, 1721); Hoskyns' will in TNA, PROB 11/665/183; litigation in TNA, C 11/54/1.
34 List of Freemen of the Royal African Company of England, 23.6.1720, in TNA, T 70/1507; *Weekly Journal or British Gazetteer*, 18.2.1721.
35 *The special report, from the Committee Appointed to Inquire into, and Examine the several Subscriptions for Fisheries, Insurances, Annuities for Lives, and all other Projects carryed on by Subscription, in and about the Cities of London and Westminster; and to Inquire into all Undertakings for purchasing Joint-Stocks, or Obsolete Charters* (London, 1720).
36 On the Hollow Sword Blade Company see Helen J. Paul, *The South Sea Bubble: An Economic History of Its Origins and Consequences* (London and New York: Routledge, 2011), 48. On Symonds and Trollop: litigation in TNA, C 11/1707/6.
37 Plomer's will in TNA, PROB 11/726/330.

1720, each partner found they could afford the substantial sum of £1,000 to invest in a new venture, it seems plausible that they all were enjoying or anticipating profits from the boom – though they may have differed in the benefits they expected from investing in the economic development of a German principality. However, the manifest commercial rationale of the company points to the multiplicity and complexity of the impulses to innovate and experiment that were touched off by the boom: the plans that these men committed themselves to involved more than spinning money.

It nevertheless seems likely that the partners envisaged a financial spin-off from the manufacture. Shortly after the articles of association were signed, a communication reached the Duke's councilors urging that the increase in commercial activity that would surely follow the establishment of the English company called for the creation of a bank in Braunschweig. With a proposed capital of 4 million Banco-Thaler and a range of services, the bank could be expected to generate "4 à 5 casks of gold" for the ducal treasury and attract deposits from all over Germany ("ganz Teutschland"). The unnamed author promised to provide a detailed plan for the bank, though for the eyes of the Duke and his council only. Other evidence indicates that the proposal originated from Thomas Pindar and Company, but no more detailed plan has survived, if it ever existed.[38] In any event, the bank proposal was not pursued, while real preparations were made for setting the linen manufacture in motion. Meanwhile, both dimensions of the Londoners' plan were challenged by the emergence of a second, new project in Braunschweig.

New Projects: Corr's Lottery

The proposal for a second enterprise, a lottery authorized by the Duke of Braunschweig and to be drawn in Braunschweig but selling tickets in London, was devised by a certain Ebenezer Corr. It was submitted to and approved by Duke August Wilhelm in August 1718, as Hopmann was following up his first representations to the Duke. The initial patent for the lottery provided for an honorarium of £500 to the Duke, which he was committed to spend on charitable purposes, and substantial personal fees for the Braunschweig civil servants who would be responsible for administering the draw. But Corr's scheme was more

38 Anonymous communication, n.d. [June/July 1720], in NLA WO, 2 Alt 6542, 59–60. Cf. Ducal rescript to Hopmann, 7.10.1721, in NLA WO, 2 Alt 6545, 55–60. The handwriting on the proposal matches that of the author of the German version of the partners' 23.6.1720 letter to the Duke.

complex and offered a promise of still greater wealth for the territory. The lottery project was followed in June 1720 by a proposal for a joint-stock bank, in which purchasers of lottery tickets would automatically qualify for shares but which would also sell stock to "all persons of any rank or nation".[39]

In spite of the coincidence of timing, there is no evidence of an original connection between the company scheme and the lottery/bank scheme. Corr reported in late August 1720 that when Thomas Pindar applied to him for some lottery tickets, Pindar promised Corr that he could help him deal with the ducal court,[40] but no other (or earlier) personal connection between Corr and the company networks has come to light. Corr was clearly an adventurer riding the Bubble. In the summer of 1720, while the tickets were being sold for the Braunschweig lottery, he also was playing the market in South Sea stock, mainly with other people's money. In February 1721, he enrolled as a Freeman of the Royal African Company, and a few years later we find him fitting out a ship for "the coast of Africa and beyond," while finding excuses not to pay for the cargo he had contracted for.[41] Stephen Ram, the goldsmith who acted as agent and treasurer for Corr's lottery, had been treasurer for a joint-stock marine insurance scheme to which John Martin and Henry Voguell were party in 1718, though in that case his actions had not been such as to make friends of the shareholders; he was charged with embezzling their subscriptions.[42]

Although they were distinct, the two undertakings, Corr's lottery and the linen manufacture, rapidly became linked in the minds of both English and German actors. It is conceivable that the intimation of a bank scheme from Thomas Pindar and Company inspired August Johann Mattenberg to invite Corr's bank proposal. Mattenberg was one of the Ducal councilors responsible for the economic affairs of the city of Braunschweig. He was one of the named agents of Corr's lottery but closely involved in negotiations over both English schemes. He wrote to a fellow councilor that the establishment of a bank was a logical ingredient in any plan to revive the Braunschweig economy, though he had doubts about some aspects of Corr's scheme.[43]

---

39 Corr's outline statements of June – July 1720 in NLA WO, 2 Alt 6543, 3 – 4, 6, 8 – 11, and full draft scheme (undated, in German and French) in NLA WO, 4 Alt 358.

40 Corr to Mattenberg, 20.8./10.9.1720, in NLA WO, 2 Alt 6543, 15.

41 List of Freemen of the Royal African Company of England, 9.2.1721, in TNA, T 70/1507; litigation of 1728 in TNA, C 11/241/24.

42 *The special report*, 20, 60. On Ram, see also William R. Scott, *The Constitution and Finance of English, Scottish and Irish Joint-Stock Companies to 1720* (Cambridge: Cambridge University Press, 1912), 3:399 – 401.

43 Mattenberg to Hochwohlgebohrener Herr, 28.7.1720, in NLA WO, 2 Alt 6543, 12 – 13.

With his lottery going ahead in late summer of 1718, Corr had a head start on Hopmann; but, by the time Thomas Pindar and Company was established, Corr's scheme was in crisis. At the end of August 1720, Corr announced that all the tickets had been sold, claiming that the purchasers included members of the English royal family, directors of the South Sea Company, and other prominent Londoners, and he pressed his scheme for establishing a bank on the proceeds.[44] But Braunschweig never saw that money, and neither did the holders of Corr's lottery tickets. As the lottery draw was repeatedly postponed, it became apparent in London that its organizers had been maneuvering to drive up the price of tickets. There was a public outcry, and subscribers demanded their money back.[45] Hopmann was just able to prevent a lawsuit being brought against the Duke. Corr's bank scheme, which the Duke had sent to a committee of privy councilors for consideration, was roundly rejected by a resolution of 20 November 1720.[46] It was too late, however, to prevent the fate of Thomas Pindar and Company from being colored by the Braunschweigers' doubts about Corr. Set against the background of this unfolding financial crisis, the result was increasing mutual suspicion between the English and the German actors.

Interferences

Two months earlier, in late September, Faber had noted to the Duke's secretary that Corr's lottery was so obviously a fraud that people were beginning to withdraw their money. Adopting a new vocabulary from the events in London, where South Sea stock prices were falling fast, he commented that the Duke's "hand and seal are profaned by this business that amounts to so-called bubbles". He also reflected on the position of Thomas Pindar and Company:

> I regret that the other society, from which much good might most probably arise for the public, did not either present their own proposal before this one came in or wait until time had proved this one unworthy, for since the two cannot flourish side by side and the general view is that we are in so deep with lottery-men and bankers that we cannot step back, I'm afraid the good seed will fall among the tares and be smothered.[47]

44 Corr to Mattenberg, 20.8./10.9.1720, in NLA WO, 2 Alt 6543, 15.

45 *The Case of great Numbers of His Majesty's injured Subjects, drawn in by the Artifice of Stephen Ram, of London, Goldsmith, and Agents, to become Proprietors of Lottery Tickets, Pretended to be Brunswick* [London, 1720]; litigation in TNA, C 11/1787/17.

46 Relatio ad Sermum die von dem Engländer Everhard Corr vorgeschlagene Actien Banque in Braunschweig und andere Hazard-negotia betreffend, in NLA WO, 2 Alt 6544, 19–26.

47 Faber to Geheimer Sekretär (unnamed), 20.9.1720, in NLA WO, 2 Alt 6543, 33–35.

Even after Corr's bank scheme had been rejected, the fact that the Duke initially showed more favor to Corr than he manifestly deserved informed the growing tension in negotiations around the linen manufacture. In late September 1720, Mattenberg and Faber met representatives of the company, who had arrived in Braunschweig "surprised and troubled [verwundert und affligiert]" at the fact that, in spite of Hopmann's assurances, there had been no practical response to their proposal. They worked out a compromise that met the English partners' key demands, including a 21-year exemption from import duties on sugar and yarn as well as other concessions on tariffs and duties.[48] But the company had still not made any moves to establish a physical presence in Braunschweig by the beginning of 1721, when it submitted a new set of requests; these were in many respects a reiteration of their infrastructural needs (i.e. warehouses and bleaching facilities), but they also stated the hopes that the concessions might be extended and that the company might be allowed to set up operations in other territories.[49] Faber was persuaded of their good faith, but he warned Edward Morgan that those who had been in favor of Corr's scheme:

> are now attempting to convince your supporters either that you are not in a position to pay the high costs that the business calls for or that you never had any better intentions than Mr Corr, and that everything you said about the linen manufacture and refinery served only to cover up your real objectives.[50]

The English investors, in their turn, expressed themselves indignant at being trumped by Corr and doubtful of the good sense and good faith of the Braunschweigers. Nevertheless, the company went into production, confirming the entrepreneurial intentions of at least some of the partners. In November 1720, the factors Potgiesser and Rosenhagen were appointed on three-year contracts, and, by December, they were contracting spinners and weavers in Braunschweig. Certainly, Potgiesser and Rosenhagen believed they were operating a real enterprise. In April 1721, the first samples of linen reached London; it was of good quality but still unbleached, because the manufacture still had no facilities of its own – no warehouse, no offices and no bleaching yards.[51] By October, the factors employed 35 spinners and weavers in Braunschweig and in seven surrounding towns and villages, and they had, by their own account, produced over 8,000

48 Faber to Duke August Wilhelm 26.9.1720, in NLA WO, 2 Alt 6543, 36–52.

49 Translation of a letter signed Thomas Burgess, with Hopmann's comments, in NLA WO, 2 Alt 6544, 59–60.

50 Faber [?] to Morgan, probably January 1721, in NLA WO, 4 Alt 5, Nr. 358.

51 Thomas Burgess to Potgiesser and Rosenhagen, 5.5.1721, in NLA WO, 2 Alt 6545, 20.

yards of linen cloth. In explanation of *why* they had gone outside of Braunschweig to recruit workers, the factors reported that they could not find men and women with the requisite level of skills in the city. They also asserted that they needed to be licensed to import skilled workers, if necessary – a point which the company had stipulated in January 1721 and which is further evidence of the seriousness of the project.[52] There was still no firm basis for proceeding with full production, however, not least because by the time the samples arrived in Braunschweig, the London equity market had already crashed, dampening optimism on both sides and resetting the terms of mutual trust.

The Aftermath of the Crash

Many of Thomas Pindar and Company's principals personally lost in the crash. One was reportedly bankrupted, and, more importantly, much of the ground capital invested in South Sea stock was lost. Some of the investors also lost money in Corr's lottery scheme.[53] But once Corr was out of the way, the partners were prepared to keep trying. Burgess later admitted that the company needed considerably more than four times the original capital, and in order to raise new funds, Hopmann proposed in December 1720 that a lottery be established to be drawn in Braunschweig, with five percent of the income going to the Duke and five percent to the company.[54] (In a later communication to the Duke, he added that his recent marriage would give him the means to help finance the new scheme.)[55] The terms and timing of this lottery now became the focus of negotiations between the Duke and the company. The key sticking point was the question of oversight. The Duke wanted his councilors to be able to audit and indeed co-manage the accounts, while the English investors insisted that the lottery funds remain in London and treated the Duke's proposal as illegitimate meddling. A counter-proposal emerged in August 1721, that holders of lottery tickets should be entitled to a share in the profits of the company. This echoed Corr's scheme, and, while avoiding a commitment to the joint-stock form, it is an example of the kind of experimentation with mixed forms

52 Rosenhagen and Potgiesser, Noat Was von uns der privilegirten Englischen Companie bestellte Factoren zum Anfange unternommen worden, in NLA WO, 2 Alt 6545, 47–48.

53 Thomas Pindar to Duke August Wilhelm, 2.4.1722, in NLA WO, 2 Alt 6546, 67–68; Hopmann to Duke August Wilhelm, 2.12.1720, in NLA WO, 2 Alt 6544, 28.

54 Hopmann to Duke August Wilhelm, 20.12.1720, in NLA WO, 2 Alt 6544, 31–32. Cf. Burgess to Potgiesser, 17.3.1721, in NLA WO 2 Alt 6545, 2.

55 Hopmann to Duke August Wilhelm, 19.1.1721, in NLA WO, 1 Alt 6, Nr. 85, 65.

of finance that was characteristic of the boom years.[56] What is interesting here is that the proposal came from Braunschweig and was rejected by the English partners, only to reappear in October as a promise that ticket-holders who drew blanks in the lottery would receive shares in the company.[57]

As this new round of negotiations dragged on, the Duke expressed his state of mind in a rescript to Hopmann dated 7 October 1721; he found it "displeasing" that the company now objected to oversight of their accounts, having never made an issue of it (for example) in their original bank proposal. He characterized his stipulations as a means of "securing our reputation and the public credit here". Noting that the company was "already partially dissolved", he expressed a real anxiety about Hopmann's middleman role. He reminded Hopmann of his own responsibility, should the company renege on all its as-yet-unfulfilled promises, and of the need to ensure that the anticipated lottery fund not be:

> ~~aveuglement~~ blindly put at risk, and so much hazarded for so little on the basis of a simple promise, particularly when we have not the slightest information about the state of the whole company, and should God call upon your person we [...] would not even know to whom we should address ourselves in so distant lands.[58]

The mistrust that now prevailed in Braunschweig was expressed directly by Faber shortly afterwards; somehow or other, he wrote, the company must be forced:

> to show us their inmost minds [ihr Innerstes herauszukehren] and once and for all make clear whether they are or have ever been serious about taking the enterprise forward, or whether they were simply looking to make a heap of money dishonestly at the cost of His Grace and others.[59]

For the sake of his own reputation, Privy Councilor Count Conrad Detlev von Dehn, who was the Duke's favorite and in effect his deputy in commercial affairs, refused to put his initials to any positive statement about the lottery.[60]

Against this background, Potgiesser and Rosenhagen attempted to seize the initiative, first pressing for completion of the lottery and then offering to bypass the company and run both the manufacture and the lottery themselves on the

---

56 Condorelli, *The 1719–20 Stock Euphoria.*

57 MS draft of a lottery ticket, n.d., in NLA WO, 2 Alt 6545, 67.

58 Ducal rescript to Hopmann, 7.10.1721.

59 Faber to Privy Councillors, 19.10.1721, in NLA WO 2 Alt 6454, 68–70.

60 MS note attached to MS draft of public announcement of the lottery, n.d. [October 1721], in NLA WO 2 Alt 6454 [with 65–66].

Duke's terms, with the lottery as a separate operation.[61] They were in a particularly exposed position, since they were running out of ready cash. Waiting to be paid themselves, in September 1721, they also faced a complaint from the Braunschweig weavers' guild that they were underpaying local weavers and deliberately bringing lower-skilled weavers in from the outside.[62] These factors would be the last of the actors to retain some hopes of the project. In March 1722, they produced a highly detailed plan for running the manufacture themselves, citing their own experience and the results of some market research.[63] This was dismissed by the Privy Council, and the last pages of the file on Thomas Pindar and Company are concerned with the factors' efforts to extract payment from the company partners. By the summer of 1723, the only men in the story who had done any real work were kicking their heels in Braunschweig and falling out with each other and with the agents of the Duke, who at one point wrote personally (but in vain) to King George I in hopes of getting the men compensated and re-established elsewhere.[64] In late July 1723, Potgiesser appealed to the council against Elisabeth, the younger of Rosenhagen's two sisters, who was refusing him access to the company accounts. Relations in their (apparently shared) household had broken down so far that Mattenberg reported on his interview with the sisters: "I [...] found them in such a state that interviewing them *en detail* would produce a whole book of notes [...] When Secretary Alberti tried to make peace between them recently [Elisabeth] offered [her sister Anne Sophie] a box on the ears instead of the intended hand of friendship."[65]

By this time, Thomas Pindar and Company was no longer in existence. Hopmann's response to the Duke's strictures of late 1721 was to distance himself from his English partners without giving up the project. In January 1722, observing that the company project had been spoiled by the wave of "ill managed" stock-jobbing, he proposed moving the business out of the hands of the English partners and setting up a Braunschweig import-export office in London, under his own management and linked to a joint-stock bank with commercial, lending

61 Rosenhagen and Potgiesser to Duke August Wilhelm, 20.10.1721, in NLA WO, 2 Alt 6546, 1–2.
62 Geschworene Elteste und sämtliche Meister des Löblichen Leineweber-Handwerks to Duke August Wilhelm, 15.9.1721; Councilor (unnamed) to Duke August Wilhelm, 11.11.1721, in NLA WO, 2 Alt 6546, 10–11 and 8–9, respectively.
63 Rosenhagen and Potgiesser to Duke August Wilhelm, 4.3.1722; Rosenhagen and Potgiesser to Councilors, 9.3.1722, in NLA WO 2 Alt 6546, 40–45 and 52–54 respectively.
64 Duke August Wilhelm and Cabinet to George I, 8.4.1723 and reply 31.5./11.6.1723, in NLA WO 2 Alt 6546, 84 and 82.
65 Potgiesser to Privy Councilors and statement of Duke and Cabinet, 22.7.1723, in NLA WO, 2 Alt 6546, 86, 88–89.

and insurance functions.[66] On 3 February, Hopmann, Pindar, Morgan, Hoskyns, Tench and Burgess met at Hopmann's lodgings in Pall Mall to dissolve their partnership. By mid-February, Hopmann had been dismissed from the Duke's service.[67]

Learning Curves

Amid the dwindling mutual trust and increasing skepticism that characterized the fortunes of Thomas Pindar and Company after 1720, we can sense the aftershocks of the stock market crash itself, which discredited the business of *Actienhandel* and the joint-stock form and which left those who had been drawn into (or placed themselves at risk of being drawn into) it bruised. The emotional dimensions of this are most apparent in the discussions that Corr's bank proposal generated, but the company suffered moral as well as material damage from the crash. In order to understand this aspect of the episode, we need to consider the expectations and resources that informed the responses of the Duke and his councilors to the English projects. There was an awareness of risk on both sides, and this added to the challenges of maintaining a dialogue between actors with different levels of knowledge and different approaches to economic development.

In September 1720, Hopmann was in Hanover with two deputies from the company. Learning of the progress of Corr's bank plan, he rode to Wolfenbüttel, seeking the Duke – in vain – at both of his palaces to warn against the scheme. He then contacted Privy Councilor Dehn; it was not his purpose, he wrote, simply to denounce Corr. Rather, "I would say this clearly to his face and to the whole world, because I understand the principles of this stock-trading business. Above all I can predict that within a year the very first subscribers to the scheme will have sold their shares and the money will have gone out of the country".[68] This was Hopmann self-consciously articulating his role as broker between two political economies. His intervention echoes a leitmotif of the contemporary German pamphlet and periodical literature, which, building on a presumption that most Germans were ignorant of joint-stock operations, repeatedly raised the question: who knows what about *Actienhandel?*

66 Hopmann to Duke August Wilhelm, 13.1.1722, in NLA WO, 2 Alt 6546, 20–22.

67 Notes on the dissolution of the partnership, in NLA WO, 2 Alt 6546, 31; Ducal rescript to Hopmann, 3.2.1722, in NLA WO, 1 Alt 6, Nr. 85, 67.

68 Hopmann to Dehn, 20.9.1720, in NLA WO, 2 Alt 6543, 26–29.

As Hopmann's own financial entanglements show, he was indeed experienced in stock-trading, and he had already invoked this expertise once before in his correspondence with Braunschweig. His December 1719 diplomatic dispatch to Duke August Wilhelm, for example, included a report on new companies being set up in London and on the presence on the London markets of French investors who had made profits on the Mississippi scheme.[69] In April 1720, he offered to invest in the South Sea scheme, which he called a "second Mississipi," on the Duke's behalf. He asked for a ten percent commission on the profits, which were bound to be substantial – "because I fully understand the business".[70] There is no evidence that the Duke responded, but it suggests that the Braunschweig courtiers were not quite as innocent of knowledge about stock-trading and its consequences as contemporaries claimed. It is nevertheless significant that in September 1720, deploying his claim to technical knowledge to see off the competitor Corr, Hopmann referenced an argument that would be most likely to appeal to a German territorial ruler (or anyone else educated in the mercantilist tradition): a catastrophic threat to the money supply.

It is not surprising that the Duke and his councilors initially welcomed the English proposals. Financial incentives and concessions, funding of infrastructural development, and even the encouragement of inward investment were familiar instruments of economic policy in the early modern German lands. Since the sixteenth century, the Dukes of Braunschweig-Wolfenbüttel had found ways to promote the economic development of their territory. After the city of Braunschweig lost its independence to ducal authority in 1671, they showed considerable energy in developing local commercial life. Faber and Mattenberg led the negotiations with Thomas Pindar and Company because they were members of a commission that had been set up in 1674 to manage the city's commercial affairs. (Faber was in charge of the city treasury, and Privy Councilor Dehn chaired the commission). Braunschweig's thriving semi-annual trade fairs were further testimony to the enterprising spirit of August Wilhelm's forebears.[71] With the decline of the Hanse, these fairs were, perhaps, the main mechanism through which the local economy was linked with supra-regional and even international trade networks. That said, August Wilhelm and his immediate predecessor Anton Ulrich had not been particularly energetic in maintaining developmental momentum, beyond promoting the growing and processing of tobacco as well

69 Report dated London, 20.11./1.12.1719, in NLA WO, 1 Alt 6, Nr. 85, 23–24,

70 Hopmann to Duke August Wilhelm, 7.4.1720, in NLA WO, 1 Alt 6, Nr. 85, 50–51.

71 Nils Brübach, *Die Reichsmessen von Frankfurt am Main, Leipzig und Braunschweig (14.–18. Jahrhundert)* (Stuttgart: Steiner, 1994).

as a fayence manufacture, whose best workmen were repeatedly poached by wealthier princes. By the second decade of the eighteenth century, the court was heavily in debt.[72]

In 1718, then, the Wolfenbüttel court was open to developmental projects, but both of the English proposals exceeded recent experience. Corr's lottery looked like a familiar form of short-term fundraising,[73] which probably helped him to get his foot in the door; but the joint-stock bank was something entirely new. Thomas Pindar and Company envisaged an indefinite foreign presence, with manufacture subcontracted to local producers but also the freedom to import labor. The trading company also proposed to continuously import from and export to a global market. One precedent for this was the operations of the English Merchant Adventurers, some of which involved linen manufacture but which had ended a century earlier and never had a presence in Braunschweig.[74] Similarly, the attendance of foreign merchants at the Braunschweig trade fairs was seasonal, temporary and (like the income it generated from fees and duties) easily controlled; indeed, a key question that councilors asked about the English company in 1718 was whether its retail operations would interfere with or supplement the benefits already provided by the fairs. And ducal concessionary and taxation policies up to then had been informed by the mercantilist principles of protectionism and of the augmentation of the money supply.

In the German-speaking lands, the alternative vision of dynamic economic expansion fueled by the progressive circulation of wealth that informed the fiscal experiments of 1719 to 1720 was associated with cameralist political economy. Cameralism, as such, came into its own as the 'user's manual' for territorial rulers later in the century, but its earliest proponents were already active at the time of the bubbles. Some commented on events in Paris and London, and, among these, it was Paul Jacob Marperger who was most active both in disseminating detailed information about the ways in which the stock market worked and in trying to explain to the German public the underlying rationale of such fiscal ex-

72 Karl Heinrich Kaufhold, "Die Wirtschaft in der frühen Neuzeit: Gewerbe, Handel und Verkehr," in *Geschichte Niedersachsens: Politik, Wirtschaft und Gesellschaft von der Reformation bis zum Beginn des 19. Jahrhunderts*, ed. Christine van den Heuvel and Manfred von Boetticher (Hannover: Hahn, 1998), 351–636, here 362–366.

73 On lotteries, see Hans-Peter Ullmann, *Der Staat, die Spieler und das Glück: Lotterien im Deutschland des 18. und 19. Jahrhunderts* (Berlin: de Gruyter, 1991).

74 Wolf-Rüdiger Baumann, *The Merchants Adventurers and the Continental Cloth-trade (1560s–1620s)* (Berlin: de Gruyter, 1990), 151–154, 183–189, 329–330.

periments and their potential benefits in a globalizing economy.[75] In Braunschweig, the archival record attests to the serious and informed consideration that the Duke's councilors gave to the possibilities as well as the risks involved in the English schemes, and one measure of their level of technical sophistication might be the extent to which they engaged with the writings of Marperger and other cameralists. The evidence is limited but suggestive: Of Marperger's pamphlet on the Mississippi scheme, which was published in the imperial financial centers of Frankfurt and Leipzig in at least five editions over the course of 1720, there is no contemporary copy in the Ducal library.[76] In an unsigned commentary on Corr's bank plan written at the end of 1720 or at the beginning of 1721, one of the councilors (very likely Faber) invokes the authority of "a certain author" in condemning "Billet-Banquen" as "a desperate measure best left to the despotic French government".[77] From the context, it is clear that the commentator thinks that "Billet-Banquen" refers to joint-stock banks; in fact, the reference is to banks issuing paper money. The "certain author" was Marperger, but it was the Marperger of ten years earlier, writing in his *Neu eröffnetes Handels-Bericht oder wohlbestelltes Commercien-Collegium.*[78] A standard text on commercial law and practice, based on a 1688 work by Jacques Savary, the *Handels-Bericht* was probably ready at hand in the Braunschweig treasury office as well as in the Ducal library, but it had nothing to say about stock trading.

The same manuscript commentary on Corr's plan, however, refers knowledgeably to the policies of local governments in Holland and Hamburg, which denied foreigners the right to buy shares in new joint-stock enterprises, and also to the failure of the Mississippi scheme. The author cites a recent issue of a Hamburg news-sheet. If the Braunschweig councilors had a lot to learn, it is clear that they kept themselves informed. The Treasury files[79] contain notes on local, regional and global geography (including products of the British Empire to which the new company might give access), enquiries into the dimensions of and income from the local yarn and linen trade, and excerpts from economic

75 Rosenhaft, "'All That Glitters'." On the relationship between cameralism and European global expansion, see Sophus A. Reinert, *Translating Empire: Emulation and the Origins of Political Economy* (Cambridge, Mass.: Harvard University Press, 2011).

76 The copy currently in the holdings of the Herzog August Library in Wolfenbüttel was acquired as part of the library of a Hanoverian aristocratic family in 1993.

77 Anmerckungen bey dem Banco-Project, in NLA WO, 4 Alt 5, Nr. 358.

78 See Paul Jacob Marperger, *Neu eröffnetes Handels-Bericht oder wohlbestelltes Commercien-Collegium* [...] (Hamburg, 1709), 261–262. In this work, Marperger advocated the creation of banks with lending and other facilities, managed by civil society agents and operating on a cash basis.

79 NLA WO, 4 Alt 5, Nr. 358.

literature. On the cover of a folder of historical documents on relations between the English Merchant Adventurers and the Hanse cities, the compiler noted that he had been prompted by his readings in English and German commercial law to copy them out from the archives. He did so in order to understand "what needs to be taken into consideration in deciding about the proposed establishment of an English company in Braunschweig". Notes on the history of banks and banking law are accompanied by the printed prospectus for an imperial bank (not a joint-stock enterprise), set up by Holy Roman Emperor Charles VI in 1715. The Duke and his councilors also received the news about other bubble projects. The files include a printed German pamphlet on the South Sea scheme and one in German and Dutch on joint-stock insurance projects.[80] Printed copies and manuscript extracts from Dutch newspapers carry reports about London bubble companies in 1720 and the 1721 Hessen-Kassel projects, and there are manuscript reports from London about the emerging South Sea scandal and the Harburg lottery – another English project linking a lottery with a development scheme in Germany, which lasted from 1720 to 1723 and about which Hopmann reported personally to the Duke in February 1722.[81]

We thus see the Braunschweig actors poised between acknowledging the value of new projects and looking for ways to assess the risk. This is particularly apparent before the crash of the equity market in London, but, even in its aftermath, they sought to understand their own situation in light of what was going on elsewhere. As late as September 1720, Faber was pointing out in entirely cameralist terms the advantages of the new company, not only for stimulating trade and industry but also for giving the citizens of Braunschweig direct access to English and colonial consumer goods.[82] It is all the more striking, then, that the crash drove them back to a position that was entirely pessimistic. The descriptions in the councilors' report on Corr's bank scheme are particularly dramatic.[83] Expressing unalloyed horror at the very notion of a joint-stock company, they wrote of the:

> pernicious destructiveness, the miserable and ruinous consequences which paper commerce of that kind has really brought with it in France, England and Holland and is still bringing, since while a few have made themselves rich in a short time most have been to-

80 These are in the form of uncut galley sheets and show no signs of having been read.

81 Hopmann to Duke August Wilhelm, 26.2.1722, in NLA WO, 2 Alt 6546, 38–39. On the Harburg lottery, see A.J.G. Cummings, "The Harburgh Company and Its lottery 1716–1723," *Business History* 28 (1986): 1–18.

82 Faber to Duke August Wilhelm, 26.9.1720.

83 Relatio ad Sermum die von dem Engländer Everhard Corr vorgeschlagene Actien Banque in Braunschweig und andere Hazard-negotia betreffend, 20.11.1720, in NLA WO, 2 Alt 6544, 19–26.

> tally ruined so that there is nothing left but breakdown, confusion, desolation, poverty, misfortune, misery and despair, with such deplorable effects on powerful kingdoms and opulent republics that they are bemoaned there as a *flagellum divinum.*

Still more interesting is the way in which they answered the vision of industrial and financial regeneration that was common to both English projects by painting a landscape of ineluctable backwardness. Whereas Corr proposed that various other financial institutions, like assurances, could be rolled out alongside the bank, they commented:

> Insuring ships and cargoes at sea has always been a highly dangerous business [...] and anyway Braunschweig lacks the object of insurance, namely navigation [...] Lending banks are instituted not for profiteers but for the poor[...] and it will be difficult to introduce life annuities here because there are too few unmarried people and people are not familiar with them.

Similarly:

> Anyone who looks to make Braunschweig into a leading commercial center is flattering themselves, because it's completely incomprehensible what kind of merchants might move to the city, expand and flourish, given that there are already more than enough in Holland, Hamburg, Bremen, Lübeck, Leipzig, Nürnberg, Augsburg, Frankfurt am Main.

And finally:

> What might move the English and Dutch to abandon their usual water routes to the Prussian east and make an expensive detour for the sake of a Braunschweig bank? How does the author expect the Silesians, Poles and Prussians, who transport their merchandise by water to Hamburg, Holland, and England, to prefer the overland trek via Braunschweig?

In 1718, the Duke's councilors were thinking with their English partners about ways to compete with Hamburg's confectioners; and, even as the bubble was bursting in London, Corr's joint-stock scheme had its supporters in Braunschweig. By November 1720, anxiety at the prospect of being drawn into a new project whose risky, and indeed disastrous, nature appeared now confirmed seems to have forced the Duke's councilors into a rhetorical stance that rejected all prospects for improvement and hopes for competing with established markets. And, in their reservations, they articulated quite vividly their own conviction of being at a disadvantage in a two-speed Holy Roman Empire.

Conclusion

The terms of the November 1720 report were certainly colored by the urgency of disassociating the court from Corr's project, but the affect they carry seems real, particularly in the light of longer-term developments. The end of Thomas Pindar and Company was not by any means the end of economic projects in London or Braunschweig, let alone in the Holy Roman Empire as a whole. In Braunschweig, in the wake of the squabbles between Potgiesser and Elisabeth Rosenhagen, the council gave Potgiesser sole authority to go on managing the linen manufacture, and Potgiesser (who at some point married Anne Sophie Rosenhagen) remained a respected figure in the city's linen trade for at least another fifteen years.[84] This bespeaks the ducal administration's continued commitment to supporting the local economy. There would be no new experiments for another decade, though, until the accession of Duke Carl I. His long reign (1731–80) was characterized by an exceptionally intensive program of cameralist reforms, among which were the foundation of a highly successful porcelain factory, the introduction of a fire insurance scheme, and the formation in 1765 of a lending (or development) bank.[85] But none of these was a joint-stock enterprise.

Johann Gerhard Hopmann continued to build his career as a diplomat in London, and his projecting did not end with the bubble. In 1727, he presented Prime Minister Robert Walpole with a complicated scheme for funding the planned new bridge between Putney and Fulham.[86] In a letter of 1722, reflecting on his dismissal from the Duke's service, he observed: "Important business like this is never accomplished in haste [...] It's well known how much patience and careful nurture is going into the Ostend business in Vienna."[87] "The Ostend business" was a reference to one of the most ambitious new projects of the day, a trading company that aimed to challenge the English and Dutch in the East Indies and at the same time to revitalize the Holy Roman Empire's inland ports and trading centers. Established on a joint-stock basis in 1722, after several years of testing the competition, the Ostend Company continued to operate profitably until succumbing to political pressure from England in 1727/31.[88] It was a manifestation of the projecting spirit of the bubble years, as well as the global vision

---

84 NLA WO 4 Alt 5, Nr. 375 and 383; 2 Alt 18320; Burial notice of Anne Sophie Potgiesser née Rosenhagen, *Braunschweigische Anzeigen*, no. 103, December 1746, 2382.

85 Kaufhold, "Wirtschaft," 366–367.

86 Hopmann to Sir Robert Walpole (with scheme), 6.4.1727, in Cambridge University Library, Cholmondeley (Houghton) Papers, Correspondence/1419.

87 Hopmann to Hofrat, 31.7.1722, in NLA WO, 2 Alt 6546, 72–76.

88 Georges-Henri Dumont, *L'Épopée de la compagnie d'Ostende* (Brussels: Le cri, 2000).

and enthusiasm for innovation that fed it all over Europe; it also demonstrates that even the shock of the crash did not bring an end to new projects for improvement.[89] In spite of disappointments and failures, the same can be said for Braunschweig and its bubble companies.

89 Condorelli, *The 1719–20 Stock Euphoria*, 19, reports examples of stock prices in local projects remaining unaffected by the crash in London.

Malick W. Ghachem

The Mississippi Bubble in Saint-Domingue (Haiti)

In April 1720, just as speculation in the stock of the French Indies Company was reaching feverishly high levels, the Abbé Joseph Lambert penned a scathing denunciation of the Mississippi Bubble. Some of his rhetoric was only to be expected from a Catholic priest, lecturer at the Sorbonne, and Prior of St. Martin de Palaiseau, near Versailles. Lambert adhered to an especially austere version of Jansenism, the French Catholic reform movement that, inspired by the theology of St. Augustine, opposed papal and royal absolutism and promoted a relatively direct relationship between God and the individual Christian conscience. In keeping with these commitments, Lambert argued that the evils of the rue Quincampoix – the narrow street near the central Parisian markets at Les Halles, where shares of the Indies Company were traded – were a function of the shares themselves. He dutifully subjected these instruments to a "theological decision," condemning both their "injustices" and "inequities" in ancient Christian terms that evoked the sins of luxury and financial excess.[1]

Lambert's discussion of the speculators' complicity with the slave trade, by contrast, sounded distinctly modern. His critique flowed from the definition of a share (*action*) itself: "in the language of commerce," Lambert explained, a share is "a right that one acquires to share the profits that can flow from a particular business; whence it is apparent that a share places us in society with a number of persons who acquire, with us, one or more actions."[2] The share, in other

---

1 Joseph Lambert, "Décision théologique sur les actions de la Compagnie des indes," April 1720, in The Historic New Orleans Collection, Mss. 735. A digital version is available at http://hnoc.minisisinc.com/thnoc/catalog/3/13693. The appearance of the pamphlet is noted in the 25.4.1720 entry of Mathieu Marais's *Journal de Paris* (Saint-Etienne: Presses universitaires de Saint-Etienne, 2004), 1:104. Lambert's critique of the System is analyzed in Arnaud Orain, *La politique du merveilleux: Une autre histoire du Système de Law (1695–1795)* (Paris: Fayard, 2018), 238–248. Lambert also was affiliated with the Cardinal de Noailles, the archbishop of Paris and brother of the Duke de Noailles, one of John Law's principal rivals. Lambert's text thus likely reflected both theological and political opposition to Law's System. For a concise synopsis of the complexities of Jansenist theology, see Gemma Simmonds, CJ, "Jansenism," in *The Cambridge Encyclopedia of the Jesuits*, ed. Thomas Worcester, S.J. (New York: Cambridge University Press, 2017), 414–415.

2 Lambert, "Décision théologique," fol. 2.

https://doi.org/10.1515/9783110592139-006

words, draws the investor into a relationship of profit and loss with the Company's business, thereby creating a community (or society). Even the most individualistic profit-seeking investor is unable to avoid the coordinated nature of the market.

According to Lambert, this social dimension of investing had especially pronounced moral implications when the business in question encompassed the commodification of human beings. Combining France's various commercial monopolies to create the Indies Company enabled France to extend its trade "to the four corners of the world," in the words of a May 1719 act of merger.[3] But the Company's power over others was at its zenith in one particular region, West Africa:

> The buying and selling of men [is a trade] that accords poorly with the Christian religion. The invasion of lands and countries occupied by other men, the violence, the extortion, the fraud and shock inflicted by the Company's clerks are the profits that revert to the Company.

Lambert believed that investors with the fear of God in them would recognize that, just as they were liable as shareholders for any embezzlement that occurred within the company, they were responsible for renouncing any dividends derived from the theft of other humans. Thus, although a potential investor had multiple reasons to abstain from the Indies Company craze, avoiding complicity with slavery was an independent and sufficient reason for putting one's money elsewhere.[4]

Appearances to the contrary, Lambert's version of what we would today call socially responsible investing did not merely reflect one set of theological commitments. Other forms of Judeo-Christian doctrine could just as easily have been used to defend slavery and social hierarchy.[5] In its very focus on the sin of slavery, Lambert's *Décision théologique* transcends its Jansenist provenance and becomes a statement about the individual's responsibility for the acts of a community in the era of joint-stock speculation. Lambert's sense of the interdependence of slavery and the System (as the effort to revamp French public finances between 1716 and 1720 has become known) made him not only a religious voice

3 Lambert, "Décision théologique," fols. 7–8. According to Edgar Faure, these words were penned by John Law himself. Edgar Faure, *La banqueroute de Law, 17 juillet 1720* (Paris: Gallimard, 1977), 195.

4 Lambert, "Décision théologique," fol. 7.

5 David Brion Davis, *Inhuman Bondage: The Rise and Fall of Slavery in the New World* (Oxford and New York: Oxford University Press, 2006), 64–69, 187.

but also a kind of financial prophet: an oracle revealing to the generation of 1720 the present and future of financial capitalism.

Like most prophets, Lambert was almost certainly without honor in his hometown. He need not be representative of the Parisian moral climate of the time, however, for us to see that his interpretation of the System also has implications for the historiography of the bubbles. By and large, the scholarly literature on John Law's System has described an essentially Parisian story of paper money, speculative frenzy, and stockjobbing followed by financial collapse, liquidation, and recrimination. This Parisian orientation reflects a predilection for an econometric and financial-historical interpretation of the System: was the Bubble rational or irrational, and what were its fundamental financial and economic underpinnings (if any)? The leading studies of the System – those by Larry Neal, François Velde, Antoin Murphy, and Peter Garber – share an interest in John Law as an economic theorist, and they typically resort to economic theory to explain why Law's own models failed to work out as planned.[6] (The literature on the South Sea Bubble, though not the subject here, displays a similar tendency, albeit with seemingly more room for disagreement among competing economic theories.)[7]

The colonies typically are placed outside the mainstream of these financial histories, relevant only insofar as they signaled the fantastic profits to be reaped from the vast Louisiana territory or the potential of the *asiento* contract to promote investment in the South Sea and Indies companies.[8] There are some nota-

---

6 See, e.g., Antoin E. Murphy, *John Law: Economic Theorist and Policy-maker* (Oxford and New York: Clarendon Press, 1997); Larry Neal, *The Rise of Financial Capitalism: International Capital Markets in the Age of Reason* (New York: Cambridge University Press, 1990); François R. Velde, "Was John Law's System a Bubble? The Mississippi Bubble Revisited," in *The Origins and Development of Financial Markets and Institutions: From the Seventeenth Century to the Present*, ed. Larry Neal and Jeremy Atack (New York: Cambridge University Press, 2009), 99–120; François R. Velde, "French Public Finance between 1683 and 1726," in *Government Debts and Financial Markets in Europe*, ed. Fausto Piola Caselli (London: Pickering & Chatto, 2008), 135–165; Faure, *La banqueroute de Law*; and Nicolas Buat, *John Law: La dette ou comment s'en débarrasser* (Paris: Belles lettres, 2015). Buat's book appears as part of a series that classifies Law as no less than a "penseur de la liberté" (a thinker of freedom) – a puzzling label for a man held universally and almost single-handedly responsible for creating the first major stock market crisis.

7 See, e.g., Helen J. Paul, *The South Sea Bubble: An Economic History of Its Origins and Consequences* (New York: Routledge, 2011); and Richard Dale, *The First Crash: Lessons from the South Sea Bubble* (Princeton: Princeton University Press, 2016).

8 On the marketing of the lower Mississippi Valley and South America as untapped repositories of wealth, see Rik Frehen, William N. Goetzmann, and K. Geert Rouwenhorst, "Finance in the Great Mirror of Folly," in *The Great Mirror of Folly: Finance, Culture, and the Crash of 1720*, ed. William N. Goetzmann et al. (New Haven: Yale University Press, 2013), 72–79; and Carl Wenner-

ble exceptions, perhaps the most important of which is Marcel Girard's extraordinarily detailed study of the System's implementation in Louisiana.[9] On the whole, however, we have lost sight of the extent to which Law's vision for the future of France extended "to the four corners of the world," encompassing such unexpected places as modern-day Haiti, Algeria, India, Quebec, and China.

Haiti, or Saint-Domingue as it was known in the colonial era, is a particularly instructive theatre for exploring the ramifications of this greater Mississippi Bubble. Already becoming the heart of the French Atlantic economy by the 1720s, Haiti was the site of an extraordinary second life for the System that unfolded several years after the 1720 Bubble burst in France. In 1722 and 1723, the French Indies Company attempted to implement the monopoly over the slave trade that it originally received in 1719. Law was gone from office by the time the System finally was enforced in Saint-Domingue, but the vision of an integrated West African slave trade that permitted the exploitation of a greater Caribbean economy extending from Haiti to Louisiana was emphatically his. It was this vision that came under attack in the Caribbean in the early 1720s. It was equally the cornerstone of the larger global system that Lambert underscored in his *Décision théologique*. Yet, the most important study of the consequences of Law's System in Saint-Domingue, written by Charles Frostin, treats it as a chapter in the history of local (white) creole revolts in the colony, rather than as an essential part of the Mississippi Bubble writ large.[10] As I will argue here, integrating Saint-Domingue into the history of the System is a matter of moving in two directions at once, or synthesizing a metropolitan and a colonial historiography that have been largely compartmentalized.

The first major financial crises of the north Atlantic were also moments at which France and Britain, in competition with each other and with Dutch interlopers to supply the Spanish American slave market through control of the *asiento* contract, committed themselves to a decisive expansion of and investment in the slave trade.[11] This commitment had many repercussions in the Atlantic

lind, *Casualties of Credit: The English Financial Revolution, 1620–1720* (Cambridge, MA: Harvard University Press, 2011), 197–234.

9 Marcel Giraud, *Histoire de la Louisiane française*, vol. 3, *L'époque de John Law, 1717–1720* (Paris: Presses universitaires de France, 1966). My impression is that this book serves as a reference point for historians of Louisiana and French colonization in the Americas more than it does for historians of the System or of financial and economic history.

10 Charles Frostin, *Les révoltes blanches à Saint-Domingue aux XVIIe et XVIIIe siècles* (Paris: L'École, 1975; Rennes: Presses Universitaires de Rennes, 2008), chs. 3–4.

11 Under the 1494 Treaty of Tordesillas, sponsored by the Papacy, the Spanish and Portuguese crowns effectively divided the world beyond Europe into two largely exclusive spheres. Spain would have control of nearly all of the Americas, while Portugal would control the African

world, one of which was a massive revolt against the French Indies Company in Haiti in 1722 and 1723. Another was the revival of the rhetoric of free trade in opposition to the resurgence of monopoly trading companies following the peace of 1713, which brought an end to the War of the Spanish Succession. Though it drew liberally on seventeenth-century controversies over the legitimacy of the Indies companies, this revival also should be read in light of competing French, British and Dutch efforts to control the Atlantic slave trade in an era of still-rampant piracy and contraband. The north Atlantic struggle to tie the West Africa trade successfully to an emergent plantation complex in the West Indies extended into the East Indies and reverberated in the domestic markets of northern Europe. Along with Britain's Royal African and South Sea companies and the Dutch West Indies Company, the French Indies Company – the only slave trading company that controlled a global commercial network in its own right – fought to inherit the transatlantic rewards of the post-war era. This struggle came to a climax in the 1720s, with dramatic consequences for British, Dutch, and French slave traders alike.[12]

Seen in this light, it is difficult to interpret the bubbles of 1720 as strictly metropolitan affairs primarily involving the restructuring of French and British state debt – which is how the extant scholarship has, by and large, described them.[13] Instead, the French West Indies (and, to a lesser extent, the British Caribbean islands) emerge as a crucial theatre of what contemporaries understood as a revolutionary shift from mercantilism to free trade. The shift away from corporate mercantile control in Saint-Domingue and elsewhere in the North Atlantic during this period was indeed a momentous – if hardly unidirectional or foreordained – change. But, if "free trade" was supposed to represent a radical departure from company monopolies in the colonial context, the picture looked far more ambiguous from the perspective of the slave trade and the emerging plantation system.

---

slave trade and the East Indies. This left the Spanish monarchy in the position of having to grant licenses (*asientos*) to foreign powers for the exclusive right to supply the Spanish territories in the New World with slaves. Robin Blackburn, *The Making of New World Slavery: From the Baroque to the Modern, 1492–1800* (London: Verso, 1997), 8, 141–142.

12 On the effort to reorganize the French slave trade following the Peace of Utrecht, see Robert Louis Stein, *The French Slave Trade in the Eighteenth Century: An Old Regime Business* (Madison: University of Wisconsin Press, 1979), 13–18. The resulting conflicts between colonial authorities and Caribbean colonists are outlined in Blackburn, *The Making of New World Slavery*, 295–296. Cf. John Shovlin's argument that the Mississippi scheme represented Law's effort to renegotiate the place of France in the European state system: "Jealousy of Credit: John Law's 'System' and the Geopolitics of Financial Revolution," *The Journal of Modern History* 88 (2016): 275–305.

13 A good short statement of the conventional wisdom is François R. Velde, "John Law's System," *The American Economic Review* 97 (2007): 276–279. See also the sources cited in note 6 above.

The notion of a "free" trade in slaves certainly was ironic, but it also was loaded with uncertainty and confusion about which economic policies would best promote national interests in a competitive world.[14] The stock market crises of 1720 themselves reflected this confusion and expressed a deeper, longer-term transformation of the North Atlantic economies, in which the only real certainty was that slavery and the slave trade were and would remain primary considerations for both Britain and France.

This context helps to explain why the first major stock market crash played out so differently on either side of the Atlantic basin. While metropolitan commentators very quickly came to see the 1720 crises as an aberration from a natural process of self-correcting, self-organizing credit and trade,[15] the picture looked very different from a Caribbean point of view. In Haiti, especially, it would have been very hard to agree with the marquis d'Argenson (1694–1757) that "the finances of France were soon reestablished, notwithstanding the catastrophes of the bank and the *Visa*," or that "in matters of finance, public credit and circulation find their own level, like the water of the sea, after storms and tempests."[16] For colonial subjects (and those subject to them), the true crisis period came in the years after 1720.

Expanding our sense of the political geography of the Mississippi Bubble, therefore, also requires opening up the chronological boundaries that historians have placed on this subject. The 1719 to 1720 stock market crisis was the opening chapter in a series of interlocking crises that, conservatively, ended only in 1724 or 1725. We might even understand the 1729 revolt of the Natchez Indians in the lower Mississippi Valley as part of a much longer rebellion against the Indies Company, which began in Paris in 1720, extended through Haiti in the early 1720s, and culminated in Louisiana at the end of that decade – with echoes that could be heard as late as the 1773 Boston Tea Party and the early years of the French Revolution.[17]

---

14 Cf. Steve Pincus, "Rethinking Mercantilism: Political Economy, the British Empire, and the Atlantic World in the Seventeenth and Eighteenth Centuries," *The William and Mary Quarterly* 69 (2012): 3–34, which argues that there was no mercantilist consensus in British political economy during this period (or at any point prior to the American Revolution). Also relevant here is John Shovlin's work in progress on the multiple meanings of "free trade" in late seventeenth- and early eighteenth-century French political economy.

15 See the chapter by Dror Wahrman in this book.

16 Quoted in Jonathan Sheehan and Dror Wahrman, *Invisible Hands: Self-Organization and the Eighteenth Century* (Chicago: The University of Chicago Press, 2015), 119. The authors, at 334 n.55, mistakenly describe the Visa of 1721 as part of Law's plan for dealing with the public debt.

17 See Malick W. Ghachem, "'No Body to Be Kicked?' Monopoly, Financial Crisis, and Popular Revolt in 18th-Century Haiti and America," *Law & Literature* (2016), 403–431. For the French rev-

The Rise of John Law's Commercial Empire

The road from Paris to Haiti and beyond was paved by the takeover model of mergers and acquisitions that was the *modus operandi* of Law's new trading empire. Between 1718 and 1720, Law added one company after another to his original corporate entity, the Company of the West, rechristened as the Indies Company in 1719. The very name gave away the game: this was not to be a "mere" association of adventurers to either the East or West Indies alone, but a unification of the "two Indies" – to use the phrase the Abbé Raynal would later make famous in the 1770s – into one corporate conglomerate that was perhaps the first truly global corporation. In December 1718, Law acquired the Senegal Company, which enjoyed a monopoly on the slave trade along the West African coast north of the Sierra Leone River.[18] By June 1719, his portfolio expanded to include Jean-Baptiste Colbert's former East Indies Company, the China Company, and the Africa Company, the last chartered with a monopoly over the French trade out of two North African outposts located in what is now Algeria and Tunisia. Finally, in September 1720, the Indies Company acquired the erstwhile Company of Saint-Domingue and the Guinea Company, which held the exclusive privilege to the West African slave trade south of the Sierra Leone River all the way down to the Cape of Good Hope – and thus deep into what had long been Portuguese slave trading territory.[19]

With the monetary, commercial, and colonial branches of his empire in place (although with more companies to be added in the fall of 1720), Law turned to the final structural component of the System: the financial maneuvering that would culminate in the events that we now know as the Mississippi Bubble. Here, the critical turning point was August 1719, when Law committed his Indies Company to the buy-out of the entire French national debt. This commitment had the additional, closely related consequence of making Law the monarchy's tax-collector-in-chief, responsible for roughly ninety percent of the nation's entire revenues. And, with the integration of the Banque Royale into the Indies Company in February 1720, Law was able to unite this fiscal quasi-monopoly

olutionary campaign against the (new) Indies Company resurrected by controller-general Charles Alexandre de Calonne in 1785, see, *inter alia*, Albert Mathiez, *Un proces de corruption sous la terreur: L'affaire de la Compagnie des Indes* (Paris: F. Alcan, 1920).

18 On the acquisition of the Senegal Company, see Faure, *La banqueroute de Law*, 188.

19 Velde, "Was John Law's System a Bubble?," 103–105. The Company of China had been created in 1660 by an influential and prosperous Catholic confraternity in France known as the Company of the Blessed Sacrament. Carlos M. N. Eire, *Reformations: The Early Modern World, 1450–1650* (New Haven: Yale University Press, 2016), 514–515.

with sole control over the French money supply, now denominated in units of account rather than silver coins and issued in notes of the Banque Royale. Law's position at the top of the nation's financial and economic pyramid was made official by his appointment the month before (January 1720) as controller general, or finance minister, of France.[20] In short, by 1720, John Law had recreated the French state in the guise of a company.

Slavery and the slave trade were central to the kind of company Law was developing. And Saint-Domingue occupied an especially prominent place in that vision. In a letter dated 30September 1719, the secretary to the British ambassador in Paris observed that the insatiable demand for shares in the Indies Company would oblige Law "to throw in some new thing into the company by which it may appear that that a great profit will arise to it, otherwise the actions must certainly fall. By what I can judge from his discourse it will probably be the [B]anque [royale] and the island of St. Domingo which he'll get from the king."[21] As we have seen, by September 1720, with the acquisition of the Saint-Domingue Company, this prophecy had become true. The Saint-Domingue Company was a critical piece, but only one piece, of a larger scheme to rescue the monarchy through massive public investment in the business of acquiring West African captives for plantation labor in the greater Caribbean. One after another, the companies that Law targeted for acquisition were enterprises that had a clear role in or relationship to the Middle Passage: the Mississippi Company, the Senegal and Guinea companies, and the Saint-Domingue Company, to name only those most directly involved. (The slave trade was also a critical component and extension of the East Indies trade, as Lynn Hunt has pointed out).[22] Without the Louisiana economy to expand the Company's revenue stream, the entire System amounted to a house of cards; and the Mississippi venture was itself a pipe dream without the support of the human captives provided by slaving companies.[23]

This relationship was encoded into the System by the very pattern of Law's corporate acquisitions. The slave trading companies could not alone sustain the

20 Velde, "Was John Law's System a Bubble?," 106–108.

21 Thomas Crawford to James Craggs, September 30, 1719, UK National Archives, 30.9.1719, SP 78/165/84, cited in James Buchan, *John Law, A Scottish Adventurer of the Eighteenth Century* (London: MacLehose Press, 2019), 256.

22 Lynn Hunt, "The Global Financial Origins of 1789," in *The French Revolution in Global Perspective*, ed. Suzanne Desan, Lynn Hunt, and William Max Nelson (Ithaca: Cornell University Press, 2013), 32–43, here 36–38.

23 Cf. Wennerlind, *Casualties of Credit*, ch. 6, for a discussion of the role of slavery in the coming of the South Sea Bubble.

System, even when their profits were added to those derived from the tobacco and fur trades.[24] But they were key to Law's larger design because they permitted him to crowd out the private slave traders of Nantes and other port cities of the Ponant. The acquisition of the Senegal Company's monopoly accomplished this purpose for the region north of the Sierra Leone River but not south. The aggressive lobbying campaign that Law mounted for the rights to the Guinea Company, which would shut out the Nantais merchants from this vast, southern coastal region, brought the process to a culmination in September 1720.[25] With a monopoly on the entire French trade to the west coast of Africa, Law not only secured a lock on the full profits to be reaped from the slave trade; he also established a bridge between the West and East Indies spheres of his commercial empire.[26]

It was one thing to design a theory and structure of the French slave trade from the Company's headquarters on the rue Neuve des Petits Champs in Paris. It was quite another to implement it on the coast of West Africa and in the harbors of the French West Indies. John Law's vision for the future of the French slave trade turned out not quite to match its reality for several reasons, including the Company's need to rely on private traders in cities like Nantes and La Rochelle to help it meet the annual slave import quotas. But what most obviously compromised the Company's ability to perform this role was the bursting of the Mississippi Bubble itself, the traumatic impact of which was widely felt in the kingdom. By the end of 1720, essentially all of France was in a state of open revolt against John Law and his Indies Company.

The Colonial Bubble Bursts

The crash that brought the System tumbling down in the second half of 1720 reverberated not only throughout the metropole but also overseas. For, just as the System was deeply invested in slavery, the economy of slavery was heavily invested in the System. Through familial, commercial, and financial ties, the planters of the Caribbean colonies already were becoming deeply implicated in the economic fate of France's major Atlantic port cities.

Using the wealth that they accrued from the rise of the sugar industry in Saint-Domingue during the opening decades of the eighteenth century, these

24 Albert Girard, "La réorganisation de la Compagnie des Indes (1719–1723), I: L'oeuvre de John Law (1719–1721)," *Revue d'histoire moderne et contemporaine* 11 (1908–1909): 5–34, here 20.
25 Robert Harms, *The Diligent: A Voyage through the Worlds of The Slave Trade* (New York: Basic Books, 2002), 51.
26 Faure, *La banqueroute de Law*, 195.

planters managed to become significant investors in the Indies Company. The Jesuit historian Pierre-François-Xavier de Charlevoix's 1730–1731 history of Saint-Domingue was perhaps the first published account to note the impact of the crash on the French Caribbean planter elite. Some of these planters, he suggested, managed to take up residence in France during the upswing of Law's System, only to find themselves unable to support a metropolitan lifestyle on the down cycle. Having made their way back in desperation to Saint-Domingue, these erstwhile colonial grandees, many of them advancing in years, found themselves lucky to find work as mid-level employees on plantations they once might have owned. Charlevoix implied that these economic and financial refugees from the System formed part of an increasingly disgruntled and restless population that was in no mood to commune further with the representatives of Law's failed experiment in financial engineering.[27]

Charlevoix's secondhand account of the impact of the Bubble in Saint-Domingue finds some empirical support in modern scholarship produced in the 1950s.[28] This body of work emphasizes the quite temporary but massive increase in liquidity ushered in by Law's System. The most conspicuous mechanism of that increased liquidity was the proliferation of bank notes that Law hoped would give France a widely circulating paper currency for the first time.[29] As a result of this newly available credit, exports from Saint-Domingue to France tripled between 1718 and 1720, in many cases without corresponding returns of metropolitan goods and supplies. Indeed, even after the crash of 1720, colonial

---

27 Pierre-François-Xavier de Charlevoix, *Histoire de l'Isle espagnole ou de St. Domingue* (Paris, 1731), 2:394. The South Sea crash in Britain similarly caused some who lost money on the stock market to seek a new start in the New World, far from the reach of their creditors. Daniel Horsmanden, the future chief justice of New York's high court, who presided over the 1741 New York slave conspiracy trial, was one of these casualties of the 1720 crisis. Serena R. Zabin, *Dangerous Economies: Status and Commerce in Imperial New York* (Philadelphia: University of Pennsylvania Press, 2009), 150.

28 Charlevoix's material on Haiti was based on the eyewitness narrative of Jean-Baptiste Le Pers, a fellow Jesuit priest who had lived through the revolt of 1722–1723, as well as official correspondence of the period. Le Pers arrived in Saint-Domingue in 1704 and remained through the 1720s. Charlevoix himself had passed through Saint-Domingue in September and October 1722, but he departed for France just prior to the outbreak of the rebellion. On Charlevoix's connection to Le Pers, whom Charlevoix met during his novitiate years in Paris, see J.-Edmond Roy, "Essai sur Charlevoix," in *Proceedings and Transactions of the Royal Society of Canada* 1 (1907): 55.

29 Cf. Philippe Haudrère, *La Compagnie française des Indes au XVIIIe siècle*, 2nd ed. (Paris: Les Indes savantes, 2005), 1:78, cautioning against overestimating the extent to which Banque Royale notes and shares of the French Indies Company were diffused beyond a narrow circle of the financially active public.

trade continued its upward march unperturbed for some time.[30] As Robert Lacombe explains, the resulting imbalance of payments was an exceptional situation; at nearly every other moment of the eighteenth century, Saint-Domingue planters were the debtors and French merchants the creditors.[31]

The mechanism for mediating and ultimately resolving this imbalance of payments was Law's Banque Royale. Headquartered in Paris, the bank established five branches in different parts of the kingdom, including one (founded in December 1718) in La Rochelle, a major Atlantic trading port in the second half of the seventeenth century. Although the Bank's archives have been lost, notarial documents survive that describe the commercial relationships handled through this branch, including critical transactions with the French Caribbean islands. Marcel Delafosse has patiently reconstructed the story that these documents tell of the flow of payments between Saint-Domingue and the metropole.[32] When public confidence in Law's System began to crumble in early 1720, Rochelais merchants, seeking to forestall losses, suddenly sought to pay off their debts to Saint-Domingue planters by redeeming their holdings of Banque Royale notes at the bank's La Rochelle branch. Residing, as they did, at such distance from the scene of the metropolitan financial cataclysm, colonial planters were all too unaware of the precipitous collapse in the value of Law's bank notes. These planters suddenly found themselves creditors of large sums expressed in bank notes and held on the books of the La Rochelle bank. Denominated in the *écu* units of Banque Royale money, these notes now held only a quarter of their face value and paid trivial amounts of interest.[33]

Reactions ranged from resignation and despair to anger and nonimportation – a tactic that British American colonists would take up in the years after the Stamp Act of 1765. Planters residing in the Antilles were in no position to seek immediate legal or financial redress in the metropole for their losses.[34] For their part, absentee planters residing in France, who held the same worthless paper as all other victims of the Bubble, could no longer sustain a metropolitan

---

30 Marcel Delafosse, "Planteurs de Saint-Domingue et négociants rochelais au temps de Law," *Revue d'histoire des colonies* 142 (1954): 1–21, here 14–15, 17.

31 Robert Lacombe, "Histoire monétaire de Saint-Domingue et de la République d'Haïti, des origines à 1874," *Revue d'histoire des colonies* 152 (1956): 273–337, here 292.

32 The records at issue were created by the notaries Rivière and Soullard and can be consulted in the Archives départmentales de la Charente Maritime in La Rochelle, 3E/1803 and 3E/1816, *inter alia*.

33 Delafosse, "Planteurs de Saint-Domingue et négociants rochelais," 1–18. See also Lacombe, "Histoire monétaire de Saint-Domingue," 292–293.

34 Delafosse, "Planteurs de Saint-Domingue et négociants rochelais," 20.

livelihood. In Charlevoix's account, many of these forlorn planters, returning in tatters to Saint-Domingue in 1721, struggled simply to find gainful employment:

> After twenty or thirty years of labor in a boiling climate, having flattered themselves that they would be able to enjoy wealth in their homeland, which they had acquired by the sweat of their brow, [they] found themselves forced to return poor to a colony from which they had departed most opulent, and too happy to find at the age of sixty years a position as bursar or steward.

At the same time, the colonists believed themselves to have been hoodwinked by metropolitan merchants with much easier access to the banking system and greater ability to manipulate notarial services. According to one historian, Haitian planters laid low by the Mississippi Bubble, and seeking revenge in the only way left to them, managed to organize a boycott of metropolitan goods that lasted several years and succeeded in triggering a number of significant French mercantile bankruptcies.[35]

Monopoly and Slavery

The discontent that John Law's System produced in the Caribbean was embedded in a longer transition extending from the 1660s to the 1730s, during which Haiti evolved from a decentralized and vulnerable frontier society to an organized colony on the verge of a massive economic takeoff. This transformation was an enormously complex one with many components, including the siphoning of silver from the Spanish Main, the rise of contraband networks linking Saint-Domingue to the Dutch and British islands, and the development of basic institutions of colonial governance like taxation and a fugitive slave patrol system.[36] The emergence of a creole resistance movement hostile to monopoly companies was the glue that held all of these developments together. And no event in early Haitian history did more to solidify the colonists in their determination to organize Saint-Domingue around the demands of the sugar revolution than the uprising against John Law's Indies Company.

In light of the rocky history of commercial monopolies in Haiti, it may seem remarkable that the Indies Company believed it had any chance of success in Saint-Domingue. Negative examples of the fate of slave trading companies

35 Lacombe, "Histoire monétaire de Saint-Domingue," 293.

36 Much of this history is traced in Karsten Voss's recent study of the Saint-Domingue Company from 1698 to 1715: *Sklaven als Ware und Kapital: Die Plantagenökonomie von Saint-Domingue als Entwicklungsprojekt* (München: C.H. Beck, 2016).

were everywhere to be observed by the end of the second decade of the eighteenth century: in the Caribbean, Britain, Spain, the United Provinces, and France itself. How did John Law's monopoly expect to succeed where Colbert's West Indies Company, the Senegal Company, the Saint-Domingue Company, and Britain's Royal African Company (among others) had all failed?

Part of the answer is that John Law's vision for Haiti was a product of the heady times that preceded the final crash of late 1720. It certainly was not for lack of trying that the implementation of Law's System was so long delayed in Saint-Domingue. As Law conceived his empire, Saint-Domingue and French commercial outposts along the entire West African coast would have been up and running before the end of 1720, as the Afro-Caribbean linchpin of a plan to unite the two Indies into a single commercial system. The decisive step for Saint-Domingue came on 10 September 1720, when the Conseil d'État approved Law's proposal to buy out the rights and settle the debts of the existing Company of Saint-Domingue for approximately six million fifty thousand *livres tournois.*[37] An independent group of private investors, acting on behalf of the Indies Company, was to pay six million *livres* to a notary, who would distribute that amount among the directors and shareholders, with the balance used to pay off any remaining private debts incurred in France and elsewhere.[38] The Indies Company also would pay roughly fifty thousand *livres* directly to the Crown for purposes of extinguishing the Saint-Domingue Company's royal debts.[39] The imminent bankruptcy of John Law's own company, as well as the plight of its reign in the West Indies, thus were foreshadowed by the earlier failure of the Saint-Domingue Company.

But the Indies Company had additional, more specific reasons for banking on the success of its gamble in Saint-Domingue. First, where the Saint-Domingue Company apparently lacked a fleet of vessels sufficient to sustain an expanding trade in both slaves and Caribbean raw goods, the Indies Company had econo-

---

37 "Arrêt du Conseil d'État, qui subroge la Compagnie des indes aux droits et pretentions appartenants à la Compagnie de Saint-Domingue," 10.9.1720, in Méderic Louis Elie Moreau de Saint-Méry, *Loix et constitutions des colonies françoises de l'Amérique sous le vent* (Paris and Cap Français, 1784): 2:692–696. On the Saint-Domingue Company, see Voss, *Sklaven als Ware und Kapital.*

38 The exact terms of the distribution are set forth in the "Arrêt du Conseil qui fixe l'indemnité crée par la Compagnie des indes," 12.9.1720, in Archives nationales d'outre-mer (ANOM), Aix-en-Provence, F/2 A/11, folder entitled "Compagnie de Saint-Domingue, 1706–1720," no. 84.

39 "Arret du Conseil d'État, qui subroge la Compagnie des indes," 10.9.1720, in Moreau, *Loix et constitutions*, 2:695–696.

mies of scale, vast resources, and a seamless network of interconnected hubs.[40] Above all, it brought to the table a special relationship with the French monarchy, which held out the company as "the most important institution (*établissement*) of the State".[41] Second, the new Company would enjoy highly favorable tax treatment in the colony, in the form of a total exemption from export duties for any goods generated by the labor of slaves brought to Saint-Domingue by the Company – thereby incentivizing the Company to expand its participation in the slave trade.[42] Third, the Company would enjoy an "exclusive privilege" in Saint-Domingue.

But an exclusive privilege to do what, exactly? Here, the term "monopoly" is of limited use in understanding the Company's position in Saint-Domingue. Strictly speaking, the Company's exclusive privilege to trade with the French colony was limited to the southern territory over which it had proprietary jurisdiction. That is, the Company had the authority to prohibit private French traders from landing ships on the island's southern coast and to ban planters in the southern territory from exporting colonial goods on any other than a Company ship. The strictly territorial component of this authority was not insignificant. As the creole jurist Médéric Louis-Élie Moreau de Saint-Méry reminded his readers at the end of the eighteenth century, the *arrêt* of 10 September 1720 gave the Company the authority to sell for its own profit any terrain not previously conceded to local planters by the Saint-Domingue Company. Moreover, the privilege vested the Indies Company with the right to enter and occupy any uncleared lands.[43] These commercial and territorial powers flowed from the act subrogating

---

40 Cf. Robert Harms, *The Diligent*, 48, contrasting the Indies Company with its bankrupt predecessors on the grounds that the former had a "worldwide reach".

41 "Arrêt du Conseil d'État, qui subroge la Compagnie des indes," 10.9.1720, in Moreau, *Loix et constitutions*, 2:695.

42 "Arrêt du Conseil d'État, qui subroge la Compagnie des indes," in Moreau, *Loix et constitutions*, 2:694. The Saint-Domingue Company had been granted what seems like a more limited tax exemption: viz., immunity from the *droits d'octrois*, as well as all import and export duties, for purposes of any materials associated with the construction, equipping, and supplying of its trading vessels. It also enjoyed an exemption from metropolitan entry and exit duties for goods brought back to France for reexport to other countries. "Edit en forme de Lettres-Patentes," Sept. 1698, in Moreau, *Loix et constitutions*, 1:616–617 (arts. 32–34).

43 Médéric Louis-Élie Moreau de Saint-Méry, *Description topographique, physique, civile, politique et historique de la partie française de l'isle Saint-Domingue* (Philadelphia, 1797–1798), 1:627. Contrary to Moreau's suggestion, however, it was not simply these "new ideas of hindrance and constraint," nor even the arrival of the Company's officers in October 1722, that triggered the revolt. See Moreau de Saint-Méry, *Description topographique*, 1:628.

the Indies Company to the rights and privileges of the Saint-Domingue Company as formalized in the latter's 1698 charter.[44]

The resentment created by these prerogatives remained alive and well, even after the Saint-Domingue Company ceded them to John Law. In April 1721, arsonists set fire to the warehouses of the defunct Saint-Domingue Company in the southern port of Jacmel.[45] That same month, the French government effectively offered a bribe to colonists who agreed not to mistreat one of the Indies Company's incoming agents.[46] Royal and company administrators alike were attuned to the sensitivity of the situation and expected a difficult road ahead, even if they hardly could have anticipated the full scope of the storm to come.

Notwithstanding all of this, the privilege that the Indies Company inherited from its ostracized predecessor was very far from a monopoly on the whole of trade to and from Saint-Domingue. It was only in the critical area of the slave trade that the Company enjoyed what local colonists would come to understand (and denounce) as a monopoly. Hence the significance of a fourth and final advantage that the Company enjoyed over its predecessors. Law's acquisition of the Guinea Company, less than three weeks after acquiring the Saint-Domingue privilege, gave the Indies Company control – in perpetuity – over a newly unified French slave trade, one no longer divided between different companies and territories or dependent on the largesse of the Spanish Crown.[47] More than any other area of colonial policy, the slave trade reveals that even as the French state yielded ever greater control of the economy to John Law, it did not abandon the tenets of mercantilist capitalism altogether. In the tradition of Richelieu and Colbert, the French monarchy empowered commercial companies not simply to enrich themselves, but to expand the nation's economy and enhance the state vis-à-vis its major competitors, Holland and England.[48]

The arrangement that the Regency worked out with the Indies Company permits us to see the persistence of this tradition in the very detailed specifications

---

44 The Saint-Domingue Company's exclusive commercial jurisdiction over its southern territory was enshrined in Article 2 of the "Édit en forme de Lettres-Patentes," Sept. 1698, in Moreau, *Loix et constitutions*, 1:611.

45 Philippe Haudrère, *La Compagnie française*, 1:102; Conseil de Marine to the Commissaires du Conseil de la Compagnie des indes, 20.8.1721, in ANOM, B/44, fols. 77v–78r.

46 Conseil de Marine to d'Arquian, 30.4.1721, in ANOM, C/2/196, no. 41.

47 "Arrêt du Conseil d'État, qui accorde et réunit à perpetuité à la Compagnie des indes, le Privilège exclusif pour le Commerce de la Côte de Guinée," 27.9.1720, in Moreau, *Loix et constitutions*, 2:698–701.

48 See Charles Woolsey Cole, *Colbert and a Century of French Mercantilism*, 2 vols. (New York: Columbia University Press, 1939); Cole, *French Mercantilism, 1683–1700* (New York: Columbia University Press, 1943); and Girard, "La réorganisation de la Compagnie des Indes," 8.

that were made for the adequate provisioning of Saint-Domingue with slaves. The heart of the Company's "exclusive privilege" was the right to import 30,000 Africans (*nègres*) from "foreigners" on a tax-free basis for a period of fifteen years. The privilege was good for the entirety of Saint-Domingue, not just the southern peninsula; but it applied only to Saint-Domingue, in deference to the concerns of planters on other French Caribbean islands. At two thousand slaves per year, this was not, in the eyes of the local planter community, an especially demanding quota, even if it amounted to a nefarious monopoly. But the privilege also had a sunset clause attached to it: if the Company reached its cap of 30,000 imported Africans before fifteen years passed, its right to import slaves on an exclusive basis would expire, and private traders could step in to fill the gap.[49] In a sign of just how closely the colonial administration sought to monitor the ongoing contraband slave trade to Saint-Domingue, the privilege also included a condition on the resale of Africans imported by the Indies Company: no such resale could occur without the seller producing an invoice that showed he had paid the Company full price for the slave. And, in the event the Company was forced to resort to non-French slavers to obtain the requisite number of African captives, it was required to pay for those slaves either in metropolitan merchandise legally imported from France or in molasses produced in Saint-Domingue.[50]

In short, the Company enjoyed, as of September 1720, what we might call a privilege to provide: a right coupled with a duty that local colonists had no trouble understanding, by the fall of 1722, as a simple, perfidious monopoly.

Toward a Free Trade in Slaves

But how exactly did a monopoly work, as a matter of institutional practice, in the area of the slave trade? And why the delay between the initial grant of the privilege in 1720 and its implementation in Saint-Domingue in 1722? The work of Robert Louis Stein and, more recently, Robert Harms on the early eighteenth-century French slave trade can help us to get a handle on these questions. The disarray introduced by the collapse of the System, followed by the experience of corporate receivership and reorganization, account for at least some of the time lag between 1720 and 1722. The lack of financial resources may have been compounded by concern that the Company likely would receive a hostile recep-

49 "Arrêt du Conseil d'État, qui subroge la Compagnie des indes," 10.9.1720, in Moreau, *Loix et constitutions*, 2:694 (clause 13)
50 Ibid. (clauses 8 and 10).

tion from the Saint-Domingue colonists.[51] But another part of the answer – perhaps the major part – has to do with how and why the Indies Company continued to negotiate with and rely on private traders even in the era of the new privilege.

The end of the War of the Spanish Succession in 1713 created an opening for private traders to make inroads on territory that had previously been monopolized by France's Senegal and Guinea (or Asiento) companies. With the signing of the Treaty of Utrecht and the transfer of the *asiento* contract from France to Britain in 1713, the Guinea Company entered a long process of liquidation. Slave traders from Rouen, La Rochelle, Bordeaux, Saint Malo, and Nantes, for their part, began to push for the liberalization of the French slave trade on the grounds that the monopoly companies had failed to supply the French colonies with adequate numbers of African captives.[52] French planters had been forced to switch from sugar to less labor-intensive indigo cultivation because of the shortage of slave imports, argued the *négociants* of Nantes. These same representatives saw no irony, tragic or otherwise, in the claim that the French slave trade ought to be opened up in order to counteract the high mortality rates of the Middle Passage. Finally, private traders rebutted the traditional defense of the monopoly companies that having too many competing firms negotiate with suppliers along the West African coast drove up prices for everyone.[53]

Such claims hit their intended target, and, in January 1716, the Regency government responded with letters patent that effectively opened up the Guinea trade to merchants from the Ponant cities of Rouen, La Rochelle, Bordeaux, Saint Malo, and Nantes.[54] Liberalization, in this context, retained a distinctly mercantilist framework of passports and permissions. Merchants interested in outfitting slave ships were required to pay a tax of twenty livres for each captive imported into the colonies. These revenues were earmarked for the upkeep of the former Guinea Company's fort at Whydah. The arrangement constituted a *quid pro quo*, insofar as the private traders were able to finance their purchases of African captives with French metropolitan goods exported on a duty-free basis. An

---

51 Haudrère, *La Compagnie française*, 1:102; Stein, *The French Slave Trade*, 18.

52 Stein, *The French Slave Trade*, 13–14.

53 Harms, *The Diligent*, 37–39. For the origins of these claims in lobbying before the Council of Commerce by the merchants of Nantes and Rouen between 1695 and 1701, see Lionel Rothkrug, *Opposition to Louis XIV: The Political and Social Origins of the French Enlightenment* (Princeton: Princeton University Press, 1965), 409–419; and Cole, *French Mercantilism, 1683–1700*, 254–269.

54 Le Havre, Honfleur, and other ports soon were added to the list. The Senegal monopoly was retained only because of concerns that revoking it would compromise France's special position in the gum trade north of the Sierra Leone River. Stein, *The French Slave Trade*, 13–15.

additional incentive came in the form of a fifty percent exemption from duties attached to the traders' subsequent export of sugar and other Caribbean goods to France.[55]

With John Law's acquisition of the Senegal privilege in September 1718 and of the Guinea monopoly in September 1720, a restoration of the status quo ante seemed at hand. Indeed, the latter privilege brought with it not only an exemption from the private trader tax of twenty livres per captive, but also an affirmative bonus of thirteen livres for each slave successfully delivered to the French Caribbean colonies.[56] But limitations on the Indies Company's own shipping capacities and the effectiveness of the private traders' lobbying campaign prevented the Company from enjoying a genuine monopoly. In 1718 and 1719, the Company resorted to commissioning merchants from Saint Malo and La Rochelle to help it fit out its slave ships.[57]

The collapse of 1720 did not entirely negate the Indies Company's ability to engage in slave trading or merchant shipping more generally. Between 1 January and 15 April 1721, the Company dispatched from Lorient seven ships to make the Senegal-Antilles-Louisiana circuit, two for the East Indies and one for China.[58] In total, thirteen slave ships were sent out during the Company's first two years. But these numbers were clearly inadequate to meet the quota of two thousand slaves per year as specified in the Guinea privilege, and they were made to seem all the worse in light of the ongoing campaign of the private traders. The Company therefore was compelled to issue permissions to the *négociants* (especially those of Nantes) to help fill the gap in supply. The arrangement required the private traders to pay twenty livres for each slave delivered to the islands, an amount that was cut back to ten livres in 1720. Nantes alone supplied seventeen expeditions in 1720, another twenty-four in 1721, and twelve in 1722.[59] In this way, by fits and starts, a hybrid public-private slave trading operation resumed the course that the monarchy began to set with the return of peace to Europe after 1713.

---

55 Harms, *The Diligent*, 40; Stein, *The French Slave Trade*, 14. See also James S. Pritchard, *In Search of Empire: The French in the Americas, 1670–1730* (New York: Cambridge University Press, 2004), 221.

56 The bonus would be paid upon the Company's presentation of a certificate issued by the intendant of the receiving colony. "Arrêt du Conseil d'État," 27.9.1720, in Moreau, *Loix et constitutions*, 2:699–700 (arts. 6 and 8). See also Harms, *The Diligent*, 52.

57 Stein, *The French Slave Trade*, 18.

58 Haudrère, *La Compagnie française*, 1:85. See also Stein, *The French Slave Trade*, 17.

59 Harms, *The Diligent*, 52.

Meanwhile, the Company's monopoly privileges in West Africa and the Caribbean remained on the books, there to be activated if and when the right moment arrived. That moment came in the late fall of 1722, by which time the Company managed to increase its shipping capacity to the point that it could fulfill independently the quotas envisioned in the September 1720 Guinea privilege. The Company's slaving voyages increased dramatically after 1 January 1723, when the directors stopped issuing permissions to private traders. Some sixty Company slave vessels departed France for West Africa, the Caribbean, and Louisiana over the next few years.[60] These were, indeed, the peak years of the slave trade to Louisiana, whose enslaved population grew during the 1720s at a rate not paralleled either before or after.[61] The ships that carried out this belated implementation of the Company's monopoly, moreover, were not just any vessels. Averaging about three hundred tons, they held more than double the human cargo of the typical private ship.[62] But then, suddenly, in the late summer of 1725, the surge in corporate trading ended. The Company once again reversed course and resumed issuing passports to private merchants to carry out the slave trade.

Conclusion

The French Indies Company remained active in the French slave trade for another four decades after 1725, but the writing was on the wall by the end of that year.[63] Noting the abrupt and definitive shift to a private, free trade in 1725, scholars of the Middle Passage have offered various explanations for it.[64] Robert Louis Stein hypothesizes that the Company "had apparently overextended itself," in particular by failing to control outfitting costs.[65] Robert Harms suggests that the Company was weighed down by inefficiencies associated with its larger ship-

---

60 Stein, *The French Slave Trade*, 19; Harms, *The Diligent*, 52.

61 See Gwendolyn Midlo Hall, *Africans in Colonial Louisiana: The Development of Afro-Creole Culture in the Eighteenth Century* (Baton Rouge: Louisiana State University Press, 1992), chs. 2–3.

62 Stein, *The French Slave Trade*, 19; Harms, *The Diligent*, 59.

63 For an overview, see Yves Banallec and Jean Yves Le Lan, "La Compagnie des Indes et la traite des noirs," *Bulletin et Mulletin de la Société Polymathique du Morbihan* 132 (2006): 95–120.

64 Stein and Harms both emphasize the post-1725 shift towards private trade as definitive for the remainder of the Old Regime. Stein, *The French Slave Trade*, 19; Harms, *The Diligent*, 61. The Indies Company continued to trade along the West African coast as one private company competing with others, until 1744, when it ended slaving operations everywhere except for the occasional Mascarene expedition. Stein, *The French Slave Trade*, 21.

65 Stein, *The French Slave Trade*, 19.

ping capacity, which yielded only 40 percent more captives than private ships with less than half the tonnage.[66] Neither scholar considers the role of events and forces unfolding in the Caribbean itself during the period, which preceded this dramatic shift of course.

There is not space here to give a detailed narrative of the events in Haiti between 1722 and 1725 that brought down the curtain on the Indies Company.[67] The extraordinary uprising commenced by women and vagabonds in the fall of 1722 grew into an extended, planter-led, Caribbean precursor to the Boston Tea Party over the course of 1723, complete with boycotts of newly-arrived slaving vessels, the deportation of Indies Company officials, and the destruction of Company property. This was neither the first nor the last such display of creole resistance under French colonial rule, but it was by far the most consequential before the revolutionary era, and it proved to be the single most important pivot in France's turn away from company control of the slave trade. For Haiti, the impact was enormous: privatized slaving ushered in the spectacular rise of Haiti's large-scale sugar plantation economy in the 1730s and after. This nexus between an early eighteenth-century rebellion in Haiti and a transformation in the Atlantic slave trade is one of the stories that a fuller understanding of John Law's Slave System helps us to grasp.[68]

Another such story is the very close connection between eighteenth-century high finance and the slave trade: how decisions about state debt and monetary policy reverberated in the colonies, and vice versa. Lambert's *Décision théologique*, for all of its spiritual and political intensity, was a highly abstract rendering of this connection, which is difficult to grasp from the vantage point of the rue Neuve des Petits Champs in Paris. The revolt against the Indies Company in Saint-Domingue gives us a more concrete sense of the relationship between

66 As Harms explains, filling a ship with three hundred slaves meant forcing crews to wait for months on end in unwelcome conditions until the vessel was fully loaded and ready to make the crossing. Harms, *The Diligent*, 60.

67 I am at work on a book-length study. The most important extant account is Frostin, *Les révoltes blanches à Saint-Domingue*, chs. 3–4.

68 The point applies also to the South Sea Bubble, whose Caribbean dimensions – notwithstanding the wartime interruption of Britain's holding of the *asiento* from 1719–1721 – are beginning to come into sharper focus thanks to the work of scholars who have written about the politics of the *asiento* and the slave trade in Jamaica and Barbados. See Abigail L. Swingen, *Competing Visions of Empire: Labor, Slavery, and the Origins of the British Atlantic Empire* (New Haven: Yale University Press, 2015), ch. 7; and Gregory E. O'Malley, *Final Passages: The Intercolonial Slave Trade of British America* (Chapel Hill: The University of North Carolina Press, 2014), 219–263. Also important is the older study by Elizabeth Donnan, "The Early Days of the South Sea Company, 1711–1718," *Journal of Economic and Business History* 2 (1930): 419–450.

high finance and slavery. The term "Mississippi" in the phrase Mississippi Bubble turns out to be an even more pliable phrase than its already expansive eighteenth-century meaning would suggest. More than the entire middle third of the territory that eventually became the United States, "Mississippi" also connoted the greater Caribbean, which looked east across the Atlantic to Africa and, from there, to the East Indies and beyond. The Mississippi scheme was, in other words, a truly global enterprise, perhaps the earliest such entity of its kind – and we should not, in the end, be surprised to learn that it marked a fundamental turning point in the history of the slave trade and the development of financial capitalism alike.[69]

What did the world of the Mississippi Bubble look like in some of these other theaters of Law's empire? How did the System play out in the port cities of West Africa, the French comptoirs along the Malabar and Coromandel coasts, the fur trading centers of New France, or the warehouses of the former Company of China? In all of these places the Indies Company had an active presence. We are only at the beginning, rather than the end, of tracing a genuinely global history of events like the Mississippi Bubble.

Part of what we can learn from such an exercise is how to think more broadly about financial capitalism in later eras, including in our own day. "When the financial crisis began 10 years ago in the United States, followed by the United Kingdom, many initially thought it would not affect Africa – or at least not so much," observes a recent commentary on the 2007 to 2008 subprime meltdown. "Not so […] the poorest countries were not immune to the crisis."[70] As in Saint-Domingue during the 1720s, the crisis manifested not as a dramatic metropolitan stock market crash but, rather, in the form of lower commodity prices and ex-

---

69 Despite an effervescence of recent scholarship on slavery and capitalism, much of it focusing on the nineteenth-century United States, there is still a good deal to learn about the role of slavery in state finance, monetary policy, and the rise of the stock market (as well as vice versa). This is particularly the case as regards the late seventeenth/early eighteenth-century period that witnessed the birth of those institutions we associate with financial capitalism. For a sampling and review of recent scholarship on the slavery/capitalism nexus, see Sven Beckert and Seth Rockman, *Slavery's Capitalism: A New History of American Economic Development* (Philadelphia: University of Pennsylvania Press, 2016); and John J. Clegg, "Capitalism and Slavery," *Critical Historical Studies* 2 (2015): 281–304. On the birth of financial capitalism in the late seventeenth and early eighteenth centuries, see the essays collected in William N Goetzmann and K. Geert Rouwenhorst, *The Origins of Value: The Financial Innovations That Created Modern Capital Markets* (New York: Oxford University Press, 2005).

70 Dirk Willem te Velde, "Africa 10 Years After the Global Financial Crisis: What We've Learned," *Overseas Development Institute* (blog), 11.9.2018, https://www.odi.org/comment/10680-africa-10-years-after-global-financial-crisis-what-we-ve-learned, last visit 11.5.2019.

change rate problems in countries like Nigeria and South Africa. For many citizens of the world today (Haiti very much included), this is what financial crisis continues to look like.

The global character of financial capitalism should serve to temper some of the more polemical certainties that figure in our current historiographical as well as political debates.

Critics of the financial market system tend to suggest that capitalism operates according to a singleminded will of its own, independently of forces like racial ideologies, national identities, religious chauvinism, and the rest. The pursuit of profit is inseparable from slavery but no single force caused slavery's rise or sustained its long life. Defenders of the market system, for their part, respond that capitalist institutions have been responsible for rescuing large portions of humankind from the lives of deprivation that seemed to be their permanent condition prior to industrialization.[71] It is far from clear that this thesis holds true for places like Haiti. But the point is neither to condemn nor to embrace capitalism and modern finance. We all breath their air and play by their rules. And we all should be able to see the debt that capitalism, as it has actually developed over time and space, owes to places like Haiti. If one of the rules of market capitalism is that one is supposed to honor one's debts, then here is a debt that still has to be repaid.

71 See, e.g., Deirdre N. McCloskey, *Bourgeois Equality: How Ideas, Not Capital or Institutions, Enriched the World* (Chicago: University of Chicago Press, 2016).

II. Engaging with Traditional Narratives

Richard A. Kleer

When First We Practice to Deceive: An Alternative Account of the South Sea Bubble

In early 1720 the South Sea Company approached the British parliament with a proposition for a major change in the nation's system of public finance.[1] Those holding long-term public debt would be invited to convert it into newly-issued shares in the Company. The government would continue paying out as much interest as before, but to the Company instead of to its present numerous creditors. The Company in turn would pass the cash along, perhaps in large part to those same creditors, in the form of dividends on its new shares. Parliament eventually accepted the proposal. There followed an almost tenfold increase in the price of South Sea Company shares later that year and, in the fall, a subsequent rapid collapse back very near to its original level.

The *Investopedia* entry on the South Sea Bubble nicely captures the still-prevailing view, repeated for three centuries now, that it was a "stock scam" driven by Company management, who "continued to issue shares in response to seemingly insatiable demand".[2] This chapter argues that the genesis and course of the Bubble was much more complex and interesting than this. It maintains that Company officials were among the Bubble's foremost victims. Driven by a general public mania, rapidly increasing share prices presented the directors with enormous problems of financial management that in the end they were unable to overcome. But neither were they blameless. Working hand-in-hand with the government, they had set out quite deliberately to mislead the general investing public about the underlying debt-conversion project: a deception that eventually got away from them.

1 This paper recapitulates, in summary form, findings originally presented in Richard Kleer, "'The Folly of Particulars': The Political Economy of the South Sea Bubble," *Financial History Review* 19 (2012): 175–197 and Richard Kleer, "Riding a Wave: The Company's Role in the South Sea Bubble," *Economic History Review* 68 (2015): 264–285.

2 See James Chen, "South Sea Bubble," *Investopedia*, www.investopedia.com/terms/s/south seabubble.asp, last visit 26.1.2018.

https://doi.org/10.1515/9783110592139-007

The Company's Motivations

In 1720 the Company was engaged in a project to convert a large part of Great Britain's public debt, some £31 million of a total £50 million,[3] into South Sea stock and to raise a further £7.7 million for a one-time cash payment to the Exchequer. The traditional story holds that the cash payment was offered in prospect of still greater gains that the Company stood to make from the debt-for-stock conversion. This interpretation turns on the facts that: a) the Company would be permitted to issue an amount of stock, rated at its par price of £100, equal the value of whatever amount of public debt was offered for conversion; and b) for the purposes of actually exchanging debt for Company stock, the latter would be rated at its current market price. On this telling, the higher the market price of Company stock rose above £100 (it was at £121 when the project was first announced), the less stock would have to be offered in exchange for the £31 million in public debt, leaving more "surplus" stock that the Company might sell for its own profit. The story isn't credible, however, since anyone buying surplus stock would still expect to be paid dividends upon it – meaning the proceeds from such sales would have to be placed in some profitable line of investment and so would not be available for distribution as "profit". An alternative, much more plausible, version of the story is that the directors hoped to profit personally by quietly buying up stock on their own account before the conversion project was announced, using that project as an opportunity to manipulate the market price upward, and then selling their personal holdings at some later date.

But the directors, collectively, stood to benefit from the debt-stock conversion by much more direct, and far less shady, means. To grasp this point we must first understand a little about how banking and public finance operated in Britain during this period. From the mid-1600s onward, paper notes had come to play an increasingly-prominent role in bank lending. Loans came to be paid out more in notes (or bank account credits that might later be withdrawn in notes) than in specie (coined gold or silver). As long as the general public was confident the notes of a given bank could readily be exchanged for specie as occasion required, monetary transactions might be conducted mainly in paper rather than in gold or silver coin, the notes being presented for encashment only after passing through numerous hands. Banks' capacity for providing credit expanded accordingly, by some multiple of their specie holdings. But, for their

3 Peter G.M. Dickson, *The Financial Revolution in England: A Study in the Development of Public Credit, 1688–1756* (London: Macmillan, 1967), 93.

long-term security, banks also needed to insert themselves into one or more regular specie flows, to create channels for returning whatever coin had left them through withdrawals.

In London at this time, the principal such flow of specie centered on the Exchequer. Until at least 1707, almost all tax payments and public loans were received into the Exchequer in specie.[4] And payments of principal and/or interest upon public debt were transacted in the same currency. Even after Exchequer bills (interest-bearing, transferable IOUs issued by government to its lenders) were introduced, during the War of the Spanish Succession, as an alternative currency for public transactions, the Exchequer continued to be a key channel of specie flow in London. Ownership of public debt was therefore an important source of credit capacity in the British banking sector at this time; interest payments upon government loans were a regular and highly dependable source of specie.

The Bank of England had managed to acquire access to a large proportion of the specie flows associated with public debt; indeed, the supply and management of public credit were at the very core of its business model from its inception in 1694.[5] The Bank benefited directly from the interest it earned on its several long-term loans to the state. By the end of 1719 these loans totaled £5.4 million and brought it payments from the Exchequer of £288,751 per annum.[6] The Bank collected the cash weekly as it arrived on the relevant tax accounts.[7] From the beginning the Bank was also heavily invested in Exchequer tallies (an earlier form of interest-bearing, transferable IOU issued by the government to its lenders), which it could count upon to be repaid in specie at predictable intervals (though not, like Exchequer bills, convertible into cash upon demand). The Bank was a key player in the issue of £5.6 million in new Exchequer bills from 1707 to 1713,[8] which it "circulated" (i.e. guaranteed to convert into Bank notes or specie upon demand) on the government's behalf in return for regular interest payments, in cash, from the Exchequer. And in 1717 the Bank entered into an agreement with the Treasury to begin managing payment of £11.1 million in public annuities. Since that business had until then been handled by the Ex-

---

4 See Richard Kleer, "A New Species of Money: British Exchequer Bills, 1701–11," *Financial History Review* 22 (2015): 179–203.

5 See Richard Kleer, *Money, Politics and Power: Banking and Public Finance in Wartime England, 1694–96* (London: Routledge, 2017), ch. 3.

6 The National Archives (TNA), T 1/225.

7 3 George I, c. 8.

8 Dickson, *Financial Revolution*, 373.

chequer,[9] this immediately brought the Bank new public cash flows (payable quarterly) of £552,108 per annum.[10] Though in principle the Bank was required to pay the annuities out again as soon as possible after it received them, it would have benefited by the opportunity to substitute its notes for any specie received from the Exchequer. It could benefit too if annuitants decided to leave their payments on deposit and/or manage their money transactions via Bank account transfers rather than by withdrawing cash.

The South Sea Company's 1720 debt-conversion project was an attempt to redirect a massive portion of British specie flows through its own coffers and thereby dislodge the Bank of England from its place at the center of the British public finance. The directors had already taken steps in this direction upon the Company's creation in 1711, when some £9.5 million of Exchequer tallies was converted into an equivalent amount of stock in the new corporation. As the government's debt to the Company was to carry interest at 6 percent, there would be a regular flow of some £570,000 per annum of public cash through its vaults. The plan probably had been to harness this cash flow to the credit-generating capacities of the Sword Blade Company – a banking partnership, the first two of whose three owners (George Caswall, John Blunt and Jacob Sawbridge) became leading officers for the South Sea Company.[11] Unsuccessful in this first attempt, the group tried again in 1720.

If the Company was able to draw in the whole £31 million of public debt targeted for conversion in 1720, it would gain access to a further £1.5 million per annum of public cash flow. Under the terms of the authorizing statute, it would be entitled to collect this money weekly from the Exchequer as revenues came in upon the appointed taxes;[12] but it would pay out the proceeds in dividends only semi-annually. Much of this new specie flow would have come at the Bank of England's expense. Of the debt to be converted, £13.7 million represented the capital value of public annuities that had been administered by the Bank since 1717.[13] More importantly, the Company's one-time cash payment to the Exchequer would be used to buy back £3.8 million of other public debt held by the Bank itself. Since the £188,751 in annual interest on these particular loans was collectible weekly at the Exchequer and paid out only twice a year by way of shareholder dividends, this would have been a very significant blow to

9 3 Geo. I, c. 7.

10 TNA, T 1/225.

11 See Stuart Bell, "A Masterpiece of Knavery? The Activities of the Sword Blade Company in London's Early Financial Markets," *Business History* 54 (2012): 623–638.

12 6 Geo. I, c. 4.

13 *Journals of the House of Commons* (London, 1803), 19:314.

the Bank. After the conversion was complete, it would retain only £100,000 per annum of public specie flow – the interest on its founding loan of £1.2 million, later increased to £1.6 million without further interest charge.[14] With all the extra cash flow at its disposal, the South Sea Company, working together with the Sword Blade Bank, could then have supplanted the Bank of England and assumed its status as the state's principal lender.

One piece of eye-witness testimony supports this proposition. In September 1720, when the Bubble first began to collapse, the Treasury learned that Company directors had neglected to set aside a specie reserve sufficient to meet the present surge of Exchequer bill holders wanting to have their bills cashed. This violated a clear Treasury expectation for any bank handling public business. On 1 October, Chancellor of the Exchequer John Aislabie summoned to the Treasury those Company officials who had been appointed (together with a matching number of Exchequer officers) to look after circulating Exchequer bills. A minute of the meeting, highly unusual in its length and detail, indicates how very angry he was with them. Aislabie asked what their failure in this matter, involving a relatively small sum of money, implied about "their great promises to this Board of supporting publick credit & furnishing money for the current service upon any exigency or demand from the Treasury".[15] Since the Company had never before served as the Treasury's lender of first resort, the promises in question must have been made in conjunction with the debt-conversion proposal.

Since, following this interpretation, the directors did not need increases in the price of South Sea stock to profit from the debt-for-stock swap, it should not surprise us that the available records afford little evidence of their working behind the scenes to engineer such increases.[16] Those who charge the directors with price-rigging maintain that they: a) engaged in "underhand buying" of stock and "systematic use of forward purchases at high prices" to induce "market optimism"; and b) lent vast sums to those interested in buying Company stock.[17] Director trading in the spot market for South Sea stock does not follow the simple pattern we would expect if they were trying to manipulate the market upward. Had this been their goal, presumably they would have bought large quantities of stock just before South Sea share prices spiked significantly, and cashed out large amounts shortly afterward. Alternatively, they might have bought large quantities before the scheme was announced publicly and started

---

14 Dickson, *Financial Revolution*, 374.

15 TNA, T 29/24 A.

16 For the details see Kleer, "Riding a Wave."

17 Dickson, *Financial Revolution*, 144–145; Richard Dale, *The First Crash: Lessons from the South Sea Bubble* (Princeton: Princeton University Press, 2004), 98–101.

selling out once prices reached their peak in June. But the directors did not build up their stock inventories before any major price surges or sell out large parts of their holdings during the peak months of the Bubble. Nor is there much evidence to support Peter Dickson's claim that they made "systematic use of forward purchases at high prices". Only 2.9 percent (by transaction value) of the South Sea shares bought by Company officials in 1720 were for future delivery. Of these, a small number were indeed at prices significantly ahead of the market rate, but the rest were negotiated for prices at or below the going market rate.[18] Finally, the first two of the three main surges in Company lending (late April, mid-June, and late August) came *after* large spikes in the market price. Thereafter stock prices stabilized near their previous peaks (April and June) or even declined (August), rather than increasing as they should have were the directors working to manipulate the market upwards.

The Debt-Conversion Project's Central Dilemma

If the foregoing account is correct, we must look to forces other than deliberate market manipulation by Company insiders to understand what drove the Bubble and led to its eventual collapse. This section locates the key causes in the very structure of the debt-conversion project itself.

The scheme unfolded in the context of an initiative by the British government, already several years underway, to reduce the cost of servicing the public debt that had built up during the War of the Spanish Succession (1701–14). Peacetime always provided financial breathing room for such measures, most welcome to a public that had absorbed significant new taxes during the war. Projects of this nature were a kind of competitive undertaking, clearing financial headroom vis-à-vis neighboring powers for whatever military conflict might be coming next. The administration began its efforts in 1717, when the interest rate on a large portion of the debt was lowered from 6 to 5 percent per annum.[19] At the time, some were pushing for the rate to be lowered still further to 4 percent[20] and for the legal maximum on all private debt contracts to be reduced accordingly.[21]

18 See Kleer, "Riding a Wave."

19 Dickson, *Financial Revolution*, 84–87.

20 [Daniel Defoe], *Fair Payment No Spunge: or, Some Considerations on the Unreasonableness of Refusing to Receive Back Money Lent on Publick Securities [...]* (London, 1717), 37–39, 57–59; [William Paterson], *An Enquiry into the State of the Union of Great Britain and the Past and Present State of the Trade and Publick Revenues Thereof. With Schemes for the Speedy Payment of the*

For a while there was little support for further reductions in the interest rate on public debt. Everything changed in 1719 when John Law, the new finance minister in France, set to work to lower the carrying charges on public debt in that country. To bring this about, Law created a large new financial holding company, the so-called *Compagnie des Indes* (successor to the better-known *Compagnie du Mississippi).* He issued large quantities of new shares in the *Compagnie* in order to raise a massive loan for the French Crown at 3 percent interest. He used these funds in turn to redeem the bulk of existing French public debt (which had been running at much higher interest rates). Finally, Law engineered a price bubble in the Paris stock market with the goal of reducing the rate of return on *Compagnie* shares to 2 percent per annum.[22] His aim in so doing was to lower interest rates generally. *Compagnie* shares would be almost the sole public asset remaining for purchase in France. Unable to earn more than 2 percent from investing in public securities, lenders would have had to settle for less also on loans to private borrowers. Law's design was realized by the final day of December 1719, when the market price of *Compagnie* stock stabilized around 10,000 *livres* per share and the dividend payout for the coming year was set at 200 *livres* per share. In March 1720 Law issued an edict fixing the legal maximum interest rate on private debt contracts at this same rate.[23] British diplomats residing in Paris were wringing their hands while Law's system unfolded, worried that the new measures would greatly enhance France's financial capacity for making war. They warned London that unless something were done to match Law's bold new initiatives, "his majesty [George I] cannot long continue the arbiter of Europe".[24] The administration resolved late in 1719 upon the relatively staid measure of undertaking to lower the interest rate on British public debt to 4 percent per annum.

This was the core purpose of the South Sea Company debt-conversion project, which (after a bidding war with the Bank of England) was approved by the

---

Heavy Debts the Nation Groans Under. By the Wednesday's Club in Friday Street, 2nd ed. (London, 1717), 82, 90–91, 97, 116, 144–145.

21 [Archibald Hutcheson], *Some Considerations Relating to the Payment of the Publick Debts, Humbly Offer'd to the Commons of Great-Britain in Parliament Assembled. By a Member of the House of Commons* (London, 1717), 16.

22 Larry Neal, "The Monetary, Financial and Political Architecture of Europe, 1648–1815," in *Exceptionalism and Industrialisation: Britain and Its European Rivals, 1688–1815*, ed. L. Prados de la Escosura (Cambridge: Cambridge University Press, 2004), 173–189, here 184.

23 Edgar Faure, *Le banqueroute de Law, 17 juillet 1720* (Paris: Gallimard, 1977), 401; *The Present State of the French Revenues and Trade, and of the Controversy betwixt the Parliament of Paris, and Mr. Law. Containing the Parliament of Paris's Remonstrance to the King, April 17, 1720 against Reducing Annuities [...]* (London, 1720), 1–19.

24 TNA, SP 78/166, 16.10.1719.

British Parliament in early February 1720. At base the conversion was nothing more than an exercise in reducing the government's per-pound debt-servicing costs. The latter objective could have been accomplished by lowering the interest rate on the existing principal, by keeping the interest rate constant and increasing the principal (i.e. in effect affording the government a new, interest-free loan), or of course by some combination of the two. The Treasury and the South Sea Company chose the second route. After the public debt in question had been converted into stock, the crown would pay as much interest to the Company as it had been paying out to the holders of public debt. But, depending on how much debt was actually converted, the Company would make the Crown a one-time, interest-free payment of up to £7.7 million. Given the £43.4 million in existing interest-bearing public debt that the Company would end up holding, the Company would be affording the Crown a loan of £51.1 million in total. Since there was to be no additional interest beyond the £2.1 million already being paid out on the existing debt, the directors were in effect offering the state a reduced interest rate of 4.15 percent per annum. The Crown could use the influx of new cash to redeem some other long-term public debt. The resulting budget surpluses were to be used over time to redeem still more debt, raising annual surpluses further, and so on. According to one MP, an earlier version of the scheme that had the Company making a one-time cash payment of only £3.5 million would have positioned the nation to retire the whole of the debt within twenty-five years;[25] with a payment of £7.7 million, the time to debt freedom would have been even shorter.[26]

From the outset the project faced two large hurdles. To appreciate their significance, one first needs to know a little about the exact structure of the debt targeted for conversion. It had two main components, of roughly equal value; contemporaries distinguished them as "redeemable" and "irredeemable". The former was named for the fact that it carried an option for the government to buy it back at par value. This kind of debt had been designed to be perpetual; owners would collect interest only and had no right to demand repayment of any portion of the principal. Given its structure, redeemable debt had a well-defined principal value of £17.1 million, upon which the nation was obligated to pay a fixed rate of interest (before 1720, 5 percent per annum for most of it) in perpetuity or until redemption. The irredeemable debt, by contrast, was so named because the government could not buy it back at will; redemption required

25 Cited in *Memoirs of the Life and Administration of Sir Robert Walpole, Earl of Orford* [...], ed. William Coxe (London, 1798), 2:181–182.

26 Abel Boyer, *The Political State of Great Britain* (London, 1720), 19:92–95.

the holders' prior permission. This portion of the debt had been sold in the form of annuities; in return for a one-time, up-front cash contribution, investors received annual payments that were a blend of principal and interest. Thus the principal would automatically be extinguished after a certain number of years, at which point all payments would cease. In 1720, the so-called "long" and "short" annuities still had another 80 and 23 years to run respectively. Given its nature, irredeemable debt did not have an agreed-upon capital value.[27] The government rated it officially at £15 million when calculating how much interest it would pay to the South Sea Company in the future. But to entice the holders into volunteering their annuities for conversion, the Company would need to offer an attractive lump-sum cash price, one that was entirely up for negotiation.

The two main obstacles to the conversion project, then, were persuading the holders of redeemable and irredeemable debt, respectively, that it would be to their advantage to swap their public assets for the stock of a private company.

The first obstacle was less problematic than the second. In theory the government could unilaterally reduce the interest rate on redeemable debt at any time. For if the holders did not like the new state of affairs, the state had the right to buy them out, using cash raised by selling debt to other investors who were prepared to accept a lower interest rate. So state creditors might be induced to make the swap even if Company stock paid a lower rate of return than holders were currently receiving on their public debt. Still, converting the whole redeemable debt would be no mean feat. While the government had the right to buy it all back, it did not necessarily have the financial capacity to do so. £17.1 million was an immense sum of money at the time. Unless the crown or the Company could amass a significant portion of this sum in liquid funds, the threat of being bought out simply would not be credible. The willingness of the holders of redeemable debt to accept a lower interest rate or a proffered conversion to Company stock would be correspondingly reduced.

Converting the irredeemable debt was bound to be a bigger hurdle for the Company. Owners could not be compelled to trade debt for stock; rather they would have to be offered terms sufficiently attractive to induce them to make the exchange of their own free will. Worse still, the further the general interest rate should fall, the higher the price the Company could expect to have to pay the owners of irredeemable debt. For instance, because interest rates fell be-

27 Though many commentators write as though it did, the irredeemable debt did not have an agreed interest rate either. Dale, for instance, (*First Crash*, 73) states that it was "costly to service" because yields on the original annuities had been 7 to 9 percent. But those interest rates had long ago ceased being relevant. All that mattered now was the present value of a long stream of annual payments, which depended only on *current* market interest rates.

tween 1714 and 1716, short annuities rose in value from 10.4 to 14 years' purchase over this same period.[28] (At this time, annuity prices were quoted as multiples of the annuity payment – hence the term "years' purchase".) If as a result of the conversion project the general rate of interest were to fall to 4 percent, owners of short annuities were likely to hold out for a price of at least 14.4 years' purchase (even though by then the scheduled end-date of such annuities was four years closer than it had been in 1716). And the years'-purchase price of long annuities would likely rise from 21.25[29] to something like 24. So the holders of irredeemable debt were positioned to capture the whole of whatever increase in the market value of their assets would be generated by the interest-rate reduction the debt-conversion project itself. This would leave the directors with less to offer the holders of redeemable debt.

Given these obstacles, state creditors would have to believe that the debt-conversion project was something more than just a straight-up swap of debt for stock. Otherwise the holders of redeemable debt would have had absolutely no motivation to make the exchange. The Company would be receiving only 4 percent interest on its new holdings of public debt. So unless the conversion project would somehow open up profitable new lines of business for the Company, the holders of redeemable debt had to expect a lower return from Company stock than they were receiving from that debt. Their expected return would be even lower if the owners of irredeemable debt were able to drive a hard bargain for themselves.

For the conversion to succeed, there had to be a general expectation that something more and better was in store for state creditors, post-conversion. In this connection, the Company might have pointed to its prospects for dominating the British banking sector. Banking-related earnings could have been used to supplement dividend payouts and sustain a rate of return at least as good as what the holders of public debt were currently earning. But banking was a complex business; it would have been well beyond the ken of the average investor to place a value upon its likely returns. It was probably for this reason that the Company decided instead to rely upon a general expectation that the price of South Sea stock was destined to rise as the conversion unfolded. There was a clear, rational foundation for this expectation, given that the project was built around an attempt to lower the interest rate on public debt. The dividend rate on South Sea stock was not expected to decline as a result of the debt-conversion project. In a world where the interest rate attainable on Britain's dominant asset

---

28 John Castaing, *Course of the Exchange* (London, 1714–1720).

29 According to John Freke, *Prices of the Several Stocks* (London, 1720), its value in early 1720.

class, public debt, was expected to fall, this would make prospective investors willing to pay more to obtain a share of Company stock. But it is unclear whether the typical public creditor was sophisticated enough to grasp this logic. And in the end it may have been unnecessary that they do so. Everyone had the recent French example clearly in view, where the price of *Compagnie* stock had risen twentyfold in a mere seven months for reasons no one there really understood or cared about. That project had not yet unraveled when, in February 1720, the British parliament approved its own iteration. Even after the Mississippi Bubble collapsed in May, many unsophisticated investors in London remained certain that the price of South Sea stock was destined to rise. Blind, unreasoning enthusiasm among at least a part of the investing public was what the Company was counting upon to get them over the conversion hump: the conviction that there was *some* reason why prices could be expected to go on rising for a time.

Company and Treasury therefore resorted to deception. They crafted a simple story that stood to get the job done more effectively than any carefully-reasoned financial analysis might. No mention was made of an interest-rate reduction. Instead the one-time payment to the Exchequer was represented as the Company's generous offer to share with the state some part of the benefits that would accrue to it from the conversion operation. Hints were given that the profits needed to fund the payment would flow from the gap between the par and market prices of South Sea stock and from the sale of any stock thereby made "surplus". The common run of state creditor, unlikely to have thought the whole thing carefully through, might well have been taken in by this fiction. Certainly the Company's foremost contemporary critic, Archibald Hutcheson, was unable to undermine it, despite repeatedly publishing detailed calculations showing that, on the announced terms, those converting were sure to lose from the operation.[30] Even if they knew better or at least had their doubts, state creditors may have been persuaded to join in the exercise anyway – as long as they expected others to believe that share prices were destined to rise. The resulting prospect for capital gains could have made conversion worth their while.[31]

Company officials, and any government officials or parliamentarians in the know, could have justified the ruse to themselves on the grounds that it was essential for Britain to keep pace with recent rapid declines in the cost to the

---

30 See for instance Archibald Hutcheson, *An Abstract Shewing the Loss to the New Subscribers to the South-Sea Stock, at the Several Prices Following; and the Yearly Profits on Trade Necessary to Make Good the Said Loss* [...] (London, 1720).

31 See Larry Neal, *The Rise of Financial Capitalism: International Capital Markets in the Age of Reason* (Cambridge: Cambridge University Press, 1990), 80 – 82 for a statistical test of the premise that the Bubble was "rational" in this sense.

French government of servicing its own national debt. Their consciences might also have been eased by the expectation that, when the dust had settled, investors would be no worse off than if they had voluntarily accepted a reduction in the interest rate on their holdings of public debt to 4 percent per annum. This attitude is well captured in a letter written in May 1720 by Archbishop William King in Dublin to MP Robert Molesworth in London:

> I send you the queries about the South Sea, but would not on any account have it known that I am concerned in it, for I think, if the debts of the nation may be paid by the folly of particulars [...] it will be very well for the publick, and I know no obligation on me to hinder it. Perhaps what would be spent this way would be spent on gaming or on luxury, and I am of opinion that most that go into the matter are well aware it will not [succeed], but hope to sell before the price fall.[32]

Riding a Wave: Company Management of the Bubble

What then are we to make of those actions by Company directors that until now have been viewed as evidence they were deliberately trying to inflate the Bubble? This section argues they were increasingly-desperate attempts to keep the price of South Sea stock from collapsing before state creditors could be locked into contracts for converting their holdings of public debt into Company stock.

First a bit of background on the debt-conversion process. The Company's one-time payment to the Exchequer had two parts: a flat fee of £4.2 million levied in view of the redeemable debt (which everyone assumed would be converted *in toto*) and a payment equal to 4.5 times the annual payout on any irredeemable annuities offered for conversion – potentially another £3.5 million.[33] Those individuals seeking to exchange public debt for new Company stock were termed "debt subscribers". The Company also had to sell some stock to so-called "money subscribers", to raise the cash needed for the Exchequer payment.[34]

The directors scheduled three debt subscriptions: one in late April for about two thirds of the irredeemable debt, another in mid-July for the same proportion

---

32 Cited in William R. Scott, *The Constitution and Finance of English, Scottish and Irish Joint-Stock Companies to 1720* (Cambridge: Cambridge University Press, 1912), 1:424.

33 6 Geo. I, c. 4.

34 The term "subscriber" applied since the several classes of investor all indicated their intent, and simultaneously their legal commitment, to deal with the Company by signing their names in large books kept for this purpose. See Gary S. Shea, "Financial Market Analysis Can Go Mad (in the Search for Irrational Behaviour During the South Sea Bubble)," *Economic History Review* 60 (2007): 742–765, here 745–747, for a discussion of the exact legal commitments involved.

of the redeemable debt, and one more in early August for the rest of both.[35] The sequencing and proportions seem sensible. The irredeemable debt would be hardest to bring in and so needed to be addressed first. Limiting the initial subscription to about two thirds would have made potential subscribers fear being excluded and thus eager to get involved early on. Should the price of South Sea stock increase in the meantime, the regret of those excluded from the first subscription would position the Company well to bring in the remaining irredeemable debt at a later date. The Company targeted next that portion of the redeemable debt currently being handled by the Bank of England. This too made sense, since the Company was interested in stealing from its chief rival the cash flow associated with that debt. The directors left for last those redeemable annuities being handled by the Exchequer, which were less important since acquiring them would not help weaken the Bank.

In principle there should have been only one money subscription, designed to bring in whatever amount the Company expected to have to pay the Exchequer (i.e. no more than £7.7 million). But in fact the directors appointed four money subscriptions, opened on 14 April, 28 April, 17 June, and 24 August, for £6.75, £6, £50, and £12.5 million respectively. These were the net results of offering £2.25, £1.5, £5 and £1.25 million new shares (rated at their par value of £100 per share) for sale at official prices of £300, £400, £1,000 and £1,000 per share respectively. Both the decision to hold four subscriptions, and especially the very large size of the final two, ought to have been a puzzle for previous commentators and require explaining (as attempted below).

The Company's central aim in 1720 was to get as much as possible of the relevant public debt converted into South Sea stock. A corollary objective, and indeed the Company's principal strategic problem during 1720, was to prevent any significant decline in the price of South Sea stock while the conversion was under way. If later subscribers were to feel confident offering their debt for conversion, the market price of South Sea stock could not fall below whatever official value the Company had set upon the stock when converting the debt of earlier subscribers. Otherwise potential investors would fear large capital losses should they have to resell their new South Sea shares in the open market. So the Company became particularly vulnerable after 19 May, when the directors announced they would be valuing South Sea stock at £375 per share for the purposes of converting the irredeemable debt subscribed in late April.[36]

35 British Library (BL), Add. Ms. 25499, 13.4., 17.6., 8.7. and 27.7.1720.
36 BL, Add. Ms. 25499, 19.5.1720.

A similar problem existed with regard to the money subscribers. For the first money subscription there were to be eight installment payments in all, the last not coming due until August 1721. Subscribers could choose at any point to decline making further payments; the maximum penalty they would suffer was the loss of their 20 percent down payment.[37] Yet the Company would need the full amount of this subscription to fund the one-time payment to the Exchequer upon which the conversion project was predicated. So once a price of £300 per share had been set, in mid-April, for the stock being sold via the first money subscription, Company officials needed the market price to stay above that threshold until all the installment payments on that subscription had come in.

For reasons already discussed, the directors needed the public to believe that stock prices were due to rise above the levels at which they had stood in early 1720. But, past a certain point, actual price increases made their lives more and more difficult. First, any given price increase made it harder for investors to believe that further increases were yet to come and thus more difficult for the Company to persuade owners of yet-unconverted public debt that capital gains were still to be had by becoming South Sea shareholders. Second, as prices rose so did the probability that the market might suffer a sharp drop. If this happened before substantial portions of the debt had been converted, and if the decline could not be reversed or at least kept from snowballing, the project would have utterly failed. Finally, the Company had to worry about the long-term sustainability of its share price in the open market. Should that price, for any reason, suffer a significant decline within a year or two of the conversion, the directors were sure to be pilloried as swindlers.

Well-informed individuals began worrying very early on about the rising price of South Sea stock. Already in mid-February 1720, when prices were still relatively low, George Middleton, a London banker serving as the agent of John Law and his brother William, wrote to Paris regarding his concerns about South Sea stock. He feared that if its price rose any higher, hostile foreigners would be able to induce a stock market crash at will.[38] In late March, as the stock price fluctuated between £300 and £350, MP William Pulteney wrote from Paris to Secretary of State James Craggs with similar concerns:

---

37 Shea, "Financial Market Analysis," Appendix IV, 24–25, available separately online only.
38 Cited in Larry Neal, "'For God's Sake, Remitt Me': The Adventures of George Middleton, John Law's London Goldsmith-Banker, 1712–1729," *Business and Economic History* 23 (1994): 27–60, here 36–37.

> Mr Law speaking last night about the rise of our stocks said we could not stand it six weeks & that we are at the mercy of three of four persons in this city [...] You may depend on it that Mr Law's design is to make such a strong and sudden push on our stocks as we may not be able to stand.[39]

The directors expressed the same concern. On 21 April, they explained to a general meeting of shareholders that in the coming months they planned to lend money on security of South Sea stock because "attempts may be made to depreciate the stock at the times of the execution of the Act".[40]

So whenever the market price of South Sea stock started to slip, the directors swung into action. The main tool at their disposal was the money subscriptions. These could serve in three ways to sustain market prices. First, the very act of setting an official price for the subscriptions, usually somewhat higher than the going market rate, seems to have been interpreted by investors as inside information: evidence that the directors continued to have confidence in the Company's longer-term prospects. Second, to the extent the public bought large quantities of South Sea stock at prices set by the directors, they too were testifying to an expectation of further price increases: a demonstration effect that usually helped buoy the market price for existing stock. Finally, the money subscriptions raised large amounts of cash which the directors were quite prepared to lend to investors intent upon buying Company stock. Since the directors took existing stock, or the "receipts" issued to those making installment payments on new money-subscription stock, as security for such loans, this kind of lending also had the side benefit of reducing the supply of South Sea assets in the open market, thereby helping to sustain the market price.

In closing, this section provides a short account of key moments in the directors' price-support campaign. Consider for example the first money subscription. On 23 March, after a large upward surge lasting some two weeks, South Sea shares peaked at £350. For the next two weeks the spot price hovered between £310 and £320. On 8 April (the day after the statute authorizing the debt conversion finally passed), it fell beneath £300 and thereafter settled for several days in the mid-£280s. According to a contemporary, this "occasion'd no small alarm among those who had lately bought in at a higher price".[41] On 11 April the directors scheduled the first money subscription for 14 April at an official price of £300 per share. They had planned to secure subscriptions for £2 million of stock (at par value); but the issue was oversubscribed the same day by some

---

39 TNA, SP 78/166, 10. and 11.4.1720.

40 BL, Add. Ms. 25499, 21.4.1720.

41 Boyer, *Political State*, 19:448.

£250,000. Given a 20 percent down payment, this would have brought the Company £1.35 million in new cash resources. At first none needed to be loaned out, for the subscription itself seems to have helped; the stock recovered that day to £315 and a week later reached almost £350. The directors began lending only a week later, after prices had started to slide again. A total of £1.7 million was given out over the next two weeks. Once the stock recovered to £350 in early May, the volume of lending fell right off.

On 29 April, half way through this lending surge and probably with a view to rebuilding the Company's war chest, the directors opened a second money subscription. By pricing this subscription at £400, when the stock stood that day in Exchange Alley at £340, the directors may have been hoping to buoy the market again. In any case, with a down payment set at 10 percent, the new subscription immediately raised another £600,000. Since prices stabilized shortly thereafter, the directors held onto most of this cash.

The third money subscription likewise came after the price of South Sea stock experienced a sudden surge and was starting to slip back. On 19 May the directors offered terms to the April debt subscribers, for this purpose valuing South Sea stock at £375. Perhaps much to their surprise, the price of South Sea stock began a very sharp ascent the next day. From £375 on 19 May it steadily rose to £595 by the end of the month and to £770 on 3 June. Over this period the directors did engage in some further lending, but only for the relatively small sum of £400,000. Prices held reasonably firm during the next week. But the second installment on the first money subscription was due on 14 June and investors may have been worried about the impact on the spot price for South Sea stock, should subscribers be unable to meet their payments. On 10 June, the spot price having declined to £735, the directors resumed lending in a major way, issuing out a total of £2.7 million. At first they probably used some of the £1 million in Exchequer bills received from the Treasury on 8 June. These bills had been authorized by the underlying statute and were intended from the outset to be used as part of a price-support campaign. The market nevertheless continued downward, reaching £700 on 13 June. A day later, several of the wealthier Company directors were asked to borrow from their correspondents in Amsterdam, and the cashier was instructed to "take care to support the Company's stock by buying the same at £700 or under as far as the Company's cash will permit".[42]

On 15 June, with their cash reserves having been seriously depleted by all the new lending, the directors laid plans for a third money subscription on 17 June.

---

42 House of Lords Record Office (HLRO), HL/PO/JO/10/5/64.

With the issue officially priced at £1,000, a 10 percent down payment, and subscriptions for £5 million (par value) actually received, the Company should have gained £5 million in new cash resources. The official price set by the directors may itself have induced market optimism. For when the new subscription became public knowledge on 15 June, South Sea stock immediately climbed to £750. The directors loaned a further £2.7 million the following week, including a massive £1.7 million on 22 June. During this week too, and especially on 21 June, Company officials bought large quantities of "refusals" with a strike price of £1,000, thereby signaling that they believed prices would eventually rise above that threshold.[43] Further support operations became unnecessary after 22 June, since the Company's stock transfer books closed that day – making contracts for spot delivery impossible. Lending operations and refusals purchases also halted that same day (but for one further small refusal purchased on 23 June). So in June the directors had resorted to quite desperate measures to keep the stock price relatively stable until the closing of the books. This gave the directors some much-needed breathing room until the books reopened in August, since in the interim stock holders could not officially transfer any Company shares.

Finally, the fourth money subscription and another round of Company loans were put into effect after the market price of South Sea stock again came under serious downward pressure. Share prices slowly declined in July from £950 to £850. (Note that all summer prices quotes referred to forward contracts for delivery of stock on 22 August, when the Company's stock transfer books were scheduled to re-open.) The spot price was sure to come under more downward pressure on 22 August, when many investors would need to sell stock to raise cash for settling a host of option and forward contracts then coming due.[44] So as early as 27 July the directors were exploring the idea of a fourth money subscription. Initially it was to be limited to "proprietors" of South Sea stock, including any of the existing debt and money subscribers. Money subscriptions sold to this group would be a more dependable source of cash, since the debt-conversion statute authorized the Company to sell shareholders' stock to cover any payment defaults.[45]

Meanwhile, the market price continued descending in early August, slipping to £805 on the 10th. Two days later the directors announced conversion terms for the debt subscriptions obtained in mid-July and early August, valuing stock for

43 The modern terminology for a refusal is a "call option", which entitles the buyer to purchase stock on some future date at a pre-determined value called the "strike price".
44 Boyer, *Political State*, 20:143.
45 Boyer, *Political State*, 20:133.

this purpose at £800. They also resolved in-camera to go ahead with a proprietors' money subscription, though without yet setting purchase terms or a date for opening the subscription books. The market price continued downward, reaching £780 on 18 August. That day, acting on Company instructions, Company cashier Robert Knight bought £59,000 (par value) of South Sea stock at a price (dividend excluded) of about £800 per share. A day later he was directed to buy a further £100,000 "so as to keep up the price thereof" and the directors ordered the issue of £400,000 in new corporate bonds for lending upon South Sea stock.[46] Despite these efforts, a day after the transfer books re-opened, on 22 August, the market fell further to £740. With the Company's cash reserves already low, more cash was needed. A proprietors' money subscription would have taken too much time, since the current state of stock ownership had first to be ascertained. So instead on 24 August the directors opened a standard money subscription, open to all interested investors. With £1.25 million (par value) subscribed, a 20 percent down payment, and an official issue price of £1,000, the immediate cash proceeds would have been around £2.5 million. The official issue price may have been another attempt by the directors to induce market optimism – by occasioning a public demonstration that many were still willing to buy at that price. If so, their objective was achieved when the subscription filled, in fact over-filled, the same day the books were opened. The spot price quickly rose above £800 and remained there for a few days.

Still worried, the directors loaned out £600,000 over the next few days, ordered Company officials to buy up to a further £100,000 of South Sea stock,[47] and decided on 25 August to proceed with a proprietors' money subscription on 12 September.[48] For the latter, investors would be permitted to subscribe for new purchases of up to 20 percent of the amount of stock they were already holding. The directors announced that the books would be shut from 31 August to 21 September to accommodate the accounting work needed for a proprietors' subscription. The subscription would have had several positive effects: a) bringing in a lot more cash right away; b) ensuring access to regular cash infusions in future, since any payment defaults could be raised by selling the proprietors' existing stock or subscription receipts; c) giving a plausible reason for shutting the transfer books again; and d) to the extent the public was anxious to subscribe, giving proprietors real incentive to keep their stock and subscription receipts off the market. Yet somehow the plan backfired. Perhaps the decisions to close the

46 HLRO, HL/PO/JO/10/5/64.
47 HLRO, HL/PO/JO/10/5/64, 26.8.1720.
48 BL, Add. Ms. 25499.

transfer books once more, and to let investors borrow the down payment for the proprietors' money subscription without needing to transfer actual stock or subscription receipts as security, struck investors as signs of desperation – which indeed they were. On 29 August the market price fell to £775, despite massive Company lending that day in the amount of £2.9 million. The promise of very large future dividends bruited about by the directors the next day and formalized on 8 September did nothing to forestall further declines. The crash had begun.

The very design of the later money subscriptions suggests the directors were worried that the market would collapse before their project could be completed. The third, fourth, and aborted proprietors' money subscriptions were nominally configured to bring in £50, £12.5, and £60.5 million respectively. This was far more than the Company could ever have needed or invested profitably.[49] The whole national debt was only about £50 million;[50] the Company held title to £11 million of this before the conversion began and had already obtained subscriptions for a further £26 million. And it would have been impossible to invest so large a sum in new projects, given that it amounted to roughly twice the estimated annual national income of £62 million. Instead, what the directors must have wanted were the down payments, to undertake share-price support operations. The second installments on the third and fourth money subscriptions were initially scheduled for January and March 1721.[51] By then, they hoped, the project would be virtually complete. The bulk of the irredeemable and redeemable debt had already been locked in for conversion. It remained only to secure a cash reserve sufficient to cover the £7.7 million Exchequer payment and to support market prices for some reasonable period of time – at least long enough for the debt subscribers to sell out, if that was their intention. The proprietors' subscription alone, slated to be finished by no later than 21 September, would have ensured both of these objectives. Thereafter the directors could have proceeded exactly as they did in late September after market prices tumbled: cancel all further installment payments on the four money subscriptions and renegotiate the prices of the later debt and money subscriptions at more sustainable and equitable levels.[52] But when investors panicked, the directors were forced to abort the planned proprietors' subscription. This left them without the cash needed to support the market price of their stock. Once that fell below £400, those who had borrowed upon security of South Sea stock officially rated at that price lost all incentive to

49 Patrick K. O'Brien, "The Rise of a Fiscal State in England, 1485 – 1815," *Historical Research* 66 (1993): 129 – 176, here 175.
50 Dickson, *Financial Revolution*, 93.
51 Shea, "Financial Market Analysis," Appendix IV, 24 – 25, available separately online only.
52 Boyer, *Political State*, 20:203 – 205.

repay their loans. Unfortunately, the Company needed a large share of that money, roughly £11.3 million,[53] to cover the Exchequer payment. The directors being unable to fulfill this crucial part of their bargain with the state, the project had failed.

Concluding Remarks

In short, the South Sea Company directors inadvertently did themselves in by choosing to sell their debt-conversion project with the lure of capital gains – specifically the premise that the Company would profit by selling surplus stock. This crude fiction led some part of an uninformed general public to anticipate ever-increasing share prices, which for a time became a self-fulfilling prophecy. As the market price got increasingly out of hand, the directors were confronted with a very difficult choice: either carry on with the deception or allow prices to unwind, dooming the project to failure. They chose the former course, presenting each new rise in share prices as an opportunity for the Company to profit still further. The evidence suggests that their intent was not to swindle anyone but rather to complete the debt conversion and deal at some later date with the adverse consequences to new shareholders from having bought in at very high prices. Once investors were locked into contracts to exchange their holdings of public debt for South Sea stock, the directors could have afforded to let market share prices decline to levels that might prove sustainable in the longer term and then renegotiate the conversion contracts to match – as indeed they did in September, proffering stock at £400 per share to subscribers who had earlier agreed to pay as much as £1,000 for it. Had the market price stabilized at £400, most new shareholders would have been disappointed of their hopes for large capital gains but unlikely to complain of having been cheated by the directors.

But the bubble continued to unwind, leaving the directors to face the wrath of ruined investors. Opposition politicians used the occasion to try to dislodge the current administration. The thesis that the directors had deliberately engineered the market price increases of that year proved far too convenient in the ensuing parliamentary investigation. Nor could Company or Treasury officials, having from the outset based the whole scheme on a ruse, come clean and say what had really happened. So the story came to focus on greedy directors and, by dint of sheer repetition, survived in that form to the present day.

53 HLRO, HL/PO/JO/10/2/157.

Abigail Swingen

The Bubble and the Bail-Out: The South Sea Company, Jacobitism, and Public Credit in Early Hanoverian Britain

In the summer of 1722, nearly two years after the South Sea Bubble burst, the directors of the South Sea Company wrote to their governor, King George I, to request financial assistance. The Company had been relying on the support of the King and his ministry throughout the bubble crisis, so this in and of itself was not particularly significant. But the language used in the Company's address in July 1722 suggested that some people perceived a possible connection between recent Jacobite activity and the South Sea Company. The address read: "The Enemys of your Majesty's Government, might probably take Encouragement in their Designs, from the Anxiety and Uneasiness, which the particular Losses of many of your Subjects in this Company had given us; and might hope to worke up and Inflame our Divisions to such Degree, as to lead Unwary People from their Allegiance".[1] The "Designs" likely referred to the Jacobite Atterbury Plot. Named for one of the main conspirators, Francis Atterbury, the Bishop of Rochester, the plotters intended both a domestic uprising and an invasion of armed regiments from France and Spain in an attempt to install James Francis Edward Stuart, the son of King James II, on the throne.[2] Evidence of the plot recently had been revealed and, throughout the summer of 1722, political tensions remained high. Eager to emphasize loyalty to the current Hanoverian monarch, the Company's address continued: "But Vain were their thoughts, if they Imagined that we, who at no time forgot that Your Majesty had greatly Commiserated and Releived us, should act so Inconstantly, as by Resenting Mischeifs which your Majesty neither caused nor could possibly prevent, to contribute to and assist in measures that can only Tend to the destruction of all Property, the preservation of which depends upon your Peaceable Enjoyment of the Throne".[3]

Since the collapse of South Sea Company stock in September 1720, there had been widespread rumors that supporters of the exiled house of Stuart would at-

1 South Sea Company General Court meeting minutes, Address to George I, 20.7.1722, in British Library (BL), Add. Ms. 25544, 49–51.

2 Eveline Cruickshanks and Howard Erskine-Hill, *The Atterbury Plot* (New York: Palgrave Macmillan, 2004), 91–123.

3 South Sea Company General Court meeting minutes, Address to George I, 20.7.1722, in BL, Add. Ms. 25544, 49–51.

https://doi.org/10.1515/9783110592139-008

tempt to take advantage of the disorder caused by the Bubble. In October 1720, a proclamation issued on behalf of James Francis Edward (and possibly approved by Atterbury himself) offered support to his English subjects and expressed his "Paternal concern for their sufferings" in light of "so great a Calamity" caused "by the avarice of a few Miscreants", hoping to take advantage of the chaos to orchestrate a Stuart restoration.[4] Many contemporaries eventually connected the Atterbury conspiracy to the Bubble.[5] But the Company's July 1722 address seemed to go beyond the mere implication that Jacobites might exploit the chaos created by the Bubble. It suggested there was a need for the Company's directors to distance themselves from the plot and from any hint of disloyalty to the Hanoverian regime. Why did the Company's directors not only feel the need to declare loyalty to George I but also to dissociate themselves from any idea that they participated in a treasonous uprising against the ruling monarch? Was it simply a rhetorical ploy, or did it reveal deeper anxieties about the Company and its relationship to the state?

The multiple causes and consequences of the South Sea Bubble have been explored by many historians, economists, and literary critics.[6] But there has been little scholarship on the Bubble's consequences explicitly in terms of its political implications for the still-fragile Hanoverian regime, which only had been established in 1714. It is important to remember that the South Sea Bubble of 1720 was the first major financial crisis faced by the Hanoverian monarchy. There also have been few considerations of what the South Sea Bubble might have indicated to contemporaries about the state of Britain's Financial Revolution, which was supposedly reaching a kind of maturity by the 1720s. In part, this stems from the fact that many key studies of Britain's Financial Revolution, even those that incorporate politics, focus on the decades leading up to 1720.[7]

4 "Proclamation of the Pretender," 10.10.1720, in The National Archive (TNA), SP 35/23/91; Cruickshanks and Erskine-Hill, *The Atterbury Plot*, 62.

5 Judy Hayden, "Of Windmills and Bubbles: Harlequin Faustus on the Eighteenth-Century State," *Huntington Library Quarterly* 77 (2014): 1–16, here 3.

6 The scholarly literature on the South Sea Bubble is vast. To cite just a few examples: Peter G.M. Dickson, *The Financial Revolution in England: A Study in the Development of Public Credit, 1688–1756* (London: MacMillan, 1967); Richard Dale, *The First Crash: Lessons from the South Sea Bubble* (Princeton: Princeton University Press, 2004); Julian Hoppit, "The Myths of the South Sea Bubble," *Transactions of the Royal Historical Society* 12 (2002): 141–165; Helen J. Paul, *The South Sea Bubble: An Economic History of Its Origins and Consequences* (London: Routledge, 2011); Richard Kleer, "'The Folly of Particulars': The Political Economy of the South Sea Bubble," *Financial History Review* 19 (2012): 175–197.

7 Gary S. De Krey, *A Fractured Society: The Politics of London in the First Age of Party, 1688–1715* (Oxford: Clarendon Press, 1985); Bruce Carruthers, *City of Capital: Politics and Markets in the*

Other studies of the Financial Revolution that do include considerations of the Bubble tend to empty it of its political meaning, beyond the bald pursuit of power by Sir Robert Walpole and his associates.[8] Similarly, studies of Walpole's rise to power and the entrenchment of the "Whig Oligarchy" tend to see the Bubble as a major step in that process but do not consider exactly how and why it mattered in terms of popular understandings and disagreements about public finance, the Revolutionary Settlement, and the Hanoverian Succession.[9]

The South Sea Bubble must be placed in the context of contemporary debates about the Financial Revolution and its ideological implications. At the time, there was broad consensus that the South Sea Bubble threatened public finance and credit, which put the country at serious financial risk. But that is where agreement about the Bubble ended. To some observers, the Bubble revealed public credit's volatile nature and indicated that the state should not only discourage such schemes in the future but rely on public credit either less or not at all. Others came to a different conclusion: although the Bubble had destabilized public credit, to weaken the state's support of public credit and the national debt would make matters worse. They felt that only those who wanted to subvert the government would wish for such a thing. Ultimately, the Bubble accelerated ongoing ideological debates about the state and its relationship to finance, which had major implications for British politics in the early Hanoverian era. This chapter considers the broader political significance of the South Sea Bubble in terms of how public credit and its ideological connections to political parties, factions, and policies were utilized and deployed in the wake of the crisis. Contemporaries associated Whigs and Tories (or more accurately sub-sections of those parties) with particular financial policies, ideas, and caricatures. These associations drew on a tradition of rancorous political language that had emerged in Britain during the late 1600s and blossomed during the so-called "rage of party" in the early eighteenth century.[10] Such associations had both financial and electoral consequences.

English Financial Revolution (Princeton: Princeton University Press, 1996); Natasha Glaisyer, *The Culture of Commerce in England, 1660–1720* (London: Boydell Press, 2006); Anne L. Murphy, *The Origins of English Financial Markets: Investment and Speculation before the South Sea Bubble* (Cambridge: Cambridge University Press, 2009).

8 Dickson, *The Financial Revolution in England*, chs. 6–8.

9 H.T. Dickinson, *Walpole and the Whig Supremacy* (Aylesbury: The English Universities Press, 1973).

10 J.H. Plumb, *The Growth of Political Stability in England, 1675–1725* (Atlantic Highlands: Humanities Press, 1967); Geoffrey Holmes, *British Politics in the Age of Anne*, rev. ed. (London: Hambledon Press, 1987); Mark Knights, *Representation and Misrepresentation in Later Stuart Britain: Partisanship and Political Culture* (Oxford: Oxford University Press, 2005).

This chapter argues that the South Sea Bubble had significant political significance for the Hanoverian regime, particularly in terms of the perceived danger of Jacobitism to the state. This is how many contemporaries framed their understanding of the Bubble and its effects on British society. This chapter is less concerned about the relative strengths and weaknesses of the Jacobite movement and is more interested in exploring what people *perceived* about Jacobitism, particularly in terms of its relationship to public credit and the national debt. It explores how and why these perceptions mattered amidst significant financial instability and how they contributed to the entrenchment of the Hanoverian monarchy and the Whig regime under the leadership of Sir Robert Walpole. During the crisis, anyone who seemed to wish the country harm, be it the Company's directors, the Whig ministry that implemented the original scheme, or those unwilling to adequately assist the Company after the crash, could be labeled a Jacobite. The fact that the South Sea Company had to distance itself from rumored connections to the Atterbury Plot in the summer of 1722 was one indication of how deeply these ideological associations had taken hold. I further argue that the Walpolean Whig regime's ascendancy in 1721–1722 was connected to the successful deployment of the idea that those who wished to let the South Sea Company and its subscribers fail were really Jacobites in disguise. They were helped by the fact that Jacobitism remained a real threat throughout the South Sea crisis and its aftermath.

Ideological Associations in Popular Print

Rhetoric mobilized in the public outcry over the South Sea Bubble drew from and exaggerated well-known ideological associations that had emerged during the late 1600s amidst what has become known as Britain's Financial Revolution. This Revolution included the creation of the national debt and public credit that allowed the government to pay for increasingly expensive wars, as well as other measures, via loans from joint-stock corporations such as the Bank of England, the East India Company, and the South Sea Company. In loaning money to the government, these institutions held a stake in the national debt and became political as well as financial entities.[11] Images of a politically-powerful "moneyed interest" that profited from "stock-jobbing", impenetrable investment systems that average people could not understand, and from controlling the main insti-

11 Bruce Carruthers, "Homo Economicus and Homo Politicus: Non-Economic Rationality in the Early 18th Century London Stock Market," *Acta Sociologica* 37 (1994): 165–194, here 166.

tutions of investment were widespread during the early eighteenth century. According to many contemporaries, such men and their complicated investment schemes threatened not only to fleece unsuspecting people of their money but to destabilize the constitution itself. In his famous 1719 pamphlet, *The Anatomy of Exchange Alley*, Daniel Defoe wrote that "Stock-jobbers who are guilty of the Practices I am going to detect, are eventually Traytors to King George, and to his Government, Family and Interest, and to their Country, and deserve to be used at least as Confederates with Traytors". Although such financial trickery was "litterally speaking [...] no Treason", Defoe maintained that the activities of speculative investors had the effect of "disabling the Government, discouraging the King's Friends, and [gave] visible Encouragement of the King's Enemies".[12]

Over time, such associations became explicitly party political. In the popular imagination since at least the late 1690s, the "moneyed men" were most often associated with Whigs, specifically the Court or "Junto" Whigs, who supported the creation of the Bank of England, the expansion and funding of the national debt, as well as new financial instruments of investment that the government experimented with at the time, such as lotteries, tallies, and annuities.[13] The "moneyed man", by supporting these new schemes, was seen as a greedy promoter of his own self-interest at the expense of the nation's well-being. This political stereotype became exaggerated in Tory and anti-establishment pamphlets, broadsides, poems, and ballads. In 1701, Charles Davenant wrote, "If you talk or think of the Publick-Good, you will never become a right Modern Whig".[14] One Tory/Jacobite pamphlet in 1714 claimed that Whigs were so venal that they bought and sold votes for MPs on the stock exchange: "Boroughs are rated on the *Royal Exchange*, like Stocks and Tallies; the Price of a Vote is as well known as an Acre of Land; and it is no Secret who are the monied Men, and consequently the best Customers".[15] Tory literature frequently presented Whigs as profiteering from ongoing wars against France and seeking to prolong those conflicts as a result.[16] In addition, Tory propaganda often exploited xenophobia and anti-Semitism common in contemporary Britain owing to the large number of

12 Daniel Defoe, *The Anatomy of Exchange Alley, or A System of Stock-Jobbing* (London, 1719), 25, 28.

13 De Krey, *A Fractured Society*; Carruthers, *City of Capital*; Carruthers, "Homo Economicus," 169.

14 Charles Davenant, *The True Picture of a Modern Whig* (London, 1701), 7.

15 Francis Atterbury, *English Advice to Freeholders of England* (London, 1714), 4.

16 For example, see *The Management of the Last Four Years Vindicated* (London, 1714), 19; see also Davenant, *True Picture*, 11.

families of foreign and nonconformist descent, particularly Huguenots and Jews, who were involved in the new financial system.[17] The Whiggish "moneyed interest" was regularly understood to be opposed to the "landed" interest that traditionally had been in charge of the nation's political system, and it was therefore presented as corrupt and threatening to the established pillars of the British constitution.[18]

Just exactly who was the real threat to the nation, of course, was in the eye of the accuser. While certain Tories and others skeptical of public credit felt that the "moneyed interest" made the nation vulnerable to the whims of an upstart political class, others argued that those who were unwilling to support public finance were the real risk to the state. In contrast to the ideas outlined above, supporters of the new world of finance often portrayed their Tory and "country" Whig counterparts as dangerously out of touch with the new realities of governance, particularly in terms of waging international wars. The military needs of the British state required far more revenue than had been the case in earlier generations and, therefore, they argued, to do away with the structures and institutions that helped pay for those realities would be dangerous. In fact, Whiggish propaganda maintained that Tories would erase the national debt and undermine public credit, if given the chance. According to Benjamin Hoadly, the future Bishop of Bangor and ardent defender of the Whig position, Tories would use a "*Political Spunge* to wipe out the Debts of the Nation".[19]

In effect, in the Whig imagination, Tories and others skeptical of the new financial realities of the early 1700s were no better than Jacobites. To wipe out the national debt and undermine public credit would result in a major destabilization of the constitution, thereby undermining Britain's Revolutionary Settlement and the Protestant Hanoverian Succession. This notion made its way into Whig

---

17 See, for example, *The Battle of the Bubbles: Shewing their several Constitutions, Alliances, Policies, and Wars; From their first Suddain Rise, to their late Speedy Decay* (London, 1720), 5; Carruthers, "Homo Economicus," 172; De Krey, *A Fractured Society*, 219–222; Nicholas Rogers, *Whigs and Cities: Popular Politics in the Age of Walpole and Pitt* (Oxford: Clarendon Press, 1989), 23; Geoffrey Holmes, "The Sacheverell Riots: The Crowd and the Church in Early Eighteenth-Century London," *Past and Present* 72 (1976): 55–85, here 61–62; Tim Harris, *Politics under the Later Stuarts: Party Conflict in a Divided Society, 1660–1715* (London and New York: Longman, 1993), 196–202.

18 Geoffrey Holmes, *British Politics in the Age of Anne*, ch. 5; Perry Gauci, "The Clash of Interests: Commerce and the Politics of Trade in the Age of Anne," in *British Politics in the Age of Holmes*, ed. Clyve Jones (Oxford: Wiley-Blackwell, 2009), 115–125; Dickinson, *Walpole and the Whig Supremacy*, 143–144.

19 Benjamin Hoadly, *The Fears and Sentiments of all True Britains; With respect to National Credit, Interest, and Religion* (London, 1710), 8, 9.

propaganda and exploited the fear that a Stuart restoration would result in catastrophic consequences for the national debt. The most famous depiction of this fear was Joseph Addison's 1711 image of "Publick Credit" as a "beautiful Virgin seated on a Throne of Gold", in the *Spectator*. When she was adequately supported by the "Acts of Parliament as had been made for the Establishment of Publick Funds", she maintained her strength and stability. But when threatened with Tyranny, Anarchy, Bigotry, Atheism, as well as a "young Man of about twenty-two Years of Age" – referring to James Stuart, who carried "a Sword in his right Hand" and a "Spunge in his left" – she "fainted and dyed away at the sight".[20] Similarly, as religious freethinker John Toland argued, "I never heard any Man argue for reducing the Interest of the Funds, that was not an Enemy to the Cause towards the support of which these funds were given".[21] In other words, failure to support public finance was likely the design of clandestine Jacobites, who opposed the war against France and had been aiding the exiled House of Stuart. This Whig construct equated the Jacobite cause not only with returning the Catholic Stuart line to the throne and undermining Parliamentary authority but with threatening the economic security of the nation.

Plenty of Tories (or those writing for Tories) argued that such portrayals were unfair and that all sensible people, regardless of party affiliation, adequately supported public credit and the national debt. Daniel Defoe, writing on behalf of the Tories in 1710, maintained that the health of public credit, rather than relying on one political party, depended on "just and honourable Dealing" and the proper constitutional balance between Parliament and the monarchy.[22] Nevertheless, this Whig political construct persisted, in spite of the active involvement in finance of a number of men with Tory sympathies, such as Sir Mathew Decker, Sir Richard Hoare, and Sir Theodore Janssen. It was also despite the fact that, throughout the period, joint-stock companies often became associated with Tories and Tory politics. When he came to power in 1710, Robert Harley envisioned the South Sea Company as a Tory counterweight to the Whig-dominated Bank of England and East India Company, on which the government could rely for loans. Similarly, the Royal African Company had been associated with Tory politicians

20 Joseph Addison, *The Spectator*, no. 3, 3.3.1711, in *The Spectator in Four Volumes*, ed. Gregory Smith (London and New York: Dent, 1964), 1:10–13.

21 John Toland, *The Grand Mystery Laid Open: Namely, By dividing of the Protestants to weaken the Hanover Succession, and by defeating the Succession to extirpate the Protestant Religion* (London, 1714), 36–37.

22 Daniel Defoe, *Essay upon Publick Credit* (London, 1710), 13. See also Abel Boyer, *An Essay Towards the History of the Late Ministry and Parliament* (London, 1710), 5, 58.

and political ideologies since the 1680s.[23] But, during the early eighteenth century, Whig propaganda repeated this idea that Tories had a dangerous financial agenda, just as Tories repeated the notion that the Whig "moneyed man" was the real threat to the nation.

As historian Mark Knights argues, such stereotypes, particularly that of the "grasping and unscrupulous Whig financier", reflected anxieties not only about new institutions of finance but also of the state of post-Revolutionary politics more generally. As Knights has written, in the popular imagination, "Fraudulent politics and fraudulent money-making went hand in hand". Knights also points out that such exaggerated rhetoric had both financial and "electoral consequences".[24] Taking a cue from Knights, I argue that the use of such dire language about Britain's nascent financial system revealed a significant amount of anxiety about the state of the financial sector. Tories mostly worried that the economic and political effects of ongoing financial change would be detrimental to traditional British society, whereas Whigs mostly worried about the potentially catastrophic consequences if Tories had the chance to undermine the financial system. These characterizations, however much they were embellished, were deliberate and meaningful. Such hyperbole betrayed a significant level of anxiety not only about the potential dangers associated with having a government that relied so heavily on public credit, but also about the uncertain nature of the Financial Revolution, especially among those who most forcefully supported it. Rhetoric that equated dismantling public credit with a Jacobite invasion or uprising indicated that the success of the Financial Revolution was by no means guaranteed as far as its supporters were concerned. Many historians, however, have not taken the use of such language seriously when analyzing the significance of the Financial Revolution or the consequences of the South Sea Bubble. Economic historians, in particular, have ignored the political (and politicized) contexts of such debates and, instead, have argued that most politicians in power, when confronted with credit crises and other financial problems, ignored party-political divides and platforms and passed laws aimed at securing financial institutions, thus entrenching the new world of financial capitalism.[25] This

---

23 Carruthers, "Homo Economicus," 170 – 171; Carl Wennerlind, *Casualties of Credit: The English Financial Revolution, 1620 – 1720* (Cambridge, Mass.: Harvard University Press, 2011); Abigail L. Swingen, *Competing Visions of Empire: Labor, Slavery, and the Origins of the British Atlantic Empire* (New Haven: Yale University Press, 2015), ch. 5.

24 Knights, *Representation and Misrepresentation*, 310, 317, 320.

25 B. W. Hill, "The Change of Government and the 'Loss of the City'," *Economic History Review* 24 (1971): 395 – 413; Murphy, *Origins of English Financial Markets*; Anne L. Murphy, "Demanding 'Credible Commitment': Public Reactions to the Failures of the Early Financial Revolution," *Eco-*

idea of a broad consensus about state finance in the early eighteenth century obscures the reality of how polarizing such changes actually were.

Such rhetoric contributed to an atmosphere of political divisiveness and likely had financial and electoral consequences. Indeed, financial decisions were never merely economic in the early eighteenth century. As Bruce Carruthers has demonstrated, investors made a political as much as a financial calculus when making investment choices.[26] Some scholars have even suggested that contemporaries might have equated the threat of Jacobite activity with financial instability, specifically downward trends in the stock market. A number of social scientists have determined that during moments of Jacobite activity, or amid rumors of such activity, markets reacted negatively not only because of the threat posed in terms of possible war, but because it was widely believed the exiled Stuarts had an economic platform that repudiated the national debt. These scholars conclude that Jacobitism came to be associated by investors with negative behavior in the stock market.[27] The actual threat of Jacobitism mattered less than what people perceived about the relationship between a possible Stuart restoration and their investments. These ideological constructs became amplified following the South Sea crisis.

The South Sea Bubble and the Public Response

Not surprisingly, the Tory construct of the nefarious "moneyed interest" was repeated in books, pamphlets, poems, and broadsides published in the wake of the South Sea Bubble. Many argued that the original South Sea scheme had been based on imaginary wealth, meant to deceive the public. One pamphlet claimed that the Bubble had been orchestrated by "a Set of crafty Men having undertaken to delude the World into an Opinion, that they can, by a little

---

nomic History Review 66 (2013): 178–197; James MacDonald, "The Importance of Not Defaulting: The Significance of the Election of 1710," in *Questioning Credible Commitment: Perspectives on the Rise of Financial Capitalism*, ed. D'Maris Coffman, Adrian Leonard, and Larry Neal (Cambridge: Cambridge University Press, 2013), 125–146.

26 Carruthers, *City of Capital*; Carruthers, "Homo Economicus."

27 John Wells and Douglas Wills, "Revolution, Restoration, and Debt Repudiation: The Jacobite Threat to England's Institutions and Economic Growth," *Journal of Economic History* 60 (2000): 418–441; David Stasavage, "Partisan Politics and Public Debt: The Importance of the 'Whig Supremacy' for Britain's Financial Revolution," *European Review of Economic History* 11 (2007): 123–153.

hocus pocus Management, make a single Unit become a good Ten".[28] Many tried to emphasize the distinction between landed wealth and wealth based on stock. "There is a wide difference between the *South-Sea* stock, and a Landed Estate", claimed the author of *The South Sea Scheme Detected.* "A Man will certainly enjoy the Products of his Land for the Maintenance of his family, when he can make nothing of his *South-Sea* stock; and one is a real security for the borrowing of Money, and the other perhaps no Security at all".[29] Others likewise highlighted the imaginary nature of the scheme. Ned Ward in his *South Sea Ballad* proclaimed:

Five Hundred Millions, Notes and Bonds;
Our Stocks are worth in Value,
But neither lie in Goods or Lands,
Or Money, let me tell ye.
Yet tho' our Foreign Trade is lost,
Of mighty Wealth we vapour,
When all the Riches that we boast
Consist in scraps of Paper.[30]

To these observers, the South Sea Bubble confirmed the dangerous consequences of letting the "moneyed interest" run the country. As one writer exclaimed, "Who can enough lament the Misery of a Nation surrounded with such People who wait for nothing but to prey on the Body of the Publick, and yet still to be under a necessity of making use of them!"[31] Another author wrote that "our Trustees, who should have known the nature of Credit better, should never have attempted at one blow to have destroy'd it".[32] John Trenchard in one of the first of *Cato's Letters* referred to the South Sea directors as a "class of ravens, whose wealth has cost the nation its all, as they are manifest enemies to God and man, no man can call them his neighbours".[33] One pamphleteer purported to have "accidentally" been an "Eye-witness to many proceedings" of the

28 *A Letter to a Conscientious Man: Concerning the Use and the Abuse of Riches, and the Right and Wrong Ways of acquiring them* (London, 1720), 14–15.
29 *The South Sea Scheme Detected* (London, 1720), 14.
30 Edward Ward, *South Sea Ballad, or, Merry Remarks upon Exchange-Alley Bubbles* or *The Looking Glass for England* (1720).
31 *A Letter to a Friend, Concerning the Proposals for the Payment of the Nation's Debts* (London, 1720), 12.
32 *An Appeal to Common Sense: or, some Considerations offer'd to Restore Publick Credit* (London, 1720), 8.
33 John Trenchard, *Cato's Letters*, no. 3, 19.11.1720, in *Cato's Letters*, ed. Ronald Hamowy (Indianapolis: Liberty Fund, 1995), 1:44.

South Sea Company directors, whose ultimate aim was not just getting rich. "Money alone now was not the only thing our Gentlemen aimed at; they began to look much higher: the Creature Money, which before they adored, was now only regarded as subservient to greater Ends".[34] According to these observers, political ambition directed the scheme from the very beginning.

Debates about the government's role in finance and its implications for state power occurred since at least the 1690s but became more fiercely politicized after the South Sea Bubble.[35] For many, the Bubble and its aftermath revealed that Britain was too dependent upon public credit and that its precarious foundations were dangerous to the national interest. One pamphlet containing a plan to stabilize the economy through the issuance of government bills argued, "As for Publick Credit, if the above scheme be followed, we shall have no Occasion to make use of it; and happy it had been for the Nation if we never had; we never then should have laboured under the Burthen we now feel, and our Taxes had ended with our Wars".[36] For many, the dishonest nature of the South Sea Bubble indicated that public credit and finance were likewise based on fraud and that those behind the scheme were no better than traitors.[37] A petition from the city of Coventry to the Commons blamed those who orchestrated the design with threatening the constitution and putting Britain in danger from foreign and domestic enemies. "But look likewise with the utmost Concern upon the Shattered, Discontented, and in a manner Defenceless Condition of the Nation in General", it warned, "should any Revengeful Neighbour, take this Opportunity of our Weakness to Insult us, and we cannot believe that those Wicked Engineers, who have brought us into this State, design'd to undermine us for our Wealth alone, but to blow up our happy Constitution too".[38] The South Sea Bubble and other financial projects deemed erroneous weakened Britain and made it vulnerable to potential foreign and Jacobite threats.

Still, many of these pamphlets that labeled the South Sea Company directors as "traitors" simultaneously argued that for the government to do nothing in the face of a major financial crisis would make matters worse. "Let these Traytors (if they be so) be brought before that great Tribunal, the Parliament", argued one writer, "and if their Treason be prov'd, we need not doubt but the legislature

34 *The Nation Preserved; or, the Plot Discovered* (London, 1720), 2.

35 Dickson, *The Financial Revolution in England*, ch. 2.

36 *The Rise of the Stocks The Ruin of the People, Plainly Demonstrated, In Three Letters to a Member of Parliament* (London, 1721), 10.

37 *The Naked and Undisguis'd Truth* (London, 1721), 1.

38 *A Collection of the Several Petitions of the Counties, Boroughs, &c, Presented to the House of Commons* (London, 1721), 21–22.

will do Justice, in the mean time let us see what we have left, and by what means it may be improv'd to our Advantage".[39] Another declared, "As the Breach of Publick Faith is the Terror and Apprehension of People in all Revolutions, so nothing can more effectually preserve the Honour of a King, and render him beyond all Attempts secure in his Possession of his Throne, than the keeping of all Parliamentary Affairs, especially relating to Money, inviolable".[40] Even if the directors were traitors, if they were dealt with by the law, this presumably would be adequate punishment. Perhaps the real "Jacobite" threat lay not with the Company's old directors or with government ministers who had allowed the scheme to take place but with those who refused to allow the government to try to ameliorate the situation. This would be the position adopted by the King's ministry as it attempted to stabilize public finance in 1721.

Rescue Plans Justified and the Entrenchment of the Ministry

While nearly everyone agreed that public credit was not functioning properly as a result of the South Sea Bubble, there was considerable disagreement about what, if anything, to do about it. According to many observers, if the Bubble threatened public credit and made the country vulnerable, then it was all the more important for the King's ministry to rescue the Company and secure public credit. The King opened Parliament on 8 December 1720 and implored the legislature to "consider the most effectual and speedy methods to restore the National Credit, and fix it upon a lasting Foundation".[41] Both Houses immediately set to work, forming committees charged with scrutinizing the Company's subscription books to find out what exactly had caused the scheme to collapse.[42] Thomas Brodrick, selected by fellow MPs to head the Secret Committee, was a longtime critic of the Company. He relished his investigative role and uncovered the corrupt actions of many of the Company's directors and of a number of high-placed politicians in the ministry, including First Lord of the Treasury the Earl of Sunderland; Chancellor of the Exchequer John Aislabie; Treasury Secretary Charles Stanhope; Postmaster General James Craggs, Sr.; and the last's son, James Craggs, Jr., Secretary of State for the Southern Department. By the spring of 1721, most of these men had either died, been found guilty by the Commons,

39 *An Appeal to Common Sense*, 11–12.
40 *The South Sea Scheme Detected*, 10.
41 *Journals of the House of Commons* (London, 1803), 19:377.
42 John Carswell, *The South Sea Bubble*, rev. ed. (Washington, DC: Alan Sutton, 1993), chs. 12–14.

or resigned in disgrace, and many former directors had their estates confiscated and sold by the government, the proceeds of which went to assist those who had "suffered" from the scheme.[43] The men in charge of the Secret Committee have been labeled "Whiggish, yet anti-ministerial", which was certainly the case.[44] They specifically were selected because they had no qualms going after the Company or key figures involved in the scheme. It is a distinct possibility that certain members of the government knew exactly that Brodrick and his committee would do this, resulting in the final removal not only of the Company's directors but also of important members of the Stanhope-Sunderland faction, which had been in charge of the ministry since 1717 and which subsequently allowed the South Sea scheme to become law in early 1720. Such men included Sir Robert Walpole (currently serving as Paymaster of the Forces), who skillfully took advantage of the situation. Although Walpole tried to protect certain men involved in the scheme from prosecution, he emerged as the clear leader of the ministry and in April 1721 was appointed First Lord of the Treasury.[45]

In fact, Walpole had been working throughout late 1720 and early 1721 to come up with ways to save the Company and stabilize public credit. Walpole's rescue plans have been analyzed by many scholars, although most focus primarily on their economic rather than their political and ideological significance.[46] The main financial problem in need of solving was the fact that the South Sea scheme had been designed so that the Company would hold most of the nation's debts, as people swapped debt owed to them by the government for Company stock. Essentially, the directors had hoped that the Company would function not only as a bank but as the main bank that the government relied on for loans, eventually replacing the Bank of England.[47] Therefore Walpole and his allies, in trying to rescue the Company, also hoped to break the Company's "monopoly" on state debt. During the initial Parliamentary inquiry, it was revealed that the Company's debts totaled over £14 million.[48] Many of Walpole's proposals in late 1720 and early 1721 involved distributing this debt away from the South

---

43 James Craggs, Sr., died on 16 March and Craggs, Jr., died on 16 April. Dickson, *The Financial Revolution in England*, 171–176; Linda Colley, *In Defiance of Oligarchy: The Tory Party, 1714–60* (Cambridge: Cambridge University Press, 1982), 196.

44 Carswell, *The South Sea Bubble*, 182.

45 Julian Hoppit, *A Land of Liberty? England 1689–1727* (Oxford: Clarendon Press, 2000), 406–407.

46 Dickson, *The Financial Revolution in England*, chs. 7–8; Dale, *The First Crash*, ch. 8; Carswell, *The South Sea Bubble*, chs. 10–11, 13–14.

47 Kleer, "'The folly of particulars'."

48 Carswell, *The South Sea Bubble*, 203.

Sea Company to other entities such as the Bank of England and the East India Company. He first proposed this kind of plan in the autumn of 1720, which involved an "engraftment" of South Sea stock by the other two corporations.[49] In some notes, likely written by Walpole to the King, he argued that the involvement of the Bank and the East India Company was crucial because it would dilute rather than concentrate political and financial power in one entity. "The Publick has been & frequently must be obliged to apply to these Corporate Bodies for the support of Publick Credit", he argued, and "the Publick will not be under a necessity to accept the hard terms which one single powerfull body might be inclinable to impose, when all three are in a condition to aid & assist upon any emergency".[50]

Walpole's proposal faced plenty of resistance. A number of pamphlets described the plan as economically reckless and politically dangerous. Some feared that rather than breaking a monopoly, the act would create a "union" of the three companies, which one writer argued could become a strong political force and "Influence our Elections".[51] According to *Cato's Letters*, "the uniting the three great companies in one interest" would result in "the forming such a potent conspiracy against the whole kingdom".[52] Another writer expressed concern that the scheme would harm the other two companies by cutting into their profits, "for the Bank and East-India Company will not be able to make so great Dividends as now they do, [and] therefore Stock will be less in value".[53] Still another concluded that the engraftment plan, like the original scheme itself, was based on fraud. "Tho' by crafty Management, of *Broker's* false Reports (that the *South-Sea* Company gets much by this Bargain) Stocks may rise, it may decieve many and Encourage that Ruinous Trade of buying and selling Stocks for more then it's real Value".[54] Despite these warnings, the plan became law on 23 March 1721. However, the law only made the scheme legally possible; it did nothing to compel

49 Dickson, *The Financial Revolution in England*, 170–171; Dale, *The First Crash*, 146; Paul, *The South Sea Bubble*, 102–103.

50 "Some Thoughts & Considerations concerning the present Posture of the South Sea Stock humbly laid bare before his Majesty," c. late 1720/early 1721, in BL, Add. Ms. 74066, fols. 3v–4r.

51 *Now or Never: or, a Familiar Discourse Concerning the Two Schemes for Restoring National Credit* (London, 1721), 4.

52 Trenchard, *Cato's Letters*, no. 9, 31.12.1720, in *Cato's Letters*, 1:72.

53 *To The Right Honourable House of Lords: The Humble Petition of Merchants and Traders of Great Britain, and others interested in the Bank, East-India, or South-Sea Company, Sufferers by the Fall of Stock* (London, 1721).

54 *Reasons against Ingrafting the South-Sea Fund with the Bank and East India Company* (London, 1721), [2].

either the Bank of England or the East India Company to engraft any South Sea stock.[55]

After another engraftment scheme was pursued and abandoned that spring, Walpole and William Lowndes, the main secretary at the Treasury and one of Walpole's key allies in that department, came up with a new rescue plan that abandoned engraftment altogether. In July 1721, they introduced a proposal that forgave £7 million of the Company's debts to the government, canceled some of the Company's loans, and further assisted some subscribers who had purchased shares at high prices, particularly those who had held "irredeemable" debts from the government exchanged for Company stock.[56] It was strictly an arrangement between the Company, its investors, and the government. In the Commons, Walpole explained the necessity of the plan by stating (somewhat disingenuously) that, although at the start of the crisis the government "were of Opinion, That no Relief or Abatement could properly be prescribed, or given, but from the South Sea Company" itself, things had dramatically changed. "The Discontents of the People daily increasing", Walpole continued, "and the uncertain and doubtful Events that threatened very great and valuable Properties, creating such infinite Anxieties and Dissatisfaction, as had a most fatal and general influence upon all publick and private Credit, [therefore] the Interposition of Parliament became unavoidable".[57]

It is telling that Walpole's justification for this plan had to do with the "Discontents of the People", which was soon evident in the halls of the House of Commons. On the final day of debate (3 August 1721), "a Croud of People were got together, in a tumultuous and riotous Manner, in the Lobby, and Passages" of the Commons.[58] Among the protesters were "several Hundreds of the Proprietors of the Short Annuities, and other Redeemable Publick Debts, of Both Sexes, who in a rude and insolent Manner demanded Justice of the Members".[59] They presented a long petition detailing the "Unreasonableness" of the plan because it did nothing to relieve their sufferings but instead offered assistance to holders of the "irredeemable" debt only. They argued that the Parliamentary bail-out was unconstitutional because it "interrupt[ed] the common Course of the Laws" and

---

55 Dickson, *The Financial Revolution in England*, 171; Dickinson, *Walpole and the Whig Supremacy*, 61–62.

56 Carswell, *The South Sea Bubble*, 230–231; Dickson, *The Financial Revolution in England*, 176.

57 *Journals of the House of Commons*, 19:638–639.

58 *Journals of the House of Commons*, 19:643–644; Abel Boyer, *The Political State of Great Britain* (London, 1721), 22:158; Carswell, *The South Sea Bubble*, 233.

59 Boyer, *Political State*, 22:149. Thanks to François Velde for bringing this to my attention.

"open[ed] a wide gap in our constitution".[60] Justices of the Peace and their constables were called in "to go forthwith, and disperse the said riotous croud; and to take care to prevent the like Riots for the future", indicating a reading of the Riot Act.[61] The following day, the rescue plan passed the Commons and, unlike the previous plan, it was put into operation.[62]

It makes sense that the Riot Act was utilized as a tool of repression while Walpole attempted to get his bill passed. The Riot Act had become law in August 1715, in response to widespread protests that occurred in the wake of the Hanoverian Succession.[63] According to the law, an assembly of twelve or more people could be deemed a riot by local magistrates if the crowd refused to disperse after being read a portion of the act. It was significant because it made the act of assembly, rather than "outrages against persons or property", punishable.[64] The Riot Act was part of a broad platform implemented by the Whig government that in the words of historian J.M. Beattie was "designed to deal vigorously with disorder, including crime, if that posed a threat to the stability of the regime".[65] As historian Nicholas Rogers has shown, popular protest in the early eighteenth-century was often tinged with anti-Hanoverian (if not clearly Jacobite) sentiment, particularly when such protests involved economic concerns.[66] It is highly likely that the ministry perceived this particular protest not only to be dangerous to the proceedings in the Commons but also to be tinged with anti-Hanoverian sentiment. It could easily become outright Jacobitism as far as the government was concerned.

---

60 Boyer, *Political State*, 22:155.

61 *Journals of the House of Commons*, 19:643–644; Carswell, *The South Sea Bubble*, 233.

62 *Anno Regni Georgii Regis, An Act for making several Provisions to restore the Publick Credit, which suffers by the Frauds and Managements of the late Directors of the South-Sea Company, and others* (London, 1721).

63 Adrian Randall, *Riotous Assemblies: Popular Protest in Hanoverian England* (Oxford: Oxford University Press, 2006), 24–25. For details on the anti-Hanoverian riots in 1714–1715, see Nicholas Rogers, *Crowds, Culture, and Politics in Georgian Britain* (Oxford: Clarendon Press, 1998), ch. 1.

64 Randall, *Riotous Assemblies*, 26.

65 J.M. Beattie, *Policing and Punishment in London, 1660–1750* (Oxford: Oxford University Press, 2001), 429; Hoppit, *A Land of Liberty?*, 48–49; Rogers, *Whigs and Cities*, 29–31; Nicholas Rogers, "Popular Protest in Early Hanoverian London," *Past & Present* 79 (1978): 70–100, here 74–75.

66 Rogers, "Popular Protest," 72; Rogers, "Riot and Popular Jacobitism in Early Hanoverian England," in *Ideology and Conspiracy: Aspects and Jacobitism, 1689–1759*, ed. Eveline Cruickshanks (Edinburgh: John Donald Publishers, 1982), 70–88.

Exploiting the Fear of Jacobitism

The specter of Jacobitism once again emerged in 1722, in the wake of Parliamentary elections that spring. Some of the political implications of the South Sea Bubble and the government's responses to it had played out during the general election. Many expected that Tories and others disaffected from the Court party would unseat the Whig majority, or at least cause a major change in the ministry. Not surprisingly, a number of Tory and Jacobite tracts published in the lead-up to the election recalled the evils of the South Sea Bubble, blaming the Whigs who seemed to benefit from the scheme. Some went so far as to lay responsibility on George I and claimed the scheme was designed "not to discharge National Debts but to support Foreign Interests".[67] One Jacobite pamphlet maintained that "When the Stock began to Decline by the Knavery of the Directors, and the vast Sums Exported to Hannover", the King refused to return to England because he was busy using that money "Building a Magnificent Palace at *Herenhausen* [...] and either was kept Ignorant of our situation or did not think fit to come".[68] It, of course, did not help the King's cause that he and his mistresses had been involved in the scheme, having been allocated stock in early spring 1720.[69] Pamphleteers writing on behalf of the Whig ministry were quick to respond, one agreeing that the Bubble "had brought credit very low". This pamphlet continued that, although a Whig government had been behind the passage of the original South Sea bill in 1720, a different Whig ministry was now in charge, and it should not be blamed for the crisis: "Therefore it must be concluded highly unjust to stigmatize all those who are in the Administration of Publick Affairs, or all the *Whigs* in a Place, as Approvers and Encouragers of the Acceptance of the Scheme".[70]

Despite the efforts of those opposed to the ministry, it became apparent during the elections that a sweeping anti-ministerial victory was not likely. People took to the streets to protest the likelihood of another Whig government. From London, Anglo-Irish politician John Perceval noted that "The Mob which is generally High Church have where they are strongest been insufferably rude, as at Westminster, Reading, Stafford &c and never was a dead Parliamt so abused in Pamphlets & news papers". He also noted that such words of abuse "is all

67 *An Historical Account of the Advantages that have Accru'd to England by the Succession in the Illustrious House of Hanover* (London, 1722), 36; *The Second Part of the Advantages That have Accrued to England but Succession in the Illustrious House of Hanover* (London, 1721), 41.

68 *The Second and Last English Advice, to the Freehoulders of England* (London, 1722), 37.

69 Carswell, *The South Sea Bubble*, 104, 106.

70 *Advice and Considerations for the Electors of Great Britain* (London, 1722), 12, 15.

that Party have for it".[71] In other words, the anti-establishment faction did not seem to have any real cohesion or platform beyond the message that the current ministry was corrupt and that it ignored the needs of British people at the expense of European interests. This was not enough to secure an electoral victory, and Whigs managed to maintain their majority in 1722.[72]

It is important to remember that fears of Jacobitism continued to play a major role in British politics and in how people understood ideas about finance. It is therefore plausible that Whigs maintained their majority in part because the ministry had successfully exploited fears of Jacobitism in the wake of the South Sea Bubble by constantly reminding the public that those Tories and "country" Whigs who refused to assist the Company and shore up public credit were likely crypto-Jacobites. It was easy to paint those opposed to the ministry, like the protesters storming Parliament in 1721 or those noted by John Perceval, as a Jacobite mob. In fact, Whigs had successfully promoted the idea that Tories had incited violent anti-Hanoverian/Jacobite "mobs" since 1714.[73] This connection became easier to believe when the Atterbury Plot came to light in the weeks following the general election. According to a recent history of the plot, it initially was planned to take place during the election, "when the army had by law to be withdrawn from the constituencies and there was the greatest excitement on each side". The invasion was postponed, however, for a lack of adequate funding. Instead, the plotters planned to invade while the King was in Germany in late summer.[74] When the conspiracy became known, many assumed that the plotters were attempting to take "advantage of the general uneasyness occasioned by the fall of the South Sea".[75] There were reports that the conspirators planned to seize "the Tower, & having arm'd their accomplices there, to march streight to the Bank, South Sea & India Houses, whose Treasure being seiz'd would have enabled them to engage a greater multitude in pay".[76] Attacking such places was highly symbolic because they were the financial institutions that the Hanoverian state relied on so heavily. Since the accession of George I in 1714, many anti-Hanoverian protests had gathered at the Bank or the Stock Exchange because they

---

71 John Perceval to Charles Dering, London 27.3.1722, in BL, Add. Ms. 47029, fols. 110–111r; Cruickshanks and Erskine-Hill, *The Atterbury Plot*, 66.

72 Cruickshanks and Erskine-Hill, *The Atterbury Plot*, 89–90; Hoppit, *A Land of Liberty?*, 408; Dickinson, *Walpole and the Whig Supremacy*, 161.

73 Rogers, "Riot and Popular Jacobitism."

74 Cruickshanks and Erskine-Hill, *The Atterbury Plot*, 119–121.

75 John Perceval to Charles Dering, London 10.5.1722, in BL, Add. Ms. 47029, fols. 121v–122r.

76 John Perceval to his brother, London 2.6.1722, in BL, Add. Ms. 47029, fols. 124–125r; Cruickshanks and Erskine-Hill, *The Atterbury Plot*, 129.

were popularly understood as symbols of government corruption and the "moneyed interests".[77] Cracking down on potential unrest was therefore essential for the government while the invasion itself was still expected in the late summer or fall.

It was in this tense political atmosphere that the South Sea Company wrote to the King asking for further financial assistance in July 1722, as referenced at the start of this chapter. The request came after the finalization of one last rescue plan orchestrated by the Company and the Bank of England. Known as the "Bank Treaty", the proposal involved a direct transfer of capital from one entity to the other and allowed the South Sea Company to begin to pay its debts to the government. This had the effect of stabilizing its stock price for the first time in nearly two years.[78] Still, the Company's directors felt the need to request further financial allowances from the King. In doing so, they alluded to the fact that Jacobite plotters might have hoped that subscribers and directors of the South Sea Company were so dissatisfied with the government's rescue plans that they would have joined the Atterbury conspiracy. In addition to explaining to the King how mistaken these assumptions were, the directors provided an interesting explanation as to why they had remained loyal to George I and the Hanoverian Succession. The address continued:

> Your Majesty's sacred and Inviolable Regard to our Laws and Religion, makes it the Universal Duty of your whole People to Render your Government Easy, and to defend you against all Traiterous Conspiracies; But your strict and constant Regard to Publick Funds makes it more Immediately the Duty of those subjects whose Estates are Engaged in the Publick Funds, and particularly of this corporation, Interested in so great a share of the whole National Debts; And we should have been wanting to our Own Interest and preservation, as well as Duty to your Majesty, and our Country, if we had not taken first opportunity of convincing the World of the Folly and Weakness of their Expectations, who thought our Divisions proceeded from, or could be raised up to a Disaffection to your Majesty.[79]

The reasons stated for remaining loyal to the Hanoverian monarch are illuminating. In addition to invoking the usual language of laws, property, and religion, this address suggested that an important reason why the South Sea Company re-

---

77 See, for example, Petition of John Blackwell to the Treasury, 26.9.1716, in TNA, T 1/200, no. 33.

78 Dickson, *The Financial Revolution in England*, 179–180; South Sea Company Court of Directors meeting minutes, 7.6.1722, in BL, Add. Ms. 25544, 39–41; 19.6.1722, in BL, Add. Ms. 25544, 42–44; Peter Leheny to Robert Walpole, 15./26.6.1722, in BL, Add. Ms. 74066, no. 6.

79 South Sea Company general court meeting minutes, Address to George I, 20.7.1722, in BL, Add. Ms. 25544, 49–51.

mained loyal to George I was because of his assistance and "relief" of the Company when it was at its most vulnerable. Mentioning the King's "strict and constant Regard to Publick Funds" as a motive for the loyalty of the Company's directors, as well as all those "whose Estates are Engaged in the Publick Funds", demonstrated the intimate connections that existed between politics and finance, specifically the Hanoverian regime and its Whig allies and their support of the national debt and public credit. Despite the financial losses resulting from the Bubble, or any lingering dissatisfaction with the rescue plans, it was imperative to demonstrate loyalty to the Hanoverian regime. After all, only those who wished to undermine public credit and finance were the true Jacobites.

Conclusions

The South Sea Bubble exposed two major sources of anxiety for the Hanoverian regime: the perceived fragility of public finance that the state relied upon so heavily and the possibility of Jacobite unrest. The rescue plans revealed a strategy by Walpole and the ministry to not only calm financial markets (which included such outsized responses as the implementation of the Riot Act) but also to continue taking advantage of the longstanding ideological association of Tories with undermining public credit, violent protest, and ultimately Jacobitism.[80] The specters of Jacobitism and anti-Jacobitism, both real and imagined, remained ever-present in a variety of different social, political, and economic settings in the early eighteenth century.[81] The apparent chaos caused by the South Sea Bubble not only offered a potential opening for Jacobite conspirators; it also provided an opportunity for the Walpolean Whigs to, in turn, use the threat of Jacobitism to entrench themselves in power. They did this in a variety of ways, such as passing laws limiting elections and popular protests as well as successfully perpetuating the idea that public credit and finance were essential to the post-Revolutionary constitutional settlement and that those opposed to supporting them adequately were simply enemies of the state. The idea of the "moneyed man" might have remained a potent political construct, but the threat of Jacobitism and the possibility of undermining government finance and the constitution seemed to outweigh those concerns. In other words, Whigs seemed to win not

---

80 Hoppit, *Land of Liberty*, 389–392.

81 For other examples, see Hayden, "Of Windmills and Bubbles"; David Parrish, "A Party Contagion: Party Politics and the Inoculation Controversy in the British Atlantic World, c. 1721–1723," *Journal for Eighteenth-Century Studies* 39 (2016): 41–58.

only the political battle but also the rhetorical battle over who was the real threat to the nation.

Daniel Menning

The Economic Effect of the South Sea Bubble on the Baltic Sea Trade

Reflecting on the economic situation in London late in 1720, Peter Godfrey remarked in a letter to John Scattergood, then active as a country trader in the Indian Ocean: "We are now at a full stop in Trade."[1] Already a few weeks earlier, the president of the Swedish Commercial College, a government agency, had written to the country's ambassador Carl Sparre in the British capital:

> since [...] it may not be unknown to you, what scarcity of good and skillful manufacturers and artisans this Empire is laboring under, and, therefore, necessity demands that all means and solutions should be thought about, how such [i. e. manufacturers and artisans] can be recruited from foreign places, I have thought about, whether under the current circumstances in England some craftsmen could be found, which because of the current plight would be willing to move from there and settle preferably in this Empire.[2]

Further contemporary comments could be added attesting to the difficult economic conditions in London after the bursting of the South Sea Bubble. In addition, complaints of the scarcity of money, meaning specie, can be found in numerous letters from late 1720 and early 1721. While the stock market crash regularly was considered to be the cause for this want of coins, the lack of gold and silver also seemed to bring about economic problems, as a letter from the Directors of the East India Company to their staff in Madras in February 1721 evidences:

> When We took up in August last [1720] the large quantity of Shipping [...] it was upon the Prospect of our Trade being carry'd on with its usual currency, but some little time after that a General Stagnation of Credit overspread all these Parts of Europe. Holland France Spain & Italy as well as Britain have felt the sad Effects of it each Countrey affecting the others, insomuch that Bullion was not to be gotten thô We thought We had made a sufficient Provision for it.[3]

I would like to thank François Velde (Chicago) for reading and commenting on this chapter.

1 Peter Godfrey to John Scattergood, London 31.12.1720, in British Library (BL), Mss. Eur. 387/3, 91.

2 Magnus Julius Delagardie to Carl Sparre, Stockholm 15.11.1720, in Swedish National Archives, Diplomatica Anglica 254, unfol., 2–3.

3 General Letter to Fort St. George, London 24.2.1721, in BL, IOR/E/3/100, 520–521.

https://doi.org/10.1515/9783110592139-009

The East India Company directors, therefore, had to devise measures, which could keep their trade running and which would circumvent the lack of specie.

Surprisingly, however, and in contradiction to these statements, scholars of the history of finance and economic historians have claimed for the last decades that the bursting of the South Sea Bubble did not really impact the larger economy. Julian Hoppit, for example, emphasizes that British imports and exports hardly fell after the stock market crash and re-exports actually grew by 17 percent. At the same time excise data shows differing results – for some the revenues grew, for others they declined. He concludes: "neither trade nor industry was universally or dramatically upset by the chaos of the summer and autumn of 1720."[4] While the number of bankruptcies increased, Hoppit continues, the development was not particularly significant. The 87 petitions that reached the House of Commons in the spring of 1721 complaining of the detrimental economic effects of the bursting of the bubble should be thought of as a call to punish the Directors of the South Sea Company rather than as evidence of widespread economic dislocation, he opines. Though he does acknowledge that the market for international bills of exchange swung wildly during 1720, for Hoppit, this was only a matter of "high finance."[5] Helen J. Paul follows Hoppit's argument, suggesting that "if share-trading was mostly centered around the London area, it is not clear how the crash could have devastated the goods trade at the periphery."[6] She adds that "the incentives to overstate financial distress were clear."[7]

There may, however, be good reasons to maintain that the bursting of the South Sea Bubble caused significant economic difficulties. Part of this argument can be made by challenging the data used by Hoppit who looked at national statistics. As the economic effect of the post-speculation troubles may have been larger in London than in the rest of the country, his data possibly attenuates the dislocation in the capital. In addition, the British import and export statistics historians can use regularly started on Michaelmas of each year, i.e. 29 September. Thus, for example, what we look at for 1720 are actually imports from October 1719 to September 1720. Furthermore, taking into account the speed of sail and the seasonal freezing of harbors in New England and the mid-Atlantic colonies, British ships with their cargoes may have left ports there and in the West Indies before news of the crash in London reached overseas merchants. Thus,

4 Julian Hoppit, "The Myths of the South Sea Bubble," *Transactions of the Royal Historical Society* 12 (2002): 141–165, here 152–153.

5 Hoppit, "The Myths of the South Sea Bubble," 158.

6 Helen J. Paul, *The South Sea Bubble: An Economic History of Its Origins and Consequences* (London and New York: Routledge, 2011), 106.

7 Paul, *The South Sea Bubble*, 106.

economic effects may have been delayed. Finally, as Thomas S. Ashton in his book on economic fluctuations in England pointed out more than fifty years ago: "The bill drawn on the reputable London house [... was] the means by which transactions were settled not only between the provinces and the metropolis, but between one provincial area and another. It was through them that conditions of plenty or shortage at the center were transmitted to the periphery."[8] Trouble in the capital, thus, usually also had an impact elsewhere.

More specifically, though, to understand the ways in which the stock market crash could have had an effect on the economy at large in 1720, one needs to consider London merchants' usual behaviors in times of prosperity and crises. Again, following Ashton:

> When men were optimistic they tended to hold goods or securities, and cut down their holdings of ready money, relying on their ability to discount bills if they needed more cash. They would allow others to draw on them at dates far ahead, and might be willing to renew bills payable to themselves when these reached maturity.[9]

However, in times of crises, unsure whether one would be able to sell goods in the future at a decent or, preferably, even higher price (especially if they were perishable), merchants emptied their warehouses. If many did so at the same time, prices decreased significantly and losses resulted. At the same time, with economic dislocation on the horizon, merchants sought liquidity as a form of security against future contingencies. This had multiple effects. For one thing, it meant that the willingness to prolong bills and lend money decreased, since it was unclear whether debtors would be able to honor their debts in the future. For another, outstanding loans were called in and bills, if possible, cashed.[10] Restricting credit and hoarding specie, of course, meant that less trade could be conducted. The procedure had, however, dissimilar effects in the different regions with which London merchants traded. Partners in areas where Londoners' had a positive balance of trade, e. g. Pennsylvania, were asked to settle outstanding loans after a crash. Colonial dwellers, constantly faced with specie shortages,[11] sometimes tried to make up for their obligations by sending additional

8 Thomas S. Ashton, *Economic Fluctuations in England 1700–1800* (Oxford: Clarendon Press, 1959), 107.

9 Ashton, *Economic Fluctuations*, 108.

10 Ashton, *Economic Fluctuations*, 108–110.

11 There is a debate as to whether the North American colonies truly labored under a lack of specie. More recent research maintains that such a shortage existed. Roger W. Weiss, "The Issue of Paper Money in the American Colonies, 1720–1774," *Journal of Economic History* 30 (1970): 770–784; John R. Hanson, "Money in the Colonial American Economy: An Extension,"

goods – though these ran the risk of encountering a glutted market in the British capital. London merchants, looking for cash and not additional supplies in their warehouses, may have gotten rid of these goods at cheap prices quickly, explaining the growth of re-exports in 1721.[12] On the other hand, trading areas wherein London merchants had a negative balance of trade, e.g. the Baltic Sea, felt the effects of a crisis differently. Not willing to lose specie in order to settle trading accounts, British merchants could temporarily restrict their orders. Thus, the London merchants' preference for liquidity and willingness to lend had major impacts on the development of trade and, in extension, the public perception of an economic crisis. It is not, in this light, possible to read the effects of a crisis in a simple, straight-forward statistical manner. Instead, one has to pay attention to the ways in which different arenas of trade were affected by economic downturns and restrictions of credit.

While the dynamics of areas with a positive balance of trade can be traced in a qualitative fashion using merchants' letters combined with a variety of other material, those in areas of trade deficits are examined more easily using serial data – especially if it has not been aggregated annually. One such source is the Sound Toll Registers. During the early modern period, any ship passing through the strait between Denmark and Sweden had to pay the Sound Toll to the Danish king. To collect it, all ships were stopped by Danish officials, who recorded the name, origin and destination, date of passage through the Sound, and cargo of the vessel. The files emanating from the Sound Toll were preserved, recently have been digitized, and now are available online. This chapter uses this data to search for effects of the South Sea Bubble on the development of the British Baltic Sea trade. To do this, it first considers the importance and structure of the trade for the British economy as well as the political situation in the trading region. Afterwards it looks at the development of the mercantile exchange between 1713 and 1727 so as to consider the bubble year 1720 and the post-crash phase within its broader context and thereby judge the effects of the failed speculation and the duration of signs of economic crisis on the larger economy.

Economic Inquiry 17 (1979): 281–286; Peter L. Rousseau, "Backing the Quantity Theory, and the Transition to the US Dollar, 1723–1850," *AEA Papers and Proceedings* 97 (2007): 266–270.

12 I am currently working on an article on the economic effects of the South Sea Bubble in Pennsylvania, which will spell out these problems in more detail.

Britain and the Baltic Sea Trade

Looking at trade between Great Britain and the Baltic Sea, one captures a significant share of overall British foreign trade in the early 1700s. Accounting for roughly £530,000 annually in the first decade of the eighteenth century it made up about 12 percent of imports. Though the overall volume grew to a yearly average of £660,000 over the next decade, the relative amount decreased to 10 percent of all British imports. The main reason for this was that the shipment of goods from Asia and the West Indies simply grew at a quicker pace. Nevertheless, the Baltic trade remained economically important. This was not only true for Britain itself but also for countries like Russia and Sweden. After the Dutch, British merchants were the most important group trading to the Baltic and their relative share was increasing during the eighteenth century.[13] While the Eastland Company had a monopoly on commercial interchange with parts of the region until the second third of the seventeenth century, the trade mostly was laid open by 1672, when the entrance fee to the Company was reduced to a nominal amount of 40 shillings.[14] The same applied to the Russia Company, which reduced its entrance fee to £5 and admitted new merchants by 1699, basically opening up trade within its monopolized area as well.[15] The importance of St. Petersburg (founded in 1703) for British ships grew quickly during the eighteenth century, with British merchants also regularly trading in Danzig, Stockholm and Riga. Ships also visited numerous other ports along the coastline, albeit less frequently. As a subgroup within the London Baltic trading community, merchants of German origins naturalized as British citizens played an important role.[16]

On their outbound trips, British ships usually took colonial and East India goods to the Baltic. The most important return freights were iron and copper, especially from Sweden, as well as wood and its products, like pitch, tar and turpentine. In addition, hemp and flax were carried on homebound journeys. These 'naval stores' all were especially important for the British shipping industry and

13 Michael North, *Geschichte der Ostsee: Handel und Kulturen* (München: C.H. Beck, 2011), 149–153, 180–187; J.A. Faber, "Structural Changes in the European Economy During the Eighteenth Century as Reflected in the Baltic Trade," in *From Dunkirk to Danzig: Shipping and Trade in the North Sea and the Baltic, 1350–1850*, ed. W.G. Heeres et al. (Hilversum: Verloren, 1988), 83–94.
14 Adam Anderson, *An Historical and Chronological Deduction of the Origins of Commerce* (London 1787), 2:521–522.
15 Margrit Schulte Beerbühl, *Deutsche Kaufleute in London: Welthandel und Einbürgerung (1660–1818)* (München: Oldenbourg, 2007), 127.
16 Schulte Beerbühl, *Deutsche Kaufleute*, 218–306.

the Royal Navy. There had been recurrent attempts to cultivate/produce these commodities in the British North American colonies since the 1600s. One way to encourage production was through bounties, which the House of Commons introduced in the early eighteenth century and debated again in the very spring of 1720.[17] While these resulted in increased imports from the colonies, the quality of products originating from the Baltic Sea countries was deemed far superior, and the Royal Navy preferred to use the latter.[18]

A second way to encourage the colonial production of naval stores, already proposed in 1704, appeared to be the chartering of joint-stock companies. It was claimed that such, due to their larger capital base, would be able to hire specialists who's presence would encourage an increase of not only the quantity but also the quality of colonial naval stores, especially tar.[19] The idea resurfaced in 1720, when investors were asked to subscribe to companies for "importing naval stores from Nova Scotia and Virginia", "for pitch and tar, from America and Scotland" or "for hemp and flax from Pennsylvania".[20] In the short run, however, nothing came of these initiatives.

One of the main reasons for these attempts to supplement colonial for north-eastern European goods was the adverse payments balance that the purchases of naval stores created for the overall British Baltic Sea trade. A 1716 balance sheet, for example, showed that exports to the value of £262,865 stood against imports of £511,760. With regard to Denmark and Norway, the deficit amounted to roughly £15,000. From the East Countries, or the modern-day Baltic States and Polish coastline, £38,000 more were imported than exported, whereas these digits increased for Russia to £84,000 and Sweden to £112,000.[21] British merchants usu-

---

17 *Journals of the House of Commons* (London 1803), 19:281–359, passim.

18 Julian Hoppit, *Britain's Political Economies: Parliament and Economic Life, 1660–1800* (Cambridge: Cambridge University Press, 2017), 249–276; Schulte Beerbühl, *Deutsche Kaufleute*, 221–226; Sven-Erik Åsträm, "English Timber Imports from Northern Europe in the Eighteenth Century," *Scandinavian Economic History Review* 18 (1970): 57–71; Joseph J. Malone, *Pine Trees and Politics: The Naval Stores and Forest Policy in Colonial New England 1691–1775* (Seattle: University of Washington Press, 1964), 24, 28–46; Sinclair Snow, "Naval Stores in Colonial Virginia," *Virginia Magazine of History and Biography* 72 (1964): 75–93; Justin Williams' "English Mercantilism and Carolina Naval Stores, 1705–1776," *Journal of Southern History* 1 (1935): 169–185.

19 Malone, *Pine Trees and Politics*, 24, 28–46.

20 *The South Sea Bubble and the numerous fraudulent projects to which it gave rise in 1720 [...]* (London, 1825), 78. One Pennsylvania company already possessed land in the colony. James Logan to Simon Clement, Philadelphia 25.11.1721, in Historical Society of Philadelphia, Logan Family Papers, Coll. 379, Vol. 10, 231.

21 Adam Anderson, *An Historical and Chronological Deduction of the Origins of Commerce* (London, 1801), 3:70.

ally paid for the difference in value between imports and exports by drawing on their colleagues in the United Provinces – the latter having a positive balance of trade with the merchants along these eastern shores.[22] Thus, from a British perspective, trade with the Baltic Sea usually required the availability of a certain amount of either cash in London or claims on such in the hands of Dutch correspondents who then could transfer it east via bills of exchange.

Finally, one needs to keep in mind that, during the time of the South Sea Bubble, the Great Northern War was fought out in the Baltic Sea region. Since 1700, Sweden had been trying to retain its hegemonic position in the east. It was opposed by changing coalitions that included Russia, Poland-Saxony, Denmark and Prussia. These were joined by King George I, acting in his role as elector of Hanover in 1714, with Great Britain only formally entering the conflict in 1717. The war had been going badly for Sweden since its defeat at Poltava in 1709. Most of its overseas possessions were captured by enemies. Yet, after the death of Charles XII of Sweden during the winter campaign to Norway in 1718, Britain and Hanover switched sides. Contemporary British politicians hoped to shift the balance of power back in Sweden's favor, because Czar Peter's Russia appeared to be growing too powerful and capable of achieving a hegemonic position in the Baltic, especially with regard to naval stores. British support for Sweden took the form of sending a fleet to the Baltic and of attempting to form a pro-Swedish coalition. Meanwhile, Czar Peter's troops used small boats in 1719 and 1720 to ravage and plunder the Swedish coast around Stockholm and to the north. Sweden's Navy and troops proved incapable to stop these attacks, and the British fleet was partially unwilling and partially unable to engage with Russian ships, because the water in the Gulf of Bothnia was too shallow for larger British ships.[23]

---

22 Artur Attman, "The Bullion Flow from the Netherlands to the Baltic and the Arctic," in *The Interactions of Amsterdam and Antwerp with the Baltic Region, 1400–1800*, ed. Johanna Maria van Winter (Leiden: Nijhoff, 1983), 19–21; Jennifer Newman, "Anglo-Dutch Commercial Cooperation and the Russia Trade in the Eighteenth Century," in *The Interactions of Amsterdam and Antwerp with the Baltic Region, 1400–1800*, ed. Johanna Maria van Winter (Leiden: Nijhoff, 1983), 95–103; Schulte Beerbühl, *Deutsche Kaufleute*, 223–224.

23 Eckardt Opitz, "Vielerlei Ursachen, eindeutige Ergebnisse: Das Ringen um die Vormacht im Ostseeraum im Großen Nordischen Krieg 1700 bis 1721," in *Wie Kriege entstehen: Zum historischen Hintergrund von Staatenkonflikten*, ed. Bernd Wegner (Paderborn: Schöningh, 2000), 89–107; David Denis Aldridge, *Admiral Sir John Norris and the British Expeditions to the Baltic Sea 1715–1727* (Lund: Nordic Academic Press, 2009); Walther Mediger, *Mecklenburg, Rußland und England-Hannover, 1706–1721*, 2 vols. (Hildesheim: Lax, 1967); James Frederick Chance, *George I and the Northern War: A Study of British-Hanoverian Policy in the North of Europe in the Years 1709–1721* (London: Smith, Elder, and Company, 1909); James R. Moulton, *Peter the*

The war, however, did not seriously interfere with trade. There were intermittent clashes between the Swedish and the Russian Navy, the latter usually winning the engagements during the last years of the war. In addition, King Charles XII of Sweden sent out privateers to capture enemy ships.[24] But the British government, as long as it officially was fighting Sweden, simply formed convoys that were protected by the Royal Navy. Such arrangements, of course, had an influence on the rhythm of British ships sailing into and out of the Baltic Sea, but it, again, does not seem to have depressed the trade in general. Also, once George I switched sides, Czar Peter officially proclaimed that British ships still would be welcome in Russian-controlled ports, as he did not want to lose the business. He also announced that he would not hinder British merchant ships from going to Sweden, so long as they did not carry goods that could be used in the military conflict.[25] David Aldridge, who has studied the role of the British fleets in the Baltic Sea in the 1710s and 1720s extensively, concludes that, in 1720/21, regional military engagements had no influence on trade from England, Scotland and Wales.[26]

Thus, overall the Baltic trade was an important branch for British merchants, albeit one that showed a heavy deficit that had to be made good by either sending specie or drawing bills, usually on Amsterdam merchants. Its volume also was not significantly impeded by political events around 1720, though the rhythms of ship sailings sometimes were impacted.

Great and the Russian Military Campaigns During the Final Years of the Great Northern War, 1719–1721 (Lanham: University Press of America, 2005); Lucjan R. Lewitter, "Poland, Russia and the Treaty of Vienna of 5 January 1719," *Historical Journal* 13 (1970): 3–30; Jeremy Black, *Continental Commitment: Britain, Hanover and Interventionism 1714–1793* (London and New York: Routledge 2005), 48–59.

24 Lars Ericson, "Economic Warfare or Piracy? Swedish Privateering Against British and Dutch Trade in the Baltic During the Great Northern War 1710–1721," in *Britain and the Baltic: Studies in Commercial, Political and Cultural Relations 1550–2000*, ed. Tony Barron and Patrick Salmon (Sunderland: University of Sunderland Press, 2003), 111–118.

25 Moulton, *Peter the Great*, 42, 53, 64, 84–85.

26 David Aldridge, "English East Coast Trade with the Baltic in the Closing Years of the Great Northern War 1714–1721," in *Britain and the Baltic: Studies in Commercial, Political and Cultural Relations 1550–2000*, ed. Tony Barron and Patrick Salmon (Sunderland: University of Sunderland Press, 2003), 119–129.

Baltic Sea Trade and the 1720 Bubble

So how did the British trade to the Baltic Sea develop during and after the South Sea Bubble, as exemplified in the data provided by the Sound Toll registers? The figures gathered by Danish officials can be analyzed in a number of ways, zooming in from the general European level to focus on the specific development of trade to and from London, the center of share trading in England, as well as comparing London commerce to that of other major European ports. Seasonal developments also can be taken into account and will provide further insights into the economic situation in London in 1720/21. Finally, the economic effects of the bubble can be seen within the longer-term trajectory of the Baltic Sea trade – allowing estimates as to the duration of any economic dislocations.

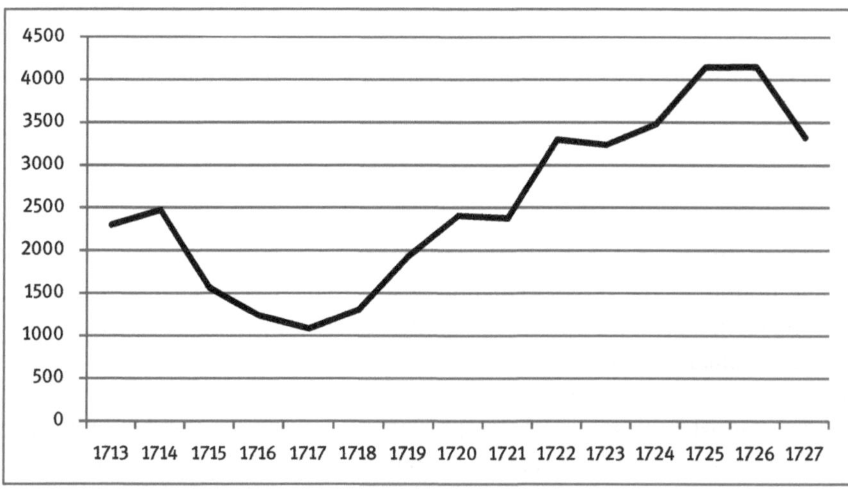

Graph 1: Absolute number of ships passing through the Sound (1713–1727). Analysis of the data provided by Sound Toll Registers Online: http://www.soundtoll.nl/index.php/en/, last visit 4.6.2014.

As the joint-stock euphoria in 1719/20 was a pan-European phenomenon with hyper-speculation and crashes in other parts of the continent besides London, the general development of the Baltic Sea trade provides a good point to start looking at the effects of the stock market frenzy on other parts of the economy. One can see the expansive volume of the overall Baltic Sea trade across the fifteen years covered by Graph 1. Looking closer for effects that the bursting of speculative bubbles may have caused, it is conspicuous that voyages to and from the eastern shores through the Sound steadily increased between 1717

Graph 2: Ship voyages passing through the Sound to and from London (1713–1727). Analysis of the data provided by Sound Toll Registers Online: http://www.soundtoll.nl/index.php/en/, last visit 4.6.2014.

and 1720. The following year saw a small dip, with 26 ships or a drop of slightly more than one percent, but this does not suggest any serious pan-European economic trouble in the post-speculation year. Although, considering that traffic grew again in 1722, there may still be a more significant impact of the bubble hidden in the small decrease. Thus, one cannot discern signs of a serious economic downturn in the general Baltic Sea trade from Graph 1.

In contrast to this general development, one can see a marked difference when focusing on trips through the Sound to and from London (Graph 2). First, the number of passages catalogued by Danish toll officials that named the British capital as their port of origin or destination went down by almost 50 percent in 1721 as compared to the previous year. The files provide data for 187 ships in 1719 and 193 bottoms in 1720; but the number of vessels coming from or sailing to London went down to 105 in 1721. The capital was the most important British harbor for trade with the Baltic, but, even when we exclude London and consider the rest of England and Wales, the picture is quite similar. In 1720, Danish officials counted 214 of such voyages, while in the subsequent year there were only 120. These numbers certainly provide evidence of a serious strain in London's, England's and Wales's Baltic Sea trade during the post-bubble year. At the same time, the longer perspective indicates that this was a short and abrupt aberration – not a general trend – as numbers increased again for London by 1722 and grew by more than 75 percent until 1726. England (excluding

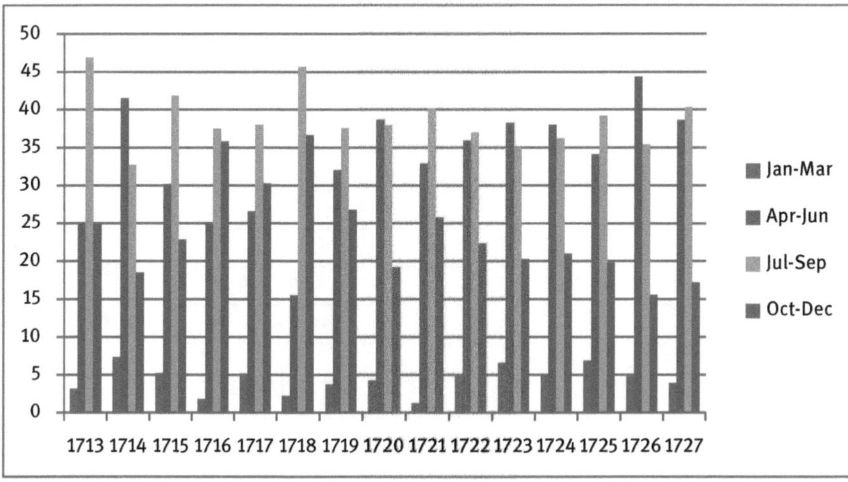

Graph 3: Seasonal development of the overall Baltic Sea trade in percentage (1713–1727). Analysis of the data provided by Sound Toll Registers Online: http://www.soundtoll.nl/index.php/en/, last visit 4.6.2014.

London) and Wales also saw this upward tendency, with 309 voyages by 1722, though their trade was growing differently from the capital's. Thus, the data for these areas does indicate that the bursting of the South Sea Bubble may have had serious economic consequences on the economy at large.

Zooming in on the situation in 1720 and 1721, it also is important to consider the seasonal ebbs and flows of the overall Baltic Sea trade. The weather and especially the freezing of parts of the waters east to the Sound had a large influence on the rhythms of trade. The number of voyages in different months, therefore, fluctuated markedly over the years. Yet, looking at the overall data in Graph 3, the relative number of ships passing through the Sound does not show particularly unusual variations for 1720 or 1721. Therefore, no bad weather conditions or sea ice at unusual times seem to have influenced shipping in general. Keeping in mind that the weather most likely was not a serious influence in the bubble and the post-crash years, the more specific analysis of the London trade in 1720 and 1721 is quite revealing.

As London was the center of the British economy and the most important port for the English Baltic Sea trade, any post-crash economic crisis must have had the strongest impact there. This chapter thus now will focus on the British capital (Graph 4). Considering seasonal voyages from London to the Baltic, relative numbers were significantly above average during the second quarter (April to June) of 1720. During the years considered in this paper (1713–1727),

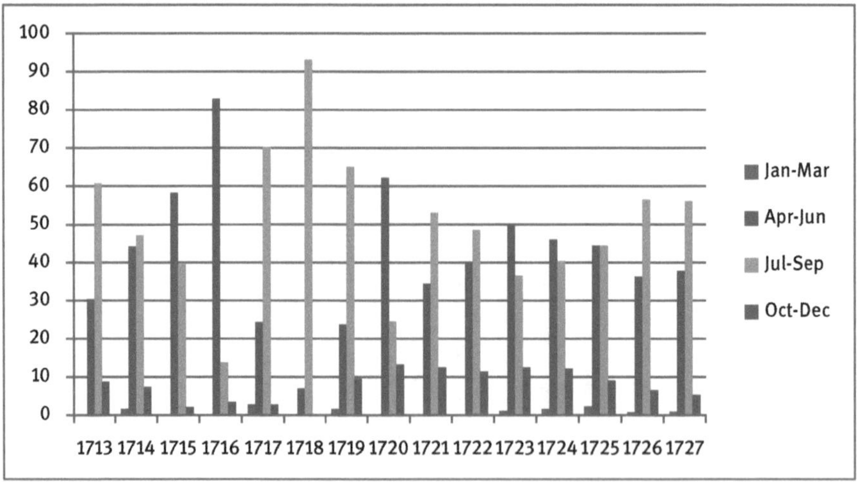

Graph 4: Seasonal development of ships going from London to the Baltic Sea in percentage (1713–1727). Analysis of the data provided by Sound Toll Registers Online: http://www.soundtoll.nl/index.php/en/, last visit 4. 6. 2014.

they were only higher in 1716 and slightly lower in 1715. These, however, were unusual years as, due to Swedish privateers, British ships travelled to the Baltic in convoys. This caused unusual concentrations of movements on particular days. Taking this abnormality into account, early 1720 appears to have been an exceptionally strong season for shipping to the countries east of the Sound. On the other hand, the number of voyages in the third quarter (July to September) of the South Sea Bubble year is particularly low – again, with the exception of the convoy year 1716. If one keeps in mind that ships needed some time to sail from the British capital to the Sound, the data, thus, suggests that merchants and captains in London tried to get their vessels at sea early in the bubble year. Thus, as stock prices were rising, the overall economic climate in London seems to have been favorable as well. During the speculative climax over the summer, however, numbers were much lower. Of course, ships that had left earlier in the year could not leave again. But it is noteworthy that the decline in voyages evident in the Danish officials' documents also coincides with complaints of critics of the joint-stock boom, who lamented a decline of economic activity more generally due to the share trade in the summer of 1720. For example, a London correspondent of the Dutch *Mercure historique et politique* reported in July 1720:

> Moreover it is to be noted that trade has completely slowed down, that more than one hundred ships moored along the river Thames are for sale, and that owners of capital prefer to

> speculate on shares than to work at their normal business. The consequence of all this could be very prejudicial to the nation, all the more so if foreigners sell as many shares as possible and send their profits out of the kingdom in specie.[27]

Complaints like these, thus, may not only have resulted from a specific kind of criticism of stock market speculation. Rather, the Sound Toll Registers suggests that they were based on facts.

Compared to 1720, developments in the post-bubble year were exactly opposite. The relative number of ships sailing from London to the Baltic was quite small between January and June, again it was mostly convoys that caused lower numbers. On the other hand, over the next three-month period, noticeably higher digits are evident – though of course the absolute number was much lower than in the previous year, as shown above in Graph 2. While the seasonal variation in 1721 is not as exceptional as in 1720, keeping in mind that the absolute number of ships passing through the Sound in the first half of 1721 was particularly low, the London data does provide hints at economic troubles in London that persisted into the post-bubble year. In fact, it looks like many London merchants and captains early in 1721 were still unsure how trade would develop. Instead of taking chances, they hesitated and acted according to Ashton's description. For a region like the Baltic Sea, which was burdened by a trade deficit, this meant restricting commercial exchange, since it had a negative impact on liquid assets, i.e. specie.

Only towards the summer did prospects for trade again look brighter, and ships were sent to the Baltic Sea in a rush, before winter arrived. Newspaper reports provide more general confirmation for this interpretation. For example, shortly before Christmas 1721, *The American Weekly Mercury* reprinted an article from London dated 9 September that stated:

> We now see with Pleasure, that the Custom House Bills of Entry of Goods imported and exported which are published daily in Print, begin to encrease considerably, particularly with respect to the Exports of our Woolen Manufacture, great Quantities whereof are shipped for Portugal, Italy and Russia but especially to Spain. People flatter themselves, that when Credit is a little better revived, Trade will consequently flourish.[28]

With regard to credit, London merchants' behavior in late 1720 and 1721 thus seems to have complied with usual proceedings during times of crises, as described in the introduction of this chapter.

---

27 Cited after Antoin E. Murphy, *Richard Cantillon: Entrepreneur and Economist* (Oxford: Clarendon Press, 1986), 170.

28 *The American Weekly Mercury*, 19.12.1721.

Calling in outstanding loans and searching for liquidity may not only have resulted from a general economic downturn after the crash, but it could have been a matter of necessity for many of London's Baltic Sea merchants as well. We will, of course, never know how many of them entered the hectic trade with shares of the South Sea Company in 1720. But the London Germans, who were important to the English Baltic trade, certainly were involved in share transactions around 1720 more generally, as Margrit Schulte Beerbühl has shown.[29] In addition, the ledgers of the Bank of England provide evidence that London merchants were the most active speculators in Bank shares in 1720 and most likely suffered heavy losses from such engagements, though we do not know how many of these 'merchants' also traded with countries bordering the Baltic Sea.[30] Nevertheless, as with trade more generally, speculators difficulties eased somewhat towards the fall of 1721 as well. This reading is supported by the observations of the Saxon-Polish ambassador Jacques LeCoq in the fall of 1721, who reported to his king:

> Since parliament has made its arrangements, everyone now has a clearer impression of his personal financial circumstances. People have also had time to see clearer into the circumstances of others. The necessity which one feels for one another in trade has the effect that people begin to stir a bit again. This leads to a return of trust and credit so that in a country full of resources as this, one cannot doubt that trade will soon return to its normal pace again.[31]

Thus, the parliamentary reorganization of the South Sea Company in the late summer 1721 appears to have engendered trust and facilitated the revival of trade – something that is evident in data on the Baltic Sea trade.

Movements of ships in the other direction (Graph 5), namely past the Danish officials to the British capital, do not show any marked variations for 1720. The more unusual ones are the convoy years of 1716 and 1718. The post-crash year 1721 also followed a fairly usual trajectory during the first two quarters of the year. The third quarter, however, was much weaker, again leaving the convoy years aside. The most likely explanation for this deviation is that ships which had not left Britain early in the year could, of course, neither return timely. As

29 Schulte Beerbühl, *Deutsche Kaufleute*, 128 – 140.

30 Ann M. Carlos and Larry Neal, "The Micro-Foundations of the Early London Capital Market: Bank of England Shareholders During and After the South Sea Bubble, 1720 – 25," *Economic History Review* 59 (2006): 498 – 538, here 519.

31 Report of ambassador Jacques LeCoq to king August II, London n.d. [fall 1721], in Hauptstaatsarchiv Dresden, 10026, Geheimes Kabinett, Loc 2674 – 11, 27.

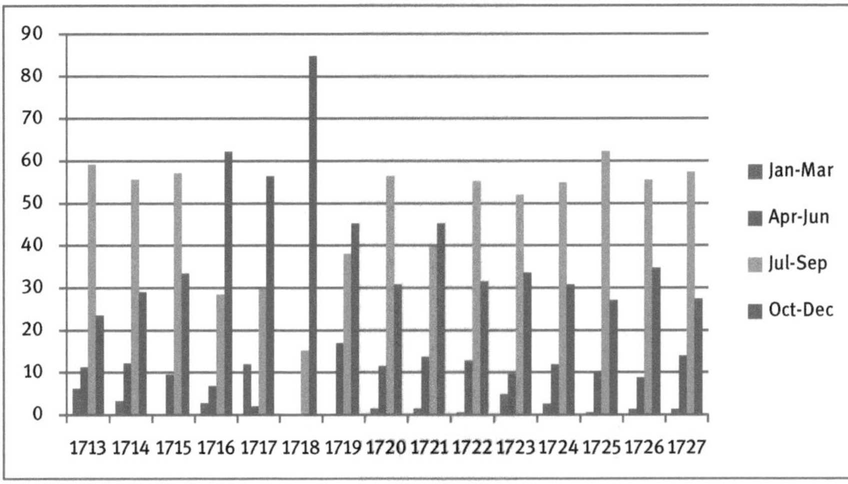

Graph 5: Seasonal development of ships going to London from the Baltic Sea in percentage (1713–1727). Analysis of the data provided by Sound Toll Registers Online: http://www.soundtoll.nl/index.php/en/, last visit 4.6.2014.

many ships left London fairly late, they only returned between October and December 1721, making it a very strong quarter, disregarding convoy years.

Thus, the data for London indicates firstly that, following the bursting of the South Sea Bubble, the number of ships plying the sea between London and the Baltic decreased significantly and secondly that ships' voyages were spread unevenly over the two years, with an early start concomittant to the rise of share prices in 1720 and a late start after the crash. Only in the summer of 1721 did the Baltic Sea trade in London revive.

The assumption that the bursting of the stock market bubble caused variations in the London data receives further support when looking at Sound passages to and from other major European ports (Graph 6).[32] Amsterdam's trade in 1721 showed an increase of almost 20 percent compared to 1720. The Dutch city's share of the Baltic Sea trade thereby grew from 35 to 42 percent (838 to 999 voyages). Even though it, too, had been a center of share speculation in 1720, this may indicate that the Dutch economy was less severely hit by the post-bubble crisis, as Oscar Gelderblom and Joost Jonker have claimed.[33] Though considering

32 Due to the war, St. Petersburg and Stockholm are not taken into account here.

33 Oscar Gelderblom and Joost Jonker, "Mirroring Different Follies: The Character of the 1720 Bubble in the Dutch Republic," in *The Great Mirror of Folly: Finance, Culture, and the Crash of 1720*, ed. William N. Goetzmann et al. (New Haven: Yale University Press, 2013), 121–139.

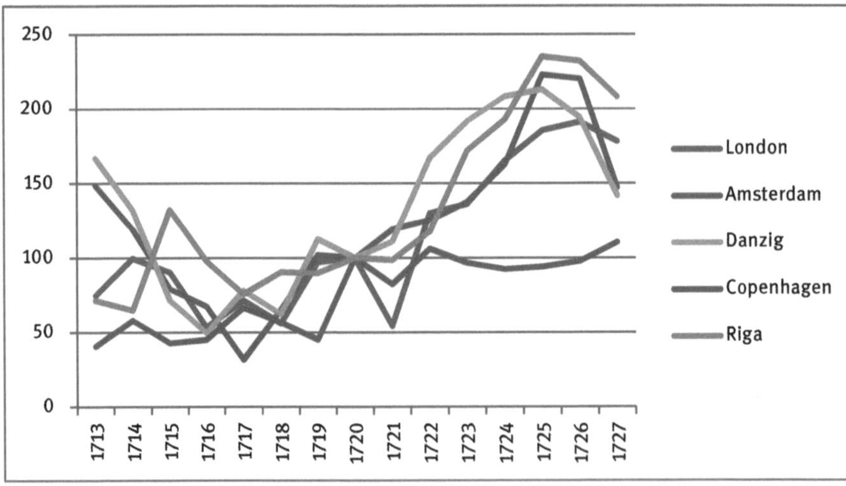

Graph 6: Sound passages to and from major ports in percent (1713–1727, 1720 = 100%). Analysis of the data provided by Sound Toll Registers Online: http://www.soundtoll.nl/index.php/en/, last visit 4.6.2014.

that Dutch merchants had a positive balance of trade with the Baltic Sea region and, therefore, could expect specie from that commercial exchange, whereas Britain faced a negative balance and had to make up for it in bills or precious metals, the differing effect of the events in 1720 on the two nations' trades certainly needs more investigation. The number of voyages to and from Danzig also grew in 1721, though not as much. Riga showed a small decrease and Copenhagen a larger one, while the number of voyages to and from London, as already discussed, fell significantly, although it had been moving parallel to Danzig and Amsterdam over the previous years. London voyages did catch up with Amsterdam again in 1722, when they also returned to a synchronous development with Riga and Danzig. The comparison thus provides further evidence for a serious dislocation in the British capital's Baltic Sea trade after the bursting of the South Sea Bubble. The data, however, also testifies to the brevity of this dislocation.

One final factor for the striking London development in 1721 can be ruled out as well. Russian troops had ravaged the Swedish shores in 1719 and 1720, destroying coastal villages and iron production facilities as well as sinking stocks of bar iron. One might thus assume that the war caused the decrease in the British capital's trade. Yet, the import and export statistics show that not only the trade to Sweden was affected by the downturn. It is true, imports from the Nordic country fell by 20 percent between 1720 and 1721; but, at the same time, numbers for Russia went down by 18 percent. From the East Countries, imports again decreased by 20 percent. Compared to this, exports of English merchandize east to Russia and the East Countries were up 24 and 7 percent respectively when compared to 1720, perhaps signifying attempts to avoid a negative balance outstanding at the conclusion of the trading season. On the export side, only those to Sweden fell by 13.5 percent.[34] While this could have been a result of the war, comparing London and Amsterdam is again instructive. The number of ships travelling from the Swedish kingdom and Finland to the Dutch emporium went down 12 percent between 1720 and 1721. Yet, for London, the overall number of voyages decreased from 67 to 26 – a 62 percent decline. In the opposite direction – to Sweden and Finland – the number of ships sailing from Amsterdam increased by 8 percent and fell by 59 percent for those departing from London.[35] This again underlines that the Great Northern War most likely was not the cause of the poor performance of London's Baltic Sea trade in 1721. Rather, the effects of the stock market crash seriously influenced London's trade.

Conclusion

Was there an economic crisis following the bursting of the South Sea Bubble? While researchers over the past two decades frequently have denied the impact of this event beyond 'high finance', data on the Baltic Sea trade from England and Wales, and more particularly London, provides evidence to the contrary. It shows that the number of voyages to the east declined significantly – by almost 50 percent – between 1720 and 1721. As the Great Northern War can be ruled out as a causal factor, there is, thus, good evidence that the slowdown of the Baltic Sea trade in the British capital was due to the stock market crash. In addition, the decline in the volume of trade possibly already began during the later summer of the bubble year. Following the stock market crash, merchants also did not send early ships to the Baltic in 1721. The number of bottoms sailing only picked up in the second half of the post-bubble year. Therefore, the Baltic trade seems to have suffered mostly between the summers of 1720 and 1721. Considering that this was a major branch of the British commercial exchange, it is hard to believe that its significant slowdown had no parallel in other arenas of trade and no effects on businesses and workers in London/Eng-

34 This data calculated from the Ledgers of Imports and Exports for 1720/21, in The National Archive, CUST 3/21–22.

35 Calculated from the data of the Sound Toll Registers Online: http://www.soundtoll.nl/index.php/en/, last visit 4.6.2014.

land more generally. Overall, however, this slowdown was short and abrupt. The Baltic Sea trade quickly returned to its trend line in 1722, and the reorganization of the South Sea Company most likely was the cause for this revival of trade and credit.

Finally, the development of the British Baltic Sea trade is in stark contrast to other parts of Europe – especially Amsterdam, which actually saw its business with the eastern shores increase in 1721. While this may be due to the Dutch economy being less affected by the speculation crises of 1720, the particular balance of trade that both countries had with the Baltic region may be another explanation for the difference. For British merchants, the trade to the east created a deficit as, value-wise, more was imported than exported. This meant that merchants had to pay the difference either with specie or bills, usually drawn on Amsterdam. As both money and good bills were precious in times of crisis, merchants in London probably were reluctant to part with either after the crash. Dutch traders, on the other hand, expected money inflows from their trading in the Baltic Sea, as the States General had a positive balance of trade with the countries of northeastern Europe. Thus, increasing the trade east could have helped alleviate any distress experienced after the bursting of the Dutch bubbles in late 1720, whereas for Britain it threatened increasing economic difficulties.

Amy M. Froide

The Long Shadow of the South Sea Bubble: Memory, Financial Crisis, and the Charitable Corporation Scandal of 1732

It is the early eighteenth century and the shareholders of a popular joint-stock company are clamoring for redress. They have woken up one day to find their money and profits gone, and they are blaming the directors of the company for their greed. News of fraudulent practices, a company employee who has absconded with the company's books, and the possible involvement of government ministers will soon leak out. The public will demand that the government bail out the shareholders and punish the directors by confiscating their personal estates. What is the year and the financial crisis? If you guessed 1720 and the South Sea Bubble, you would be wrong. It is 1732 and the scandal of the day involves the Charitable Corporation.

Although the South Sea Bubble was one of the most infamous and well-documented financial collapses, it was not unique or one of a kind in the heady early decades of the stock market. The South Sea Bubble was neither the first nor the last example of the excesses of the Financial Revolution. Nevertheless, for Britons its shadow lingered, and its memory was evoked when further financial meltdowns occurred. The South Sea Bubble became an important point of reference for financial crises. A mere twelve years later, contemporaries evoked the Bubble as a way to understand and contextualize the collapse of the Charitable Corporation in 1732. Just over a decade after the South Sea Bubble, history seemed to repeat itself with the financial failure of another joint-stock company, shareholders blaming fraudulent directors, and demands for government redress. Although the two financial crises shared many similarities, there were also some important differences. This chapter will examine the Charitable Corporation scandal of 1732, and how the ways in which contemporaries perceived the situation were very much influenced by their memory of the South Sea Bubble.

To begin with, some of the financial crises of the first few decades of the Financial Revolution, well before the South Sea Bubble, will be discussed so as to provide some context for this particular financial crisis, and tease out recurrent themes. From here, the discussion will move on to an explication of the financial scandal most linked and compared to the South Sea Bubble, the Charitable Corporation scandal of 1732. Finally, a comparison of these two financial scandals will reveal some common elements: blaming the directors of the companies, cre-

https://doi.org/10.1515/9783110592139-010

ating support for the victims, a focus on the level of fraud, the need for government redress, and the public utility of these ventures.

Corporation Scandals in the Early Financial Revolution

From its very start in the coffeehouses of London's Exchange Alley, public trading in stocks and shares was inherently risky. The first few decades of the Financial Revolution in Britain witnessed multiple examples of corporate mismanagement, failure, and malfeasance. While the bubble that burst – but did not sink – the South Sea Company in 1720 is the most well known example, it is far from the only one. Examples of rampant speculation and corporate fraud began four decades before the South Sea Bubble, in the 1680s.

One of the first notable cases of swindled public investors involved London's Court of Orphans.[1] The Court of Orphans had been established as far back as the thirteenth century as a safe place to store the inheritances of the minor children of London's deceased freemen. By the early modern era, London's chamber regularly loaned out this store to private individuals for a low rate of interest. Between 1628 and 1682, London's freemen lodged almost £1.5 million of their children's inheritance money in the Chamber. In the seventeenth century, the corporation's many financial troubles (due to the Civil Wars, the Great Fire, and the city's growth) led it to dip into the Orphans' Fund to pay its own bills. By 1682, things were so bad that the corporation could no longer pay interest on the principal of the orphans' money. It turned out that false accounting had hidden the fact that the corporation had been using the Orphans' Fund to cover its losses for decades, and employing new orphans' money to pay out old.

Charles Carlton, who has produced the only major study of London's Court of Orphans, notes that in 1688 the Chamber owed £508,355 to 617 different families, which he estimates meant that over 2,300 orphans were touched by this financial calamity. At the time, a petition to the House of Lords mentions 1,400 'distressed orphans.' Thus, thousands of Londoners were affected by the loss of their inheritance money out on loan to the corporation. The 'Orphans' banded together to recover their capital by going to the courts, petitioning Parliament, appealing to the monarchs Charles II and James II, and trying to sway public opinion

---

1 For a history of London's Court of Orphans, as well as the financial crisis, see Charles Carlton, *The Court of Orphans* (Leicester: Leicester University Press, 1974), esp. ch. 3. For a longer discussion of the London Orphans' Fund financial crisis, see Amy Froide, *Silent Partners: Women as Public Investors During Britain's Financial Revolution, 1690–1750* (Oxford: Oxford University Press, 2017), 164–167.

through the press. Although various bills were introduced in Parliament to redress these wrongs, it was not until 1694 that an "Act for the relief of orphans and creditors of the City of London" combined the corporation's debts into an Orphans' Fund which was publicly traded and which paid four percent interest. It took until 1832 for the corporation to pay off all of the orphans through this Fund. This first major corporate financial crisis in the era of the Financial Revolution introduced several themes which would reappear in the context of future bubbles and crises. These included corporate mismanagement, the plight of poor oppressed victims who had loaned or invested money in good faith, and government intervention.

The 1690s witnessed numerous financial bubbles as the quantity of publicly traded companies rapidly expanded for the first time. According to Anne Murphy, between 1685 and 1695 a hundred or so "new joint-stock companies were established, giving investors the opportunity to commit their capital to projects ranging from the manufacture of paper and textiles to the hunt for sunken treasure ships."[2] Mining companies in particular were popular speculative ventures. One of the most fraudulent of these was the Mine Adventurers' Company. In 1698, Sir Humphrey Mackworth, known as a pious Tory gentleman and founder of the Society for the Promotion of Christian Knowledge, bought and reorganized this enterprise. He established a lottery to recapitalize the company, and shareholders flocked to subscribe money. After the lottery, there were 700 proprietors of shares in the Mine Adventurers' Company, and total investment capital somewhere near £250,000.[3] However, it turned out that Mackworth and the manager of the company, William Waller, embezzled much of the lottery profits, and funneled its prizes to their friends. Meanwhile, the company's mining business was not doing so well either. A Parliamentary investigation found that Mackworth had withheld news of mine failures and had propped up share prices so he and his friends could sell theirs at a profit. The company's shareholders began to team up and make demands. They ultimately petitioned Parliament, which discovered major mismanagement, fraudulent bookkeeping, and a lack of funds. The government found the company's directors, including Mackworth, guilty of fraud, and seized their assets to help pay off the company's debt. The company's creditors wanted a different financial settlement, but even though the one they got was probably a disappointment, it meant that they got something back. Parliament passed the 1711 Mine Adventurers' Act which reduced

---

2 Anne Murphy, *The Origins of English Financial Markets: Investment and Speculation before the South Sea Bubble* (Cambridge: Cambridge University Press, 2009), 1.

3 William R. Scott, *The Constitution and Finance of English, Scottish, and Irish Joint Stock Companies to 1720* (Cambridge: Cambridge University Press, 1912), 2:447, 456.

the company's shares by a third while bondholders saw theirs written down by a fifth. Thus, creditors received back between 20 and 33.3 percent less than they had originally invested. Despite these financial troubles, the company continued its existence, and amazingly Mackworth even enjoyed a short-lived return as a manager (until he fell back into his criminal ways).[4] Like the Orphans' Fund, the Mine Adventurers' Company scandal introduced themes that reoccurred in later financial crises: the role of active shareholders in petitioning Parliament for redress, the punishment of criminal directors and managers and the confiscation of their estates, as well as partial financial bailouts orchestrated by the government.

The Charitable Corporation Scandal

While the Orphans' Fund and Mine Adventurers' Company scandals predated the South Sea Bubble, financial crises continued after 1720 as well, and these were now compared to the South Sea disaster. The financial scandal that merited the most press coverage and comparison to the South Sea Bubble was that of the Charitable Corporation in 1732. The full title of the company was "the Charitable Corporation for the relief of the industrious poor by assisting them with small sums at legal interest".[5] Established in London in 1707, its founder, William Higgs, created the institution to aid the working poor, and to protect them from predatory lenders who often charged as much as 30 percent interest. The Charitable Corporation would provide small loans at six percent in return for a pledge of property for security. Higgs' innovation was a rare Protestant example of the Catholic concept of a *monte di pietà* ('mount of piety,' a charitable fund established to combat usury, or high rates of interest). This English model was not a philanthropic institution run by the Church, however; instead, it was a profitable venture. The working poor paid interest, investors could buy shares in the enterprise, and the company was designed to pay out a dividend. While the corporation was deemed 'charitable' because it offered low interest loans

4 For an account of the Mine Adventurers' Company fraud, see Froide, *Silent Partners*, 167–171; Koji Yamamoto, "Piety, Profit and Public Service in the Financial Revolution," *English Historical Review* 126 (2011): 806–834.

5 There is not much modern scholarship on the Charitable Corporation. See Beverly Lemire, *The Business of Everyday Life: Gender, Practice and Social Politics in England, c. 1600–1900* (Manchester: Manchester University Press, 2005), ch. 3; and Peter Brealey, "The Charitable Corporation for the Relief of Industrious Poor: Philanthropy, Profit and Sleaze in London, 1707–1733," *History* 98 (2013): 708–729.

in contrast to the exorbitant rates charged by individual pawnbrokers, it was still a business. It was more akin to today's 'social choice funds' where investors put their capital into companies which further social or ethical causes. At the same time, while investors could think of themselves as 'doing good,' they could also turn a nice profit by investing in the Charitable Corporation. In fact, the company "declared a dividend after the rate of 10 per cent" between 1725 and 1730, which dropped to a more modest six percent the year after.[6]

After some difficulties in getting off of the ground, the Charitable Corporation began to catch on with investors in the 1720s. Perhaps not coincidentally this is the same period that the company began to diverge from its original mission. Instead of focusing on small loans to the poor, in 1718 the upper limit of a loan was raised to £1,000. This was a considerable sum of money at the time, and indicates that the wealthy were beginning to use the corporation as a piggy bank. New directors pushed up the value of the stock, and diverted funds to buy other stocks. At the same time, employees engaged in sloppy, if not downright suspect, procedures. Safety checks ceased, books were kept irregularly, and pledges went unrecorded. Investigators would find that £200,000 went out on loan with no pledges recorded for security. By 1730, the company seems to have had a capital stock of £600,000, and the proprietors of this stock numbered in the low 300s.[7] In October 1731, rumors began to circulate about the corporation; shortly thereafter, one of the officers, John Thompson, hid the company's books and fled to the continent. The General Court of shareholders held a meeting only to find money, pledges, and accounts all missing. At this point, the shareholders appealed to Parliament for redress. And the whole sordid story of mismanagement, fraud, and embezzlement began to leak out – thereby making the scandal one in a longer list of similar financial crises.

The British press – primarily the London papers but also some from Edinburgh – covered the story avidly over the next 18 months. The Charitable Corporation was one of, if not the, top story in 1732. In January of that year, the *Daily Journal* reported: "There having been an extraordinary Demand for our Paper of Wednesday last, on Account of the Report of the Committee appointed to inspect the Affairs of the Charitable Corporation, the same is this Day re-printed, and may be had of T. Cooper, in Ivy-Lane."[8] People evidently could not get enough of the news about the Charitable Corporation. Another example of how popular the topic was: A search of the most mentioned name in the *Gentleman's Maga-*

---

6 *A Short History of the Charitable Corporation: From The Date of Their Charter, to Their Late Petition* (London, 1732), 15.

7 Brealey, "The Charitable Corporation," 717; Froide, *Silent Partners*, 172.

8 *Daily Journal*, no. 3447, 21.1.1732.

zine for 1732 comes up with various monarchs followed by John Thompson.[9] Thompson was the Charitable Corporation's warehouse keeper, who had embezzled from the company and absconded to the continent. There was a reward on his head, and accounts of Thompson's escape and sightings of him in France and Italy was regularly reported.

The Charitable Corporation and the South Sea Bubble

As news of the Charitable Corporation continued to dominate the periodicals, comparisons to the Bubble of 1720 were almost inevitable. The financial crisis resulting from the fraudulent practices of the managers of the corporation stirred up renewed interest in the South Sea Bubble. In March of 1732, right at the moment that news of the Charitable Corporation scandal was appearing daily in the papers, an advertisement announced: "This Day is Published, *Remarks on the Occurrences of the Years 1720 and 1721; relating to the Execution of the South-Sea Scheme*."[10] It seems more than a coincidence that a publication about the South Sea Bubble, which had occurred 12 years earlier, would suddenly appear in the midst of a new bubble. Moreover, just to the right of the advert for the publication on the South Sea Scheme was another announcing "This Day is Published, *A Short History of the Charitable Corporation*." Pamphlets about the two companies were coming out simultaneously. And some of these publications referenced both the South Sea Company and the Charitable Corporation. For instance, in May 1732, the following pamphlet appeared:

> This Day is Published,
> The Un-Charitable Corporation: or, A New Way for the Mother of the Charitable Corporation to raise a Fund to retrieve the Treasure imbezzled by the late Directors. To which is annex'd The Charitable Directors, a Satyr: And a Speech of a Ghost of a South Sea Director in the Year 1720. With a new Ballad. To the Tune of, To you fair Ladies now on Land. Occasioned by the Resolution of securing the Estates of the discarded Directors.
> Sold only by S. Slow, over against Devereux Court without Temple Bar.[11]

---

9 This is based on a search of the name index of the *Gentleman's Magazine* 2 (1732). It is worth noting that Thompson's actions in the wake of the Charitable Corporation scandal were quite similar to that of the South Sea Company's cashier, Robert Knight, who also fled to the continent after the bubble burst. John Carswell, *The South Sea Bubble* (London: Cresset Press, 1960), 225.
10 *Daily Journal*, no. 3509, 30.3.1732.
11 *Daily Journal*, no. 3540, 10.5.1732. Unfortunately, this pamphlet does not seem to be extant.

This publication satirized the embezzling directors of the Charitable Corporation while at the same time evoking the "ghost of a South Sea Director" in comparison. A direct link was being made between the two joint-stock companies and their fraudulent managers.

When contemporaries began to compare the Charitable Corporation scandal to the South Sea Bubble, they were in some sense equating them. It is telling that writers and commentators considered no other financial crises severe enough to compare to the Charitable Corporation. They may well have evoked the South Sea Bubble as a rhetorical strategy to garner sympathy and attention for the victims of this new financial scandal. In the early 1730s, it was these two financial bubbles that stood out from the rest; they were continually referenced and compared to one another. In fact, it is surprising how little discussion there is of other contemporary financial scandals such as France's Mississippi Bubble, or the more domestic affair of the Mine Adventurers' Company. What stands out is how contemporaries noted similarities in the particulars of the South Sea and Charitable Corporation bubbles. They emphasized company mismanagement, the fraud and greed of directors, a need for punishment of those at fault, government redress for innocent victims and shareholder losses, and a departure of the companies from their original business rationale.

Blaming the Directors

Contemporaries placed the blame for both the Bubble of 1720 and the financial scandal of 1732 squarely on the shoulders of the corporate directors. One of the earliest connections between the South Sea and Charitable Corporation bubbles came just two months after the latter financial scandal broke. In 1731, the *Gentleman's Magazine* republished a piece from *The Craftsman* dated Saturday, 11 December, and entitled "On the Charitable Corporation." The unnamed author stated: "[I]f there is such a thing as a parallel between two cases, that of the S. Sea Directors in the Year 1720, and of the Managers of the Charitable Corporation at present, is such."[12] He – the author noted he was male – went on to note the amount shareholders had lost, how this wealth had been stolen, the relative responsibility of the shareholders and the corporation, the innocent victims worthy of compassion due to their losses, and the effect this scandal might have on public credit. In conclusion, he cautioned that, "[s]o notorious a Breach of Trust should [not] pass unexamined or unpunished." He called for a government in-

12 *Gentleman's Magazine* 1 (1731): 516.

vestigation and consequences for the malefactors just as the British people had in 1720. It is worth noting that *The Craftsman* was an opposition, pro-Tory periodical, and may have enjoyed critiquing a crisis that was unfolding on the government's watch.[13]

The *London Journal* was *the Craftsman*'s political opposite, however it also agreed that corporate mismanagement was a key problem in these financial bubbles. It ran a piece entitled "A Caveat against Bubbles" in which the author stated that people are "continually exclaiming against fraudulent Practices in the Management; and observe that the Managers generally forfeit the good Character they had in a private Life. Men are not thoroughly known 'till tried by Power, Want, or Opportunities of gaining Wealth unfairly. Many who wou'd not be Rogues for a small Matter, stick at no Villainy when the Prize is large enough."[14] The writer thus reflected that even good men could be tempted into corporate malfeasance.

By 1732, the culpability for the Charitable Corporation scandal had fallen directly on the managers of the company. "Yesterday the Proprietors of the Charitable Corporation deliver'd their Case to the Members of the House of Commons, whereby they lay the entire blame on the Gentlemen in the Direction, viz. Seven Committee Men and Eleven Assistants [...]."[15] Once again, there was a similarity drawn between the Directors of the Charitable Corporation and of the South Sea Company. The newspaper called on Parliament to bring the offenders to justice and added: "The Punishments inflicted upon the famous South-Sea Directors in the ever memorable Year 1720, are fresh in everyone's Memory, but their Crimes are but small when compar'd with these Charitable Gentlemen, who have stript the Poor quite naked."[16] Perhaps as a rhetorical device, the new scandal was claimed to be worse than previous financial scandals.

The House of Commons seems to have been persuaded by, or agreed with, this rhetoric about corporate fraud – though it is unclear whether they shared the opinion that this case was similar to that of the South Sea Bubble. When they summoned and examined the various officers of the Charitable Corporation, they did so to explicitly ask them about the "proceedings of the managers

---

13 *The Craftsman* ran from 1726 to 1752, and, according to Simon Varey, was "the unofficial mouthpiece of the opposition" to Sir Robert Walpole's government. It was started by Lord Bolingbroke and William Pulteney and was pro-Tory and Church of England in its stance as well as sympathetic to the Jacobite cause. Simon Varey, "The Craftsman," *Prose Studies* 16 (1993): 58–77.

14 *Gentleman's Magazine* 2 (1732): 649–650.

15 *London Evening Post*, no. 653, 3.2.–5.2.1732.

16 *London Evening Post*, no. 653, 3.2.–5.2.1732.

of the Charitable Corporation."[17] In other words, the members of Parliament specifically focused on the actions of the directors. To do so, they questioned the junior officers about the managers, the committeemen, and the assistants of the corporation.

The level of disrepute in which the directors of the Charitable Corporation – and of the South Sea Company – were held is illustrated by their comparison to another major news story in 1732. Along with the Charitable Corporation scandal, another account stirred the public's imagination in that year: an incident involving vampires. In March, the *Gentleman's Magazine* included foreign news from Medreyga, Hungary that "certain dead bodies called Vampires had killed several persons by sucking out all their blood."[18] Commentators quickly found a way to link the two major stories of 1732. In May 1732, the *Gentleman's Magazine* re-ran an article from *The Craftsman* entitled "Political Vampyres." Ridiculing "romantick Stories" of stakes being driven through the hearts of corpses, this essay pointed out that the vampire was a useful political analogy. Caleb D'Anvers, the editor of the *Craftsman*, noted that stories of vampires came from the East, which region is "always remarkable for the Allegorical style. The States of Hungary are in Subjection to the Turks and Germans and govern'd by a pretty hard Hand; which obliges them to couch all their Complaints under Figures." In other words, vampires or entities who sucked the blood out of the living, were interpreted as more symbolic than real. Likewise, D'Anvers thought a certain "ravenous Minister, in this part of the World, is compared to a Leech or a Blood-sucker, and carries his Oppressions beyond the grave by anticipating the public Revenues, and entailing a Perpetuity of Taxes, which must gradually drain the Body Politick of its Blood and Spirits." The writers of the *Craftsman* did not stop at characterizing the government minister Sir Robert Walpole and his party's tax policies as acts of bloodsucking. They also noted that "Private Persons may be vampyres, or Blood-suckers, i.e. Sharpers, Usurers, and Stockjobbers [as well as ...] some *S. Sea Directors, and the Managers of the Charitable Corporation.*" Contemporaries were quick to apply the vampire analogy to both politicians and stockjobbers in England, especially the corporate directors of two companies thought to have fleeced their shareholders. And although it was 1732 and the managers of the Charitable Corporation were the current talk of the town, to emphasize the level of their rapacity they were linked once again to the South Sea Directors.

---

17 *Fog's Weekly Journal*, no. 173, 6.2.1732.

18 *Gentleman's Magazine* 2 (1732): 681. Italics my own for emphasis.

Victims of the Bubbles

If the Directors were the villains, then the South Sea Bubble and Charitable Corporation scandals also had their innocent victims. In the aftermath of both these financial crises, bilked shareholders became known as 'sufferers.'[19] The victims of the 1732 scandal sought to explain their plight to the public in a pamphlet entitled *The Present State of the Unhappy Sufferers of the Charitable Corporation Consider'd* (1732). They asserted that they were due compassion because

> *Persons of all Degrees, Sexes, and Ages* have had their Fortunes swallowed up by the late fraudulent Management, *many of them such as were willing to secure the regular Interest of what they had saved thro' the Course of an industrious Life, that it might afford them a comfortable Support in their Declining Years* [...] *Orphans and Widows*, the most helpless and distressed Characters in ordinary Life, have, from These Frauds, had their Misfortunes doubled, and their Small Pittances of Support utterly dissipated [...][20]

The author of the above-mentioned "A Caveat against Bubbles" also emphasized that certain people were particularly likely to become victims of Bubbles and fraudulent companies: "Single Women and others uncapable of Trade, or the Management of great Estates, whose Substance is in Money, and Income but small, have the most plausible Excuse, for venturing into these Projects."[21] However, even single women and those with modest amounts of cash to invest who could or would not work – that is, widows, orphans, the aged, and the clergy – were admonished by him:. "But let these consider whether a secure Interest, tho' small, is not better than to run the Risque of losing their All in hopes of a greater, and whereby they are often left without Means of repairing a broken Fortune." According to this author, even innocent victims of corporate fraud were perhaps partially responsible due to their greed and hopes of "greater" profit rather than being satisfied with secure investments that produced a lower rate of interest. The author also implicitly offered some sound financial advice; he was of the opinion that these investors should diversify their holdings rather than putting all their eggs in one basket, which could lead to a "broken Fortune."[22]

The perception that financial scandals had a particularly hard effect on women and children was at least somewhat rooted in reality. For instance,

---

19 Parliamentary proceedings referred to the "South Sea Sufferers." Helen J. Paul, *The South Sea Bubble: An Economic History of Its Origins and Consequences* (London: Routledge, 2011), 90–91.
20 *The Present State of the Unhappy Sufferers of the Charitable Corporation Consider'd* (London, 1732).
21 *Gentleman's Magazine* 2 (1732): 649–650.
22 *Gentleman's Magazine* 2 (1732): 649–650.

women were relatively well represented among those who held South Sea stock at the time of the Bubble because the company had taken over managing much of the National Debt in 1720. In a debt for equity swap the South Sea Company offered the holders of government annuities shares in its company. The terms of the swap looked attractive, and South Sea stock enjoyed easy liquidity, so the company persuaded many annuitants to exchange their government loans for company stock. As I have shown elsewhere, single and widowed women who invested in public stocks and shares were especially attracted to government annuities.[23] Their purchase of these annuities, which were then converted into South Sea shares, led to significant numbers of women holding South Sea stock right before the Bubble burst, and these female victims as well as minors affected by the calamity then became one of the main concerns in the aftermath of the disaster. Public commentary on the South Sea Bubble brimmed with examples of women and families who lost fortunes and livelihoods due to the Company's collapse.[24]

Women and children once again figured prominently in public commentary after the Charitable Corporation scandal. One might postulate that authors exaggerated the number of single women and minors affected by this scandal, as well as the extent of their suffering, to provoke a sympathetic response toward shareholders. However, the proportion of women hurt by the 1732 crisis really was quite high. It is possible to assess actual numbers of female investors defrauded by the Charitable Corporation due to the existence of sources such as the 1734 "List of the Sufferers [...] entitled to Relief from a Lottery granted for that purpose."[25] It included 304 individual names, 116 of which were women, thus revealing that 38.16 percent of the people swindled by the directors of the Charitable Corporation were women. This is the highest percentage of female participation in any public security (besides the government debt) for the period up to 1750.[26] Such numbers suggest that women were disproportionately disadvantaged by this particular financial scandal.

The List of Sufferers also corroborates concerns that women and children may have invested their entire savings or inheritance in one company, which when it imploded meant the loss of their life savings. As early as December 1731, commentators were emphasizing the compassion which the "many poor

---

23 See Froide, *Silent Partners*, esp. ch. 5.

24 For a discussion of the effect of the South Sea Bubble on women investors in particular, see Froide, *Silent Partners*, ch. 6.

25 "A List of the Sufferers by the Charitable Corporation, Entitled to Relief from the Lottery granted for that purpose," *Gentlemen's Magazine* 4 (1734): 235–237.

26 Froide, *Silent Partners*, 172.

Widows, Orphans, and young Ladies, whose Fortunes are embark'd in this Corporation" deserved.[27] We can get some sense of the extent of fortunes involved. For instance, only 20 out of 116 female investors in the Charitable Corporation held less than £50 in company stock. Another 21 women invested between £50–99, 27 between £100–199, 14 between £200–299, and 12 between £300–499. Perhaps they had not put all of their capital in this one investment; nevertheless, these were large sums of money to lose when the cost of living for a single gentlewoman in eighteenth-century London was between £100–200 a year.[28] Moreover, almost 20 percent of women had purchased more than £500 in the Charitable Corporation stock, with a few investing thousands of pounds. This could easily have been their entire savings and it was lost due to the fraudulent actions of company directors and managers.

Level of Fraud and Loss

Contemporaries leveled accusations of fraud against both the South Sea Company and the Charitable Corporation. The author of the aforementioned 1732 *London Journal* piece entitled "A Caveat against Bubbles" emphasized the role of intentional mismanagement in both crises: "Our Times have abounded with fraudulent Management of Companies and Corporations, and Visionary Schemes to gain Wealth; and notwithstanding the fatal Consequences that attended such Practices about 12 Years ago, we have seen People as eagerly engaged in the same Measures [...]."[29] Thus, according to the *London Journal* – which was largely a government mouthpiece – fraud, greed, and speculation were at the heart of both the South Sea and the Charitable Corporation bubbles. Despite the seriousness and the "fatal consequences" of the 1720 Bubble, the same corporate malfeasance was occurring once again.

"Greed, fraud, and speculation" might have been the watchwords for both financial bubbles, but on a more detailed level, the crises were not the same. Helen Paul notes that the South Sea Bubble was caused by inflated stock prices.[30] When it came to the Charitable Corporation, however, it was not that but the misuse of the fund on the part of greedy directors and the embezzlement of money and pledges by greedy officers that were the issue.

---

27 *Gentleman's Magazine* 1 (1731): 516.
28 Froide, *Silent Partners*, 146.
29 *Gentleman's Magazine* 2 (1732): 649–650.
30 Paul, *The South Sea Bubble*.

Commentators not only emphasized the level of fraud in these bubbles, they also noted the level of financial loss. In November 1731, just one month after the Charitable Corporation scandal broke, the *London Evening Post* reported: "We hear that the Charitable Corporation hath, by their late misfortune, suffer'd the Loss of above 200,000 l."[31] But this early assessment was revised up to between £500,000 and £600,000.[32] The debts of the Charitable Corporation were considerable but in no way equivalent to those of the South Sea Company's, which the inquiry by the House of Commons estimated to be over £14 million.[33]

Despite lower overall monetary losses, however, a number of commentators thought the Charitable Corporation disaster was proportionately worse than the South Sea Bubble. The author of one pamphlet averred that "[t]he late Management of the Charitable Corporation is agreed by all Mankind, to have been the most unheard of Villainy that ever was projected or perpetrated in any Country." He continued by noting that, comparatively,

> [e]ven by the fatal South Sea Scheme, less Mischief was done in Proportion. Men of great Estates and large Fortunes, with Men of Business educated in Trade, and never left without the Means of Subsistence, were the Persons engaged in those Transactions. [...] If the Company's Stock was sunk from stupendous Price, to less than its original Value, still the Stock remained, and it bore some Price. But here the Sufferers are the most completely unhappy, the most unsparingly plundered, and absolutely undone.[34]

Thus, the 1732 crisis was supposedly worse than the South Sea Bubble because the 1720 Bubble had primarily affected the prosperous who had other money or livelihoods to fall back on, and because the stock they held was still worth something after the Bubble. The victims of the Charitable Corporation, on the other hand, came from more modest backgrounds, and lost all of their invested capital. The author continued to make his case that the 1732 financial disaster was more grave because "[i]n this Corporation, most of the Proprietors had no other Substance, than the Value of their Shares. Here the Widow and the Orphan, the helpless Women, and Persons in no Trade or Employment, lodged their little Fortunes, flattered with the vile Assurances of large and uncommon Improvements."[35]

The question of which of the two financial disasters was worse was of less interest to contemporaries, however, than noting the similarities between the

31 *London Evening Post*, no. 617, 11.11.–13.11.1731.
32 *London Evening Post*, no. 640, 4.1.–6.1.1732.
33 Carswell, *South Sea Bubble*, chs. 12–14.
34 *Free Briton*, no. 131, 1.6.1732.
35 *Free Briton*, no. 131, 1.6.1732.

two. As a rhetorical strategy to emphasize the serious nature of the Charitable Corporation scandal, commentators evoked the South Sea Bubble as a yardstick. Contemporaries compared the financial losses incurred by the shareholders and creditors of each company, but they focused even more on the relative fraud and 'knavery' of the two failures as well as their relative impact. Contemporaries either perceived – or for rhetorical purposes claimed to perceive – that the Charitable Corporation crisis was similar to, if not worse than what they had experienced just twelve years earlier.

Government Redress

During both the South Sea Bubble and the Charitable Corporation scandal, commentators raised concerns about the effects on public credit and the larger economy.[36] In reference to the Charitable Corporation's impact on the stock market, one writer said: "It deserves Consideration, whether this Affair may not affect the public Credit, if so notorious a Breach of Trust should pass unexamined or unpunished".[37] This may again have been a rhetorical strategy to persuade Parliament to action – something that investors were hoping for.

In previous financial scandals, shareholders and investors had turned to the government for both justice and assistance. This was true for the victims of the Orphans' Fund, as well as the shareholders of the Mine Adventurers' Company and the South Sea Company. Perhaps this is why it only took three months for the proprietors of the Charitable Corporation to beseech Parliament for assistance. After an internal investigation, the shareholders of the company – as opposed to the managers – were "determined to seek Redress in Parliament." In January 1732, they decided to petition the House of Commons, "humbly imploring their assistance in detecting the Frauds by which this Corporation is reduced to so deplorable a state, and for giving them such relief as in their wisdom they shall think meet."[38] In modern parlance, the shareholders were asking for a government bailout.

The shareholders justified their request of Parliament by referring to the severity and the extent of the financial crisis and the plight of the Charitable Cor-

36 The reality of the South Sea Bubble's effect on the larger economy is more up to debate. See Julian Hoppit, "The Myths of the South Sea Bubble," *Transactions of the Royal Historical Society* 12 (2002): 141–165, here 155; and Daniel Menning's chapter in this volume.

37 *Gentleman's Magazine* 1 (1731): 516.

38 *The Present State of the Unhappy Sufferers of the Charitable Corporation Consider'd* (London, 1732).

poration's victims. *The Present State of the Unhappy Sufferers of the Charitable Corporation Consider'd* (1732) took issue with anyone who said that the situation could not be "stiled a public calamity." The Sufferers included "*Persons of all Degrees, Sexes, and Ages,*" those who had saved money up from a life of industry, the elderly, the orphaned, and the widowed. In other words, these were precisely the type of people who needed and deserved Parliament's protection and intervention.[39] They were not bailing out rich male investors who engendered no sympathy (or if they were, they were not emphasizing that).

According to the author of "A Caveat against Bubbles," it was the government's responsibility to stop these financial scandals. The pro-government *London Journal* stated: "The more flagrant and injurious Vices are to the Publick the more Care will a wise Government take to discountenance and prevent them."[40] This statement appeared in March 1732, right as Parliament began to investigate the Charitable Corporation affair and hold its managers accountable. We can read this as a gentle encouragement for the government to do the right thing and punish fraud. Even more importantly, the author urged Parliament to prevent future financial crises, something that had not occurred after the South Sea Bubble. Though in 1732, the government would again fail to act in any preventative way.[41]

The creditors of the Charitable Corporation now waited for Parliament to make up their financial losses. There were, however, other types of loss as well. The authors warned that "several struck with the vast and unexpected shock of their whole fortune being destroyed, have added the loss of life to the miseries induced by the late wicked management," while there remained some hundred of distressed families who had no other support for their hopes "but that confidence they place in the equity and tenderness of the British Legislature towards British Subjects."[42] Just as they did in the aftermath of the South Sea Bubble, commentators focused on suicides and deaths due to corporate greed. For instance, in January of 1732, three months after the scandal broke,

---

39 *The Present State of the Unhappy Sufferers of the Charitable Corporation Consider'd* (London, 1732).

40 "A Caveat against Bubbles," *Gentleman's Magazine* 2 (1732): 649–650.

41 Anne L. Murphy says that despite repeated calls for regulation, little was done in the early decades of the Financial Revolution. Anne L. Murphy, "Financial Markets: The Limits of Economic Regulation in Early Modern England," in *Mercantilism Reimagined: Political Economy in Early Modern Britain and Its Empire*, ed. Philip J. Stern and Carl Wennerlind (Oxford: Oxford University Press, 2013), 263–281.

42 Italics my own for emphasis. *The Present State of the Unhappy Sufferers of the Charitable Corporation Consider'd. With Reasons humbly offer'd for their Relief* (London, 1733), 18, 24.

the *London Evening Post* reported that "on Tuesday last, at his Father's in Golden Square, died Mr. Burroughs, a young Gentleman of a pretty good Fortune: It is said the Loss he sustained in the Charitable Corporation broke his heart."[43]

Despite the general atmosphere of death and despair, Parliament appears to have been unable to recoup the money lost, or at least all of it. The method they chose to pay back the 'sufferers' of the Charitable Corporation was a lottery; that cure-all for the British government when it was low on funds. This lottery issued 125,000 tickets at £4 each for a sum of £500,000. But only £79,120 out of the total was allotted to pay the subscribers who had suffered at the hands of the Charitable Corporation, while over £400,000 was reserved for lottery benefit tickets or prizes. If the expenses for prizes had been twenty percent lower, the corporation's shareholders could have been paid back in full. Instead, most corporation shareholders probably received less than half of what they had originally invested. At least this is what a "List of the Sufferers by the Charitable Corporation entitled to Relief from a Lottery granted for that purpose" published in the *Gentleman's Magazine* in 1734 suggests.[44] It was something, but if the money lost represented a person's life savings, and if the sufferers were indeed single women, widows, and orphans, the loss was most severe, and Parliament's approach uncharitable.

It is worth noting that after both the South Sea Bubble and the Charitable Corporation scandal, Parliament made a show of actively investigating these companies, helping sufferers, and punishing the malefactors. Once scapegoats had been found, and the managers of the companies had been personally punished, through the garnishing of their estates and the loss of their reputation and position, Parliament seems to have thought their job done. The mitigation of the financial losses of shareholders was impartial at best in both bubbles. And there was no move to ensure that such financial frauds could not occur again.

The Public Benefit of these Ventures

Comparisons of the Charitable Corporation and the South Sea Company also noted the originally-intended public utility of both ventures, and how corporate greed had trumped and abused this notion.[45] The Charitable Corporation chose

---

43 *London Evening Post*, no. 640, 4.1. – 6.1.1732.

44 "A List of the Sufferers by the Charitable Corporation, Entitled to Relief from the Lottery granted for that purpose," *Gentlemen's Magazine* 4 (1734): 235 – 237.

45 Koji Yamamoto argues that in seventeenth-century England it was common for for-profit ventures and their projectors to assert their public utility and their improvement of society as a way

to emphasize its purported philanthropic bent through its very name. Throughout the spring of 1732, the press sarcastically referenced "[t]hose Charitable Gentlemen" who ran the corporation, and pamphlets with titles such as "The Un-Charitable Corporation" appeared.[46] A purported proprietor of the Charitable Corporation claimed in a letter to the *Daily Journal* that he (or she) invested in the company because:

> I thought the Design was honourable and compassionate, that great Benefit might flow from thence to the necessitous Poor, and that the Exigencies of thousands might be relieved; I thought it would be an Assylum for the Trader in any unexpected Distress, and that it would keep him out of the Hands of the Pawnbrokers [...] I protest these Reasons had so much Weight with me, they made me then subscribe most of my Fortune into it [...].[47]

This author felt deceived in more ways than one, and the company found itself satirically mocked for its hypocrisy.

It might seem that the South Sea Company, based as it was on profit and slave trading, would have little to do with charity. Yet this was apparently the case, since one author connected the South Sea and Charitable Corporation debacles by observing how they both started out as offering some social good but in the end swindled the nation. This writer's essay "Of Charity" appeared in *The Craftsman* of 19 January 1732, and we can suppose that in that year any reference to the word 'charity' would have conjured up the story of the moment – the financial scandal of the Charitable Corporation. According to the author, "True Charity consists in Publick or Private Beneficence; but there have been so many instances of false Charity that this celestial virtue is almost brought to Contempt."[48] One might assume the author was thinking of the Charitable Corporation when he referenced 'false charity,' but he was actually referring to the South Sea Bubble: "The South Sea Scheme was a charitable Project to relieve the Publick from the Burthen of their Debts; and some Miscarriages happening in the Execution of it, a certain worthy Gentleman generously screen'd the Delinquents from the Rage of The Multitude, The Bank Contract, and the Remission of the 7

---

to assuage concerns about their venality. See Koji Yamamoto, *Taming Capitalism Before Its Triumph: Public Service, Distrust, & Projecting in Early Modern England* (Oxford: Oxford University Press, 2018).

46 See, for instance, *Daily Post*, no. 3875, 17.2.1732.

47 *Daily Journal*, no. 3491, 13.3.1732; *The London Magazine, or Gentleman's Monthly Intelligencer* 1 (1732): 105.

48 *Gentleman's Magazine* 2 (1732): 572–573.

Millions were excellent Improvements on the Original Scheme." The writer then goes on to relate that

> [t]he Charitable Corporation for the Relief of Industrious Poor have been twitted with an Observation that a Poor Tradesman must be very industrious to have any Transactions with them and not be undone; and turbulent People have Nick-nam'd the Managers, Gentlemen of the Industry, offering to prove that they have disposed of several thousand Pounds, by way of Alms upon Themselves, their Relations and Creatures [...] the World cannot shew a Set of more elemosinary Gentlemen than those concern'd in the Management of the Charitable Corporation.[49]

In other words, both the South Sea Company and the Charitable Corporation had set out to serve the 'public good,' to relieve the nation of debt, or to assist poor tradesmen by providing low-interest loans, respectively. But in the end, the only assistance the companies provided was to their own directors, and their families and friends.

Conclusion

This comparison of the South Sea Bubble and the Charitable Corporation scandal illustrates how the memory of the former Bubble influenced and informed the discussion of and response to subsequent financial crises. The South Sea Bubble has served as a yardstick against which corporate frauds were judged from the 1730s to the present day. In comparing the two financial bubbles, a number of factors stood out as significant to contemporaries: the role of company directors and managers and their responsibility for fraud and losses; the sympathy for financial victims of corporate malfeasance, especially women and children; the necessity of government investigation, punishment, and restitution. One difference is that, perhaps surprisingly, given that the Charitable Corporation involved fewer people and lower monetary losses, some considered the level of fraud worse than that which had occurred in the South Sea Bubble.

Despite the many similarities which contemporaries saw between these bubbles, the fates of the South Sea Company and the Charitable Corporation were quite different. The South Sea Company rallied to a certain degree and continued its operations into the nineteenth century, with modest success. The Charitable Corporation likewise tried to survive but was more financially and socially scarred than the larger and more well-connected South Sea Company. The actual

49 *Gentleman's Magazine* 2 (1732): 572–573.

Charitable Corporation faded away although its shadow lingered for decades.[50] In her 1756 conduct book *The Wife*, Eliza Haywood presented a scenario in which a wife must react to and weather a "vexatious accident" brought on by her husband. Her example is set "[i]n the beginning of that too memorable year, in which the failure of the Charitable Corporation ruined half those who had not been undone by the fatal South Sea scheme [...]."[51] The husband described in this work has invested his new wife's entire dowry of £7,000 in the scheme, only to lose it all. Evidently, even in the mid-eighteenth century, the South Sea Bubble and the Charitable Corporation scandal continued to be linked, and still resonated as the paramount examples of financial folly and catastrophe in the minds of the British reading public.

50 Brealey, "The Charitable Corporation," 728.

51 [Eliza Haywood], *The Wife: By Mira. One of the Authors of the Female Spectator* (London, 1756), 232–235.

III. Understanding Speculation – Micro to Macro

Marlene Kessler

"L'on entend tant dire pour et contre, que le plus habile doit agir au pure hasard." A Case Study on one Investor's Decision-making in the Mississippi Bubble

As evidenced by the image on the cover of this book, in late 1719, large crowds of foreigners and French provincials decided to go try their luck in the *Rue Quincampoix*, a street in the commercial center of Paris where the contemporary stock market was concentrated. One of these wannabe-stockholders was the bill trader Jean Vercour (d. 1721) from Liège. On 9 November, two days after he arrived in Paris, Vercour sent a letter to a business partner of his, the merchant Ferdinan Dellesem. In it, Vercour gave Dellesem a detailed account of the *Rue Quincampoix*, which he had visited on his first full day in the French capital:

> It is impossible for me to tell you with what eagerness, avidity and fury one trades with shares. From 7 o'clock in the morning until 9 o'clock in the evening, the *Rue Quincampoix* is so full of bankers, brokers, and merchants who sell and buy stock that it is not possible to pass, nor to see exactly what is going on, for the great confusion of everyone [...]. To tell the truth, my head is spinning. I am hesitating over whether I should buy shares [now] or whether I should wait. In one day, the price alters: [yesterday,] it was rumoured that the Company [of the Indies] would issue new shares for 50 million *livres* in order to establish a new enterprise for the North. This made the equity price fall from 295% [≙1,975 l.] to 245 to 250% [≙1,725 l. to 1,750 l.]. In the afternoon, a contrary information came in which made the equity price rise again to 293% [≙1,965 l.] [...]. This is most frightful, it just needs one idea to make the stock price rise to 300% [≙2,000 l.] or even more, and no more than another idea may suffice to lower the price by 100% [≙500 l.]. I consider this trade to be a great risk.[1]

1 "Il m'est impossible de vous décrire avec quelle empressement, quelle avidité et quelle fureure l'on négocie les actions. La rue Quimquempoix depuis le 7 heure [du] matin jusqu'à 9 heures du soir est si pleine de banquiers, de courtiers, de marchand qui vendent et achettent des action qu'il n'est pas possible d'y passer, ny même voir au juste ce qui s'y passent [sic] pour la trop grande confusion du monde [...]. à la vérité, la tête me tourne. Je suis en balance d'acheter ou d'atendre. En un même jour, cela varie de prix : [hier,] il avoit couru un bruit que la Compagnie [des Indes] alloit créer encor pour 50 millions de nouvelles actions à effet d'établir une autre entreprises pour le nord. Cela fit d'abord baisser les actions de l. 295 d'agio sur l. 100 à l. 245 à 250. L'après-midy, il vient une nouvelle contraire qui le fit là même remonter à l. 293. [...]. Cela est de plus fatal, il ne faut q[u]'une pensée qui le feroit hausser à 300 et plus, est [sic] il ne faut qu'une autre pour le faire baisser de cent pour cent; je regarde ce négoce pour

https://doi.org/10.1515/9783110592139-011

This extract from Vercour's letter reads like a textbook example of stock exchange during a time of 'mania'. Vercour describes an overcrowded bourse, where traders eagerly deal with equity, while mere rumors cause share prices to rise or fall sharply from one hour to another. To Vercour, the high volatility apparently came as a surprise: his wording indicates that the experience left him bewildered and perhaps even fearful. Yet, although he insisted on his unease and confusion, Vercour did not bring up the question of whether he should buy stock but merely expressed uncertainty about when he should do so. And, indeed, in the first week after Vercour wrote this letter, he went on to invest about 30,200 l. in shares on his and Dellesem's joint account. Thus, he became an active participant in what is nowadays, at least in Anglophone literature, often designated as the 'Mississippi Bubble',[2] which took place in Paris in 1719 and 1720.

Why did Jean Vercour choose to trade in shares, even though he perceived the stock market as a highly uncertain undertaking and bemoaned its contingency as early as in the very first letter that he sent from Paris? On what imaginaries of the future did he ground his decisions? This case study will explore these questions by following the trajectory of Jean Vercour's share-trade activity during the Mississippi Bubble, one of the first stock market booms and collapses. Before that, however, a short overview on the state of research and a comment on the sources will be given.

State of Research and Own Approach

The question of how actors dealt with the uncertainty of the stock market touches on, but ultimately differs from, the dominating approach to investor behavior

---

un grand risque". Jean Vercour to Ferdinan Dellesem, Paris 9.11.1719, in Archives de l'Etat à Liège (AEL), Banque Sauvage-Vercour (BSV), Register 3.

2 In French historiography, the same events are rather seen as part of a larger political undertaking, namely 'Le Système', carried out in France during 1716 to 1720 and (co-)authored by the Scottish economist John Law (1671–1729). For the sake of brevity, the often-explored, complex history of these events shall not be recapitulated here. Amid the most important accounts are: Edgar Faure, *La banqueroute de Law, 17 juillet 1720* (Paris: Gallimard, 1977); Paul Harsin, *Crédit public et banque d'Etat en France du XVIe au XVIIIe siècle* (Paris: Droz, 1933); Paul Harsin, *Les doctrines monétaires et financières en France du XVIe au XVIIIe siècle* (Paris: F. Alcan, 1928); Emile Levasseur, *Recherches historiques sur le Système de Law* (Paris: Guillaumin, 1854); Antoin E. Murphy, *John Law: Economic Theorist and Policy-maker* (Oxford: Clarendon Press, 1997); François R. Velde, "Government Equity and Money: John Law's System in 1720 France," (2004), http://www.heraldica.org/econ/law.pdf.

in the 1719/20 bubbles, which asks whether investors acted according to 'rational' or to 'irrational' expectations. From the point of view of rational-choice-theory, which has been the standard framework used by the economic sciences to explain decision-making since the 1970s, the assumption alone that stock market bubbles occur is somewhat challenging. According to rational-choice-theory, the best way to model economic behavior is to assume that every market participant weighs alternative courses of action on the basis of all available (or even of all-embracing) information and then decides in favor of that option which promises maximum personal benefit. If the model were a perfect description of stock markets, equity prices would correlate with the fundamental value of the securities. In the case of bubbles, however, this presumably is not true, as, according to the standard definition, bubbles arise when market prices considerably exceed the asset's fundamental value.[3] Consequently, the 1719/20 bubbles have been considered a sort of test case for verifying the applicability of rational-choice-theory. Researchers have debated whether or not 'rational' economic reasons for the movement of share prices and for the behavior of investors can be identified. No consensus has yet been reached, partly because reliable empirical data is difficult to collect and partly because varying definitions and criteria exist both for rational and irrational expectations and for what constitutes a bubble.[4]

---

3 Markus K. Brunnermeier, "Bubbles," in *The New Palgrave Dictionary of Economics*, ed. Garett Jones, 3rd ed. (London: Palgrave Macmillan, 2018), 1114–1121, here 1114.

4 Even amongst supporters of the 'rational behaviour' or 'irrational behaviour' view, the arguments and the nature of the sources that are used to tackle the issue sometimes differ. 'Irrational behaviour' scenarios are, for example, put forward by: Edward Chancellor, *Devil Take the Hindmost: A History of Financial Speculation* (London: Macmillan, 1999); Richard S. Dale, Johnnie E.V. Johnson, and Leilei Tang, "Financial Markets Can Go Mad: Evidence of Irrational Behaviour During the South Sea Bubble," *Economic History Review* 58 (2005): 233–271 and Charles P. Kindleberger and Robert Z. Aliber, *Manias, Panics and Crashes: A History of Financial Crises*, 6th ed. (London: Palgrave Macmillan, 2011). 'Rational behaviour' scenarios are put forward by: Peter M. Garber, "Famous First Bubbles," *The Journal of Economic Perspectives* 4 (1990): 35–54; Peter M. Garber, *Famous First Bubbles: The Fundamentals of Early Manias* (Cambridge, Mass.: MIT Press, 2000); Gary S. Shea, "Financial Market Analysis Can Go Mad (in the Search for Irrational Behaviour During the South Sea Bubble)," *Economic History Review* 60 (2007): 742–765; Larry Neal, *The Rise of Financial Capitalism: International Capital Markets in the Age of Reason* (Cambridge and New York: Cambridge University Press, 1990); Helen J. Paul, *The South Sea Bubble: An Economic History of Its Origins and Consequences* (London: Routledge, 2011) and Hans-Joachim Voth, "Blowing Early Bubbles: Rational Exuberance in the South Sea and Mississippi Bubbles," in *The Great Mirror of Folly: Finance, Culture, and the Crash of 1720*, ed. William N. Goetzmann et al. (New Haven: Yale University Press, 2013), 89–97.
For a critical analysis of the debate, see William Deringer, "For What It's Worth: Historical Financial Bubbles and the Boundaries of Economic Rationality," *Isis* 106 (2015): 646–656.

Meanwhile, judging behaviors as 'rational' or 'irrational' is problematic because differentiating between these terms requires an after-the-fact perspective and largely ignores the contingency of the situation from the actors' point of view. Thus, the classification covers up one of the central characteristics of share markets, the uncertainty of future price developments. In 1719, this degree of uncertainty was especially high: not only was the stock market a relatively recent phenomenon, but thousands of inexperienced traders participated in it. There was little didactic financial information available to them, let alone information which would have allowed them to correctly determine the fundamental value of stock. Hence, the circumstances hardly allowed shareholders to identify the optimal course of action – even though they certainly wanted to do so. Instead, they had to deal with the reality that the outcome of their decisions was difficult to foresee.

In his book 'Imagined futures', the sociologist Jens Beckert tackles precisely this question of how economic actors cope with uncertain futures. Relying himself on earlier works on this topic,[5] Beckert argues that, under conditions of uncertainty, actors cannot be expected to accurately predict future market developments or to make valid probabilistic assessments.[6] If actors are nevertheless able to make decisions and to act with relative confidence, this is because they imagine a future state of the world and project themselves into the idea that this scenario will become reality. Beckert suggests that the expectations that actors form are contingent and thus of a fictional character – hence, their working can be analyzed using similar means as it is done with fictional texts.[7] The possible futures that actors create in their imaginations can then touch them emotionally and have a motivating effect, especially because – and here, the parallel to fictional oeuvres ends – it is possible that the imagined scenario indeed turns real.[8] If many actors act according to the same expectations, this may (but does not automatically have to) come to serve as a *self-fulfilling prophecy* and cause the formerly purely imagined future to become reality. For this reason, actors such as politicians or business enterprises might also purposefully try to create, develop, influence or spread certain fictional scenarios. In Beckert's view, the more an

5 Mainly John M. Keynes, *The General Theory of Employment Interest and Money* (1936; London: Macmillan, 1973) and Frank H. Knight, *Risk, Uncertainty and Profit* (Boston and New York: Houghton Mifflin Company, 1921).

6 Jens Beckert, *Imagined Futures: Fictional Expectations and Capitalist Dynamics* (Cambridge, Mass.: Harvard University Press, 2016), 10 and 41–42.

7 Beckert, *Imagined Futures*, 1–2, 9–10, 61–64 and passim.

8 Beckert, *Imagined Futures*, 9, 68, 75–79.

actor is able to influence the expectations of others the way he wants to, the more powerful he is.[9]

It seems promising to apply Beckert's theory of imagined futures to John Law's 'System'. Efforts to stimulate certain expectations accompanied the System from the very beginning and certainly contributed much to the boom-and-bust(s) of the Mississippi Bubble. For one thing, John Law was "influencing, if not manipulating, the price of his company's shares" in order to enhance the appeal of the stock market, as François Velde has stressed.[10] For another, Arnaud Orain recently has shown that the media played an important role in propagating the System. Orain claims that this was a purposeful campaign, directed not only at potential stockholders but at French society as a whole. Accordingly, a circle of 'Moderns' planned to radically transform French society with the System they co-authored. In order to propagate their ideas, they made use of the "puissance merveilleuse de la fiction" and employed a vast range of media, such as maps, theatre pieces or newspaper articles.[11]

This chapter's exploration of an investor in the Mississippi Bubble allows us to investigate this topic from the ground-up and to examine on a micro-level the ways in which the expectations and practical decision-making of investors were influenced by such larger efforts.

While debates over 'rational' and 'irrational' expectations seek to clarify investment behavior during the 1720 Bubbles in order to make general statements about market efficiency, little research has been done that examines individual investors and their experiences during the Mississippi Bubble on a micro- or meso-level. This lack is especially apparent in comparison with the number of studies in which the behavior of certain groups of investors or of individual shareholders during the almost simultaneous 'South Sea Bubble' is explored.[12]

---

9 Beckert, *Imagined Futures*, 10 – 12, 79 – 85, 156 – 158.

10 François R. Velde, "Was John Law's System a Bubble? The Mississippi Bubble Revisited," in *The Origins and Development of Financial Markets and Institutions: From the Seventeenth Century to the Present*, ed. Jeremy Atack and Larry Neal (Cambridge and New York: Cambridge University Press, 2009), 99 – 120, citation 110.

11 Arnaud Orain, *La politique du merveilleux: Une autre histoire du Système de Law (1695 – 1795)* (Paris: Fayard, 2018), citation 221.

12 E. g. J.V. Beckett, "Cumbrians and the South Sea Bubble, 1720," *Transactions of the Cumberland & Westmorland Antiquarian & Archaeological Society* 82 (1982): 141 – 150; Ann M. Carlos, Karen Maguire, and Larry Neal, "'A Knavish People …': London Jewry and the Stock Market During the South Sea Bubble," *Business History* 50 (2008), 728 – 748; Ann M. Carlos, Karen Maguire, and Larry Neal, "Women in the City: Financial Acumen During the South Sea Bubble," in *Women and Their Money 1700 – 1950: Essays on Women and Finance*, ed. Anne Laurence, Josephine Maltby, and Janette Rutterford (London and New York: Routledge, 2009), 33 – 45; Anne

The diverging state of research certainly mirrors a general trend in recent investigations of the two major 1719/20 bubbles, but it also has to do with the archival situation. Most of the administrative records relating to the liquidation of John Law's System were burned in public in 1722, and the remaining records of the Royal Bank and of Law's Indies Company suffered the same fate five years later.[13] As a consequence, any statistical examination of the Mississippi Company's shareholders is difficult. However, about some leading investors, prosopographical information is available.[14]

Investigations into the individual experiences and agency of single investors further are hampered by the fact that there is no systematic record of the personal papers of shareholders that incidentally survived in private or public archives.

A handful of studies that examine individual Mississippi investors does exist nonetheless. One major contribution is Herbert Lüthy's pivotal work on what he called the 'Banque Protestante' in France, which he studied for the period from 1685 until 1789. Meticulously referencing mainly administrative and notarial re-

Laurence, "Lady Betty Hastings, Her Half-sisters, and the South Sea Bubble: Family Fortunes and Strategies," *Women's History Review* 15 (2006): 533–540; Anne Laurence, "Women, Banks and the Securities Market in Early Eighteenth-Century England," in *Women and Their Money 1700–1950: Essays on Women and Finance*, ed. Anne Laurence, Josephine Maltby, and Janette Rutterford (London and New York: Routledge, 2009), 46–58; Anne Laurence, "Women Investors, 'That Nasty South Sea Affair' and the Rage to Speculate in Early Eighteenth-Century England," *Accounting, Business and Financial History* 16 (2006), 245–264; Larry Neal, *'I Am Not Master of Events': The Speculations of John Law and Lord Londonderry in the Mississippi and South Sea Bubbles* (New Haven and London: Yale University Press, 2012); Andrew Odlyzko, "Newton's Financial Misadventures in the South Sea Bubble," (2018), http://dx.doi.org/10.2139/ssrn.3068542; Peter Temin and Hans-Joachim Voth, *Prometheus Shackled: Goldsmith Banks and England's Financial Revolution After 1700* (Oxford: Oxford University Press, 2013), esp. 109–124; Patrick Walsh, *The South Sea Bubble and Ireland: Money, Banking and Investment, 1690–1721* (Woodbridge: The Boydell Press, 2014), esp. 59–109; Koji Yamamoto, "Beyond Rational vs Irrational Bubbles: James Brydges the First Duke of Chandos During the South Sea Bubble," in *Le crisi finanziarie: Gestione, implicazioni sociali e conseguenze nell'età preindustriale. Selezione di ricerche*, ed. Giampiero Nigro (Firenze: Firenze University Press, 2016), 327–357.

13 Velde, "Government Equity" 36–37, fn. 41. For existing sources with regard to the South Sea Company's investors, see Walsh, *Ireland*, 60–61.

14 E.g. Thierry Claeys, *Dictionnaire biographique des financiers en France au XVIIIe siècle*, 3rd, compl. ed., 2 vols. (Paris: SPM, 2011). Claeys lists numerous financiers who were also actively involved in John Law's System. Paul Harsin, "La création de la Compagnie d'Occident (1717): Contribution à l'histoire du Système de Law," *Revue d'histoire économique et sociale* 34 (1956): 7–42 names the first subscribers in shares of Law's Company of the West. Jean Villain, "Le rôle de la capitation extraordinaire de 1722," *Revue historique de droit français et étranger* 32 (1954): 108–116 draws up a list of 274 'Mississippiens' whose supposedly enormous gains were imposed with a penalty tax in 1722. Many of them were finally granted amnesty.

cords, Lüthy recreated the activities of numerous Protestant bankers, especially of Genevan origin, some of whom also were involved in the Mississippi Bubble.[15] Antoin E. Murphy, in turn, has written a biography of the economist and international banker Richard Cantillon. Cantillon, whom Law relied on at times and considered an opponent at other times, succeeded in making a fortune during the 1719/20 bubbles, albeit not only because of his actual share trading activities but even more so thanks to speculation on the foreign exchanges.[16] Furthermore, Larry Neal has retraced the interlinked investment behavior of John Law and Thomas Pitt Jr., Lord Londonderry, in the Mississippi and the South Sea bubbles. These two men notably concluded an enormous forward contract on shares of the English East India Company, which plunged John Law deep into debt.[17] Lastly, references to stockholders also can be found in some studies dedicated to topics that are more general.[18]

Sources

The case of Jean Vercour offers another, slightly different perspective on the Mississippi Bubble. Jean Vercour played a more marginal role in the Paris share market than most of the investors in France who have been studied thus far, as he did not count amid the eminent figures of the speculation episode. More importantly, the character of the source material left on Jean Vercour is intriguing. It mainly consists of the correspondence that Jean Vercour exchanged with his (potential) investment partners during his sojourns in Paris. These letters not only allow us to retrace his activities on an almost day-to-day level. Vercour's writings also offer precious insights into the constraints, hopes and doubts that stood behind his decisions to buy and sell. The style of writing indicates that Vercour re-

---

15 Herbert Lüthy, *La Banque protestante en France de la révocation de l'Edit de Nantes à la Révolution*, 2 vols. (Paris: S.E.V.P.E.N., 1959/1961), esp. 1:294–295, 311–312, 331–413.

16 Antoin E. Murphy, *Richard Cantillon: Entrepreneur and Economist* (Oxford: Clarendon Press, 1986). In passing, Murphy also addresses the activities of other prominent stockjobbers, especially Joseph Gage and Lady Mary Herbert. The twosome had gotten advice from Cantillon and first won, then lost greatly. Later, they conducted litigation against Cantillon lasting several years.

17 Neal, *Not Master of Events.*

18 Guy Chaussinand-Nogaret, *Les financiers de Languedoc au XVIIIe siècle* (Paris: S.E.V.P.E.N., 1970), esp. 126–157; Philippe Haudrère, *La Compagnie française des Indes au XVIIIe siècle: 1719–1795*, rev. ed., 2 vols. (Paris: Les Indes Savantes, 2005), here 1:43–44, 59, 64–67, 79–80; Marcel Giraud, *Histoire de la Louisiane française*, 5 vols. (Paris: Presses universitaires de France/L'Harmattan, 1953–2012), here esp. 3:32–36, 209–220.

ported relatively spontaneously and in a forthright manner what he thought. As for the reactions of his correspondents, they can only be discerned indirectly, because the letters that Vercour received are not preserved.

Vercour's outgoing correspondence has survived in the form of copies noted down in letter books, three of which have been preserved. These encompass the letters that Vercour sent to diverse business correspondents between 1714 and mid-1721, albeit with a gap from February to October 1719.[19] No private correspondence to family members is included in the letter books, although some drafts that his family sent Jean Vercour while he was in Paris can be found therein. The reason for this particularity is that Vercour left the letter books back home each time he went away. Many, but not all, of the letters that he wrote during these trips are included because Vercour relayed most of his outgoing letters through his family, who duplicated them before passing them on to their addressees.

The copies of Vercour's letters are largely devoid of punctuation and contain frequent 'spelling mistakes'. There are also grammatical anomalies, which probably stem from the fact that there was a diglossia situation in Liège. It seems likely that the Vercour family conversed in Walloon and used French mainly as a written language. In this chapter, the French citations retain their original spelling, except for some small interventions without special marking in order to improve readability, like the addition of punctuation marks, apostrophes and accents. The letters i and j are rendered according to modern orthography, and the use of upper and lower case also conforms to modern principles.

So far, Jean Vercour's correspondence has been almost entirely unexplored. The historian Jean-Jacques Hémardinquer drew on this source for a conference paper from 1970, but the resulting article was less interested in Vercour's share trading activity than in the economic impact of Law's System in the French region of Champagne.[20]

---

19 The first two letter books cover Jean Vercour's correspondence for the period from 9.11.1714 to 10.2.1719. After that, Vercour seems to have kept another book, which now is lost. For this study, the third one of the surviving letter books is central. It embraces the period from 20.10.1719 to 29.7.1721 and thus covers the time when Vercour traded with Indies shares.
The material has been preserved because Vercour was at the origin of an important Liégois banking house, Sauvage-Vercour, which lasted well into the nineteeth century. The Archives de l'Etat de Liège (AEL) conserve 194 "registers" for this house. These large volumes chronologically cover the bank's outgoing correspondence for 1714 until 1836. The only major gap occurs in the time between 1721, the year Jean Vercour died, and 1732.

20 Jean-Jacques Hémardinquer, "Law, Liège et la reconstruction industrielle d'Arcis-sur-Aube en 1720," in *Actes du 95e congrès national des sociétés savantes, hist. mod., Reims, 1970* (Paris: Bib-

Risk and Opportunity. Initial Considerations

Vercour followed the stock market and the political developments in France for months before he finally resolved to go to Paris.[21] According to a later letter, a friend had tried to convince him to buy shares as early as spring 1719, but, back then, Vercour had dismissed "the advantages that [this friend] illustrated as a fantasy".[22] Shortly before he departed for Paris, Vercour still had some doubts with regard to the goings-on in France, because he suspected powerful vested interests to be working in the background. On October 20, Vercour wrote to a correspondent: "A few days ago, the Company of Paris [i.e. the Company of the Indies] again created shares for 100 million. I believe that in the end, the regent and the Company will have all the money of the kingdom and the private individuals will have the paper".[23] Vercour's reservations probably were not directed against dealing with shares or paper money in-and-of itself. As a bill-trader, he had in-depth experience with paper-based credit, even if mainly in the form of bills of exchange. Instead, Vercour likely adopted a common objection against 'Le Système', which supposed that the French sovereign was sure to exploit the institutions that John Law had created for his own interests. This caveat was linked with a widespread view in the early eighteenth century: the belief that the French kingdom lacked the necessary legal certainty for a sound credit-based financial system because its monarch held 'arbitrary power'.[24]

liothèque nationale, 1974), 2:23–43. On p. 32–43, Hémardinquer gives extracts of some of Vercour's letters.

21 The first explicit mention of John Law in one of Vercour's letters dates from 13.1.1719. By then, Vercour already took a negative stance towards Law's activities. Vercour to Herwegh, Liège 13.1.1719, in AEL, BSV, Reg. 2.

22 "Il y a passé 6 mois qu'un amis [sic] de Dinant vouloit m'y engager, mais je regardois les avantages qu'il me figuroit comme un songe". Vercour to Herwegh, Liège 30.10.1719, in AEL, BSV, Reg. 3.

23 "Depuis quelques jour, la Compagnie de Paris at [sic] encor créé des actions pour 100 million. Je croy qu'à la fin, le régent et la Compagnie auront toute [sic] l'argent du roiaume et le particulier les papiers". Vercour to Théophile Thellusson, Liège 20.10.1719, in AEL, BSV, Reg. 3.

24 E.g. ex negativo, *Considerations Occasioned by the Bill for Enabling the South-Sea Company to increase their Capital Stock, &c. With observations of Mr. Law, Comptroller general of the Finances of France* (London, 1720), 6: "if those superficial Reasoners, who telling us every Day, there can be no Security under a despotick Government, and that the Regent may at once cancel all the Bank Bills, now Current in France, had Capacity enough to weigh the Probability of such an Accident, they would be ashamed of their weak Assertions". Also cf. [Daniel Defoe], *The Chimera, or, the French Way of Paying National Debts, Laid open* (London, 1720), esp. 4–5. Law hence undertook considerable effort to explain that such caveats were inaccurate with regard to the Sys-

Nevertheless, the rising share-prices in Paris evidently intrigued Vercour, and he ended up regretting that he had not benefitted from them.[25] At the end of October 1719, after having "weighed and balanced this affair for a long time",[26] Vercour decided to try his luck in the share market. Shortly before, his most important correspondent in Paris, a merchant-banker named Du Hamel, had told him that the time was still opportune to acquire stock.[27] Du Hamel's advice probably mattered all the more to Vercour because the banker, who was established on the *Rue Quincampoix*,[28] already had invested in shares with some success.[29] Apparently, Vercour expected that experienced people were capable of giving valid advice. For his own part, by contrast, he felt that he did not fully grasp the functioning of the share market, because he had not yet experienced it in-person. "I [...] intend to come to your place in order to see with precision how one deals with it", Vercour announced to another banker in Paris on 30 October.[30]

Apart from Du Hamel's advice, Vercour had other reasons to assume that, in the near future, investments would still be rewarding. In October, rumors about a new share issue circulated in Liège and elsewhere, and Vercour took the possible occurrence of such an event as a promising prospect.[31] He probably expected

tem: Cf. Thomas E. Kaiser, "Money, Despotism, and Public Opinion in Early Eighteenth-Century France: John Law and the Debate on Royal Credit," *The Journal of Modern History* 63 (1991): 1–28. After the downfall of Law and the System (or perhaps, as Saint-Simon himself claimed, even before this event), however, even the Duke of Saint-Simon as a high-ranking courtier opined that an absolute monarchy could never refrain itself from abusing a public bank and that, for this reason, John Law's projects had been doomed to fail from the outset. Marc Hersant, "Saint-Simon et Law: Poésie des finances, poésies du financier," in *'Gagnons sans savoir comment': Représentations du Système de Law du XVIIIe à nos jours*, ed. Florence Magnot-Ogilvy (Rennes: Presses universitaires de Rennes, 2017), 279–288, here 281–282.

25 Vercour to Herwegh, Liège 30.10.1719 and Vercour to de Geyr, Paris 14.11.1719, in AEL, BSV, Reg. 3.

26 "il y a bien du tems que j'ay pesé et balancé cette affaire". Vercour to Herwegh, Liège 30.10.1719, in AEL, BSV, Reg. 3.

27 Vercour to Du Hamel and to Herwegh, Liège 30.10.1719, in AEL, BSV, Reg. 3.

28 Vercour to de Geyr, Liège 30.10.1719, in AEL, BSV, Reg. 3.

29 Vercour to Herwegh, Liège 30.10.1719, in AEL, BSV, Reg. 3.

30 "J'ay [...] dessain de me rendre chez vous afin de voir à fond comme[nt] l'on s'y prend". Vercour to Darius, Liège 30.10.1719, in AEL, BSV, Reg. 3.

31 Vercour to Du Hamel, Liège 30.10.1719, in AEL, BSV, Reg. 3. An *Arrêt du Conseil* was published on 12 October that contradicted the continuing rumours about new share issues (Cf. Velde, "Government Equity," 22), but the decree had not yet reached Liège. Vercour only mentions this contrary announcement when he already is in Paris (to Dellesem, 13.11.1719).

that the new shares initially would experience a similar success as the older ones had, and he therefore planned to buy new stock shortly after its issuance.

Yet, Vercour's wording also indicates that he surmised that the price increase would be short-lived. For example, one day before he set off, on 30 October, Vercour explained to a close business partner that he "prepare[d] to depart for Paris *although at a late moment*".[32] This indicates that Vercour supposed that the increase in prices would reverse at some point and thus bring about losses for latecomers – in other words, he already conjectured some sort of stock market crash.

To sum up, when Vercour departed Liège, he did so in pursuit of the latest price increases in Paris. Even if he reckoned that eventually a price drop would occur, he was motivated by the expectation that, in the short term, prices were still going to rise. Apparently, Vercour deemed it possible to foresee developments on the share market. He expected to understand the stock trade better once he was on-site, and he believed in the idea that experts like Du Hamel were capable of giving valid advice. As soon as Vercour arrived in Paris, however, he started to question many of these assumptions.

Between Hopes and Doubts. Vercour's First Phase of Investment

When Vercour reached the French capital on 7 November 1719, after a one-week journey,[33] he was one amid many foreigners and French provincials who reportedly rushed to Paris in the last months of 1719.[34] Thus, he experienced the *Rue Quincampoix* right in the midst of what nowadays is described as a 'bull market'. Almost immediately, Jean Vercour invested considerable funds in shares. By 13 November, he was in possession of 15 *soumissions,* that is fully tradable share options which had been sold during the fourth issue that started on 23 September. At prices ranging between 292 percent [≙1,960 l.] and 314.5 percent [≙2,072 l.

32 "Quoy que tard [...], je me dispose à partir". Vercour to Herwegh, Liège 30.10.1719, in AEL, BSV, Reg. 3. Emphasis added.

33 Vercour to Théophile Thellusson, Liège 31.10.1719 and to Dellesem, Paris 9.11.1719, in AEL, BSV, Reg. 3.

34 Cf. Stefano Condorelli, "La presse étrangère et le Système de Law (1716–1720)," in '*Gagnons sans savoir comment*': *Représentations du Système de Law du XVIIIe à nos jours*, ed. Florence Magnot-Ogilvy (Rennes: Presses universitaires de Rennes, 2017), 183–206, here 191–192; Lüthy, *Banque protestante*, 347–350; Murphy, *Cantillon*, 105–106. In a later justification, John Law stated that foreign investments had amounted to 1/40 of the funds that Frenchmen had invested. "Mémoire justificatif de Mai 1723," in John Law: *Œuvres complètes*, ed. Paul Harsin, 3 vols. (Paris: Recueil Sirey, 1934), 3:204.

10 s.],[35] these had cost 30,200 l. in total.[36] Vercour divided the sum equally with a co-investor, the merchant Ferdinan Dellesem from Liège, but his half still represented a substantial amount of money and would have been sufficient, for example, to acquire a house in the *Les Halles* Quarter in Paris.[37]

During the first two months that he spent in Paris, Jean Vercour alternated between hopes and doubts. It already has been shown that, in the first letter that he sent to Dellesem, Vercour conceded a certain trepidation, triggered by the discovery that share prices followed rather erratic trends. In a second letter to his co-investor, dated 10 November, Vercour nevertheless was relatively optimistic. Vercour composed this note the morning after he had given the order to purchase *soumissions* for up to 16,000 l., and he opined that this was a good decision because the current price trend was positive and because the general view was that the newly created *soumissions* would experience a similar success as the shares of older issues had.[38] Vercour also was impressed by talk of the fortunes that had been made, and he indulged in the idea of the earnings that he could have made.[39] In this context, he also reported that he attended what seems to have been a stage play named "Les agioteur[s]". The story revolved around two stockjobbers – one a grubby-looking man, the other a wealthy man dressed in velvet. The plot was rather simple: the latter generously offered the former to buy all his stock, only to learn that his shabbily-dressed counterpart owned the large amount of 20,000 l. in shares.

The punchline of the play was similar to that of many other carnivalesque stories circulating at that time in different forms (e.g. songs, theatre pieces, letters or newspaper articles). These stories often focused on people from the 'lower

---

35 Cf. Velde, "Government Equity," Appendix, 7–8 for the two different methods which existed for quoting *soumission* prices. Vercour mostly uses what Velde calls the exclusive method: "[The two] methods quote the price as x percent premium over the face value of shares, which is also the initial down-payment, of 500 L. [The exclusive] method quotes the net percentage premium over the face value of 500 L, exclusive of any payments made: the cash price is then $5x + q$, where q is the sum of all payments made including the initial down-payment ($q = 500$ until January 1720, $q = 2000$ from January to March)".

36 Vercour to Dellesem, Paris 13.11.1719, in AEL, BSV, Reg. 3. Jean Vercour gathered these *soumissions* in several stages, cf. Vercour to Dellesem, Paris 10.11., 11.11. and 13.11.1719 in AEL, BSV, Reg. 3.

37 According to Vicomte G. d'Avenel, *Histoire économique de la propriété, des salaires, des denrées et de tous les prix en général, depuis l'an 1200 jusqu'à l'an 1800,* 7 vols. (Paris: Imprimerie nationale/Leroux, 1894–1926), 2:11, in 1719, one house on the *Rue de la Poterie* was priced at 11,000 l.

38 Vercour to Dellesem, Paris 10.11.1719, in AEL, BSV, Reg. 3.

39 Also cf. Vercour to de Geyr, Paris 14.11.1719 and Vercour to Herwegh, Paris 16.11.1719, in AEL, BSV, Reg. 3.

classes' who turned into *nouveaux riches* thanks to stock-jobbing.[40] It is difficult to tell with what intention these stories were told. Originally, they possibly were circulated as part of a deliberate attempt to trigger optimistic expectations with regard to the System.[41] They may also have been used to voice disapproval of the social changes that Law's System presumably entailed.[42] As to Jean Vercour, he did not further comment on the play he had seen, but the way he embedded his remark in his letter suggests that he found the plot amusing or even encouraging. Hence, both the play and the accounts he heard of fortunes made likely stimulated positive imaginations for him.

The next letters that Jean Vercour composed were, in comparison, of a less confident tone. Vercour remained concerned about the volatility of the market, and the fact that opinions differed greatly with regard to future price developments unsettled him.[43] Estimates focused on the fallout that upcoming payments for the *soumissions* would have. For each *soumission*, a subsequent payment of 1,500 l. was required every three months, the first due in December 1719. The idea was that once the face value of a normal share, which amounted to 5,000 l., was fully deposited, the *soumissions* would convert into a normal, dividend-yielding share. If, however, one instalment was missed, the *soumissions* were to become void.[44]

This technical provision gave rise to varying expectations of different complexity. For example, the merchant-banker François Darius, Vercour's most important advisor and money provider in Paris,[45] followed a rather complicated consideration, as Vercour outlined to Dellesem on 11 November:

---

40 E.g. Barthélemy M. Du Hautchamp, *Histoire du Système des Finances, Sous la Minorité de Louis XV pendant les années 1719 & 1720*, 6 vols. (The Hague: Pierre de Hondt, 1739), 2:51–53, 105–109; Elisabeth-Charlotte, Duchess of Orléans, to Raugravin Luise, St. Cloud 3.12.1719, in Elisabeth Charlotte Herzogin von Orléans, *Briefe aus den Jahren 1676–1722*, ed. Wilhelm L. Holland, 6 vols. (1877; Hildesheim: Olms, 1988), 4:331–334; *Le Nouveau Mercure*, October 1719, 200–204 and November 1719, 207–209 and 211–213.

41 Cf. Orain, *Politique du merveilleux*, 113–115 and 212–221.

42 Cf. Henri Duranton, "La ficelle de Law," in '*Gagnons sans savoir comment*': *Représentations du Système de Law du XVIIIe à nos jours*, ed. Florence Magnot-Ogilvy (Rennes: Presses universitaires de Rennes, 2017), 111–125, here 120; Céline Lamy, "Le carnaval des agioteurs: Critiques du pouvoir dans les récits de la banqueroute de Law," in *Fantaisie poétique et dérision des puissants: Études transversales*, ed. Élisabeth Gavoille (Tours: Université François Rabelais, 2011), 89–103, here 95–99.

43 Vercour to Dellesem, Paris 11.11., 13.11. and 15.11.1719, in AEL, BSV, Reg. 3.

44 Cf. Velde, "Government Equity," Appendix, 4–6.

45 François Darius advanced Vercour substantial sums, even though they barely were acquainted before November 1719. It seems likely that Isaac Thellusson (1690–1755), a prominent banker with whom Vercour was, at least, loosely acquainted and who likewise occasionally provided

> Mr. Darius advices me to hold on to my shares[46] and to buy more of them, even at 300 % [≙2,000 l.] [...]. Monday, I will see which decision I will take. However, I do not venture to buy such a great many because next month, the three payments will need to be made. Some people say that these payments will make the shares decline whereas Mr. Darius considers that they might rise. The reason he gives is that several people defer purchases because they wait for this time and that once that time has come, everyone will be willing to pay and it will not be easy to find purchasable shares. In short, Sir, it is impossible to tell you the effect this will have, providence must work for us. What is certainly true is that from one hour to another, share prices rise.[47]

It is typical in such situations of fundamental uncertainty that actors estimate different future developments for the market, be it because they have access to different information or because, even though they share the same information, they have different opinions about it.[48] Vercour, however, was not fully convinced of the credibility of any of the scenarios. By 13 November, when Dellesem and he owned 15 *soumissions*, he declared that he would leave it at that, because he already was overwhelmed by the idea that Dellesem and he might have to come up with another 22,500 l. as instalment payments.[49] Shortly thereafter, Du Hamel, who had acquired one *soumission* for Vercour, supposedly discarded this *soumission* at a small profit, against Vercour's will and to his annoyance.[50] Thereupon, Vercour stopped working with him.[51]

Vercour with advice, established the contact. Behind "Darius & Cie." stood a commercial partnership established between Thellusson, his associate Jean-Claude Tourton (1655–1724), Darius and Jean-Jacques Fenel (1666–1736) in May 1719. Consulted by Thellusson, Darius conducted the society's operations. In February 1721, the society was prematurely terminated. One of the reasons given for the dissolution was that several debtors had gone bankrupt. Lüthy, *Banque protestante*, 1:401–403.

46 By 'actions', Vercour mostly refers to *soumissions*, which were also popularly called 'actions de 500' because the initial down payment amounted to 500 l.

47 "M[onsieu]r Darius me conseille de [...] garder [mes actions] et d'en acheter d'autre même à 300 d'agio sur cent [...]. Je verray lundi à quoy me déterminer. Je n'ose pourtant point acheter si grosse partie à raison qu'au mois prochain, il faudra faire les trois paiement. Il y en a qui disent que cela le[s] fera baisser et M[onsieu]r Darius est d'avis qu'ils pourront hausser, disant pour raison que plusieur[s] diffèrent d'en acheter en attendant ce tems et qu'alors, tout le monde voudra acheter et qu'il ne s'en trouvera point aisément. Enfin, M[onsieu]r, il est impossible de vous dire la suite, il faut que la providence travaille pour nous. Ce qu'il y a de vrai, [c'est] que d'heure à autre, cela hausse." Vercour to Dellesem, Paris 11.11.1719, in AEL, BSV, Reg. 3.

48 Beckert, *Imagined Futures*, 148.

49 Vercour to Dellesem, Paris 13.11.1719, in AEL, BSV, Reg. 3.

50 Vercour to Dellesem, Paris 16.11. and 25.11.1719, and to Poncelet Bonniver, Paris 5.12.1719, in AEL, BSV, Reg. 3.

51 Vercour to Dellesem, Paris 25.11.1719, and to Calefice, Paris 25.12.1719, in AEL, BSV, Reg. 3.

As share prices rose rapidly over the next couple of days – by 19 November, the *soumissions* were at 500 percent [≙3,000 l.] – Vercour's determination not to invest in any more stock weakened. While he continued to express concern about the possibility of a sudden reversal of fortune, he was pleased by the appreciation and wished that Dellesem and he were able to raise even larger funds in Paris.[52] What is more, Vercour resumed earlier efforts to convince Rudolph Adolph von Geyr and Johann Peter Herwegh, two well-situated correspondents, to co-invest in shares,[53] and he offered his services as an intermediary to another one of his contacts.[54]

Then again, Vercour's new readiness to invest only was determined by the hope that the short-term trend might continue for a while and not by a strong projective imaginary as to price development. Hence, Vercour apparently planned to get rid of his *soumissions* early enough to avoid both a possible price drop and having to make further payments for his *soumissions*. As soon as he considered that he had made a considerable profit, Vercour sold off all fourteen *soumissions* that he owned in order to secure the gains he had achieved.

According to Vercour's report from later that same day, upon his arrival on the *Rue Quincampoix* on the morning of 20 November, he had found that *soumission* prices had risen to 750 percent [≙4,250 l.] – a large leap forward compared to the closing price of 500 percent [≙3,000 l.] on the last official trading day, 18 November. Thereupon, Vercour decided to sell, only to discover that prices al-

52 Vercour to Dellesem, Paris 16.11.1719, in AEL, BSV, Reg. 3.

53 Vercour to de Geyr and to Herwegh, Paris 16.11. and 18.11.1719, in AEL, BSV, Reg. 3. For earlier offers, cf. Vercour to de Geyr and to Herwegh, Paris 30.11.1719, in AEL, BSV, Reg. 3. Both orders that Vercour subsequently got from them failed at first because Vercour did not get notice of the commissions in time, see Vercour to Herwegh, Paris 19.11. and 20.11.1719 and to de Geyr, Paris 21.12.1719, in AEL, BSV, Reg. 3. Later on, however, Vercour and von Geyr did invest together. Johann Peter Herwegh (1686–1755) was one of Vercour's closest business partners, and Vercour maintained a very friendly relationship with him. In 1720, Herwegh became one of the Burgomasters of Cologne in 1720, a position which he held again in later years, cf. Joachim Deeters, "Die Kölner Bürgermeister in der Frühen Neuzeit: Profil einer Gruppe von Berufspolitikern," in *Köln als Kommunikationszentrum: Studien zur frühneuzeitlichen Stadtgeschichte*, ed. Georg Mölich and Gerd Schwerhoff (Cologne: DuMont, 2000), 365–402, here 396. Rudolf Adolf von Geyr (1672–1752) was a Generaleinnehmer (Collector of Taxes) to Joseph Clemens of Bavaria, the Archbishop of Cologne and Prince-Bishop of Liège, cf. Maria Rößner-Richarz and Monika Gussone, "Witwen- und Vormundschaft," in *Adlige Lebenswelten im Rheinland: Kommentierte Quellen der Frühen Neuzeit*, ed. Gudrun Gersmann, Hans-Werner Langbrandtner, and Monika Gussone (Cologne: Böhlau-Verlag, 2009), 22–27, here 25.

54 Vercour to Poncelet Bonniver, Paris 16.11.1719, in AEL, BSV, Reg. 3.

ready had fallen and were now at 700 percent [≙4,000 l.].[55] Vercour nevertheless went on to dispose of his stock, as he dreaded a further price slump. The sale yielded a gain of 28,000 l. for him and his co-investor Dellesem. Hence, barely two weeks after he had come to Paris, Vercour managed to sell their stock for almost twice the sum that it originally had cost them.[56] When Vercour reported all of this to his correspondent von Geyr, who was uninvolved in the transaction, he emphasized that he was entirely satisfied with the outcome, regardless of the fact that, by the time he finished his letter, prices had increased once again. On 21 November at noon, the *soumissions* were at 820 percent [≙4,600 l.].[57]

Vercour planned to leave Paris soon. To Herwegh, who manifested his interest in buying shares, he explained that he did not consider it the right time any longer. Vercour justified his opinion by directly referring to the uncertainty of the share market:

> Therein lies so much variety that my head is spinning; one hears so many pros and cons that even the most able man must act upon pure chance [...]. Meanwhile, many people claim that the *soumissions* will be higher than 1000% [≙5,500 l.] within two weeks. Nevertheless, I have not ceased to prefer ready money at a lower price instead of waiting for a more distant and very uncertain future. Anyway, Sir, in case the shares will fall, I will buy others for your and my account. [...] On the morning of 21 [Oct.], I found [*soumission*] prices at 850% [≙4,750 l.]. [...] At this price, I would never dare to buy you any. There is so much stubbornness and fury in this, while, at the same time, one neither knows what one is buying nor why one does so.[58]

---

55 Vercour to de Geyr and to Herwegh, Paris 20.11.1719, in AEL, BSV, Reg. 3. In the letter to Herwegh, and in order to justify why he had not carried out Herwegh's order to buy an ordinary share for him anymore, Vercour states that he already had tried to sell his own *soumissions*, when the price had reached 500 percent. In the letter to de Geyr, this remark is missing.

56 Vercour to de Geyr and to Herwegh, Paris 20.11.1719, in AEL, BSV, Reg. 3. The letter where Vercour reports to Dellesem about the sale is not included in the copybook.

57 Vercour to de Geyr, Paris 20.11.1719 in AEL, BSV, Reg. 3. Vercour started to write that letter on 20 November, but, as the mail only went out at noon the next day, he added the latest developments.

58 "Il y a en cela tant de variété que la tête vous tourne, et l'on entend tant dire pour et contre que le plus habile doit agir au pure hasard [...]. Cependant, s'il faloit en croire à bien de gens, [les soumissions] seront à plus de 1000 [pour cent] avant 15 jours. Malgré cela, je n'ay pas laissé de préférer le contient [sic, probablement: comptant] à un prix plus moindre que d'atendre une avenir plus éloigné et très incertain. Enfin, M[onsieu]r, si [les actions] vienne[nt] à baisser, j'en achèteray des autre p[ou]r votre compte et p[ou]r le mien. [...] le 21 au matin, je trouve les action haussé à 850 [...]. A ce prix, je n'oserois jamais vous en acheter. Il y a en cela de l'entêtement et de la fureur tandis qu'on ne sçais ce que l'on achète ny pourquoy". Vercour to Herwegh, Paris 20.11.1719, in AEL, BSV, Reg. 3.

When Vercour declared that 4,750 l. for one *soumission* was too high a price, whereas a lower sum might be acceptable, he did not base his views on an assessment of the *soumissions'* value. Instead, Vercour regarded it as unreasonable to invest again at the same or higher price than that at which he had sold. He was only willing to reconsider this plan if, as rumors suggested, a new share issue was offered or if prices fell below 700 percent.[59] Yet, rumors of this first scenario were rather weak, whereas the last one seemed improbable, as Vercour explained on 24 November:

> One does not believe that the shares will fall because of the December payment. Given that the *soumissions* have already risen to 800% [≙4,500 l.], by selling just one or two of them, one makes enough money to nourish [i.e. make the instalment payment for] several others. If, against all expectations, the shares are to fall a lot, I could remain here longer in order to buy some, but if, as it seems, they increase in price or at least if they keep their current value, I hope to depart from here at the end of this month or at the beginning of the next one.[60]

Hence, even while Vercour insisted on the uncertainty of the share market, he still tried to form expectations for the longer term. The moment of the payments for the *soumissions* constituted a particularly important anchor point for the imaginary future states that he developed. Yet, the expectations that Vercour formed only contributed to his determination to withdraw from the share market. Due to the divergent convictions of his co-investor, Ferdinan Dellesem, however, he did not realize his plan.

Vercour's Quarrel with Dellesem

During the first weeks that he spent in Paris, all the (trackable) transactions that Vercour carried out happened in co-investment with Ferdinan Dellesem. Dellesem remained back in Liège during the whole episode, while Vercour travelled to Paris on his own. Vercour rendered Dellesem accounts of the latest developments in the stock market and reported on his own reflections and plans for

59 Vercour to Dellesem, Paris 25.11.1719, in AEL, BSV, Reg. 3.

60 "On ne croit point que les actions baisseron à cause du paiement du Xbre. Comme elle sont déjà haussée à 800 [pour cent], en vendant une ou deux actions seulement, on a pour nourrir plusieurs autres. Si les actions contre toute attente baisseroit fort, je pourrois encor rester icy pour en acheter, mais si elle hausse, comme l'aparance est, ou au moins si elle soutienne, j'espère de partir d'icy vers la fin du courant ou au commencement du mois prochain." Vercour to Dellesem, Paris 24.11.1719, in AEL, BSV, Reg. 3.

their joint venture with great regularity. Nevertheless, an information imbalance between the two associates was inevitable. Their physical distance rendered it difficult, if not impossible, for the two associates to agree beforehand on purchase and sale decisions. Whereas prices at the stock exchange were highly volatile and sometimes rose or fell sharply within mere hours, a letter between Liège and Paris needed at least three days. Even if the mail arrived promptly and if Dellesem answered immediately, Vercour only received Dellesem's opinion after about one week. Consequently, Dellesem hardly was able to control or determine the actions that Vercour took. In order to work smoothly, the joint investment therefore required a large amount of trust on Dellesem's part in Vercour's integrity and skills.[61] Yet, from the outset, dissonances accompanied the association, and when Vercour sold the 14 *soumissions* on 20 November, the tensions became aggravated.

As this sale was a spontaneous decision made under time constraints, Vercour did not ask for Dellesem's consent beforehand. Presumably, he hoped that, as they had made a considerable profit, Dellesem would approve in retrospect. Nevertheless, given that prices increased after his sale and certainly also in view of his past experiences with Dellesem, Vercour prepared himself against criticism and included long justifications for his decision when he informed Dellesem about the transaction.[62] And, indeed, Dellesem took the news quite negatively, as one of Vercour's children reported to their absent father:

> Your letter brought as much joy to Mr. Dellesem as it would have brought to a starving man, given that shares [i.e. *soumissions*] are supposed to be rising to 1200 % [≙6,500 l.], and that you sold them at 700 % [≙4,000 l.]. Dellesem told my mother that he could see that you are accustomed to earning a small brokerage.[63]

The citation indicates that Dellesem formed disparate expectations for the future development of share prices from Vercour. Yet, the two also disagreed about another, even more essential aspect of the share market: the question how calcu-

61 The relationship between Vercour and Dellesem can be conceived as a variation of the principal-agent-relationship and the so-called agency-problem that it entails. For this theory, cf. Kenneth J. Arrow, "The Economics of Agency," in *Principals and Agents: The Structure of Business*, ed. John W. Pratt and Richard J. Zeckhauser (Boston: Harvard Business School Press, 1985), 37–51.

62 Vercour to Dellesem, Paris 25.11.1719, in AEL, BSV, Reg. 3.

63 "Votre lettre a fait autant de plaisir à M[onsieu]r Dellesem qu'à une homme qui crève de faim [vu] que les action doivent hau[s]ser jusqu'à 1200 [pour cent] et que vous avez vendu à sept. Il a dit à ma mère qu'il voit bien que vous êtes accoutumé à gaigner un petit coultage [sic]". One of Vercour's children to Jean Vercour, Liège 27.11.1719, in AEL, BSV, Reg. 3.

lable these future prices were at all. Although Vercour emphasized the volatility of the share market in many letters, he had not succeeded in convincing Dellesem that it was difficult to understand and, even more so, to predict share price development. Instead, Dellesem adopted the more positive expectations of, for example, Darius (as transmitted by Vercour) and of at least one other indirect source, whom Dellesem believed to be better informed than Vercour.[64] It seems that, whenever Vercour insisted on the 'fury' of the share market and wanted to dispose of their stock, Dellesem took it as an indication of Vercour's ineptitude and faintheartedness.[65] In addition, Dellesem disputed Vercour's general understanding of the stock market, especially after Vercour sold their stock. Ironically, in the very recommendations that he gave Vercour, Dellesem sometimes unwillingly revealed the blurry character of his own understanding of the stock market. Consequently, after the selling of the *soumissions*, their written conversation became filled with reciprocal taunting and reproaches, which did not remain confined to the original dispute. Two examples show this.

Sometime in early December 1719, Dellesem advised Vercour that he should try to acquire stock at the issuance price. Thereupon, Vercour pointed out to him that such a favor surpassed a service of friendship.[66] This suggests that lack of personal experience and/or misinformation sometimes led Dellesem to imagine that it was too easy to make winnings at the stock market. Furthermore, the fact that he felt Vercour needed this advice also indicates that he held his correspondent's capacities in low esteem.

At roughly the same time, another argument took place between the two co-investors on another side-stage. The dispute emerged from an account that Vercour had given about the goings-on on the *Rue Quincampoix*. Vercour told Dellesem that, on 24 November, the traders on the *Rue Quincampoix* had been in dismay because prices slumped to 600 percent [≙3,500 l.]. Accordingly, a man named Papillon started to buy up all available shares at 800 percent [≙4,500 l.], in order to make prices increase.[67] This episode counted amid the many anecdotal stories that circulated about the contemporary share-market.[68] It seems likely that Vercour only knew the story from hearsay and had not wit-

64 One of Vercour's children to Jean Vercour, Liège 20.11.1719, in AEL, BSV, Reg. 3.

65 Cf. Marie d'Heur (Vercour's wife) to Vercour, Liège 22.11.1719 in AEL, BSV, Reg. 3; Vercour to Dellesem, Paris 25.11.1719 and to Marie d'Heur, Paris 11.12.1719, in AEL, BSV, Reg. 3.

66 "Il est impossible d'avoir des actions de la première main; il ne se trouve pas des amis au prix de là." Vercour to Dellesem, Paris 11.12.1719, in AEL, BSV, Reg. 3.

67 Vercour to Dellesem, Paris 24.11.1719 and 25.11.1719, in AEL, BSV, Reg. 3. In the version from 24.11., prices only had fallen to 770 percent [≙4350 l.].

68 The story was recounted by Du Hautchamp, *Histoire*, 2: 84–85.

nessed it himself: he told it twice – once on 24 November, once the following day – and the account grew more dramatic from the first to the second version. Besides, he insisted on an unimportant detail, the seemingly tremendous rent of 10 l. that the leaser of Papillon's office, a simple cobbler, received per day. Whether he witnessed the episode or not, Vercour recounted the story as a factual report to Dellesem. Thereby, he wanted to give him an impression of how closely joy and despair followed each other on the *Rue Quincampoix*. Yet, this went awry, and Vercour and Dellesem got in a disagreement. For Dellesem, the story was a clear indicator of Vercour's incompetence. In Vercour's eyes, Dellesem revealed his own lack of understanding with his reproaches. Infuriated, Vercour replied:

> You are saying I should buy at 600% [≙3,500 l.] [and resell to Papillon] what Papillon takes at 800% [≙4,500 l.]. Good Lord, do you think anyone would be stupid enough to give me at 600% what someone else takes and requests at 800%? Quite the contrary, this [i.e. Papillon's act of buying up] initially made the price rise to 900% [≙5,000 l.]. This here is not a trade one can do with an absent friend; one has to see it to believe it.[69]

At first glance, the argument seems to display Dellesem's misconception of the share market. Yet, it might also be partly the result of poor communication on Vercour's part. In the two accounts Vercour provided, he had not stated precisely that traders disposing of their stock at 600 percent and Papillon buying at 800 percent were two chronologically separate events. Due to the vagueness of Vercour's report, it is possible that Dellesem thought that the selling at 600 percent happened at a different place on the *Rue Quincampoix* than did the purchase at 800 percent. In any case, Dellesem's reaction indicates that he was more than ready to deem Vercour stupid, and he consequently did not try to decipher what Vercour wanted to tell him. Meanwhile, neither of them inquired into what the purpose of Papillon's actions might have been. Allegedly, Papillon pursued a manipulative aim; he is said to have secretly collaborated with another man named Fleury. One of them triggered a price increase, and the other then jumped at the opportunity to sell their shares.[70] Vercour apparently did not see through this ruse.

---

69 "Vous dite que je devroit prendre à 600 [pour cent] quand Papillon vient prendre à 800 [pour cent]. Bon Dieu, croiez-vous qu'on soit assez sot pour me donner à 600: ce q[u]'une autre prend et demande à 800 [pour cent]. Bien au contraire, cela le fit d'abord monter à 900. Ce n'est pas icy un négoce à pouvoir faire avec une amis [sic] absent, il faut voire pour croire." Vercour to Dellesem, Paris 18.12.1719, in AEL, BSV, Reg. 3.

70 Du Hautchamp, *Histoire*, 2: 84–85. In Du Hautchamp's version, it sounds as if Papillon and his collaborator repeatedly carried out this strategy.

To return to the sale of the 14 *soumissions:* Vercour used the discussion on Papillon's action to deny that, far away from events, Dellesem was capable of understanding the share market. Yet, even though he stood up for his decision to sell their stock, Vercour apparently perceived the continuous reproaches as so burdensome that he ultimately gave in to his co-investor. On 4 and 5 December, he acquired another eleven *soumissions* for a total of 61,525 l.[71] He thus reinvested all of the funds that Dellesem and he had gotten back from their earlier investment. Vercour emphasized that this happened both against his own conviction and against that of Darius, who had just declined a written solicitation from Dellesem to acquire shares for him independent from Vercour. Vercour also deplored that the new investment risked a large and secure profit in exchange for the possibility of either losing all or winning hugely.[72]

It is difficult to explain why Vercour was ready to put aside his own convictions. The tone of Vercour's letters suggests that Dellesem and he stood on an equal social footing. If Vercour judged it unwise to displease his investment partner, this was perhaps because Dellesem was influential in the Liégeois merchant community. Another possible explanation is that Vercour only feigned his unease at acquiring new stock, but this seems unlikely. In the very letter where Vercour, on 5 December, informed Dellesem about the new purchase, he also urged him to end their joint venture. Vercour's flighty tone in the letters suggests a fragile emotional state. Vercour alternated from lamenting about his correspondent's directives to manifesting complete subservience to declaring that he wanted to drop out:

> I must confess to you that, throughout my life, I have never made a trade with more regret than this one; because if I am going to lose the entire stake, what will be the reason? Your obstinacy and your reproaches. Meanwhile, I will never reproach you for that, and in order to show you how strongly your reproaches have affected me, I prefer to follow your orders like a child and to sacrifice everything I own in this dangerous trade; moreover, I prefer to eat up my heart here instead of suffering your harshness at my and your place [...]. I offer you a stipulation: would you agree to take over the 15 shares [i.e. *soumissions*] that I have for your personal account by paying my wife my 14,000 *livres* of profit? [...] I only make this proposition in order to end our collaboration in a friendly manner.[73]

71 Vercour bought six *soumissions* at 1005 percent (the exact date is not told) and the other five *soumissions* at 1035 percent on 4 December. Vercour to Dellesem, Paris 5.12.1719, in AEL, BSV, Reg. 3.

72 Vercour to Dellesem, Paris 5.12.1719, in AEL, BSV, Reg. 3.

73 "Je vous avoue que de ma vie, je n'ay fait un marché avec plus de regret que celluy-cy; car si je viens à perdre le tout, qui en sera la cause ? – vostre entestement et vos reproches. Cependant, je ne vous le reprocheray jamais, et pour vous témoigner combien vos reproche m'ont piqué vivement, j'aime mieux suivre vos ordres comme une enfant et sacrifier de perdre tout ce que j'ay

Two days later, Vercour repeated his desire to end the partnership in a more measured tone, only this time he did not formulate it as a mere proposition but as a firm resolution with different possible conditions.[74] Dellesem thereupon gave his consent to proceed clearing their accounts. He agreed to take six of the eleven *soumissions* that they owned and later reimbursed the costs of their purchase, amounting to 33,600 l.. Sometime between 14 and 18 December, Vercour probably sold the other five share options. On 18 December, Vercour indicated to Dellesem that his part of the loss from this transaction amounted to 6,000 l. Hence, the sale price presumably was 15,925 l. [≙537 percent per *soumission*].[75] The putative loss of 12,000 l. that the sale caused was shared equally between Dellesem and Vercour. Afterwards, Vercour disengaged from any joint stock trading activities with Dellesem.

The example of Vercour's quarrel with Dellesem illustrates the social embeddedness of his decision-making. Not only were his own expectations socially influenced, but, in this case, the divergent expectations that another actor had made him act against his own convictions. Furthermore, the example suggests that, the less informed an actor was, the more easily he could be convinced of the predictability of the share market. At a distance, both the market's volatility and the diversity of opinions with regard to future price developments were less apparent and, hence, the uncertainty of the business was less clear. Lastly, Vercour's difficult relationship with Dellesem also might explain why he complained about the uncertainty of the stock market again and again: he probably

dans ce dangereux négoce; j'aime encor mieux me manger le cœur icy que d'aler souffrir vos dureté chez moy et chez vous [...]. Je vous propose une condition, [à] savoir : voule[z]-vous accepter les 15 actions que j'ay pour votre compte particulier en paiant à ma femme mes l[ivres] 14 000 de profit [...] ? Ce que je propose n'est que pour me tirer d'affaires avec vous en amitiéz". Vercour to Dellesem, Paris 5.12.1719, in AEL, BSV, Reg. 3. Also cf. Vercour to Dellesem, Paris 18.12.1719, in AEL, BSV, Reg. 3: "quand je vous ay dit de vouloir me séparer de vous, je ne vous ay point parlé en maître mais bien en esclave, comme une homme plin de chagrin et de déplaisir".

74 Vercour to Dellesem, Paris 7.12.1719, in AEL, BSV, Reg. 3.

75 Vercour to Dellesem, Paris 18.12.1719, in AEL, BSV, Reg. 3. It seems likely that Vercour informed Dellesem about the details of this sale in an earlier letter, not included in the copybook. It is possible that the sale price was deliberately misrepresented by Vercour. If Vercour sold the *soumissions* at 537 percent, he would have done so at the lowest moment of the month, 14 December (Cf. Giraudeau's soumission price quotations as reprinted in Faure, *Banqueroute de Law*, 685. For 14 December, Giraudeau – who only quotes one price per day, regardless of fluctuations – indicates a price of 580.5 percent, for 15 December, a price of 711 percent). It is possible Vercour told Dellesem a plausible sale price that was lower than the actual one or that he even retained the five *soumissions* on his own account and lied about their sale.

was reacting to Dellesem's conception of the share-market which, in Vercour's eyes, was unrealistic.

Second Phase of Investment

Had Jean Vercour left the share market right after his separation from Dellesem, chances are that he would have emerged from it with a profit. Considering all the transactions that he carried out on Dellesem's and his joint account, Vercour made a personal gain of about 8,000 l. Yet, Vercour decided to stay in Paris some time longer. To Dellesem, on 18 December, he explained that he wanted to compensate for the loss incurred in their second investment.[76]

Almost immediately, Vercour reinvested significant sums. He bought several *soumissions* for his own account.[77] Furthermore, he started a new joint investment, this time with Rudolf Adolf von Geyr from Cologne. For their collective account, on 22 or 23 December, Vercour acquired eight *soumissions* for a total sum of 39,000 l.[78] Potential profits or losses were to be shared equally between von Geyr and him.[79] Probably on 27 December, Vercour also procured the necessary quarterly payment of 1,500 l. per share option.[80] On 28 December, when *soumissions* were around 900 to 925 percent [≙6,500 to 6,625 l., assuming that the quarterly payment of 1,500 l. had been made[81]], Vercour informed von Geyr that he had rejected an offer to sell at 1,200 percent [≙8,000 l.] against payment one month later, because he was confident that prices would rise considerably within the next two months.[82]

Where did Vercour's renewed willingness to venture large funds, seemingly in contradiction to his former desire to leave the share market with a small profit, originate? It certainly was not because Vercour had revised his expectations re-

76 Vercour to Dellesem, Paris 18.12.1719, in AEL, BSV, Reg. 3.

77 In his letter to Herwegh, Paris 5.1.1720, in AEL, BSV, Reg. 3, Vercour mentioned that, at 700 percent [≙ 4000 l.], 780 percent [≙ 4400 l.] and 800 percent [≙ 4500 l.], he had bought several *soumissions* in addition to those that he had acquired for von Geyr. He did not give the exact date of the purchase. The number probably amounted to five.

78 Vercour to de Geyr, Paris 23.12.1719, in AEL, BSV, Reg. 3. The exact prices, varying between 850 percent and 900 percent, can be found in Vercour's letter to the same from 28.12.1719, in AEL, BSV, Reg. 3.

79 Vercour to de Geyr, Paris 9.1.1720, in AEL, BSV, Reg. 3.

80 Vercour to de Geyr, Paris 25.12.1719, in AEL, BSV, Reg. 3.

81 From this point onwards in the chapter, unless stated otherwise, the prices given for *soumissions* refer to *soumissions* for which the first quarterly payment of 1500 l. had been made.

82 Vercour to de Geyr, Paris 28.12.1719, in AEL, BSV, Reg. 3.

garding the profitability of the Indies Company. In fact, he hardly ever discussed the (imagined) future earnings of the Company in his letters. Upon enquiry, Vercour admitted to von Geyr on 9 January 1720:

> It is impossible for me to tell you, Sir, the reason why the shares rise in price, nor can I tell you what this is grounded on [...]. The most solid fact is that almost all the revenues of the kingdom are amalgamated with the Company of the Indies.[83]

This remark – the only one where Vercour ever directly discussed the fundamentals of the Indies Company – indicates that he certainly did conceptualize an 'intrinsic value' of stock but both felt unable to assess this value and doubted that the share price development had any relation to it.[84] Seemingly, the promotion of the activities of the Indies Company, especially with regard to its projects in Louisiana,[85] had not adequately encouraged Vercour's trust in the shares' value.

Yet, there also is no indication that Vercour's willingness to gamble had increased by the end of December. Instead, his letters suggest that he was ready to invest anew, because he believed the share market had changed in character. To him, it seemed that stock trading had become more reliable because John Law was again willing to steer the development of the stock market. In order to explain this, a small digression must be made.

As has already been said, John Law repeatedly intervened in the stock market, more or less openly, in order to fully realize his aim of swapping government debt into equity.[86] The functioning of many of these financial interventions can be understood as speech acts, the perlocutionary intention of which was to persuade shareholders to await further price increases. One could also say that the aim of these interventions was to reduce the perceived uncertainty of the stock market and to trigger certain imaginary expectations. Shareholders and potential

---

83 "Il m'est impossible, M[onsieu]r, de vous dire pourquoy les actions haussent ny surquoy cela est fondé [...]. Ce qu'il y a de plus solide, ce [sic] que presques tout le revenu du roiaume sont réunis a la Compagnie des Indes". Vercour to de Geyr, Paris 9.1.1720, in AEL, BSV, Reg. 3.
84 In the early eighteenth century, it was an open question and, at least in London, a subject of much debate, whether an 'intrinsic value' of stock existed at all and how it possibly could be determined. Cf. William Deringer, *Calculated Values: Finance, Politics, and the Quantitative Age* (Cambridge, Mass.: Harvard University Press, 2018), 187–226.
85 Cf. Giraud, *Histoire de la Louisiane française*, 3:129–153; Orain, *Politique du merveilleux*, 174–191.
86 Velde, "Law's System, a Bubble?," 109–114.

investors were stimulated to believe and act according to the assumption that John Law would encourage share price to rise even further.[87]

One example helps to illustrate his point. In early October 1719, the Royal Bank made a suspiciously generous offer: it declared that it was ready to buy up Indies shares for 4,500 l., i. e. above the current market value. By implication, this suggested that John Law, as the head of this bank, believed that, even though the prices for which the Royal Bank bought up these shares were above the market prices, they were still a good deal for the institution. Thus, the measure indicated to the public that John Law used some edge in knowledge: he apparently had reason to assume that prices would rise above even 4,500 l., either because he knew that the intrinsic value of the shares exceeded the current market price or because he knew that he would soon take measures that would boost the market prices. Probably as a consequence of this logic, prices on the share market thereupon rose even higher than 4,500 l. – as John Law had certainly intended all along. As this increase seemingly confirmed the shareholders' analysis, it likely reinforced their beliefs in the capabilities of Law and in their own ability to understand his plans.[88]

When Jean Vercour came to Paris in early November 1719, however, such clear signals concerning John Law's skills and intentions did not exist. At that moment, the bull market was in full swing. While prices certainly fluctuated, the overall tendency was that of an increase, even without apparent support by John Law. For Vercour, however, the lack of intervention suggested insecurity. One somewhat peculiar remark that he made on 19 November indicates that, after his arrival in Paris, Vercour felt disenchanted by his realization that John Law was less capable than he had thought.

> It is impossible for any man on earth to give advice in this undertaking. Law, who is the author of this great machine, cannot tell anything about it either; when he believes he is generating a variation of 10 %, the variation happens to be 100 %.[89]

Ex negativo, this comment suggests that Vercour initially had expected that John Law – as head both of the Royal Bank and the Indies Company – would steer

87 William R. Herring, "Neither Pistols nor Sugar-Plumbs: The Rhetoric of Finance and the 1720 Bubbles," *Advances in the History of Rhetoric* 21 (2018): 147–162, here 147 and 151–154.

88 Cf. Herring, "Neither Pistols nor Sugar-Plumbs," 147, 151–152.

89 "Il est impossible à une homme sur la terre de pouvoir conseiller dans cette entreprise. Lau [sic] qui est l'auteur de cette grande machine n'en peu rien dire luy-même; quand il croit faire une variation de dix, elle se fait de cent [pour cent]". Vercour to Dellesem, Paris 19.11.1719, in AEL, BSV, Reg. 3.

stock market development and be able to determine share prices. Yet, during the first weeks that he spent in Paris, Jean Vercour considered that this belief was erroneous and that John Law was, at best, only partly able to control price development. This gave him cause for concern, as it rendered share trade more hazardous.

In late December, the deadline for the first payment on the *soumissions* near, John Law did again intervene to prevent prices from falling. On 23 December, or the day on or after which Vercour reinvested in stock, he explained to a correspondent that it seemed like the Royal Bank and John Law were secretly buying up shares and that this was the reason why, against all odds, prices had risen before the Christmas holiday. Vercour noted that it was popularly believed that prices would rise even further as soon as the payment period for the *soumissions* ended.[90] This visible readiness to direct share prices had a reassuring effect on Vercour, and it probably is the reason why he reinvested in shares at that point.

Another intervention that Law undertook made his willingness to influence share prices even more apparent. On 2 January 1720, the Company of the Indies opened two offices on the premises of the Royal Bank for the buying and selling of shares and *soumissions*. The price level for which it would do so was announced afresh every day.[91] Vercour took this as mildly reassuring. On 5 January, he reported to Herwegh:

> The shares still increase in popularity, but neither I nor anyone would be able to tell you why. The best and most solid [assurance] presently is that the [Royal] Bank takes the *soumissions* at a profit of 920 % [≙6,600 l.]. Therefore, one hopes that there will not be such extraordinary reversals any more as seeing the price fall from 1040 % [≙5,700 l.] to 480 [≙2,900 l.] and 500 % [≙3,000 l.][92] within so few days. I have seen variations of 100 % [≙500 l.] happening in one hour. However, in order to avoid these great confusions and to preserve the stock in high esteem, the Bank has started the day before yesterday to buy shares [i.e. *soumissions*] at 900 % [≙6,500 l.] and to sell them at 910 % [≙6,550 l.].[93]

---

90 Vercour to François de Roy, Paris 23.12.1719, in AEL, BSV, Reg. 3. Also Vercour to Dellesem, Paris 28.12.1719, in AEL, BSV, Reg. 3. Two weeks later, in hindsight and in reaction to further reproaches, Vercour explained to Dellesem that, without this pegging, the *soumissions* certainly would have lost greatly around the Christmas holidays: Vercour to Dellesem, Paris 9.1.1720, in AEL, BSV, Reg. 3.

91 Faure, *Banqueroute de Law*, 307–308, 319–320, 340.

92 Here, Vercour refers to the time before the first quarterly payment has been made; hence, the *soumission* prices that are given are lower.

93 "Ce papier prend toujour faveur, cependant je ne sçauroit vous dire ny personne pourquoy. Ce qu'il y a de meilleure à présent et de plus solide, c'e[st] que la banque le prend à £920 de profit sur cent. Ainsi, on espère qu'il n'arivera plus de révolution si extraordinaire de voir tomber en si peu de jours le prix de £ 1040 à 480 et 500 [pour cent]. J'ay veu des variations en une heure

On 16 January, Vercour reflected that this new measure had convinced him that share prices would now rise steadily. Apparently, he had assumed that the prices at which the Company bought and sold shares would be adjusted to current market prices every day – and market prices, he had reasoned, forcedly would always lie at least slightly higher than the fixed prices that the office paid:

> When the Bank [...] bought shares [i.e. *soumissions*] at 1000% [≙7,000 l.], their market value was even higher at the place of trading because at worst, one could sell the shares at the Bank for 1000%, and if this had continued, the price of a share [i.e. a *soumission*] would certainly have been at least 1200% [≙8,000 l.] because the bank changed the [bid and offer] price every day and aligned it to the market price.[94]

Yet, Vercour seemingly did not want to rely too much on the price support. On 9 January, for no other apparent reason, Vercour offered to sell Dellesem his *soumissions* at 1,200 percent [≙8,000 l.], under condition of being paid in Liégeois currency.[95] Then, after the buying and selling of shares was suspended on 10 January, a price-drop of about 200 percent [≙1,000 l.] occurred and prices started to fluctuate considerably. This probably reminded Vercour of the threat of sudden reversals, and he concluded that it was best to play it safe. On 11 January, he announced to von Geyr:

> [The shutdown of the offices] does not give me great pain, because I am sure that on Monday, the *soumissions* will resume their normal course. Meanwhile, to me, this business seems very unpleasant. The fact that I have seen so many reversals in one moment has determined me to dispose of our *soumissions* when they will be high enough again that they will bring a profit of a few thousand *livres*. Or, if possible, I will sell them at credit on condition that they will be paid in one month or six weeks, as this will bring more profit.[96]

---

de 100 P[our] C[ent], mais pour éviter ces grandes confusions et pour tenir ce papier en honneur, la banque avant-hier a commencé à prendre les actions à 900 et le[s] rendre à 910 [pour cent]." Vercour to Herwegh, Paris 5.1.1720, in AEL, BSV, Reg. 3.

94 "Quand la banque [...] prennoit [les actions] à 1000 [pour cent], le cours étoit encor plus haut sur la place de négociations à raison qu'au pir, on les portoit à la banque à 1000 [pour cent], et si cela avoit continué, certainement [le prix d'une action] seroit à présent au moins à 1200 [pour cent] car la banque chang[e]oit tout le jours de prix et se régloit après le cours de la place." Vercour to de Geyr, Paris 16.1.1720, in AEL, BSV, Reg. 3.

95 Vercour to Dellesem, Paris 9.1.1720, in AEL, BSV, Reg. 3. There is no indication that Vercour had already heard about the *primes* when he made this offer. He first mentioned his worries about this new instrument on 13 January (see below).

96 "[...] cela ne me fait pas grosse peine, ne doutant pas que lundy, [les soumissions] reprendront leur train. Cependant ce négoce me paroit très désagréable. De voir ainsi en un moment tant de révolution, cela me fait résoudre de m'en défaire quand elles seront revenue à pouvoir

Ironically, Vercour's renewed belief that it was possible to foresee developments on the stock market – founded on the impression that the Indies Company again was willing to steer price developments – can best be seen by his reaction to a measure which convinced him that it was best to leave the share market for good. On 9 January 1720, the Company started to issue a new sort of bond, the so-called *primes*. *Primes* can be described as call options on shares, where the Indies Company took the role of the seller. Against a payment of 1,000 l., investors acquired the right to buy a share for the strike price of 10,000 l. within the following six months.[97] Hence, for investors, *primes* constituted mainly an interesting investment, if they assumed that, within the next half year, the price for ordinary shares would exceed 11,000 l. Vercour, probably inspired by his local advisors, considered what this meant from the opposite point of view. For the Indies Company, he reasoned, *primes* would only be lucrative if share prices remained under 11,000 l. Vercour believed that this interpretation of the new financial instrument was the main cause why the share price had declined:

> The fact which harms share prices the most is that the bank, since it is closed, promises to sell shares at 1200% [≙ 11,000 l. for a fully paid *soumission*][98] during the next 6 months. The person who buys such a promise has to pay 1000 *livres* in cash and if he then decides to buy the share, he has to pay the remaining sum. So, my dear Sir, one should not hope that, in case this becomes reality, our shares will exceed a profit of 1200%.[99]

The issue of *primes* hence worked in the manner of a speech act, even if the perlocutionary effect that this speech act had on Vercour was a negative assessment of future share price developments. In Vercour's eyes, the announcement indicated that the Company did not expect nor wish to fuel a significant price increase during the next months. Consequently, Vercour concluded that the time of great profits was over.[100] Probably, his deliberation corresponded with what John Law wished to suggest by introducing the *primes*. Reflecting back nearly five years

---

profiter quelque mille livres; ou, si je peu, je le[s] venderay à crédit pour un mois ou 6 semaines, je pouray en obtenir plus de profit". Vercour to de Geyr, Paris 11.1.1720, in AEL, BSV, Reg. 3.

97 Velde, "Government," Appendix, 18.

98 Even though the *primes* were options on normal shares, Vercour explained what the introduction of *primes* foretold with regard to the *soumission* price, as he only owned *soumissions*.

99 "Ce qui fait plus grand mal, c'e[st] que la banque, depuis qu'elle est fermée, elle donne des promesse[s] de fournir à £1200 [pour cent] pendant le terme de 6 mois. Celuy qui prend de telle promesse doit paier £1000 comptant et quand il prendroit l'action, il doit compter le reste. Ainsi, mon cher M[onsieu]r, il ne faut pas espérer, si cela a lieu, qu'avant 6 mois, nos actions passeront £1200 de profit." Vercour to de Geyr, Paris 16.1.1720, in AEL, BSV, Reg. 3. Also Vercour to de Geyr, Paris 20.1.1720, in AEL, BSV, Reg. 3.

100 Vercour to Herwegh, Paris 16.1.1720 and to de Geyr, 22.1.1720, in AEL, BSV, Reg. 3.

later, Law stated that he had issued the *primes* in order to put the brakes on speculation – precisely by dissuading share-traders that stock prices would climb higher than 10,000 l.[101]

If this had been the intention, however, Law's measure was not effective among the majority of the public. Paradoxically, while ordinary shares fell below the value of 10,000 l. as soon as the *primes* had been introduced, the *primes* themselves initially were highly sought after. Antoin E. Murphy has explained this by arguing that many shareholders (unlike Vercour) must have been so convinced that share prices would rise considerably that they sold part of their stock in order to purchase *primes*, thus multiplying their right to acquire further stock in the future.[102] Besides, Law probably had not intended to convince shareholders like Vercour that it was best to quit the market for good. For once, an attempt of John Law to channel expectations partly failed.

Vercour now slowly started to withdraw from the share market. By mid-January, when *soumission* prices were around 860 – 880 percent [≙6,300 – 6,400 l.], he succeeded in selling Dellesem five *soumissions* at 1,200 percent [≙8,000 l.], i.e. at a total cost of 40,000 l., payable in Paris one month later on 15 February 1720.[103] He then waited for another good occasion. Presumably, he was reluctant to sell as long as *soumissions* roughly were at the level at which he bought them. In early February, when the offices of the Bank were closed yet again,[104] Vercour reported that it seemed as if emissaries of the Royal Bank were secretly buying up shares, which gave the public new hope that the Bank was willing to fuel prices.[105] Vercour therefore considered it probable that prices would soon be at 1,000 percent [≙7,000 l.]. Yet, when the offices finally reopened on 10 February at 920 and 930 percent for *soumissions* [≙6,600 and 6,650 l.], the prices at which they bought and sold were lower than shareholders had hoped. Vercour, who was afraid that prices might drop further, thereupon sold the remaining six *soumissions* that he owned jointly with von Geyr at 914 percent [≙6,570 l.] for a total

---

101 "Mémoire de Law au Duc de Bourbon du 15 Octobre 1724," in John Law, *Œuvres complètes*, ed. Harsin, 3:270 – 271.

102 Murphy, *Economic Theorist*, 215 – 217. Vercour's explanation why *soumissions* and shares lost in price when the *primes* were issued therefore cannot have been (entirely) correct.

103 Vercour to Dellesem, Paris 20.1. and 22.1.1720, in AEL, BSV, Reg. 3. Vercour reacted to letters from Dellesem from 13 and 16 January. Two of these *soumissions* came from Vercour and von Geyr's joint investment, so the other three probably counted amid those that Vercour had bought on his own account.

104 For the dates of the successive shutdowns and re-openings, see Faure, *Banqueroute de Law*, 340.

105 Vercour to de Geyr, Paris 2.2. and 4.2.1720, in AEL, BSV, Reg. 3.

of 39,420 l.[106] Shortly after, he drafted an account. It stated that von Geyr and he had invested a capital of 54,322 l. and made a profit of 2,000 l. each.[107]

Yet, to Vercour's great distress, he now found that realizing his profits was difficult – due to developments that were external, but closely connected, to the share market.

Aftermath

Ever since Vercour left Liège in late October 1719, the Paris exchange rates had depreciated almost continuously – mainly because (former) investors increasingly transferred funds out of the country.[108] When, by mid-February, Vercour wanted to withdraw his funds, he thus found himself unable to do so without incurring large losses. On 30 October 1719, the exchange rate between Paris and Amsterdam (which was an important intermediary financial center for Liège and Cologne) had been 45 *deniers banco* per French *écu*. By 15 February 1720, it was 35.[109] Vercour hoped desperately that the rate would improve and speculated that the French government was ready to take corresponding measures.[110] This, however, was not the case. Instead, in order to foster stock prices, the money supply was increased by emitting paper money. Inflation only slowly started to pick up, but the measure immediately and negatively impacted rates of exchange.[111]

Sometime around mid-February, having consigned his and von Geyr's assets to the hands of Darius, Vercour left Paris. At this point, apart from paper money, he still owned two *soumissions* on his personal account.[112] Vercour reached his hometown on 25 February.[113] While he waited for better times, he reluctantly

106 Vercour to de Geyr, Paris 15.2. and 16.2.1720, in AEL, BSV, Reg. 3.
107 Vercour to de Geyr, Paris 1.3.1720, in AEL, BSV, Reg. 3.
108 For the Paris-on-Amsterdam exchange rate during 1719/20, see Neal, *Financial Capitalism*, 65. For the exchange rates that Vercour gave in 1720, see Hémardinquer, "Reconstruction," 27.
109 Vercour to Darius, Liège 30.10.1719; Vercour to de Geyr, Paris 15.2.1720, in AEL, BSV, Reg. 3.
110 Vercour to Herwegh, Liège 4.3.1720; Vercour to de Geyr, Paris 9.4. and 14.4.1720, in AEL, BSV, Reg. 3. Many other investors similarly believed that John Law would ensure that the exchange rates improved. For example, the prominent stockjobbers Joseph Gage and Lady Mary Herbert borrowed money to speculate on the exchange. Others, such as their lender Richard Cantillon, believed that the contrary would be true. Cf. Murphy, *Cantillon*, 140–147.
111 Neal, *Financial Capitalism*, 68–69; Velde, "Government Equity," 30–31, 51.
112 Cf. Vercour to de Geyr, Paris 26.3.1720, in AEL, BSV, Reg. 3. Vercour probably sold these *soumissions* shortly after he wrote that letter.
113 Vercour to de Geyr, Liège 28.2.1720, in AEL, BSV, Reg. 3.

started to look out for other uses to which he could put the funds he owned in France. Yet, to his great despair, hardly any of the opportunities he examined proved viable.[114] In February 1720, Vercour considered investing in brandy or wine, but these commodities already had risen in price.[115] A few weeks later, he reluctantly thought about playing the stock market again, because no better options seemed to exist.[116] He departed for Paris again on 12 March, only to learn that share speculation on the *Rue Quincampoix* now was forbidden, with shares being assigned the fixed monetary value of 9,000 l.[117]

Jean Vercour slowly accepted that he would be forced to stay in France, if he wanted to make some reasonable use of his remaining funds. Together with a companion from Liège, he established a brewery business, for which, in early May 1720, he rented a building in Paris. Vercour was able to pay at least the first rent with paper money.[118] Soon after that, it became increasingly difficult to make use of the *billets de banque*. In an effort to put the brakes on falling exchange prices and on slowly increasing inflation, on 21 May 1720, the government announced that banknotes and shares were to be reduced in value. This decision led to a public outcry, and, even though it was revoked only one week later, confidence in John Law's System never returned.[119] During the next months, both shares and banknotes gradually lost their value until they finally were withdrawn from the market. Simultaneously, a shortage of coin occurred. This caused general discontent, which resulted in small riots and political disturbances.[120] In September, Vercour tried, yet again, to buy commodities with his paper money, but he found no one willing to accept such payments.[121] Vercour now was filled with sorrow and self-pity. He did not perceive the difficulties in which he found himself as a personal failure; rather, he claimed that it was hardly possible for anyone to make good decisions in the present, incessantly changing conditions:

---

114 For an outline of these attempts, also see Hémardinquer, "Reconstruction," 28–31.

115 Vercour to de Geyr, Paris 15.2. and Liège 28.2.1720, in AEL, BSV, Reg. 3.

116 Vercour to de Geyr, Liège 4.3.1720, in AEL, BSV, Reg. 3.

117 Vercour to de Geyr, Paris 17.3.1720 and to Herwegh, Paris 23.03.1720, in AEL, BSV, Reg. 3.

118 Archives nationales de France (ANF), MC ET XLIX, 494, 5.5.1720: Lease contract between Jean Vercour and Anne Dufour, Veuve Labeur. Vercour also mentions his brewery plans in his letters: Vercour to Herwegh and to de Geyr, Paris 9.7.1720, in AEL, BSV, Reg. 3.

119 On this episode, see e.g. Faure, *Banqueroute*, 428–448 and Murphy, *Economic Theorist*, 244–264.

120 Cf. Murphy, *Economic Theorist*, 265–287.

121 Vercour to de Geyr, Paris 10.9.1720, in AEL, BSV, Reg. 3.

> I do not know yet which place the good God has designated as my sepulchral site. The current affairs are capable of changing one's resolution every day. Even the most able man cannot see anything solid in such a fatal conjecture and all human prudence would not suffice to avoid so many adversities. I am not ingenious or bright enough to identify the positive occasion in the downside.[122]

Jean Vercour's letter book contains very few letters after summer 1720.[123] Hence, it is unclear how he experienced the ensuing months. Some surviving administrative sources, however, indicate that they were difficult for him. Vercour probably presented his remaining paper money for the 'Visa', i.e. the liquidation process that France undertook after John Law fled the country at the end of 1720.[124] Yet, Vercour did not live long enough to see this process end in 1723. As to Vercour's brewery business, the association soon broke up due to a disagreement between himself and his companion. Vercour continued the business on his own, for which he raised a credit of 17,400 l.[125] Yet, his beer presumably was of rather poor quality.[126] At the end of 1721, during a trip home to Liège, Vercour died. When this news reached Paris, several creditors presented themselves to the competent commissary, who put his remaining property under requisition. But Vercour's daughter already had moved the most valuable of his belongings, e.g. his tapestries, out of the country.[127]

---

122 "Je ne sçais pas encor où le bon Dieu a destiné le lieu de ma sépulture. Les affaire présente sont capable de faire changer tout le jours de résolution. L'homme le plus habille ne peut rien dire de solide dans une conjucture de tems si fatal et toute la prudence humaine ne sçauroit éviter tant de contretems. Je n'ay pas assez de bon génie ni de lumière p[ou]r distinguer le bon party dans le mauvais." Vercour to Herwegh, Paris 16.9.1720, in AEL, BSV, Reg. 3.

123 The last entry that Jean Vercour made himself dates from 17.9.1720, by which time he had decided to resettle in Paris. Family members, who remained in Liège where they continued some commercial activities, composed the few letters that were entered after that date.

124 During this procedure of great complexity, all the securities that had been distributed during John Law's System were reduced and converted into government debt. Cf. François R. Velde, "Introduction," in François-Michel Chrétien-Deschamps, *Lettres sur le Visa des dettes de l'État ordonné en 1721*, ed. François R. Velde (Paris: Classiques Garnier, 2015), ix–lxiv.

125 The split-up is mentioned in a plead that Vercour wrote to the French king, wherein he asked to be received as a member of the brewery guild: ANF, G7 671, 19.2.1721. For the debenture of Vercour and his wife towards Pierre Grassin, see ANF, MC ET LVII, 306, 17.3.1721.

126 Cf. ANF, Y 14932, Minutes of the requisition from 11.12.1721: request from 9.1.1722, by Barthelemy Bruche.

127 Cf. ANF, Y 14932, Minutes of the requisition from 11.12.1721.

Conclusion

This case study has followed the trajectory of the bill trader Jean Vercour's decision-making during the 1719/20 Mississippi Bubble and especially focused on the imaginaries of the future that (co-)determined his actions.

Vercour's activities on the share market evidently were motivated by the hope that he would make significant profits. This expectation was fueled by generally positive share price developments, the omnipresent talk of the fortunes that already had been made, and by the stories which circulated about *nouveaux riches*. However, another imagination we might expect to have informed Vercour's experiences, the belief that the activities and earning prospective of the Indies Company – especially overseas – justified the rising share prices, does not seem to have played a role in Vercour's decision-making about whether and when to buy stock. At no instance did he delve into the idea of possible riches in the Louisiana territory, nor did he write enthusiastically about the trading opportunities that were open to the Indies Company. If anything, the revenues that the Indies Company generated through its tax collection activities made him believe that the shares had a measurable value, although he still suspected that stock was overvalued. Consequently, Vercour anticipated a possible price drop in the medium run. He therefore aimed for short-term gains only and constantly was concerned about the capricious character of the market. At times, he nevertheless believed that he was able to anticipate developments at the share market. This fictional scenario, that Jean Vercour certainly shared with others, was intentionally encouraged by John Law and his entourage. Whenever the institutions that Law headed, namely the Royal Bank and the Company of the Indies, signaled their willingness to manage the share market, this had a reassuring effect on Vercour. He did not perceive their interventions as manipulative but, rather, as a normal and welcome part of the game, which brought some reliability to an otherwise unpredictable, and thus dangerous, business. The interventions allowed him to convince himself that he was able to analyze John Law's plans and expectations and thus to anticipate the share price development.

Similar ideas as Vercour's also were expressed during the British South Sea Bubble. A number of investors in London had doubts about the long-term prospects of share prices but still traded in stock in the hopes of making short-term gains or even of 'riding the bubble'.[128] What is more, while many observers un-

128 E.g. Thomas Guy, Hoare's bank and James Brydges the Duke of Chandos and his brokers. See Paul, *South Sea Bubble*, 69; Temin and Voth, *Prometheus*, 114–120 and Yamamoto, "James Brydges," 339–340, 346–347 and 355.

derstood price development as largely erratic, others assumed that the Directors of the South Sea Company and their advocates in Parliament were able to support, or even determine, stock prices.[129] Just like John Law, the South Sea Directors took advantage of this notion and employed incentives that were both financial and rhetorical in order to make investors believe that they expected a price increase.[130] Untangling which images of the future (and thereby expectations for price developments) existed and how and why they changed, thus helps in developing a more nuanced understanding of what drove the speculative bubbles of 1719/20.

---

129 Deringer, *Calculated Values*, 200.
130 Herring, "Neither Pistols nor Sugar-Plumbs," 155–156; Paul, *South Sea Bubble*, 72–73.

Dror Wahrman

Order from Chaos Springs: The Bubbles of 1720 as a Turning Point in Western Conceptualizations of Causality and Order

We all know that the financial crises c. 1720, the so-called "bubbles," were a historical disruption of the highest magnitude. After all, contemporaries repeatedly told us so, insisting time and again that these events were unprecedented and extraordinary, arriving without any warning ("like a thief in the night," wrote the poet Alexander Pope), and creating unmitigated, unparalleled, existential hardship. "None can be insensible" – the words of one English sermon following the bursting of the South Sea Bubble can stand for many – "that there is a sudden run of general distress, affecting innumerable persons and families, beyond any instance within the reach of memory, and possibly within the reach of history."[1] The bubbles were a moment of great collective outcry.

It has been suggested in recent research – and contested by some, e. g. by Daniel Menning in this volume – that the actual economic, financial and social effects of the bursting of the financial bubbles were more limited in scope and extent than one could have assumed based on these emotional contemporary litanies. As can be inferred, for instance, from the surprisingly small surge of bankruptcies, by and large people did not find themselves impoverished overnight and out on the street. To be sure, many did lose money, which hurt, even if they were more often wealthy investors than individuals of modest means who might have lost their family savings.[2] But the socio-economic impact of the bursting of the bubbles, in and of itself, seems insufficient to explain the collective outburst of existential angst.

This chapter revisits one part of an argument that Jonathan Sheehan and I make in our book *Invisible Hands: Self-Organization and the Eighteenth Century*,[3] which offers a complementary explanation for the angst brought about by the period of financial booms and busts c. 1720. What was at stake for many observers

1 Pope to Atterbury, 23.9.1720, in *The Correspondence of Alexander Pope*, ed. G. Sherburn (Oxford: Oxford University Press, 1956), 2:53; John Evans, *Past Deliverances and Present Calamities Improved. In a Sermon [...]* (London, 1720), 20 – 21.

2 Julian Hoppit, "The Myths of the South Sea Bubble," *Transactions of the Royal Historical Society* 12 (2002): 141 – 165.

3 Jonathan Sheehan and Dror Wahrman, *Invisible Hands: Self-Organization and the Eighteenth Century* (Chicago: The University of Chicago Press, 2015).

https://doi.org/10.1515/9783110592139-012

and participants in these events was nothing less than their understanding and expectations regarding *the relationship of cause and effect.* And from these cognitive challenges to prevalent notions of causality emerged for some observers a new way of conceptualizing chaos and order, one founded on epistemic narratives of *self-organization.* This new way of thinking about disorder and order, providence and chance, that in the 1720s became for the first time a full-fledged cultural-cum-intellectual phenomenon in Western Europe, was an unexpected outcome of the bubbles of 1720 that remained one of its most important legacies in the modern West.

This chapter begins by mapping the challenges that the financial bubbles c. 1720 posed for European notions of causality and order. It charts various ways in which contemporaries responded to these challenges and then focuses on one of those responses: not the most prevalent one, but a radical new departure with a significant presence. This type of response conjured up stories reliant on non-linear causality and a logic of aggregation that we have described in our book as stories of "self-organization" and that may be familiar to the reader as narratives of an invisible hand. As we will see shortly, such revolutionary conceptual moves contained the cognitive difficulties presented by the crises of 1720 especially well. In order to get at evidence of such cognitive strains, parts of the following analysis are based on a wide trawl through the many hundreds of publications referring to the South Sea Bubble and related financial events primarily in Britain. To be more precise, while reading widely across European texts, the quantitative bulk of the analysis emerges from a survey of all British publications from 1720 and 1721. No less than 13 percent of these publications referred in some way to these financial events, a total of 365 texts that, discounting multiple editions, amounts to over 260 British publications.[4]

1720: A Crisis of Causality

We begin, then, with what I wish to propose as a crisis of causality. The goings-on that the bevy of hack writers and self-appointed analysts observed in the financial marketplace appeared curiously resistant to available frameworks of rational description and causal explanation. This resistance was unsettling – not least, since few had doubts as to why individuals were doing whatever they were doing in the stock market. It was news to no one that investors, in the words

4 These numbers represent a full count based on the inventory of the *Eighteenth Century Collection Online*, undertaken in August 2006.

of one writer, "know no other Principle than to get Money, and the Rule and Byass of all their Actions is Interest."[5] And yet acknowledging the individual pursuit of naked self-interest, it turned out, did not go very far in making sense of what was going on.

This inability to link causes and effects was more unsettling still, since this was, after all, the era of Isaac Newton, widely believed in his time to be a once-in-a-millennium genius of causal explanation, one "who stands up as the Miracle of the present Age" – thus spoke Addison's *Spectator* – and "can look through a whole Planetary System." Through the whole planetary system perhaps, but not through the chaos of the stock market. "*I can calculate the motions of erratic stars,*" Newton's frustration in response to the South Sea Bubble is famously quoted, "*but not the madness of the multitude.*" (Newton himself lost significant sums of money in the Bubble.)[6] Curiously, there is no actual source for this widely reproduced Newton quote. Perhaps it was put in his mouth by a generation who felt this is what Newton *must* have said, since for them he stood for causal certainty and explicability.

Rather, the basic experience of people observing these events was one of profound and unsettling disorder. In France, already in 1718, the *parlementaires* of Paris had not minced words. John Law's still-evolving System, they warned then, "produce[d] disorderliness in everything" and created "a chaos so great and so obscure that nothing about it can be known." And, if the *parlementaires* might have had in mind mystification from above more than self-generating chaos from below, this was certainly not true of the English divine who opened his finger-wagging sermon in November 1720 with "the great disorder and confusion which an eager desire of wealth has of late occasion'd amongst us." The problem, "the unhappy sources of the [present] calamities," was that the stock market made possible the "irregular pursuit" of wealth, by facilitating an "irregular traffick" and opportunities for "irregular and indirect courses to acquire it." It was not the desire for wealth in and of itself but rather all this rampant irregularity that kept our sermonizer up at night. To all intents and purpos-

---

5 Letter LIV, in *A Collection of Miscellany Letters, Selected Out of Mist's Weekly Journal* (London, 1722–1727), 2:165.

6 *The Spectator*, No. 543, in *The Spectator*, ed. D.F. Bond (Oxford: Oxford University Press, 1965), 4:442. Newton's quote (emphasis added) is often repeated, in slightly different wordings: e. g. in P. Brantlinger, *Fictions of State: Culture and Credit in Britain, 1694–1994* (Ithaca: Cornell University Press, 1996), 44 (quoting H.R. Fox Bourne, *The Romance of Trade* (London and New York: Cassell, Petter & Galpin, 1871), 292). For Newton's involvement in the Bubble, see Andrew Odlyzko, "Newton's Financial Misadventures in the South Sea Bubble," Working Paper (2018); Hoppit, "The Myths of the South Sea Bubble," 149.

es, the collective outcome of what writer Charles Gildon called "the giddy Fluctuation of the People," of the unpredictable "Humour and Whimsey, that made the Stocks run up to that prodigious Degree" and then "according to its changeable nature" sent the market back down "as fast and as unaccountably as it run up," was simply random.[7]

Jonathan Swift, poet, satirist, and sometime South Sea investor, penned these verses (as well as many others) to try to capture this particular aspect of the Bubble:

> The Bold Encroachers of the Deep,
> Gain by Degrees huge Tracts of Land,
> Till *Neptune* with one gen'ral Sweep
> Turns all again to barren Strand.
>
> The Multitudes capricious Pranks
> Are said to represent the Seas;
> *Breaking* the *Bankers* and the *Banks*,
> Resume *their own* whene'er they please.[8]

On one side in Swift's image stand the bankers and the "bold encroachers": the rational operators of the financial scene, whose actions are ordered and measured – they who "gain by degrees." But the real power to shape the outcome is not in their hands but rather in those of the multitudes, whose destructive tidal wave is unleashed like "capricious Pranks," randomly and unpredictably, "whene'er they please." The main force here is not greed, that which is the ample endowment of the bankers and encroaching speculators; it is the unfettered agency of the multitudes, their unpredictable capriciousness, irregular whimsy and giddy fluctuations, which result in randomness and chaos.

This chaos was more puzzling for being man-made and freely self-inflicted rather than the consequence of external pressures. "It will hardly be credited in future Ages," went one exclamation, that this great nation "was brought almost to the Brink of Ruin, in a few days, without the Calamities either of a Foreign Invasion, or an Intestine War." In the past, echoed another, Britons had

---

7 *Journal du Parlement par Deslisle*, interventions of 4.3. and 17.6.1718, quoted in T.E. Kaiser, "Money, Despotism, and Public Opinion in Early Eighteenth-Century France: John Law and the Debate on Royal Credit," *Journal of Modern History* 63 (1991): 1–28, here 12; Samuel Bradford, *The Honest and the Dishonest Ways of Getting Wealth. A Sermon [...]* (London, 1720), 3, 27, 31; Charles Gildon, *All for the Better; or, the World Turn'd Up-side Down [...]* (London, 1720), 10.

8 Jonathan Swift, "The Run upon the Bankers (1720)," in Jonathan Swift, *Miscellanies, in Prose and Verse. The Fifth and Sixth Volumes* (London, 1738), 1:208–209.

coped with "the malicious contrivances and unjust attempts of our enemies; but the present distresses of the nation *are directly self-made*."[9]

Wild, eccentric, capricious, irregular, giddy, changeable, unaccountable, self-made: small wonder that Newton reputedly summed it all up as the incalculable "madness of the multitude." His contemporaries, it seems, could not agree more. They were "like Men possest and frantic." "Have you really all gone mad in Paris?" asked Voltaire in response to the investors' frenzy generated by Law's actions already in 1716: "It is a chaos I cannot disentangle." The son of Robert Harley, the earl of Oxford who had invented the South Sea Company a decade earlier, reported from London in May 1720: "The madness of stock-jobbing is inconceivable. This wildness was beyond my thought." And a month later: "nothing is so like Bedlam as the present humour which has seized all parties, Whigs, Tories, Jacobites, Papists, and all sects." A Dutch observer described these events "as if all the Lunatics had escaped out of the madhouse at once." This last tableau is especially rich: it conveys the kind of chaos generated by a multitude of individuals operating each on their own steam in random directions. This was "the *many-minded Multitude*," Sir John Meres penned another evocative image, which he then resorted to Latin to explain: "the *incertum Vulgus*, of whom there is scarce any Thing certain, but this, *Quod scindet in contraria* [that which tears up in opposite directions]." Two and a half centuries later Peter G.M. Dickson, the usually tempered doyen of Bubble historians, described the behavior of those early-eighteenth-century investors, "both in the boom and after its collapse," as "apparently hysterical and ungoverned."[10] For observers then and now, contemporaries acted erratically and randomly, as if possessed, not directed by any distinguishable rationale or logic.

Was it possible, then, *pace* Newton's reputed exasperation, to disentangle this seeming chaos according to what contemporaries believed was Newtonian causal logic? Was it possible to satisfy the hope of John Theophilus Desaguliers, the foremost popularizer of Newton's work, that *The Newtonian System of the*

---

9 Erasmus Philips, *An Appeal to Common Sense: or, Some Considerations Offer'd to Restore Publick Credit* (London, 1720); Evans, *Past Deliverances*, 21 (emphasis added).

10 Elias Bockett, *The Yea and Nay Stock-jobbers, or the 'Change-Alley Quakers Anatomiz'd* (London, 1720); Voltaire to Nicolas Anne Lefèvre de La Faluère, summer 1716, in *Voltaire's Correspondence*, ed. T. Besterman (Geneva: Institut et Musée Voltaire, 1953), 1:59–60; Harley's son is quoted in Hoppit, "The Myths of the South Sea Bubble," 145. For the Dutch observer see Brantlinger, *Fictions of State*, 57. Sir John Meres, *The Equity of Parliaments, and Publick Faith, Vindicated [...]*, 3rd ed. (London, 1720), 24; Peter G.M. Dickson, *The Financial Revolution in England: A Study in the Development of Public Credit, 1688–1756* (London and New York: Macmillan, 1967), 155.

World – the title of his didactic poem – would ultimately be able to theorize disorders like the South Sea Bubble, in which "The Coin, to Day, shall in its Value rise,/ To morrow, Money sinks and Credit dies"? For many the answer was a resounding "No." This, for instance, was the implication of the following two stanzas from what is probably the best known literary reaction to this "*Madness of the Crowd*," Swift's endlessly reprinted poem "The Bubble":

> There is a Gulph where thousands fell,
> Here all the bold Advent'rers came,
> A narrow Sound, though deep as Hell,
> CHANGE-ALLY is the dreadfull Name;
> Nine times a day it ebbs and flows,
> Yet He that on the Surface lyes
> Without a Pilot seldom knows
> The Time it falls, or when 'twill rise.[11]

Newton was present in these lines through the reference to the regularity of the tides. It was his gravitational theory, after all, that famously succeeded in explaining the tides better than anyone before. Only that the tides in Exchange Alley do not follow Newtonian logic. They leave the hapless adventurer at the mercy of their unpredictable ebbing and flowing.

The South Sea Bubble, then, frustrated expectations of the natural and logical relationships of cause and effect. In the laws of nature, explained *The Director* – a short-lived post-Bubble periodical – consequences can be depended upon to follow causes in a linear and stable fashion. The recent events, by contrast, revealed the limits of these laws. "But, since we see in the World new Phaenomena rise up every Day" – this writer too was struck by how novel the developments of 1720 had been – "and that the Springs and Motions seem to be acted by Principles differing from these which we call Natural," we ultimately remain ignorant as to "the Secret *primum Mobile* of these Unaccountables." Unyielding to familiar models of causality, recent events remained "secret," "unaccountable" and "unknown."[12]

Instead, in this financial world, regularity crumbled into chance and accident. The "blind fortuitous manner" of the stock market, observed the philosopher George Berkeley in 1721, rendered it a "public Gaming Table." After all, the hero and alleged wizard of this speculative world was John Law, the ultimate

---

11 J[ohn] T[heophilus] Desaguliers, *The Newtonian System of the World, the Best Model of Government* (Westminster, 1728), 17–18; Jonathan Swift, "The Bubble," in *Gulliver's Travels and Other Writings*, ed. C. Hawes (Boston: Houghton Mifflin, 2004), 336, ll. 138–145, 338, 213.
12 *The Director, num. I, II, III, IV* (London, [1720?]), 3:16–17.

professional gambler whose "incomparable readiness in Numbers made him a perfect judge of the hazards and advantages of all Plays."[13] Most people, however, were overwhelmed by these hazards, seeing their fate subject to the accidental vagaries, the "capricious Pranks" of Swift's multitudes, inflicted "whene'er they please." They frequently underscored the randomness of these events with the language of *accident*. Could the directors of the South Sea Company, wondered one pundit, reasonably "expect that the least ill News from abroad or Accident at home, would not Tumble [the South Sea Stock] down headlong?" John Trenchard and Thomas Gordon, in their renowned *Cato's Letters*, wrote as if they were responding directly to his question: "Common Sense could have told them that Credit is the most uncertain and most fluctuating Thing in the World, especially when it is applied to Stock-Jobbing." Consequently, and inevitably, credit "always tottered, and was always tumbling down at every little Accident and Rumour. A Story of a *Spanish* Frigate or of a few Thieves in the dark Dens of the *Highlands*, or the Sickness of a foreign Prince, or the Saying of a Broker in a Coffee-House; all, or any of these contemptible Causes were able to reduce that same Credit into a very slender Figure."[14]

Many pinpointed their anxiety about current financial events on the puzzling disproportion between causes and effects. The South Sea scheme, wrote one observer, was concocted as a means to raise public credit, "but it was only a Monster like the Shadow magnify'd on the Wall by the Light of a Candle, which was no ways proportionable to its Object." The dynamics of disproportionality could hardly be more vivid. Indeed, they were mobilized by no lesser a figure than the Chancellor of the Exchequer, John Aislabie, for his own public defense. "My Lords," he speechified in parliament, "there was something very extraordinary in the Consequences of this Affair." The extraordinariness lay in the fact "that the more the *South-Sea* Company were to pay to the Publick, the higher did their Stock rise upon it." This positive feedback loop then spiraled out of control, generating an outcome out of proportion to its cause. (Economists call this dynamic a "vicious circle"). "From that Time it became difficult to govern it; and let those Gentlemen that *open'd the Floodgates* wonder at the *Deluge* that ensu'd as much as they please, it was not in one Man's Power, or in the Power of the whole Administration to stop it, considering how the World was

---

13 George Berkeley, *An Essay Towards Preventing the Ruine of Great Britain* (London, 1721); *Mr. Law's Character Vindicated. In the Management of the Stocks in France, with the True Reasons for Their Sinking* (London, 1721), 11.

14 *The South-Sea Scheme Detected; and the Management Thereof Enquir'd into*, 2nd ed. (London, 1720), 7, 12–13. John Trenchard and Thomas Gordon, *Cato's Letters*, no. 6, 10.12.1720, in *Cato's Letters*, 5th corr. ed. (London, 1748), 266.

borne away by the Torrent." The drops, by themselves, turned into an ever-expanding deluge: "the *S. Sea Scheme* was become *ungovernable*," Aislabie concluded in a suitable if ungrammatical passive construction.[15]

Few were haunted by the mysteries of causality surrounding the events of 1720 as much as Daniel Defoe. Early on, wondering about the sudden meteoric rise of the French stock market, Defoe came up with a Franco-centric explanation for the conspicuous incongruity of causes and effects: "Th[e] warmth of the *French* Temper, which prompts them to push things up to the Extremity, was certainly the Reason, I mean the Original Reason of the sudden Advance of these things, for as yet there was no weight in the things themselves, that could bear any proportion to the New Credit they assum'd." Once the British stock market followed suit, Defoe could no longer rely on the idiosyncratic extremities of the French. Furthermore, now the very parallels between events in Paris and in London themselves defied causal thinking. They were obviously similar, and happened only a few months apart, yet the causal link between them remained a mystery. In a later pamphlet, Defoe reflected again on the French and British schemes, between which "the Parallel goes on still, both were overturn'd by their own Bulk, the unperforming Machines blew themselves up by the Force of their own Motion." And what caused this self-propelled combustion? "The Overthrow of Mr. *Law* and his Schemes" arrived "when but a minute Accident gave them a Check" and brought about their collapse; which likewise happened "to Sir *John Blunt* and his Schemes, when they received a Shock from a like Accident as the other." Defoe returned to the parallel a few pages later: "Come we then to the *Circumstances* which overthrew our *South-Sea* Fabrick here, which are in Proportion the same: That which gave them the first Blow was likewise a Trifle, and from which even the longest head among them did not expect the Consequence that happen'd." Pondering the meaning of 1720 in both France and Britain, then, the most indefatigable commentator on the financial world of the early eighteenth century ended up singling out non-linear relationships of causes and effects, set in motion by unpredictable trifles.[16] We are back to accidents. And, given the centrality of accidents to Defoe's interpretation of both events, is it a coincidence that Defoe wrote the two novels in which literary

15 Sir John Midriff, *Observations on the Spleen and Vapours [...]* (London, 1721); John Aislabie, *Mr. Aislabie's Second Speech on his Defence in the House of Lords* (London, [1721]), 12, 14.
16 Daniel Defoe, *The Chimera: or, the French Way of Paying National Debts Laid Open* (London, 1720), 30; Daniel Defoe, *The Case of Mr. Law Truly Stated* (London, 1721), 8, 13, 21.

critic Sandra Macpherson finds his new logic of "profoundly accidental" responsibility – *Journal of a Plague Year* and *Roxana* – in the early 1720s?[17]

Pushed *ad extremis*, non-linear thinking could end up with the most challenging scenario of disproportionality: begetting something out of nothing. The following verses, comparing John Blunt to Moses, are typical:

> So MOSES smote the barren Rock,
> (An Emblem of the SOUTH-SEA Stock!)
> Which touch'd with his cælestial Rod,
> Pour'd a full Stream, the Work of God.

By now, the South Sea Bubble was envisaged as a challenge not only to Newton but also to God himself. This was troubling. Britons in this period of unprecedented disorder were like madmen, exclaimed a pamphlet titled *The Lunatick*, since they posit that something can emerge out of nothing without the intervention of God; but, "if there was, at some time, Nothing, how could Something ever be?" Edward Ward, typically, was one to make the point without mincing words:

> Our cunning *South-Sea*, like a God,
> Turns Nothing into All Things.

Non-linearity was shading into blasphemy.[18]

Many of these quotes from the time of the bubbles – and countless others – reverberated echoes of older anxieties that circulated since the late seventeenth century about the insubstantiality of this brave new financial world, not least in the writing of Defoe himself.[19] But now, suddenly, events seemed to prove beyond reasonable doubt that these concerns were fully justified: man-made disorder, erratic behavior, random and jittery events, unreliable lack of substance, disproportionate and perhaps imponderable relations between causes and effects, the apparent collapse of linear causality. "Stocks, and *Stock-Jobbing* [are] a Mystery born in this Age," engaged in "invisible Traffick." "What we properly call

---

17 Sandra MacPherson, *Harm's Way: Tragic Responsibility and the Novel Form* (Baltimore: Johns Hopkins University Press, 2010).

18 N[icholas] Amhurst, *An Epistle (with a Petition in It) to Sir John Blunt*, 2nd ed. (London, 1720), 10; George Flint, *The Lunatick; or, Great and Astonishing News from Bedlam* (London, [1720?]), 12; Ward, *A Looking-glass for England. A Collection of All the Humorous Letters in The London Journal*, 2nd ed. (London, 1721), 33; For South Sea Bubble critiques of the blasphemous creation out of nothing see Silke Stratmann, *Myths of Speculation: The South Sea Bubble and 18th-Century English Literature* (Munich: Wilhelm Fink, 2000), 12.

19 See Sheehan and Wahrman, *Invisible Hands*, ch. 2.

Stock-Jobbing," went another quasi-lexical definition, is a novelty only "in our Age introduc'd" and is undertaken "without any Regard to Reason or Computation" or even to "any proportional Gain."[20] The stock market and the stock-jobber (a convenient scapegoat) nullified reason, calculation and proportionality.

Invisible Causes and the Emergence of Stories of Self-organizing Order

Disaster, even the merely perceived disaster, focuses the mind. By now it is clear that the exasperation attributed to Newton in reaction to the stock market frenzy at the time of the Bubble was hardly the most original thought associated with his name. The previous section has shown that many Britons, and indeed others across Western Europe, shared in the puzzlement and anxiety of these years. "The Eyes of all the World seem to be turn'd this way," John Applebee's *Original Weekly Journal* reported from London on 1 October 1720: "the sudden Fall of our Stocks, without any visible Reason for it, is the Surprize of the World."[21] Dramatic events had transpired – chaotic, disordered, capricious – for which there was no visible reason and thus no evident cure.

But what about *invisible* reasons? Those, unsurprisingly, were invoked aplenty. Faced with the apparent triumph of chaos, randomness and erratic behavior over order and linear causality, contemporaries responded in ways that invoked invisible causes and invisible dynamics of various kinds. Some tried to invoke divine providence to explain what had transpired. In the words of one divine who can stand in for many, "if we be smitten," as by the recent events, "it is not by blind Chance, or an undirected Concurrence of second Causes, but by that mighty Hand which holds or superintends all human Affairs." Indeed, it is the very mistake of "overlooking the divine Providence, as though it were wholly unconcern'd and intermeddled not with humane Affairs," that was not only "absurd" but a dangerous way of thinking that must inevitably "destroy the Order and Harmony of the World, and bring all Things into the utmost Con-

20 Roger North, *The Gentleman Accomptant: or, an Essay to Unfold the Mystery of Accompts [...]* (London, 1714), sig. b2; *A Letter to a Conscientious Man: Concerning the Use and the Abuse of Riches [...]* (London, 1720), 13, 15.

21 *The Original Weekly Journal*, 1.10.1720, 1863. For the uses of *stupor mundi*, the surprise of the world, in the context of the frenzy and disorder of the Mississippi Bubble in France, see Stefano Condorelli, "La presse étrangère et le Système de Law (1716–20)," in '*Gagnons sans savoir comment': Représentations du Système de Law du XVIIIe siècle à nos jours*, ed. Florence Magnot-Ogilvy (Rennes: Presses Universitaires de Rennes, 2017), 183–206, here 189–194.

fusion." Others detected behind the recent financial turmoil a conspiracy of a few powerful greedy men pulling invisible strings. After all, "it cannot be imagin'd" – thus one conspiracy theorist insisted – that "all these Things have been brought to pass by a meer fortuitous Conjunction of Atoms, as Epicurus suggests the World happened to be made; that all has happen'd without the Agency of Rogues, and the Craft of Knaves." (Indeed, in Britain by 1721, this was by far the most common explanation for the bursting of the South Sea Bubble, leading to a disproportionally vigorous prosecution of the South Sea Company directors.) Others tried to contain the chaos through numbers, tables, sums, accounts, percentages and calculations; never before, perhaps, was a public crisis so painstakingly mathematized.[22]

What all these reactions had in common was the impulse to deny or to rein in those aspects of the financial crises of 1720 that were perceived as particularly unsettling: the erratic multitudes, the man-made disorder, the vulnerability of events to randomness and chance, the exposed limitations of linear causality. In this, given the nature of the events they purported to explain, they were not very successful.[23] But here I am interested in yet another group of voices who responded to the challenge differently.

Disorder for this group was not only a key problem but also a key part of the solution. Rather than explain them away, these voices embraced precisely the chaotic elements – the aggregate of erratic, independently-operating and self-interested individuals, the non-linearity and invisibility of relations of causes to effects – as the premises for new understandings of higher-level order in the aggregate, emergent from disorder itself. The various voices in this group all elaborated key components of the family of conceptual moves that Jonathan Sheehan and I group together in *Invisible Hands* under the umbrella of *self-organization*. In a sentence, what we mean by this is the fundamental insight, common to them all, that even if God was no longer the active hands-on guarantor of order, complex systems, left to their own devices, still generated order immanently, without external direction, through self-organization.

This radical breakthrough did not come in the form of an overwhelming torrent, but rather more as a scattered trickle of people experimenting with what we

22 George Smyth, *A Sermon Preach'd at the New Meeting-house in Hackney* (London, 1720), 5–7, 10, 20; *The Director, num. I, II, III, IV*, 1:4; For examples and further discussion, see Sheehan and Wahrman, *Invisible Hands*, 110–117. For the limits of mathematization during the Bubble, see also W. Deringer, "For What It's Worth: Historical Financial Bubbles and the Boundaries of Economic Rationality," *Isis* 106 (2015): 646–656. For the traces of the Directors' behavior in historiography, see Richard Kleer's essay in this volume.

23 See Sheehan and Wahrman, *Invisible Hands*, ch. 3.

prefer to call a family of self-organizing conceptual moves. Typically, their efforts were disparate and unrelated, often tentative or incomplete. Some were hedging their bets. A few may appear to belong to this group only by coincidence. The key is that these voices all responded to the same set of pressures and concerns generated by the financial crises around 1720, and came up, largely independently of each other, with similar mental experiments. Taken together, these voices, crossing a threshold in terms of the articulateness of their vision of self-organization and of the sheer number of such visions put forth within a few years in the 1720s, add up to the first appearance of self-organization as a meaningful (Western) cultural phenomenon. This was, in turn, one of the period's most distinctive and far-reaching intellectual-cum-cultural innovations.

We can begin from the end, with those who reflected on the dramas of 1720 from the distance of several years hence. These had also the benefit of hindsight and thus the knowledge of the perhaps surprising fact that order re-established itself remarkably quickly once the dust had settled, with much greater ease than the near-hysterics of 1720 could have led anyone to expect. Several retrospectives on both sides of the Channel were unambiguous in their resort to self-organization as a framework for retelling those events. Defoe is a case in point. Having been so troubled in 1720 by the mysteries of the non-linear relationships of causes and effects, as we have seen, by 1728 Defoe returned to the topic with a calmer and more confident assessment. The context was a discussion of overproduction. If particular manufactures "whether prudently, or rashly" glut the market, he wrote now, the result, despite appearances, is not "a Decay of Trade." Rather, having made "Trade a Bubble [...] it returns upon them like the late *South Sea*, and every thing goes back from its imaginary to its intrinsick Value." Although Defoe still noted that individuals paid a price during the ups and downs of the crisis of 1720, the South Sea Bubble had now become for him prime evidence for a more optimistic vision: an inevitable and beneficial aggregate process whereby – here is the key phrase – "Trade is returned to its natural Channel, after an imaginary and casual Start out of it by the Accidents of foreign Commerce" or whatever other "rash" accidents as the case may be. Production and trade are by nature self-correcting, or one may say self-organizing. By the late eighteenth century, this particular formulation, of trade overcoming accidental obstructions to resume its flow in its natural level, would become one of the most common – indeed clichéd – images for the type of self-organizing dynamic that produces a state of equilibrium.[24]

---

24 Daniel Defoe, *A Plan of the English Commerce. Being a Compleat Prospect of the Trade of This Nation [...]* (London, 1728), 265–266.

In France, the Marquis d'Argenson, an erstwhile Mississippi Company investor whose father preceded John Law as Minister of Finance, mobilized the very same image for his own retrospective evaluation of Law's schemes: "It is, however, important, to remark that the finances of France were soon re-established, notwithstanding the catastrophes of the bank and the *Visa*; so true it is that in matters of finance, public credit and circulation find their own level, like the water of the sea, after storms and tempests." With hindsight, it turned out, 1720 was describable on both sides of the Channel as a disruption soon corrected by the natural, self-organizing flow of credit and trade.[25]

Nobody looking back at 1720 was naturally more invested in demonstrating how well things turned out than John Law himself. It is thus telling that Law's *Histoire des finances pendant la Régence*, an apologia which he wrote and rewrote compulsively during his exile in the 1720s after the collapse of his System, is peppered with gestures to the dynamics of self-organization. Money for Law, as Thomas Kavanagh has aptly put it, became "a demiurgic force thriving on its own movement." Credit was even more powerful, an aggregate much greater than the sum of its parts; in Law's words, credit "multiplies by itself, and in so multiplying also multiplies the common good." The continuous self-propelled flow of credit and money counteracts disorder, "since I call disorder that which disrupts the harmony and affinity that all things must have between them, which connects them in a way that they mutually reinforce each other to produce the public good." Order and harmony are aggregate effects of the self-organizing powers of credit and money (powers, incidentally, which in Law's view were superior under an absolute ruler, who could best guarantee their smooth and equal flow). As in the case of Defoe, Law formed the germs of these ideas already before his downfall. But it was now, in the aftermath of 1720, that both seasoned economic theorists-cum-practitioners pulled together these former fragmentary insights toward a more fleshed out vision of self-organizing order.[26]

---

25 René-Louis de Voyer and Marquis d'Argenson, *Essays, Civil, Moral, Literary and Political [...] Translated from His Valuable Manuscripts, and Never Before Made Public* (Dublin, 1789), 159. The *Visa* was part of Law's efforts for dealing with the problem of public debt.

26 John Law, "Histoire des finances pendant la Régence," in *Oeuvres complètes*, ed. P. Harsin (Paris: Recueil Sirey, 1934), 3:299, 415; Thomas M. Kavanagh, *Enlightenment and the Shadows of Chance: The Novel and the Culture of Gambling in Eighteenth-Century France* (Baltimore: Johns Hopkins University Press, 1993), 87. Counter to Harsin and Kavanagh, Antoin E. Murphy in his *John Law: Economic Theorist and Policy-maker* (Oxford: Oxford University Press, 1997) doubts that Law was, in fact, the author of the 'Histoire des finances'; if he is right, then this tract was a retrospective by another informed contemporary, which makes little difference in

Nor did one have to wait for the retrospectives. One can actually find multiple instances of self-organizing thinking, however hesitant, incomplete or fleeting, already in the midst of the 1720 maelstrom itself. Even as the events of 1720 were unfolding, for example, the auditor of the Scottish Exchequer, Sir David Dalrymple, stumbled on a perhaps surprising model of prices in a market that "regulates it self," based on people's freely-formed opinions of quality and promise. As long as designing men do not meddle with price levels, this natural dynamic that determines them – Dalrymple called it "the Rule" – is capable of absorbing and correcting the temporary perturbations caused by "Accidents," be they the accidents of scarcity or novelty or whatever. Dalrymple's immediate response to the wild rise and fall of the South Sea stocks thus approached almost inadvertently a model of a self-organizing and self-correcting price system, set in motion by the free flow of multiple individually-formed opinions. Furthermore, Dalrymple also argued against the view of stocks as gambles, which fall therefore outside notions of predictable causality or liability, and thus cannot incur legal obligations in contractual exchange. Not so, said Dalrymple: "*Answer'd*, That a Chance may be bought too dear as well as other Things. *There is a Method of putting a Value upon any Chance that can happen.*" Invoking the emerging calculus of probability, Dalrymple insisted that chances could be calculated and evaluated, even if individual events are unpredictable. In short, Dalrymple was intimidated neither by erratic and accident-sensitive market fluctuations nor by the element of chance. Seen as an aggregate system, the stock market could still be expected to behave in a calculable, self-correcting manner.[27]

The status of the South Sea contracts also preoccupied an anonymous 1720 pamphleteer who was himself a stockholder. While disagreeing with Dalrymple in some details, when it came to the dynamics of the recent developments in the stock market, he reached a similar conclusion. The current situation, this writer asserted, must be recognized as unique and unprecedented. Just as the Romans "for many Ages had no Law to punish *Parricide*; it never entring into their Minds," so the ancestors of the Bubble generation could not have imagined "the Case of the *South-Sea* Contracts, [in which] Hazard and Chance is part of the Consideration, and the Value the Parties set on that not being to be

terms of the present argument. For Law's earlier views see John Law, *Money and Trade Considered, with a Proposal for Supplying the Nation with Money* (Edinburgh, 1705), e.g. 42.

27 Sir David Dalrymple, *Time Bargains Tryed by the Rules of Equity and Principles of the Civil Law* (London, 1720), 17–19, 24–25 (emphasis added). And cf. Sandra Sherman, "Credit, Simulation, and the Ideology of Contract in the Early Eighteenth Century," *Eighteenth-Century Life* 19 (1995): 86–102, here 92; Sherman has already noted an "epistemological confusion" in the financial writings of the early 1720s involving, inter alia, doubts about linearity of causality (86).

known." Now, however, unlike these ancestors and much like Sir David Dalrymple, the author could indeed imagine transactions that relied on hazard, chance, and non-linear leaps in value. His contractual solution however was different. Whereas Dalrymple relied on the new science of probability to calculate those elements of chance and thus bring them back into the fold of existing contract law, this pamphlet remained skeptical about the claims of mathematicians to make sense of the South Sea frenzy, recommending instead to treat such chance-prone contracts as equivalent to gambling debts that were free of constraints of proportionality.[28]

This writer went on like so many others to pin the blame for the bursting of the Bubble on the South Sea directors. But in explaining *why* their actions led to this result, he said something strikingly new. The problem with the directors' manipulations was that they caused all the individual operators in the market to undertake the same actions in unison. The directors were therefore guilty *not* of creating disorder but rather of eliminating it: "it is a fundamental maxim in Stock-Jobbing, that *when great numbers have the same view, no Benefit can be made.*"[29] Randomness and chaos are not threats to the stock market, he argued. Rather, it is the very randomness and chaotic nature of the actions taken by "great numbers" of operators, each pursuing their own individual path, that guarantees its beneficial functioning! What this writer presented as "a fundamental maxim in Stock-Jobbing" was in fact an abbreviated gesture at a radically new view of the market as a self-organizing system, emergent from the independent and heterogeneous actions of many individuals. The success and stability of such a market depends on that very chaos that so many other contemporaries busily were trying to make disappear.

Both this anonymous writer and Sir David Dalrymple, then, were moved in 1720 to acknowledge in a new way the role of chance as an aspect of the stock market that now became acceptable, even legitimate. This realization, in turn, pushed them to take the more far-reaching step toward the insight of self-organization, when tentatively, almost in passing, they speculated about how this unpredictable randomness of the market was in itself the basis for a new kind of aggregate order. Both, then, fit well the broader pattern I am proposing here.

The next several paragraphs, by contrast, present a text from 1721 that deals only in passing with the financial troubles of the previous year, but that spins

28 *Considerations on the Present State of the Nation, as to Publick Credit, Stocks, the Landed and Trading Interests* (London, 1720), 58–59.

29 *Considerations on the Present State of the Nation*, 40 (emphasis added).

out in more detail precisely those elements that come together in the telling of self-organizing stories. Tamworth Reresby was a military officer whose *Miscellany of Ingenious Thoughts and Reflections* was written under the acknowledged shadow of the South Sea Bubble. His sometimes-confused musings, that make him something of a poster boy for this essay, were gathered together in a section titled "Providence, Fortune, Chance."

Reresby maps the various possibilities for conceptualizing providence, fortune and chance in ways too complex to summarize here. Suffice it to say that he offers the possibility for man to accept chance while forming and executing schemes "in Spite of all intervening Accidents." If one accepts this understanding of fortune, then "we may demonstrate *Politicks* as well as *Mathematicks*, and build certain Rules upon the Contingency of human Actions, which will as little agree with the *Stoical* as the *Christian Doctrine*." Here, then, is a man who in 1721 combined the recent South Sea Bubble experience and new ideas about providence into an experimental theory that simultaneously accepts disorder at one level – that is to say, the undetermined and accident-prone contingency of human actions, "loose, irregular, and fickle" – together with order at another level, visible in the rules that govern the aggregate and that promise to make politics as predictable a science as mathematics. This maneuver brought back hope, as well as restored faith. Even "if the best methodiz'd Affairs are turn'd out of their Course, and baffled, the wisest Projects defeated, the most flattering Hopes confounded... and the humblest Condition comes to be exalted" (an unmistakable echo of the Bubble) – even then one must believe that God "has cast all Accidents into a certain Method" and hope that with His help one "shall be able to apprehend the Regularity of those Accidents, which once seem'd so confus'd."[30] Reresby's effort to reconcile accident and order was as good a prefiguration as any of the many subsequent moves toward self-organization.

By the end of his tract, it is unclear whether Reresby is fully swayed by this experimental position or whether he retreats to a certain reliance on direct divine providence. But this does not really matter. It is not surprising that stabs at self-organization in the 1720s, undertaken in the immediate aftermath of the financial crisis that had generated almost hysterical concern, were raw, tentative, and incomplete, and all the more so if their bottom line was a Panglossian belief that disorders like the recent ones all end up for the better. What is important to note here is that such experimentation was a distinctive phenomenon repeated

---

30 Tamworth Reresby, *A Miscellany of Ingenious Thoughts and Reflections, in Verse and Prose* (London, 1721), 137–139. For the South Sea affair, see especially 308.

multiple times at this particular historical juncture. It was not that such notions had never been voiced before; rather, my argument is that what we observe in the 1720s is an emergent cumulative cultural phenomenon, the echoes of which will then reverberate with increasing intensity later in the century.

That such an emergent phenomenon did occur in the 1720s is attested, inter alia, by contemporary efforts to dismiss it. Take for example one George Flint, writing in the shadow of the South Sea Bubble against "the true System of *Lunaticks.*" "Suppose a Shipwreck'd Man thrown upon an Island," he mused with Defoe's *Robinson Crusoe* freshly on his mind – an island which is "all an entire Wilderness, uninhabited by any Thing but Beasts." And suppose further that he encounters there "a beauteous Structure the most exquisite Hands ever built." According to the present-day lunatics, "he must suppose that this was built by Chance, by a mere accidental Jumbling of Things, call'd Atoms, together." Surely, Flint sneered, "*Homer* composed no Iliads, nor *Virgil* Eneids; Letters jump'd by Chance together, and form'd themselves into these Poems." Flint does not specify what particular context or author provoked his outburst against these Lucretian scenarios. But it quickly becomes a shrill tirade against those unspecified lovers of disorder, who say "*We love not Order* [...] *but will have Disorder; Huzzah! Boys Disorder for ever.*" To counter their influence, Flint appeals urgently to his audience "to own the God of Order." It does not take a huge leap to recognize in Flint's imaginary foes not only the echoes of the disorder of 1720 but also those of contemporary speculations about chance and randomness as a basis of order.[31]

There are many other such examples in the 1720s, of speakers and writers who introduced self-organizing logic into their thinking on multiple topics; some were closer to the financial bubbles (including such well-known figures as Montesquieu and Alexander Pope), some on topics further away (e.g. Mandeville, Vico, or the young Benjamin Franklin). Although each one of these instances, taken in isolation, may appear as a free-standing coincidence, when considered in the aggregate they cumulate fast enough to demand consideration as a collective phenomenon in the history of European epistemology.

For one more example of how this mode of thinking pervaded fields beyond economics (to which I will return shortly), I wish to move, perhaps surprisingly, to a tract on international relations – dealing, in the language of its anonymous 1720 author, with "the ballance of power... its necessity, origin and history." This tract introduces an earlier text as its point of departure, namely the theologian and French royal tutor François Fénelon's "Essay on the Ballance of Power,

31 Flint, *The Lunatick*, 13, 15 (emphasis added).

[which] ranges [i.e. arranges] all the different Dispositions of Power that can happen." Following Fénelon, the 1720 author identifies four possible configurations of international affairs: a single state greater than all others combined, a state greater than all others individually but not more powerful than their combination, smaller states that combine to counterbalance a bigger one, and a near equality between several great states. Our author assures his readers that the latter possibility is not only the happiest configuration; in the long run, it is also the inevitable endpoint of all others. Reason as well as the historical record, he continues, prove that, no matter what efforts different states have made to overpower others, these efforts every time "have ended in this Fourth Class" through dynamics of alliances or overgrowth-leading-to-internal-collapse that the tract explains at some length. Every state is driven only by self-interest and without a view of the whole; and, yet, the whole naturally orders itself into an equilibrium. This equilibrium is not static. The unpredictable actions of particular states destabilize it, resulting in "the Caprice of the Ballance" or "the Inconstancy of the Ballance." Yet, in the long run, stability is restored, as they all succumb to "that natural Inclination, that centripetal Force as it were, to be of the Fourth Class."[32] International relations thus turn out to be a self-organizing system, reaching equilibrium in and through the caprice of princes.

But this is in fact not at all what Fénelon originally said. Fénelon, writing around 1700, while commending the balance of roughly equal powers of the "Fourth Class" as the author of 1720 reported, had had no intention of leaving the felicitous outcome in the invisible hands of free-floating or natural dynamics. To the contrary, Fénelon believed that if states were left to their own devices, "*the most powerful will certainly at length prevail, and overthrow the rest, unless they unite together to preserve the Ballance.*" Fénelon's purpose was to offer not dispassionate reflections about a natural state of affairs but rather advice on policy making, namely how to guarantee through proactive interventions that same balance that the 1720 author believed would emerge by itself. If there was any guaranteed outcome in Fénelon's view, it was the *overthrowing* of any balance, which could only be preserved through constant vigilance. In between the end-of-the-seventeenth-century master and his proclaimed follower of 1720, then, the theory of the balance of powers acquired the dynamics of self-organization.

And to end with one more twist. The previous paragraph includes a quote from Fénelon's essay on the balance of Europe, taken from a contemporary Eng-

---

32 *The Analysis of the Ballance of Power: Wherein Its Necessity, Origin and History Is Examin'd, and Deduc'd from the Common Principles of Justice* (London, 1720), 38–56.

lish translation published at the time by a Scottish advocate named William Grant. In his added commentary to the translation, Grant, too, had something to say about the dynamic that produces said balance. The balance of powers, Grant observed, the principles of which had been elaborated so well by Fénelon, "may be demonstrated to have arisen necessarily, and from the Reason and Nature of things, as a Cure of what happen'd amiss in human Affairs." But as we already know, Grant was in fact going beyond – and even against – Fénelon in thus asserting (in his name!) that, if happenstance sends human affairs off course, this random erring would be cured by the natural self-corrective dynamic of the balance of powers. It is therefore quite suggestive, given the overall argument of this essay, that Grant published his translation of Fénelon's essay, together with these reassuring comments about the inevitability of order emerging from erratic disorder, also in that very same generative year of 1720.[33]

Prefigurations of the Invisible Hand

This essay has established that the 1720s were indeed an early – arguably the first – historical juncture in western Europe in which self-organization emerged as a recognizable cultural phenomenon – that is to say, the scene of a significant cluster of speculative ruminations about the emergence of aggregate high-level self-organizing order from lower-level disorder. It is important to stress that this wave of experimentation also rested on several game-changing developments of the previous half-century that prepared the ground for such new ways of imagining order, including new departures in understanding providence, in probabilistic thinking, and in learning to live with complexity. Looking forward, these new ways of conceptualizing order spread during the eighteenth century into multiple domains of knowledge, from science and law to society and politics. Indeed, this new way of thinking about order and disorder, provi-

---

33 François de Salignac de La Mothe-Fénelon, *Two Essays on the Ballance of Europe. The First Written in French by the Late Archbishop of Cambray, and Translated into English. The Second by the Translator of the First Essay,* [trans. William Grant] (London, 1720), 5, 31 (emphasis added). Grant's translation itself subtly added an emphasis on equilibrium to Fénelon's original text. Where Grant's translation went "unless they unite together to preserve the Ballance," as above, Fénelon had had "si les autres ne se réunissent pour fair le contrepoids" – a counterweight that did not already imply a pre-existing balance in need of preserving. See the "Supplément" to "Examen de conscience sur les devoirs de la royauté," in Fénelon, *Oeuvres*, ed. J. Le Brun (Paris: Gallimard, 1997), 2:1003.

dence and chance may well have been one of the most significant long-term effects of the financial bubbles c. 1720.[34]

The best-known example later in the eighteenth century of these long-term effects is the self-organizing logic of the science of political economy, as embodied most memorably in Adam Smith's invisible hand. It therefore seems fitting to bring this essay to an end with a trio of 1720s discussions of economic theory, now largely forgotten, that are simultaneously among the very best examples of the surge of interest in the potential of self-organizing models following the financial bubbles c. 1720, and uncanny prefigurations of Smithian political economy of half a century later.

The first appeared already in the year 1720 itself, with the ambitious title *System or Theory of the Trade of the World*. Its author was Isaac Gervaise, an Englishman of Huguenot descent and long-time merchant and director of the Royal Lustring Company. It so happened that in 1720 this monopoly-based company lost its charter, and Gervaise laid down in his only known tract a remarkably modern-sounding plea for keeping trade "natural and free." The argument was based on a careful analysis of the international trade equilibrium and of the self-regulating mechanism for the global distribution of gold and silver. What Gervaise came up with was an unflinching model of the flow of currency, labor and national riches as an interconnected self-organizing system. Having applied the self-organizing logic several times over to the social equilibrium between classes within nations and to the international balance of trade, Gervaise arrived at his final conclusion: "if Trade was not curbed by Laws, or disturbed by those Accidents that happen in long Wars, etc. which break the natural Proportion, either of People, or of private Denominators [gold and silver]; Time would bring all trading Nations of the World into that Equilibrium, which is proportioned, and belongs to the number of their Inhabitants." Here, in 1720, we find in effect the sanguine vision of Smith's invisible hand, more than half a century *avant la lettre*.[35]

Gervaise, as one economic historian puts it, was "a violet that blushed unseen for two centuries," having had no traceable echo until his rediscovery in the twentieth century. This is more or less true.[36] But it is equally important to

34 For the full argument, looking back to the seventeenth century as well as forward to the eighteenth and nineteenth centuries, see Sheehan and Wahrman, *Invisible Hands*.

35 Isaac Gervaise, *The System or Theory of the Trade of the World*, ed. J.M. Letiche (London, 1720; Baltimore: Johns Hopkins University Press, 1954), 7, 15, 18, and passim.

36 C. Wilson, "International Payments: An Interim Comment," *Economic History Review* 15 (1962): 364–369, here 368. The rediscovery was Jacob Viner's: see his *Studies in the Theory of International Trade* (New York: A.M. Kelley, 1937; New York: Harper and Brothers, 1965), 79.

note that he was not a lone blushing violet. The second text I wish to mention, published anonymously several months later, appears to have remained completely unnoticed by historians of economic thought. This is a shame, since *A True State of Publick Credit: Or, a Short View of the Condition of the Nation, with Respect to Our Present Calamities* also deserves a place on the honorary list of the precursors of Adam Smith. Written out of concern for "the Fall of *South-Sea-Stock* [that] has ruined *Credit*," its main preoccupation was the restoration of healthy credit, a goal which – so it claimed – could not be achieved by legislative intervention or administrative decree: "Credit, however it is sunk, can, from its Nature, only rise, with a general Care and Industry, *by its own Ducts and Modes*." Credit, according to this writer, was inherently a self-organizing system. Parliament, therefore, should engage in "no compulsive or unnatural Laws," but only set up favorable conditions, such as public registration of landed properties or a fund for public credit, and "the rest will be perfected by a Machine, *which will move it self*." And again: credit "must be left to itself," and, if it is, within a generally beneficial environment, it "will disperse it self, and find out just as many Channels as will be useful." "If the Legislature will but lay the Foundation Stone, the Superstructure will not want any other Assistance in raising."[37] Curiously, these repetitive assertions of the self-organizing nature of credit were all crammed into the dedication of this tract (signed 25 April 1721) but were not repeated in the body of the text. Was it because they were a meta-reflection that did not affect the writer's practical suggestions, or because they were a belated realization arrived at between penning the text and its eventual publication? Be that as it may, here was a remarkably clear economic vision responding to the perceived financial meltdown with an insistence on the self-organizing emergence of aggregate order, tending without external intervention to the public good.

Finally, the best example is the last. It is also an apt one, since nobody we have encountered in this essay, with the exception of John Law himself, was more closely entwined with and affected by the events of 1720 than Richard Cantillon. Indeed, if scruples are not a precondition for heroism, Cantillon may well be considered the unsung hero of that year of financial bubbles. Cantillon was an Irish émigré who had become one of Paris's most successful private bankers and who had subsequently turned down an invitation from John Law – a personal friend and sometimes rival – to become his deputy in running France's finances. Instead, Cantillon positioned himself to make not one but several financial

---

37 *A True State of Publick Credit: Or, a Short View of the Condition of the Nation, with Respect to Our Present Calamities* (London, 1721), 9, and dedication, unpaginated (two emphases added).

killings through canny short-term speculations – perhaps aided by insider information – in 1719 and 1720: first, twice over, in the stocks of the Mississippi company (in which his brother happened to be a central figure); and then again, after cashing in at its peak and moving his winnings out of France, in the South Sea Company.

In the late 1720s, beginning in part as a defense in a court case related to the Mississippi scheme, Cantillon wrote his *Essai sur la nature du commerce en général*, which was simultaneously a critique of Law's system, though he never mentioned the Scotsman by name, and a comprehensive view of the nature of economic systems. This treatise remained unpublished until 1755, long after Cantillon's mysterious death – his London house burnt down in 1734 but rumors persisted that he actually staged his own death and fled to Surinam – but it is likely that the manuscript circulated earlier. (Otherwise it is hard to explain how full sections of Cantillon's prose found their way, unacknowledged, into Malachy Postlethwayt's well-known *Universal Dictionary of Trade and Commerce*, published in part before Cantillon's *Essai*.) And it is in this text, little noticed outside circumscribed circles, written by an extraordinary figure in the international financial world of 1720, that we find what economists from Stanley Jevons, Cantillon's late-nineteenth-century "rediscoverer," to Friedrich Hayek have flagged as "the most original of all statements of economic principles before the *Wealth of Nations*." Its originality, they agree, "all the more remarkable because it [was] entirely devoid of providentialist or teleological content," was first and foremost in its developed notions of the self-organization of economic systems.[38]

Cantillon's self-organization thinking permeates the *Essai* throughout: in his assumptions about population (prefiguring Malthus), in his theory of value and prices (Hayek identified him as "the originator of the self-adjusting price specie flow mechanism"), in his model for the flow of money and commerce (Hume's mid-century "Of the Balance of Trade" is also reputed to have benefitted from advance access to a manuscript copy of Cantillon's *Essai*), and indeed in how all these connect to each other in a macro-economic self-reproducing equilibrating process.

At one point, for instance, Cantillon puts together a thought experiment about a region which suddenly gets more money from mines. In a long, detailed narrative, which Jevons found to be "one of the most marvellous things in the book," Cantillon shows how such a region first benefits from an economic

38 Mark Blaug quoted in Antoin E. Murphy, *Richard Cantillon: Entrepreneur and Economist* (Oxford: Clarendon, 1986); Gaetan Pirou as quoted in Friedrich A. Hayek, "Richard Cantillon," *Journal of Libertarian Studies* 7 (1985): 217–247.

boom involving increased consumption, employment and trade. But then, through multiple self-propelled processes, the boom "gradually" but "necessarily" turns to bust, as labor begins to emigrate, money flows out to foreign manufactures, local manufactures slowly decline, and the circulation of money slows down, until the state ultimately falls into ruin. This model of a self-organizing equilibrium correcting an initial disruption was historically tested, Cantillon suggests, since it was "approximately what has happened to Spain since the discovery of the Indies." But it is also a general theoretical truism, as Cantillon puts it elsewhere: "When a State has arrived at the highest point of wealth ... it will inevitably fall into poverty by the ordinary course of things. The too great abundance of money, which so long as it lasts forms the power of States, throws them back imperceptibly but naturally into poverty." Note Cantillon's insistence that such correctives take place "inevitably" and "by the ordinary course of things," without external intervention. This self-organizing dynamic occurs on every level, national and local. "If there are too many Hatters in a City or in a street for the number of People who buy hats there," Cantillon offers another illustration, "some who are least patronized must become bankrupt: if they be too few it will be a profitable Undertaking which will encourage new Hatters to open shops there and so it is that the entrepreneurs of all kinds adjust themselves to accidents in a State (*les Entrepreneurs de toutes espèces se proportionnent au hazard dans un État*)." Adam Smith could hardly have put it better.[39]

The very last sentence in Cantillon's *Essai* puts its theory back into its own historical context. It is a parting warning against manipulations of the stock market, for instance through the collusion of a bank and a minister in raising the price of public stock: "But if some panic or unforeseen crisis drove the holders to demand silver from the Bank the bomb would burst (*on en viendroit à crever la bombe*) and it would be seen that these are dangerous operations."[40] The long shadows of Law's System and of the Mississippi and South Sea bubbles (or "bombs"), those radical events that challenged common understandings of causality and opened for some contemporaries new venues of thinking about nonlinear relationships of cause and effect, could not be mistaken.

---

39 Richard Cantillon, *Essai sur la nature du commerce en général*, ed. and trans. H. Higgs (London: Macmillan, 1931), 53, 163–167, 185 (with minor changes to Higgs's translation); and S. Jevons, "Richard Cantillon and the Nationality of Political Economy (1881)," repr. in Cantillon, *Essai sur la nature du commerce*, 348. Hayek is quoted in Murphy, *Richard Cantillon*, 262.
40 Cantillon, *Essai sur la nature du commerce*, 323.

Epilogue

In the early 1730s, the poet Alexander Pope returned to the theme of self-organization, indeed in multiple references across several poems. His sharpest formulation of the logic of self-organizing order, emerging spontaneously from the chaotic pulls of different individuals, is the following:

> Hear then the truth: "'Tis Heav'n each Passion sends,
> "And diff'rent Men directs to diff'rent Ends.
> "Extremes in Nature equal Good produce,
> "Extremes in Man concur to general Use.
> (*To Bathurst*, ll. 161–164[41])

This point is echoed several times in Pope's better known *Essay on Man* that he published at the same time, for instance in the verses that sketch the analogous situation in the political realm, when the opposite pulls are those of different interests and the desired aggregate order is a harmonious polity:

> 'Till jarring int'rests of themselves create
> Th' according music of a well-mix'd State.
> (*Essay on Man* iii, ll. 293–294)

What makes these verses interesting for us here is that the immediate context for Pope's publication of the *Epistle to Bathurst* was in fact another "bubble" or financial scandal – that of the Charitable Corporation, once again a project to relieve public debts, which is the subject of Amy Froide's contribution to this volume. As Vincent Carretta has shown, Pope published the *Epistle to Bathurst* as a political intervention carefully timed to hit the streets precisely on the day before the opening of the parliamentary session; a parliamentary debate in which the leader of the campaign against the Charitable Corporation was none other than Lord Bathurst (otherwise an unlikely addressee for Pope's verses). The *Epistle*, like the discussion of the new scheme more broadly, was suffused with references to people and events involved in the 1720 bubble.[42]

Indeed, not only was the 1720 financial crisis the general background for Pope's poem as a whole; it was also the specific context of its particular verses devoted to self-organization. What precedes these verses is a long passage about the persistence of political corruption, which begins with the words: "Much in-

---

41 All quotes are from the *Twickenham Edition of the Poems of Alexander Pope.*

42 Vincent Carretta, "Pope's *Epistle to Bathurst* and the South Sea Bubble," *Journal of English and German Philology* 77 (1978): 212–231.

jur'd Blunt! Why bears he Britain's hate?" (l. 135). John Blunt had been a director of the South Sea Company, a key player during the events of 1720 who was often compared to John Law and who was subsequently one of the main figures prosecuted and punished for its collapse. Pope did not doubt Blunt's culpability, but protested his being singled out while the nefarious practices of the South Sea Bubble, with its cheating and gambling, were still alive and well. And why do people participate in such practices, even reasonable people like Pope, who had himself invested considerable sums and efforts in that financial roller coaster ride of 1720? "All this is madness, cries a sober Sage, / But who, my Friend, has Reason in his Rage?" (ll. 153–154). Pope devotes several lines to this madness, shaped as it was by individuals' ruling passions that conquered their reason, before delivering his final judgment quoted above. "Hear then the truth": the truth, significant enough for Pope to cross-reference unusually several times, was the revelation that, in fact, the frenzied disorder of the erratic actions of so many people driven by their passions ultimately comes together into an overall harmony for "general use." Pope's observations on mass behavior during the South Sea Bubble led him, too, to the discovery of self-organization, now conjured up again in response to a new "bubble."[43]

---

43 For a full discussion across Pope's several poems of the early 1730s, see Sheehan and Wahrman, *Invisible Hands*, 6–9, 96–97.

Anne L. Murphy

"We have been ruined by Whores": Perceptions of Female Involvement in the South Sea Scheme

One intriguing interpretation of the 2008 financial crisis was that the markets crashed because of excesses of testosterone.[1] Commentators argued that trading rooms contained too few women to counter the masculine, aggressive, and risk-taking discourses of trading. In consequence, predominantly male traders operated as if competition with the market and with each other was more important than preserving the global economy.[2] High salaries and bonuses became a proxy for social status. Male bonding and groupthink prevented people saying things had gone too far. Women too participated in these discourses and behaviors, but it was men who drove the system and testosterone that caused the crisis. Some commentators used this logic to argue that if you put more women in boardrooms and on dealing floors, it would bring about positive change.[3] Indeed, the *Washington Post* reported that "a healthy dose of estrogen [was the key to] fiscal recovery [and] economic strength worldwide".[4] This interpretation was not just propounded in the popular press, and, interestingly, it was not just an argument that emerged post-crisis. A 2001 analysis of approaches to investment by Brad M. Barber and Terrence Odean found that men were more overconfident than women and, in consequence, traded more than women with less success. The authors concluded that this "simple and powerful" explanation revealed why there is a prevalence of counterproductive trading in financial markets.[5]

---

1 See, particularly, J.M. Coates and J. Herbert, "Endogenous Steroids and Financial Risk Taking on a London Trading Floor," *PNAS* 105 (2008): 6167–6172.

2 Elsa Ermer, Leda Cosmides, and John Tooby, "Relative Status Regulates Risky Decision-Making About Resources in Men: Evidence for the Co-Evolution of Motivation and Cognition," *Evolution and Human Behaviour* 29 (2008): 106–118.

3 For example, Christine Lagarde, "What If It Had Been Lehman Sisters?," https://dealbook.nytimes.com/2010/05/11/lagarde-what-if-it-had-been-lehman-sisters/, last accessed 25.2.2019.

4 Quoted in Elisabeth Prügl, "'If Lehman Brothers Had Been Lehman Sisters ...': Gender and Myth in the Aftermath of the Financial Crisis," *International Political Sociology* 6 (2012): 21–35, here 28.

5 Brad M. Barber and Terrance Odean, "Boys Will Be Boys: Gender, Overconfidence and Common Stock Investment," *Quarterly Journal of Economics* 116, no. 1 (2001): 261–292, here 289.

https://doi.org/10.1515/9783110592139-013

Of course, such arguments must be treated with caution. Catherine C. Eckel and Philip J. Grossman's comprehensive review of the literature presented in the *Handbook of Experimental Economics* shows that, while greater risk-aversion in women has been confirmed in numerous field studies of risk, failure to control for such factors as wealth, knowledge and marital status may bias results. Contextualized experimentation tends to result in less conclusive findings.[6] Evidence of women as active risk-takers would not surprise historians who, in recent years, have shown that early modern women were capable of taking financial power into their own hands, skillful and knowledgeable in their actions, able to act as intermediaries for all forms of exchange, and capable of exercising power in business and financial relationships. These studies relate to women's work in domestic and business environments.[7] They also examine their behavior in the financial markets, as investors and intermediaries.[8]

This chapter adds to a growing literature by considering how female investors and speculators behaved, and how that behavior was represented, during the South Sea Bubble and in its aftermath. It shows that women engaged in the Scheme and in the market for South Sea shares, although not disproportionately

6 Catherine C. Eckel and Philip J. Grossman, "Men, Women and Risk-Aversion: Experimental Evidence," in *Handbook of Experimental Economics*, ed. Charles Plott and Vernon Smith (Princeton: Princeton University Press, 2008), 1061–1073.

7 See, for example, Hannah Barker, *The Business of Women: Female Enterprise and Urban Development in Northern England 1760–1830* (Oxford: Oxford University Press, 2006); Amy Louise Erickson, "Married Women's Occupations in Eighteenth-Century London," *Continuity and Change* 23 (2008): 267–307; Nicola Phillips, *Women in Business, 1700–1850* (Woodbridge: The Boydell Press, 2006); Jane Whittle, "Housewives and Servants in Rural England, 1440–1650: Evidence of Women's Work from Probate Documents," *Transactions of the Royal Historical Society* 15 (2005): 51–74; Jane Whittle, "Enterprising Widows and Active Wives: Women's Unpaid Work in the Household Economy of Early Modern England," *The History of the Family* 19 (2014): 283–300; M. E. Wiesner-Hanks, *Women and Gender in Early Modern Europe*, 3rd ed. (Cambridge: Cambridge University Press, 2008).

8 See, for example: Ann Carlos, Karen Maguire, and Larry Neal, "Women in the City: Financial Acumen, Women Speculators, and the Royal African Company During the South Sea Bubble," *Accounting, Business and Financial History* 16 (2006): 219–243; Ann Carlos and Larry Neal, "Women Investors in Early Capital Markets, 1720–1725," *Financial History Review* 11 (2004): 197–224; Mark Freeman, Robin Pearson, and James Taylor, "'A Doe in the City': Women Shareholders in Eighteenth- and Early Nineteenth-Century Britain," *Accounting, Business and Financial History* 16 (2006): 265–291; Anne Laurence, "Women Investors, 'That Nasty South Sea Affair', and the Rage to Speculate in Early Eighteenth-Century England," *Accounting, Business and Financial History* 16 (2006): 254–264; Rosemary O'Day, *Women's Agency in Early Modern Britain and the American Colonies* (London: Pearson and Longman, 2007); Amy Froide, *Silent Partners: Women as Public Investors During Britain's Financial Revolution, 1690–1750* (Oxford: Oxford University Press, 2017).

so. They sometimes were depicted as vulnerable and unable to make good choices, but they also were thought to be powerful manipulators of the market and of the political environment that supported the Scheme. The market itself came to be gendered in the eyes of some commentators, and speculative behavior frequently was depicted as feminine.[9] Indeed, had contemporaries thought in such ways, we might interpret the post-1720 analysis of the Bubble's bursting as having been dominated by the notion that there was just too much oestrogen in the financial markets. But, as in 2008, where toxic masculinity failed to provide an adequate explanation for a disrupted and disruptive financial system, in 1720 gendering the market and its problematic elements revealed little about female investment strategies and much about social anxieties and attempts to mend the failures of the market through the 'othering' of undesirable behavior.

Women's Involvement in the South Sea Bubble

As Amy Erickson asserts, the capital of women was necessary to the development of financial markets.[10] They operated as investors, speculators and mediators in the market. They displayed different appetites for risk, variations in knowledge and capability, and had diverse motivations for their actions. Legal freedoms available to spinsters and widows made their access to financial markets straight-forward. Single women could own property and chattels and dispose of them as they saw fit, they could make and break contracts and sue or be sued.[11] Married women were perhaps rather more vulnerable to being 'kissed or kicked' out of their property but were still able to circumvent the law of coverture and invest in financial instruments.[12] By 1720 women were a significant minority presence in the financial markets. This section will draw on studies of women's investment to paint a picture of their level of interactions with the financial markets before and during 1720. It is hampered, as are all such studies, by the destruction of the South Sea Company's books in the aftermath of the

---

9 For previous treatments of these themes, see Catherine Ingrassia, *Authorship, Commerce, and Gender in Early Eighteenth-Century England: A Culture of Paper Credit* (Cambridge: Cambridge University Press, 1998); Marieke de Goede, *Virtue, Fortune, and Faith: A Genealogy of Finance* (Minneapolis: University of Minnesota Press, 2005).

10 Amy Louise Erickson, "Coverture and Capitalism," *History Workshop Journal* 59 (2005): 1–16, here 3.

11 Erickson, "Coverture and Capitalism"; Susan Staves, *Married Women's Separate Property in England, 1660–1833* (Cambridge, Mass.: Harvard University Press, 1990).

12 Froide, *Silent Partners*, 2; Staves, *Married Women's Separate Property*, 135.

Bubble. Nonetheless, there are sources that allow us to gain an impressionistic sense of women's involvement both in the South Sea Scheme and in the financial markets more generally. It will show that, while activity increased during 1720, there is little evidence to suggest that women disproportionately were involved in the apparent folly of the Bubble.

Peter G.M. Dickson sampled a variety of stocks and government debt for the period from 1719 to 1724 and found that women comprised around one-fifth of investors in most cases. Their highest level of involvement came in the 1717 5 percent annuities, a stock which originated in the lotteries of 1711/12 and in which "many small investors would have had a flutter".[13] Women were 34.7 % of investors and held 20.1 percent of this stock. More generally, the amount of stock they held as a proportion of the total was lower than the number of investors, at around 10 to 12 percent, indicating that while women were an important minority presence in the financial market, they were generally small investors.[14] Ann Carlos and Larry Neal have gone further in their attempts to gauge the level of women's activity during 1720. Given the impossibility of using the South Sea Company's books, they turned to the extant records of the Bank of England. These survive in their entirety for the period before, during and after 1720. Carlos and Neal found that women comprised 13 percent of the market for Bank of England shares by value of transaction during 1720. They were involved in 10 percent of all sales and 8 percent of all purchases.[15] Measured by numbers of unique buyers, women comprised 18 percent of the market. These figures are, therefore, broadly consistent with the findings made by Dickson. It seems reasonable to conclude that women comprised between one tenth and one fifth of the market for shares both before and during 1720.

The transactions examined by Carlos and Neal also show that, with regard to the marital status of women investors, the majority of transactions were conducted by widows and spinsters. Women designated as wives also were active but to a far lesser extent.[16] This is consistent with what we know of wives' ability to act independently in respect of their financial decision-making. As might also be expected from Dickson's overview of investors and investment behavior during the early eighteenth century, the majority of activity was conducted by women residing in London and in the south east of England.[17] Of the 1,550 investors identi-

13 Peter G.M. Dickson, *The Financial Revolution in England: A Study in the Development of Public Credit, 1688–1756* (London: MacMillan, 1967), 282.
14 Dickson, *The Financial Revolution*, 282.
15 Carlos and Neal, "Women Investors," 209.
16 Carlos and Neal, "Women Investors," 211–212.
17 Carlos and Neal, "Women Investors," 219.

fied by Carlos and Neal, over 900 lived in London, 415 in England outside of London, and 205 outside of England. The foreign shareholders were predominantly Dutch. Switzerland also was represented by 27 female investors.[18] The preponderance of investors domiciled in London should not surprise. In a period where news flowed slowly out to the provinces and the best information circulated by word of mouth in Exchange Alley and its environs, the investors who lived closest to the City were at an advantage.[19]

Women's appetite for risk in their investment strategies varied. Amy Froide makes the salient point that, during the period under consideration here, the stock market was inherently risky, more so, indeed, than other forms of private lending.[20] Other scholars, however, have emphasized that, within the financial market and as a group, women were more cautious in their approach to investment than men. Keith Davies found that, although in 1685 women held no more than 2 to 4 percent of East India Company stock, they held nearly 20 percent of the less risky fixed-yield bonds.[21] It seems likely, given that most women would have been unable to generate alternative incomes through work, that establishing a reliable income stream was a greater priority than capital gains for the majority of women during this period. Women's turnover of stock during 1720, albeit only measured by activity in stocks other than the South Sea, was generally modest. Carlos and Neal found, with regard to Bank of England stock, that around two-thirds of women came into the market just once. The remaining third were somewhat more active, but there was no sign of speculative excess. Only eight women traded six or more times, and one of those, Johanna Cock, who we will meet again below, was a confirmed broker and jobber.[22] Furthermore, women's circumspect behavior appears to have yielded results. Carlos, Maguire and Neal have performed some analyses of trading activity in Bank of England and Royal African Company shares during 1720. They show that women did not, as a group, lose money.[23] This led them to conclude that the stock market certainly produced winners and losers, but "women were not a group who could be easily duped".[24]

---

18 Carlos and Neal, "Women Investors," 219.

19 Anne L. Murphy, *The Origins of English Financial Markets: Investment and Speculation before the South Sea Bubble* (Cambridge: Cambridge University Press, 2009), 114–136.

20 Froide, *Silent Partners*, 151.

21 K.G. Davies, "Joint-stock Investment in the Later Seventeenth Century," *Economic History Review* 4 (1952): 283–301, here 300.

22 Carlos and Neal, "Women Investors," 212.

23 Carlos and Neal, "Women Investors"; Carlos, Maguire, and Neal, "Financial Acumen."

24 Carlos, Maguire, and Neal, "Financial Acumen," 239.

This finding is supported by anecdotal evidence. It appears that women were fully cognizant of the opportunities and limitations of the South Sea scheme. Rosemary O'Day cites the case of the Duchess of Chandos, who invested wisely and sold out of stock early to buy into insurance.[25] The Duchess of Marlborough was reputed to have made £100,000 in the South Seas before exercising her "almost repellent good sense [and forcing] the Duke out of the market before the collapse".[26] The Duchess made her reasons for exiting the scheme clear:

> Every mortal that has common sense or that knows anything of figures can see that 'tis not possible by all the arts and tricks upon the earth long to carry £400,000,000 of paper credit with £15,000,000 of specie. This makes me think that this project must burst in a little while and fall to nothing.[27]

The actions of the Duchess of Rutland are another case in point. She bought stock early in the year, informing her broker in March that she was:

> allmost sure, I can mack an advantage by bying today in the South Seas with the hundred and four score pounds is still in your hands [...] so I would bye as much as that will bye today, and sell it out again next week, for [...] I have no opinion of the South Sea to continue in it [...].[28]

This is not to say that all women were so prescient. Amy Froide highlights the case of Barbara Savile, whose extant papers include details of her investments from the 1710s to her death in 1734.[29] She was active, risk-taking, and both kept careful accounts and acted on her own behalf, seldom employing agents. Despite a decade of investing and accumulating capital, she got caught up in the Bubble mania in 1720, investing in York Buildings, the Welsh Copper company and a fisheries company. She later sold out of copper to get into South Sea shares in August 1720. Her timing was poor, and she experienced a loss of over £250.[30] Her diverse portfolio of assets nonetheless seems to have cushioned the blow. Lady Mary Herbert was not so fortunate. She was one of the most celebrated speculators of the period and clearly able to deal with complexity in her trades, engaging in derivatives trading as well as straightforward sales and pur-

25 O'Day, *Women's Agency*, 222.
26 Sarah Churchill, Duchess of Marlborough, quoted in Winston S. Churchill, *Marlborough, His Life and Times* (London: Harrap, 1934), 2:1032.
27 Sarah Churchill quoted in Churchill, *Marlborough, His Life and Times*, 2:1032.
28 John Carswell, *The South Sea Bubble* (London: Cresset Press, 1960), 121.
29 Froide, *Silent Partners*, 130.
30 Froide, *Silent Partners*, 132–133.

chases. When the Mississippi and South Sea schemes collapsed, her losses were, however, tremendous.[31]

It must also be asserted that many women were drawn into the South Sea scheme neither because of overconfidence nor because of rational decision-making but simply because they had, or believed themselves to have, no choice. Those who held existing annuities in early 1720 had to make a decision about whether or not to exchange those holdings for South Sea stock and, as Dickson asserts, some may have believed themselves legally obliged to do so.[32] As a result around 80 percent of the irredeemable annuities and 85 percent of the redeemable ordinary government stock, or about £26,000,000 in nominal terms, was converted into South Sea stock.[33] In spite of the protests of public creditors after the Bubble burst, these agreements were not rescinded. In consequence, Dickson's estimates show that women comprised one-fifth of investors in South Sea stock in 1723.[34] Many of these women were 'South Sea speculators' but by accident, rather than by design.

Women were not only investors; they also were brokers of knowledge and financial advice as well as agents for others who wished to operate in the market from afar. Illustrative of the conduits for investment available to women in the provinces was Jane Bonnell, the widow of an Irish accountant-general. Bonnell moved to London in the early 1700s and, during that period, established herself as a supplier of information and goods to her friends and acquaintances.[35] Through her banker, Edward Hoare, she gained familiarity with the opportunities offered by the new financial markets and invested particularly in lottery tickets. She later purchased shares in the South Sea Company in March and April 1720 and South Sea bonds in August. Her motivation likely was to generate income, given the difficulties she had securing income from other sources.[36] Bonnell provides an interesting case study as an individual investor, but she is equally of interest to us as a source of information and as an intermediary for her friends and relatives. As documented by Anne Laurence, Bonnell was applied to by the Hastings sisters both for her advice and to arrange the sale and purchase of stocks. The sisters were conscious that "there is no judging at this dis-

---

31 Antoin E. Murphy, *Richard Cantillon: Entrepreneur and Economist* (Oxford: Clarendon Press, 1986), 111–113.

32 Dickson, *Financial Revolution*, 131.

33 Dickson, *Financial Revolution*, 134.

34 Dickson, *Financial Revolution*, 282.

35 Patrick Walsh, *The South Sea Bubble and Ireland: Money, Banking and Investment, 1690–1721* (Woodbridge: The Boydell Press, 2014), 101.

36 Walsh, *The South Sea Bubble and Ireland*, 101.

tance of these affairs" and thus they relied on Bonnell's good offices in every respect.[37]

Carlos and Neal also highlight the activities of Johanna Cock, a wealthy widow, who acted as both a broker and dealer of stocks and shares throughout the 1710s until her bankruptcy at the end of 1720.[38] She seems to have acted as a fairly small-scale dealer of stocks. Her broking activities are, of course, impossible to reconstruct, as anyone acting purely as a broker would not appear in company transfer books. Yet, she did increase significantly her own holdings between her husband's death in 1712 and 1720. Her activities during 1720 can only be traced through her dealings in Bank of England and East India Company shares. She was very active during that year, but the Bank's ledgers record a commission of bankruptcy against her in November 1720.[39]

The failure of Johanna Cock's business in 1720 should not blind us to the fact that she was a woman who was able effectively to negotiate the financial markets on her own behalf and on the behalf of others. She also demonstrates that, whatever contemporary views of the prevalence of women in the market, their involvement began long before 1720. Exploration of the extant records, however, suggests that the overarching behavior of women during this period was not very much different from their usual patterns of behavior and that, far from being led, many women were active investors and quite capable of making their own decisions both about when to enter the market and when to exit.

Perceptions of Female Involvement in the South Sea Scheme

Although we have established that women were neither an unusual presence in the market, nor disproportionately involved in the Bubble, they did attract much attention in 1720 and during the immediate aftermath of the Bubble's collapse. Archibald Hutcheson, the best known of the contemporary commentators on the South Sea Scheme, was unusual in believing women to be deserving of "the greatest compassion; for they cannot be suspected of acting with vile Views of deceiving others; but have been led by fateful Examples".[40] Other commentators and satirists painted female speculators in an unsympathetic light. Overwhelmingly, women were assigned instrumental roles in the inversion of social and eco-

37 Laurence, "That Nasty South Sea Affair," 255.
38 Carlos and Neal, "Women Investors," 205–208.
39 Carlos and Neal, "Women Investors," 207.
40 Quoted in Helen J. Paul, *The South Sea Bubble: An Economic History of Its Origins and Consequences* (London: Routledge, 2011), 91.

nomic hierarchies and power structures. They were painted as intruders in a male-dominated world, who infected that world through their manipulative behaviors.

Beginning in early 1720, comments were raised about women occupying the male world of Exchange Alley and its environs. It was reported in the *Weekly Journal* that "the Ladies from the other End of the Town have hired the China Shop at the Corner of Birchin-Lane at a Guinea per week, where they meet to buy stock and drink Tea; and at leisure Times, whilst their Agents are abroad, they Game for China".[41] A similar scene was depicted on the King of Hearts playing card (see image 1). The works of dramatists also reflected this supposed new reality. In William Chetwood's play *The Stock Jobbers*, for example, a group of women rented a shop in order that they might pursue their business in the markets away from the interference of men. These women were resolved to admit no man into their company, unless, of course, he was a trader; yet they acknowledged their desire to invade a man's world.[42] Lady Love-Picket declared:

> I do not see why these Wretches should monopolize the Pleasure of Business to themselves, it is only to keep us in Ignorance of all that's Charming in Life: Like Romish Priests, who refuse to let the Laity know anything, for fear of Usurping upon their Authority.[43]

The ladies also relished the independence that the gains from their speculation could bring. Lady Pawn-Locket viewed her profits as "better than pin-money",[44] presumably because she could spend it as she pleased, free from her husband's interference. Yet, for all these writers depicting well-informed and highly-motivated women, this was not done in the spirit of admiration. As Thomas d'Urfey insisted, "when these extraordinary events are consider'd, and Women of the Town are become Dealers in the Stocks [...] it is high time to pronounce Exchange Alley truly a Farce".[45]

When assessing the motivations of female speculators, it was their attempts to take on a less submissive role in the marriage market that were most frequently satirized. The *Original Weekly Journal* of 6 August 1720 was indeed quite explic-

---

41 *The Weekly Journal or the British Gazeteer: Being the Freshest Advices, Foreign and Domestick*, 9.4.1720.

42 W.R. Chetwood, *The Stock Jobbers, or the Humours of Exchange Alley: A Comedy of Three Acts* (London, 1720), 24.

43 Chetwood, *The Stock Jobbers*, 23.

44 Chetwood, *The Stock Jobbers*, 24.

45 T. D'Urfey, *Exchange Alley: or, the Stock-jobber turn'd Gentleman* (London, 1720), quoted in Catherine Ingrassia, *Authorship, Commerce, and Gender in Early Eighteenth-Century England: A Culture of Paper Credit* (Cambridge: Cambridge University Press, 1998), 33.

Image 1: *King of Hearts. South Sea Bubble playing cards* (London, 1720). (Courtesy of Kress Collection, Baker Library, Harvard Business School)

it about the aims of female speculation. A woman named Florentina supposedly wrote to the paper about the dilemmas of her decision to purchase a "South Sea husband".[46] She claimed to be a handsome young lady, who could not get a husband for want of a fortune. Some kind friends, however, helped her to subscribe in the first and second money subscriptions, which yielded her two thousand pounds and aided her ability to attract a man. Florentina asked how many years purchase should be given for a husband and, importantly, where to find one that was worth the money.[47]

46 *The Original Weekly Journal, with Fresh Advices, Foreign and Domestick*, 6.8.1720.
47 *The Original Weekly Journal, with Fresh Advices, Foreign and Domestick*, 6.8.1720.

Image 2: *Jack of Clubs. South Sea Bubble playing cards* (London, 1720). (Courtesy of Kress Collection, Baker Library, Harvard Business School)

Froide believes such depictions were a response to the numbers of never-married women in England. "Cultural anxiety" was generated by the notion that financial independence inverted traditional gender roles, as it allowed women to choose a husband independently or to even survive on their own.[48] Thus, satires invariably followed the *Original Weekly Journal* model and showed women – especially single, elderly women – as desirous of gaining a South Sea husband. Among the aforementioned collection of South Sea playing cards, for example, is the Jack of Clubs (see image 2), for which the motto reads:

---

48 Froide, *Silent Partners*, 30.

Her Ancient Maids, that ne'er Defil'd the Smock,
Boast of their Great Success in South Sea Stock;
Says one, when Poor, tho' Young, no Man would Sue me,
But now I'm rich, Six Irish Captains Woo me.

J.B. Gent, in *A Poem Occasioned by the Rise and Falling of the South Sea Stock*, was more explicit and even less flattering:

Numbers of those who want for charms attend,
In hopes their stocks may their stale wares commend
To the brisk Arms of some Young Vigrous Friend
The wither'd Maid lets loose her imprisoned Gold,
In stocking long immur'd in secret Hold.
Gold which for Ages past has Captive been,
Nor sun, nor moon, for numerous Years has seen,
Now travels thro' the winding Alleys free;
Rejoicing in the new gained Liberty;
Whilst with the glittering Store she seeks to Bribe
Some needy Fop to warm her frozen side.[49]

The damage that could be done to a woman's reputation by speculation was another consistent topic throughout 1720. In Thomas Foxton's *Jesina – or Delusive Gold: A Pastoral Lamenting the Misfortunes of a Young Lady of Quality Ruined by South Sea Stock*, Jesina bemoaned the ruin of her fortune and her reputation through misguided speculation. The consequence was the loss of her friends:

My dear Companions, now my Presence shun,
From her they lov'd with Eager Haste they run [...]

Well – I'll submit to this disastrous Fate,
And own my Error, tho' alas! too late.[50]

In the *Original Weekly Journal* of 23 April 1720, an obviously satirical letter appeared in which Lucinda asked whether or not it was acceptable to spend the night with a man other than her husband in order to gain South Sea shares. After all, she reconciled, her husband should not object because,

He parts with me for but one Night to a Man, whom he is sure I can never Love; and that for such a consideration, that if South Seas Stock rise, he may make by it a Fortune [... Besides

49 J.B. Gent, *A Poem Occasioned by the Rise and Falling of the South Sea Stock* (London, 1720).
50 Thomas Foxton, *Jesina, or Delusive Gold: A Pastoral Lamenting the Misfortunes of a Young Lady of Quality Ruined by South Sea Stock* (London, 1721).

> this, Lucinda was] perfectly ashamed among all the Ladies of my Acquaintance, to be the only one who have no Share in the South Sea Stock.[51]

It is difficult to judge the influence of such morality tales. Their message was consistent. The advice that Lucinda received was, of course, that she should remain faithful to her husband, as virtue and reputation were more important to a woman than profit; but whether such stories were taken as a warning is not clear. There is, however, no doubting their power to reach a wide audience. Poems, ballads and newspapers touched all levels of society "entertaining a literate elite and serving the illiterate or quasi-literate with news, information and political commentary".[52]

Personal reputation was not the only concern raised by women's involvement in the market. Other writers emphasized the ways in which an obsession with speculation was undermining social hierarchies. Women's willingness to mix with the socially undesirable to achieve their aims was commented upon, as was the fact that women were seen to bow to their social inferiors in order to get their names on subscription lists. This aroused criticism from men and women alike. The Duchess of Orléans, observing French duchesses kissing John Law's hand as they begged for shares in the Mississippi scheme, speculated what other parts of his body would be kissed by those further down the social scale.[53] Newspapers commented on the presence of aristocratic women in rue Quincampoix in Paris, where they went to purchase shares and inevitably mixed with the lower orders. These included the princess de Conti, a legitimized daughter of Louis XIV, who in September 1719 reportedly purchased sums "considérable d'actions des Indes".[54] Many contemporary ballads and poems reflect these supposed shifting social relations and the ways in which Exchange Alley had become a great social leveler:

> Our greatest Ladies hither come
>   and ply in Chariots daily,
> Oft pawn their jewels for a sum
>   to venture in the Alley.

51 *The Original Weekly Journal*, 23.4.1720.

52 Carl Wennerlind, *Casualties of Credit: The English Financial Revolution, 1620–1720* (Cambridge, Mass.: Harvard University Press, 2011), 206.

53 Malcolm Balen, *A Very English Deceit: The Secret History of the South Sea Bubble and the First Great Financial Scandal* (London: Fourth Estate, 2003), 73.

54 Stefano Condorelli, "La presse étrangère et le Système de Law (1716–20)," in '*Gagnons sans savoir comment': Représentations du Système de Law du XVIIIe siècle à nos jours*, ed. Florence Magnot-Ogilvy (Rennes: Presses universitaires de Rennes, 2017), 183–206, here 192–193.

Young harlots too from Drury Lane
approach the Change with Coaches,
To fool away the gold they gain
by their obscene Debauches.[55]

Likewise, the poet Anne Finch, Lady Winchelsea, depicted women turning from their lovers to indulge their passions for speculation with undesirable brokers:

Ombre and Basset laid aside
New Games employ the Fair,
And Brokers all those hours divide
Which Lovers used to Share [...]

With Jews and Gentiles undismay'd,
Young tender Virgins mix,
Of Whiskers nor of Beards afraid,
Nor all their Cousening tricks.[56]

The anti-Semitic tone evidenced here was not unusual. Helen J. Paul shows that while some satirical texts and images were sympathetic towards women, none were sympathetic towards Jewish speculators and brokers.[57] Moreover, depictions often showed Jewish brokers attempting to compromise apparently gentile women. The Seven of Hearts playing card, for example, shows a "Rich Jew" with a "Young Buxome Lady," to whom he is offering stock in return for expected sexual favors (see image 3). The implied vulgarity of this work also is not uncommon and arguably served a wider purpose. Indeed, Frans De Bruyn argues that writers adopted the vulgar poetic form as if their theme of the breakdown of social and gender hierarchies "demanded a matching transgression of literary decorum".[58]

Depictions of female speculators challenging accepted social roles did not come about merely as the result of social anxiety. In the early eighteenth century, women had limited opportunities for taking public roles, and, yet, legal and social conventions were powerless to keep them away from Exchange Alley and its environs. Access to this important public space, therefore, did afford women the opportunity to move out of the domestic sphere, and it is probable that some

55 *The Shepherd's Garland inc. A South Sea Ballad, or Merry Remarks upon Exchange Alley Bubbles* (London, 1720).
56 Quoted in Froide, *Silent Partners*, 152.
57 Paul, *South Sea Bubble*, 93.
58 Frans De Bruyn, "Satire in Text and Image: Bubble Publications in England and the Netherlands Compared," in *The Great Mirror of Folly: Finance, Culture, and the Crash of 1720*, ed. William N. Goetzmann (New Haven: Yale University Press, 2013), 159–174, here 159.

Image 3: *Seven of Hearts. South Sea Bubble playing cards* (London, 1720). (Courtesy of Kress Collection, Baker Library, Harvard Business School)

women appreciated this freedom and took advantage of it. It is also certain that women would have seen separate financial means as offering a degree of independence both within and outside of marriage. Yet, the depictions of women detailed above also reflect the types of critiques levelled against male traders in the aftermath of the 2008 financial crisis. This can be seen particularly in the accusations of ill-considered and peculiarly feminine motivations for speculation, the feminization of market spaces with problematic consequences, and the social climbing, which undermined the existing social and political order. Gendering these types of behavior as female allowed commentators on the collapse of the South Sea Scheme to create a narrative through which control of the market could be regained with the expulsion of women from Exchange Alley.

Gendering Credit

Elisabeth Prügl, writing of the collapse of the financial system in 2008, further elucidates the purpose of gendering crises. She argues that "inserting gender into discussions [...] enables a narrative of fall, rise and redemption through which finance capitalism is re-born both chastened and reformed".[59] This can be seen through the above-mentioned critiques of individual and group female behavior, but it is most obvious in the persistent gendering of both monied companies and the operation of credit itself. Two factors were at work here. First, gendering allowed a disavowal of the undesirable. Problematic behavior could be wrapped up in feminine traits and then dismissed as something that true men could surpass and the market could transcend. Second, depictions of credit as feminine allowed it to be controlled and mastered, sometimes in violent ways.

Attempts to assert control through gendering were, of course, directed at individuals and groups. Long before 1720, the monied man came to be seen as less reliable and less stable than he whose wealth was based in land. Land was the symbol of political and civic responsibility – a solid form of property that wedded the individual to the state in a mutually-beneficial relationship. The pursuit of money, on the other hand, was the pursuit of self-interest. The monied man indulged his desires on the strength of nothing more substantial than credit and responded to his passions, rather than to his sense of duty and responsibility. Thus, involvement in the financial markets put men in a submissive and feminine position, because it made them reliant upon opinion and reputation and subject to their passions, as women supposedly were.[60] The market robbed the monied man of his masculinity. As Thomas Gordon asserted,

> Our Evil cometh from the dull Heart of the City, and we are enchanted by a stupid kennel of Stock-Jobbers, who cheat us out of our money and our sex [...] Let us, my Brethren and countrymen either properly and patiently put on Petticoats; or resume our Manhood and shake off this shameful Delusion, this filthy Yoke, put upon our necks by dull Rogues from Jonathan's; plodding dunces![61]

Thus robbed of his masculine ability to act rationally, the monied man failed to recognize that he was being duped by the market. In particular, he failed to perceive value correctly. For critics of the early financial markets, value was something transient and almost intangible. Assets had come to be represented by

59 Prügl, "'If Lehman Brothers Had Been Lehman Sisters ...'," 21.
60 Ingrassia, *Authorship, Commerce and Gender*, 22.
61 T. Gordon, *A Learned Dissertation Upon Old Women* (London, 1720), 26.

paper, in itself valueless, and investment therefore became a business "founded upon nothing that is solid, rational or honest, but meerly upon Artifice, Trick and Catch".[62] Archibald Hutcheson, for example, observed how little the value of South Sea stock really meant and asserted that "[w]e may put what Value we please upon our Paper, and raise it [...] but we cannot hope always to make it pass with the Nations with whom we have trade and Commerce, for more than its intrinsick worth".[63]

The South Sea Bubble, however, was created by more than just trick and manipulation. Commentators argued powerfully as the Scheme collapsed that, at its heart, was deceit perpetrated by the Company and supported by both Parliament and Court. While the anger of the mob was most often directed at the directors of the South Sea Company, women in the royal household also were attacked in print and satirical imagery. They had been offered gifts of South Sea stock in return for their support of the scheme. The Duchess of Kendal, the King's mistress, and the Countess of Platen, his illegitimate half-sister, were each given £10,000 stock, and the Duchess of Kendal's two 'nieces', actually her daughters, received £5,000 stock each.[64] The Princess of Wales also was gifted stock. Countess Cowper, in her diary, recorded that,

> one of W's [Walpole's] great Arts to please the Princess has been by making her a Stock jobber in the South Sea. They bought in for her that very morning before the Great Debate and it was used to the M. of P. [Members of Parliament] as Arguments they [the Prince and Princess of Wales] were both for the Project.[65]

In the aftermath of the Bubble, the fact that gifts had been made to the Duchess of Kendal and the Countess of Platen emerged through the reports of the Committee of Secrecy set up to investigate the scheme. Robert Walpole, by then de facto Prime Minister, tried in vain to prevent the involvement of the women of the king's court becoming publicly known. His failure meant that these women became easy targets for the anger of the mob. One newspaper report indicates the prevailing mood: "We have been ruined by Whores; nay what is more

62 *A Letter to a Conscientious Man: Concerning the Use and Abuse of Riches and the Right and Wrong Ways of Acquiring Them* (London, 1720), quoted in Ingrassia, *Authorship, Commerce and Gender*, 5.

63 A. Hutcheson, *A collection of Calculations and Remarks relating to the South Sea scheme and stock* (London, 1720), 63.

64 Reports of the amounts paid to these women vary, but these seem to be the most reliable figures. *Journals of the House of Commons* (London, 1803), 19:428.

65 C.S. Cowper, ed., *Diary of Mary Countess Cowper, Lady of the Bedchamber to the Princess of Wales, 1714–1720* (London, 1824), 158.

vexatious, old ugly Whores! Such as could not find entertainment in the most hospitable hundreds of the old Drury".[66] The Duchess of Kendal became a particular target, after she was depicted in a cartoon handing papers to Robert Knight to facilitate his escape (see image 4). It seems unlikely that the Duchess was directly involved in Knight's disappearance, but the *Brabant Screen* came to represent the cover-up that money subscribers and annuitants felt had occurred. The lines that inspired the cartoon are significant:

> Should he return, the screen would useless be
> And all then the mystery would see:
> The mask thrown off, the villain would appear,
> Not Antwerp's slave, but others that are here [...][67]

The intense interest in apportioning blame at the highest levels for the failure of the South Sea Scheme indicates the extent to which the integrity of public credit was connected to the perceived stability of the country as a whole. Indeed, it was fully appreciated that success in war was dependent not on military prowess but rather on financial stability. Daniel Defoe wrote in 1711, as peace with the French was being considered during the War of Spanish Succession: "The French king [...] will recover himself, gather Strength, lessen his Debt, and lay up Money; a few Years of Peace will recover him [...] and make him the same Powerful immensely Rich Prince that he was before".[68] Speculation, which undermined England's ability to outspend its rivals, thus not only undermined the country's economic base but also placed its future in the hands of fickle, deceitful and, above all, uncontrollable forces. Numerous commentators employed female figures in text and imagery to depict these uncontrollable forces and to demonstrate the idea that "the credit mechanism ha[d] endowed society with an excessively hysterical nervous system".[69]

With this feminine hysteria was coupled the inconsistency of "Lady Credit's" affections. Lady Credit embodied "the whimsicality of the market".[70] She was sometimes honest but, in the words of Defoe, once Credit was:

---

66 *Weekly Journal*, 28.5.1721, quoted in V. Cowles, *The Great Swindle: The Story of the South Sea Bubble* (New York: Harper and Brothers, 1960), 174.

67 Quoted in Lewis Melville, *The South Sea Bubble* (New York: Franklin, 1968), 203.

68 Daniel Defoe, *A Review of the State of the British Nation*, 8.2.1711.

69 J.G.A. Pocock, *Virtue, Commerce, and History: Essays on Political Thought and History, Chiefly in the Eighteenth Century* (Cambridge: Cambridge University Press, 1985), 99.

70 Sandra Sherman, *Finance and Fictionality in the Early Eighteenth Century: Accounting for Defoe* (Cambridge: Cambridge University Press, 1996), 40.

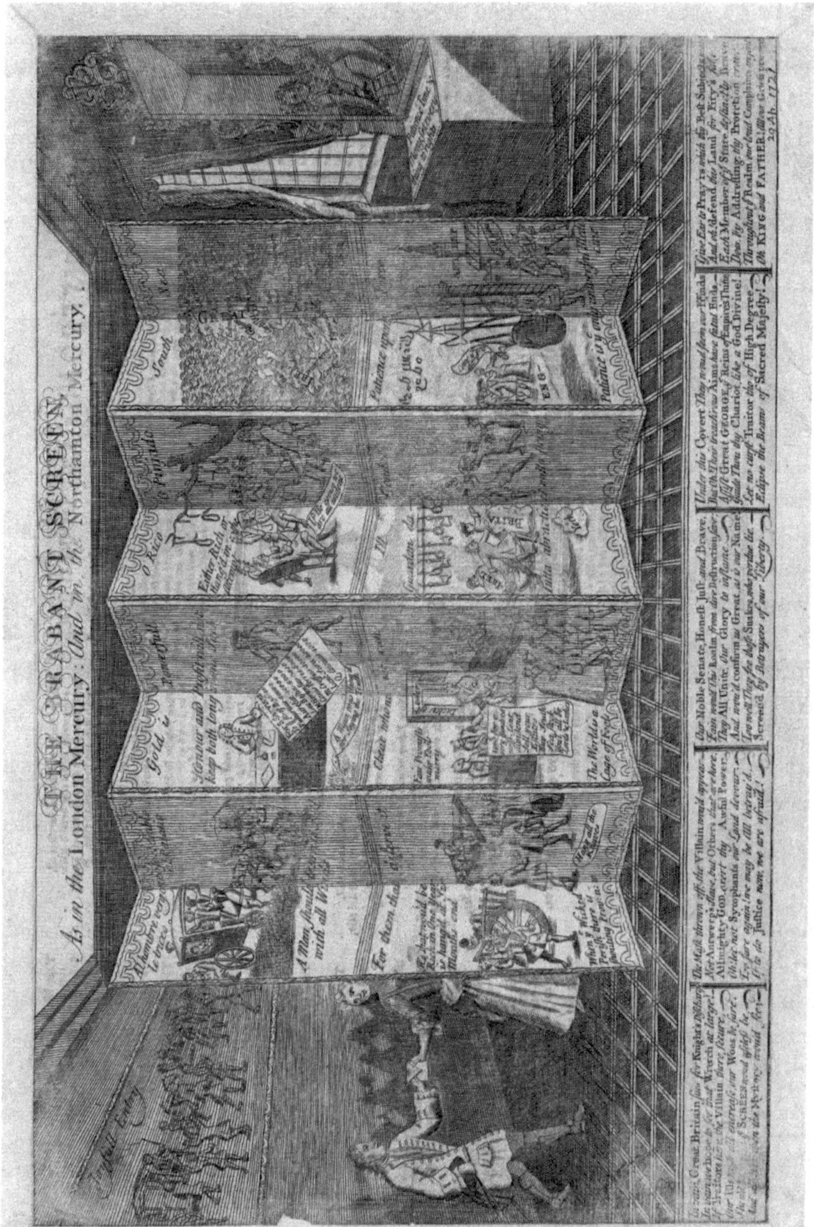

Image 4: *The Brabant Screen. As in the London Mercury: And in the Northamton Mercury* (London, 1721). (Courtesy of the British Museum)

> disoblig'd, she's the most difficult to be Friends again with us, of anything in the World, and yet she will court those most, that have no occasion for her; and will stand at their Doors neglected and ill-us'd, scorn'd and rejected, like a Beggar and never leave them: But let such have a Care of themselves, and be sure they never come to want her; for, if they do, they may depend upon it, she will pay them home, and never be reconcil'd to them, but upon a World of Entreaties, and the severe Penance of some years Prosperity.[71]

Lady Credit was, in other words, intensely volatile: one moment your friend and the next turning against you. Joseph Addison also depicted the "quick Turns and Changes in [Credit's] Constitution" and her tendency to "fall away from the most florid complexion [...] and wither into a Skeleton".[72] Credit was a vapid and vacillating woman, who was inconstant in her affections and apt to disappoint or neglect her suitors. Sandra Sherman shows that Lady Credit quickly became depicted as a whore after the collapse of a speculative market. Her "fall" mirrored the fall in public confidence that resulted from the collapse of the South Sea Scheme.[73]

It is notable that, in the aftermath of the bubble, the South Sea Company itself was also spoken of in gendered, and disparaging, terms. In the *Battle of the Bubbles*, the Company was represented by Oceania, who had "bewitch'd Thousands" and, despite having ruined them, "her Lust is not one bit abated; and She runs a whoring after new Lovers every day".[74] In the *South Sea Scheme Detected*, also published in 1720, similar images were conjured up:

> The Chief Managers of a certain Stock, may dress up their Darling Mistress once more, and send her into the World not without a tempting Aspect; but People who have already been Sufferers by their Schemes, will look upon her with a cautious Eye. A fine Lady, who had deceiv'd a Man once, will for the Future be treated as a common Prostitute.[75]

In the Dutch image *De Zuid Ze Compagnie Door Wind In Top Gerezen Beklaagt Nu Haar Verlies Met Een Bekommerd Wezen*, the Company was depicted as reclining and in a state of undress, appearing, as Catherine Ingrassia suggests, in an attitude reminiscent of eighteenth-century pornography (see image 5). Her sexual-

---

71 Sherman, *Finance and Fictionality*, 42.

72 Quoted in T. Mulcaire, "Public Credit: Or the Feminization of Virtue in the Marketplace," *PMLA* 114 (1999): 1029–1042, here 1033.

73 Sherman, *Finance and Fictionality*, 157.

74 *The Battle of the Bubbles: shewing their several constitutions, alliances, policies and wars* (London, 1720), quoted in Sherman, *Finance and Fictionality*, 53.

75 *The South Sea Scheme Detected and the Management Thereof Enquired Into* (London, 1720), quoted in Sherman, *Finance and Fictionality*, 53.

Image 5: *The South Sea Company, having Risen to the Top by Wind, now Laments her Loss with a Rueful Aspect.* (Courtesy of the John Carter Brown Library)

ized state does not indicate allurement, however, but rather the degradation of a spent whore.[76]

The fall from grace of these feminized forms of credit allowed her to be mastered by men in order to regain control. This was sometimes depicted in obvious-

76 Ingrassia, *Authorship, Commerce and Gender*, 27.

Image 6: William Hogarth, *The South Sea Scheme* (London 1721). (Courtesy of the British Museum)

ly violent forms. Daniel Defoe represented stockjobbers and brokers as the rapists of Lady Credit.[77] In William Hogarth's South Sea Scheme, published in 1721, the goddess Fortuna, often thought to be the model for Lady Credit, is seen "hanging by her hair from the balcony of London's Guildhall. Her body is being hacked by a scythe-wielding devil, who throws hunks of her flesh to the crazed spectators below" (see image 6).[78] Nonetheless, credit, being essential for the nation, cannot in the end be destroyed. As Marieke De Goede asserts, "it becomes the responsibility of financial man to make an honest woman out of her".[79] In order to do this, however, the financial man had to restrain his passions and desires. In the words of Daniel Defoe, those who wanted to entertain the virgin Lady Credit had to "act upon the nice Principles of Honour and Jus-

77 De Goede, *Virtue, Fortune, and Faith*, 34.
78 Mark Hallet quoted in De Bruyn, "Satire in Text and Image," 166.
79 De Goede, *Virtue, Fortune, and Faith*, 31.

tice".[80] Doing so allowed financial man to master an important and effective tool in the fight against Catholic Europe.

Conclusion

Women did not enter Exchange Alley for the first time in 1720. They had been active in the financial markets as investors, speculators and intermediaries long before the South Sea Scheme. They were competent, cautious investors and risk-taking speculators. In 1720, their activities were not significantly different from their typical behavior during non-crisis years. Nonetheless, social and cultural anxieties were generated by the seeming financial independence that female speculators might gain. Women's presence in Exchange Alley also allowed commentators to address the failures of 1720 by 'othering' problematic behavior. Thus, just as our twenty-first century gendering of the market as masculine allowed us to disavow its more problematic elements, depictions of speculative excess as feminine in 1720 allowed contemporaries a route to regain control of high finance.

The comparisons and contrasts between the narratives used in 2008 and in 1720 are interesting on many levels, but, most importantly, they help us to see discussions about individual and group behavior in the market for what they are and what they are not. They are critiques rooted in moral concerns about the accumulation of wealth, in social anxieties about the inversion of hierarchies that might stem from unfettered speculation, and in political anxieties about the consequences of markets grown out of control. These are not factors that explain why markets crash. Crude reconstructions of behavior that allow stigmatization of individuals and groups, whether they be wide-boys or out-of-control women, will neither help us understand why financial crises occur and recur, nor will they give us the recipe to control the financial system.

---

80 Quoted in De Goede, *Virtue, Fortune, and Faith*, 33.

Jean-Yves Grenier

To Think the Unthinkable. Early Financial Theories (Late 17th – 18th Century)

For much of the modern era, financial theory remained very separate from political economy. During the nineteenth century and a large part of the twentieth century, thinking about finance was descriptive at best, drawing on almost none of the concepts that economists then were inventing to conceptualize the production and exchange of non-financial goods and services.[1] As a result, financial theory was little able to provide a precise explanation of how the financial market worked or how asset prices formed. A major change was triggered by the discovery, problematic and gradual, that the price of financial assets followed a random walk. In an article published in 1933 in the first volume of *Econometrica,* Alfred Cowles already expressed doubt about the possibility of predicting the market through the study of the recommendations made by stock-research services.[2] Other articles, generally written by physicists or statisticians unfamiliar with financial issues, followed suit until the end of the 1950s, and all highlighted the fact that stock prices were random markets. By the late 1950s, empirical observations increasingly confirmed that the random structure of stock market fluctuations was such that any prediction of prices appeared impossible.[3] For the community of practitioners and economists of finance, this finding was difficult to accept. For practitioners, the idea that it was impossible to predict, even partially, future prices on the basis of past prices seemed to condemn as useless many professions in asset management and securities purchase. For economists, the finding implied a lack of rationality in the behavior of economic actors as well as the complete opacity of the financial market, which was reduced to a series of randomly-selected prices in contradiction with the idea that each asset had its own fundamental value.

How, then, to interpret what seemed to be an undeniable statistical fact? The solution was found by the economists who, for the first time, integrated financial markets – despite their peculiarities – into the dominant economic theory, name-

1 To mention just one example, it is remarkable that in the *History of Economic Analysis* (London: G. Allen and Unwin, 1955), Joseph Schumpeter never speaks about financial theory, and, when he alludes to speculation, he only refers to the grain trade.

2 Alfred Cowles, "Can Stock Market Forecasters Forecast?," *Econometrica* 1 (1933): 309 – 324.

3 Peter L. Bernstein, *Capital Ideas: The Improbable Origins of Modern Wall Street* (New York: The Free Press, 1992), ch. 5.

https://doi.org/10.1515/9783110592139-014

ly the neoclassical paradigm. Paul Samuelson, in his famous article of 1965, proposed returning to the insights offered by Louis Bachelier, who argued that the random nature of financial asset prices resulted from the multiplicity of new information constantly coming to the awareness of shareholders and brokers.[4] Samuelson rejected Keynes' idea that the operations of the stock market resemble those of a casino.[5] He argued, instead, that there is indeed an economic order, even in financial markets. The paradox is that a sign of its existence is precisely the random nature of asset prices, which proves that all available information is correctly interpreted by the actors since the new information is independent from the last, and what it indicates about the future is immediately integrated into market price. Paul Samuelson wrote: "What can be perceived about the future must already be 'discounted' in current price quotations."[6] Market price thus can be considered the best estimate of fundamental value, with rational agents correctly using the same model to analyze available information and to calculate the present value of expected dividends. This is the efficient-market hypothesis developed by Eugene Fama.[7] The emergence of these new concepts marked the integration of financial theory within neoclassical economic theory – an integration which therefore happened very late.

If studies about financial markets and their integration into economic science are relatively recent, there was, however, a period during which the key questions of the formation of the price of financial assets was explored. This period covered nearly a century, from 1670 to 1770.[8] The number of publications re-

4 Paul Samuelson, "Proof That Properly Anticipated Prices Fluctuate Randomly," *Industrial Management Review* 6 (1965): 41–49. Louis Bachelier's pioneering work was his mathematical thesis, "Théorie de la spéculation," which he defended in 1900.

5 "Speculators may do no harm as they are like bubbles on a steady stream of enterprise. But the position is serious when enterprise becomes the bubble on a whirlpool of speculation. When the capital development of a country becomes a by-product of the activities of a casino, the job is likely to be ill-done." John Maynard Keynes, *The General Theory of Employment Interest and Money* (London: MacMillan, 1964), 159. This image of a financial market similar to a casino appears for the first time in a statement that Keynes made before the *Royal Commission on Lotteries and Betting* on 15 December 1932. He contrasted the English, who invest for dividends, to the Americans, who do so for capital gains – that is to say, to speculate.

6 Samuelson, "Properly Anticipated," 41.

7 Eugene F. Fama, "Efficient Capital Markets: A Review of Theory and Empirical Work," *Journal of Finance* 25 (1970): 383–417.

8 For earlier financial literature, with analyses mainly based on descriptions of markets and financial practices, see Geoffrey Poitras, *The Early History of Financial Economics, 1478–1776: From Commercial Arithmetic to Life Annuities and Joint Stocks* (Cheltenham and Northampton: E. Elgar, 2000); and Neil de Marchi and Paul Harrison, "Trading 'in the Wind' and with Guile: The Troublesome Matter of the Short Selling of Share in Seventeenth-Century Holland," in *Hig-*

lated to this question remained, nonetheless, limited – so much so that Thomas Mortimer, in the first edition of his book *Every man, his own broker* in 1761, expressed surprise that this important topic had not been addressed "except in a few satirical pieces on the fatal year 1720."[9] Hence, he considered that it was important to advise the public so as to avoid being caught in situations similar to those of the 1720 financial bubble.

The first important writings on matters of finance appeared towards the end of the seventeenth century, in particular *Confusion de confusiones* by Joseph de la Vega (1688). Based on the author's personal experience (marked by failures in the stock market), this major work focused mainly on the price formation of shares traded on the Amsterdam stock exchange.[10] It is striking that this same period also saw the first developments of economic analysis, understood as a way to think about the interactions between agents. Yet, if political economists, from John Cary and Pierre le Pesant de Boisguilbert up to Adam Smith, were prolix on the questions of value and prices, they had little to say about the same questions in the specific field of finance. An author such as Richard Cantillon, despite being himself "an exceptionally successful trader in the 1719 – 20 Mississippi Bubble,"[11] devoted very little attention to the financial market in his *Essai sur la nature du commerce en général*. As for Adam Smith, he only addressed the subject in his *Lectures on Jurisprudence*. He examined there the fluctuation of prices, explaining them, rather cursorily, by the alternation between periods of peace and war and by the harmful consequences of "stock-jobbing."[12] It is noteworthy that, although Smith revisited much of his analysis from his *Lectures* in *The Wealth of Nations*, this was not the case with his considerations about financial prices. This perhaps was because he knew that he had not much more to contribute to the subject, as his approach in terms of natural prices was very far from the realities of finance. The silence, as we have seen, lasted almost two centuries.

---

gling: Transactors and Their Markets in the History of Economics, ed. N. de Marchi and M. Morgan, Annual supplement to *History of Political Economy* 26 (1994), 47–65.

9 Thomas Mortimer, *Every man, his own broker, or a Guide to Exchange-Alley*, 6th ed. (1761; London 1765), VI.

10 Joseph de la Vega, *Confusion de confusiones* (1688), ed. Hermann Kellenbenz (Boston: Publication of the Kress Library, 1957). About the author see José Luis Cardoso, "*Confusion de confusiones:* Ethics and Options on Seventeenth-Century Stock Exchange Markets," *Financial History Review* 9 (2002): 109 – 123.

11 See Antoin E. Murphy, *Richard Cantillon: Entrepreneur and Economist* (Oxford: Oxford University Press, 1986).

12 *Works and Correspondence of Adam Smith*, ed. Ronald L. Meek, David D. Raphael, and Peter Stein (Oxford: Clarendon Press, 1978), in particular 5:536 – 537.

Bringing together the early literature and the current financial science is not out of place. Some acknowledgments about the specificity of finance, indeed, are shared by both schools of thought, although interpretations of price formation differ significantly, since earlier authors proposed ways of thinking which are difficult to tread today because of the concern for consistency of financial theory with the foundations of standard neoclassical thought.

Order in Political Economy

An important element within the tradition of political economy is the notion of order, which long has underpinned economic reasoning. As we saw earlier, the notion also can be found in Paul Samuelson's work and in the early stages of neoclassical financial theory. During the Old Regime, concern with order was integral in framing how societies viewed the economic sphere.

The idea appeared first and foremost as a necessity. There are norms and rules that have to be followed to achieve the common good, or "commonwealth," and to avoid a state of social anomy. This pursuit of order, this preoccupation to impose it upon people and things, also belonged to scholastic thought. Scholastic Doctors were convinced that unregulated trade is a sure source of chaos and profound inequalities, and they thus thought it necessary to implement rules establishing a fair market, that is to say a market that grants people whatever they need to live according to the status that God had assigned them. A similar idea is found in mercantilist writings, wherein the pursuit of harmony is a central feature. Thomas Mun explained, for instance, that maintaining order within a nation is a necessary condition for winning on foreign trade.[13] Generally speaking, the notion of "good order" or "good order in merchandising" was a major concern and its absence often deplored. In the international context, order took on two meanings for mercantilists. On the one hand, it referred to market autonomy with regard to technical and legal aspects. This was a position defended, for example, by Gerard de Malynes, who considered the *Lex Mercatoria*, because it is immemorial, as more legitimate than sovereign law in matters of trade. On the other hand, it meant a structure that prevents harmful competition between traders coming from the same national community.[14]

13 Thomas Mun, *England's Treasure By Foreign Trade* (1664), ch. 10.

14 Jean-Yves Grenier, "Ordre et désordre: Échange et marchés dans le mercantilisme anglais et français (XVIIe–XVIIIe siècle)," *Vierteljahrschrift für Sozial- und Wirtschaftsgeschichte*, Beiheft 228 (2013): 83–111.

Starting in the seventeenth century, authors such as Francis Bacon in *Novum Organum* (1620) developed the idea that nature is constituted in such a way that order exists: a form of stability beyond the apparent disorder. Their aim was to discover the regularity that characterizes natural phenomena, which, at that time, was seen in terms of causes and effects. At the end of the seventeenth century, some scholars took an interest in applying the natural order idea to economic and social mechanisms. Richard Cumberland, for instance, believed that moral law, which is conducive to achieving the common good, is similar to a natural law. All human action can be analyzed in terms of cause and effect, and its consequences may be understood and considered in terms of individual and collective happiness, independently of any civil law.[15] The natural order that is thereby established carried, for Cumberland, a strong ethical dimension, which is not found among other contemporary authors using the principle of natural laws to understand economic issues. William Petty did not doubt the existence of natural laws which establish proportions and regular relationships between things. This was indeed the objective of his *Political Arithmetic:* to identify these constancies with the aid of statistics. During the same period, Boisguilbert explicitly used nature as a standard framework for investigating the regularity of economic activities. According to him, nature is eminently good, and respecting its principles leads to an order that allows all human beings to live off their work or the work of their ancestors. Opposing this good nature is the artifice of what is unnatural, starting with a number of human interventions that pretend to organize the economy.

From then on, the question of natural order became the major obsession of the eighteenth century. Indeed, for most historians, political economy only appears as a science when it adopted natural order as its key concept, such as with the Physiocrats and Adam Smith. The principle that an economic order exists was of central importance to these authors: as metaphysical evidence for the Physiocrats;[16] as a physical phenomenon – the gravitational force – for Adam Smith. It is that very certainty which was challenged, in the 1950s, when statisticians began to highlight the random nature of the series of financial prices. The advent of the concept of informational efficiency represented, from this perspective, a sort of miracle, as it offered the possibility of arguing that apparent disorder is, in fact, the very proof of the existence of an underlying order.

---

15 Richard Cumberland, *A Treatise of the Laws of Nature* (first edition in latin 1672; London, 1727), 11, § 9.

16 See the article "Evidence" by Quesnay in *Encyclopédie*, ed. Denis Diderot and Jean-Baptiste le Rond d'Alembert, vol. 6 (Paris, 1756).

However, in the decades preceding the emergence of an economy aiming to be scientific, that is before the 1770s, political economy was not so categorical. If it believed in the idea of an order inscribed in nature, it considered that this order is, to a certain extent, merely virtual and that its achievement within human affairs is never perfect. Its objective thus was to identify this order. Yet, that was particularly difficult since this early political economy also gave great importance to everything contradicting or preventing order from taking place. Richard Cantillon, who had been an insider in the major operations of Law's System, repeatedly underlined the arbitrariness reigning over the markets (which do not belong to the accuracy of geometry) and the role played by chance in price formation.[17] Later on, the Abbé de Condillac strongly emphasized that there is radical uncertainty about demand and that this has perverse effects on the organization of markets.[18] For all these authors, the question of value was secondary and much less important than the issue of price formation. The possibility of order thus was related to the risk of disorder. Yet, one essential feature was that disorder had a cause and that cause was clearly identifiable. According to Boisguilbert, although the order created by the invisible hand is effectively present,[19] the disorder which perpetually threatens it is triggered by specific factors, such as the strong tendency for hoarding or a badly distributed tax system.

Unsurprisingly, one key characteristic of the literature on financial markets – which established itself with the writings of de la Vega as well as those prompted by the 1720 events – was its search for regularities, consistency, and readability in the sequence of financial asset prices. Authors writing about finance were aware of the idiosyncrasies of that type of market, especially its complex relationship between supply and demand. This was emphasized in the long and highly critical dissertation that the Chancellor d'Aguesseau wrote on the trading of shares in the Company of the Indies, done in response to the Law affair.[20] He opposed, on the one hand, the natural trade, wherein the "natural need of the seller" is to sell at a high price and the "natural need of the buyer" is to buy at a low price; and, on the other hand, the financial market, wherein the interests of the seller and the buyer are united in the same person. If the last persons sells, explained d'Aguesseau, it would be at a low price to bring prices down

17 Richard Cantillon, *Essai sur la nature du commerce en général* (Paris: INED, 1997), part 1, ch. 13.

18 Abbé de Condillac, *Le commerce et le gouvernement* (1776), part 2, ch. 18.

19 Jean-Claude Perrot, "La main invisible et le Dieu caché," in *Une histoire intellectuelle de l'économie politique (XVIIe–XVIIIe siècle)* (Paris: Editions de l'EHESS, 1992), 333–354.

20 About the chancellor d'Aguesseau and the System, see Arnaud Orain, *La politique du merveilleux: Une autre histoire du Système de Law (1695–1795)* (Paris: Fayard, 2018), 238 sq.

even more, and, if he buys, it would be at a high price to raise prices further. Experience had taught him a peculiar characteristic – which is still valid today – namely that "raising prices, far from bringing down demand, stimulates and intensifies it," as expressed by André Orléan.[21] D'Aguesseau concluded "that the motive which drives [the trader in financial assets] to act is thus not the kind of necessity which is the link and core of the trade between sellers and buyers." It is an interest "which departs [...] from the ordinary course of trade."[22] Therefore, the confrontation between supply and demand does not lead to price regulation but to the opposite. "The fall of prices needs not have a limit, and there are also unlimited possibilities for the rise," wrote Joseph de la Vega.[23] Because it makes impossible any balance between supply and demand, and therefore any ordinary processes of pricing, the financial market is contrary to nature – in other words, it is without order.

This idea ran through various texts, and it justified the implicit representation of the financial market as a place of abnormal economic operations and impossible order. An admission in this sense was made by the abbé Terrasson, a major advocate of Law's System, who suggested that trade in financial assets, with all its repercussions, is hardly comprehensible. The ways of God are impenetrable, he continued, yet there is a harmony and a justice invisible to human beings and to their understanding: "That may shock you, but God allowed it [...] We do not always see what God's plans are, but we cannot doubt that they are just."[24] The most remarkable sign of this disorder was that changes

21 André Orléan, *De l'euphorie à la panique: Penser la crise financière* (Paris: Ed. Rue d'Ulm, 2009), 21. In *The Empire of Value*, Orléan characterises the logic of financial markets in a surprisingly similar manner to d'Aguesseau: "Ordinary markets bring together two groups with clearly divergent interests: producers and consumers. [Prices are formed as a result of the tension between these two opposed forces, the one pushing prices upward, the other downward. This is the basis for the law of supply and demand, which prevents either party from gaining too great advantage over the other.] In financial markets, by contrast, nothing of the sort occurs. There is no group of buyers that negotiates with a group of sellers; instead there is a group of individuals, each of whom acts as a buyer and a seller" (André Orléan, *The Empire of Value* (Cambridge, Mass.: MIT Press, 2014), 209).

22 Chancellor H.F. d'Aguesseau, "Mémoire sur le commerce des actions de la Compagnie des Indes," in *Oeuvres de M. le chancelier d'Aguesseau* (Paris, 1777), 10:175. Although d'Aguesseau denounces Law's System from the perspective of justice (169), he questions precisely the very characteristics of financial markets.

23 De la Vega, *Confusion de confusiones*, 14.

24 Father Jean Terrasson, *Mémoire pour servir à justifier la Compagnie des Indes contre la censure des casuistes qui la condamnent* (1720), 41. This recourse to a hidden God, whose plans for human societies are very real, reminds Boisguilbert of the economic order: i.e. an order which is only partially accessible to us and which constitutes only a partial harmony. Boisguilbert con-

in asset prices followed a *white noise:* a finding which was shared rather quickly and widely.[25] Already in the 1670s, Joseph de la Vega observed this unpredictability.[26] According to him, if a person who carries out his business wisely and without passion seeks to understand the movement of stock market prices, "at the conclusion of his observations [...] he will find that no perspicacity will divine the game and no science is sufficient here."[27] The Dutch financier had a precise understanding of white noise. Although *Confusion de confusiones* describes the Amsterdam stock exchange as a mix of science and deceits ("it is a quintessence of academic learning and a paragon of fraudulence"[28]), de la Vega did not attribute white noise to the individual irrationality of the actors or to their dishonesty. He rather argued that this phenomenon results from a collective interaction generating what he called a mystery or an "enigmatic business," terms employed throughout the eighteenth century to characterize financial markets.[29] It is therefore the very logic of finance that he called into question. The de la Vega's explanation rested on the finding – established at the beginning of the second dialogue of his book – that buyers and sellers are constantly subject to a multiplicity of non-correlated information, which produces unpredictable variations in price. The same argument was reiterated several years later by Henri

siders that a full harmony is achievable through liberalism (in order to re-establish order "the only remedy is to let it happen"). Yet, this solution seems meaningless in the financial market, since disorder appears to dominate there and since this market already is largely left free to organize itself. Let's bear in mind that Terrasson's *Mémoire* was written in response to criticisms emanating from the Jansenist camp, which was very hostile towards Law's System, in particular d'Aguesseau.

25 The term "white noise" is used here in a non-technical way to simply indicate that price variations are independent from each other, without any specific reference to variance or higher order moments, as would be the case for the strict mathematical definition of white noise. To say it in a more technical way, the price model to which we implicitly refer is a martingale model and not a strict random walk model.

26 This observation echoes the very frequent allusions, in early texts on finance, that chance presides over price formation and that the stock exchange thus is nothing more than a game of chance. This analogy was highly charged with meaning in a period when, as Thomas Kavanagh explains, pure games of chance – as compared to games which involved players' skill – were seen as a danger threatening both the divine order and the natural order. Thomas Kavanagh, *Enlightenment and the Shadows of Chance: The Novel and the Culture of Gambling in Eighteenth-Century France* (Baltimore and London: Johns Hopkins University Press, 1993), 30–36.

27 De la Vega, *Confusion de confusiones*, 12.

28 De la Vega, *Confusion de confusiones*, 3.

29 In his texts, particularly around 1720, Daniel Defoe regularly alludes to the question of mystery and secret which characterize Exchange-Alley. For example, see *The Anatomy of Exchange-Alley, or a System of Stock-Jobbing* (London, 1719). The same is true of Mortimer, *Every man*, ch. 2.

François d'Aguesseau (although he was a scholar with very different positions): "This conflict of causes which are not sought after or planned, which occurs according to the natural course of things, is precisely what currently determines the true value and current price of paper."[30] This explanation of the random nature of prices was not, in essence, without analogies to the one proposed by Louis Bachelier at the origins of modern financial theory.

Singularities of the Financial Market

The excessive nature of the phenomena arising on the stock exchange – particularly the sharp upwards and downwards variations in prices (or, to put it differently, their non-proportionality) – was, along with the unpredictability of prices, the other feature of financial markets which characterized the absence of order for contemporaries. One rather widely-shared idea, indeed, was that, within an ordered structure, things must have a specific proportion between them.

This perception of the world was rooted in Aristotelian legacy, which was still largely present in the eighteenth century, upheld by scholastic teachings that were less influential than in previous centuries yet still persisted in some aspects. It is presumably the trace of such a perspective that is found in the *circular flow of income*, a dominant contemporary economic model which claimed that prices must be in fair proportion to one another. "It is therefore the proportions [between all prices] that make up all wealth, because it is only through them that exchange and thus trade, can occur," wrote Boisguilbert in the *Factum de la France.*[31] For its part, the law itself required that the selling price be proportionate to the value of the thing sold, with the price only deviating within a limited margin. "A price that is out of proportion to the value of the thing sold is not a true price," considered Robert Joseph Pothier, an eminent jurist whose work synthesized the principles of French law during the Enlightenment.[32] The under-

30 D'Aguesseau, "Mémoire sur le commerce," 200.

31 Pierre de Boisguilbert, *Factum de la France* [...] in *Pierre de Boisguilbert ou la naissance de l'économie politique* (Paris: INED, 1966) 2:891. He reiterates this argument in his *Dissertation de la nature des richesses:* "Since wealth is therefore merely a perpetual mix between individuals, businesses, countries, and even kingdoms, it is a terrible blindness to look elsewhere for the cause of poverty than in the termination of such trade, caused by the disruption of the price ratio, which is no less essential to their maintenance than to their own construction" (991). The same type of concern is found in many eighteenth-century economic texts, such as those written by Cantillon and Forbonnais.

32 *Traité du contrat de vente, selon les règles tant du for de la conscience que du for extérieur* (Paris and Orléans, 1762), 1:20.

lying reason for this requirement was that eighteenth-century Europe considered that freedom of contract, although clearly established, had to generate reasonable exchange rates. In other words, it needed to have a legitimate cause. "Any obligations must have an honest cause" and that cause must have consequences proportionate to the values at stake. This is what usually occurred in most markets, and this is why these legal principles rarely were enforced, so as not to hinder trade and freedom of action.

In contrast, disproportion remained common in financial markets, because of the very ways supply and demand interact. After having observed that "the fall of prices need not have a limit and there are also unlimited possibilities for the rise," Joseph de la Vega proposed as an explanation the fact that anticipations have more than proportional consequences on prices: "The expectation of an event creates a much deeper impression upon the exchange than the event itself."[33] This is what d'Aguesseau explained at length in his *Mémoire*. After reminding readers that a commercial transaction is entirely void when it has no cause, he added a highly negative moral qualification to anything that might go beyond the effect of a legitimate cause: "Although an act or an obligation has a cause, if the consequence assigned to it is larger than the cause, anything that goes beyond that proportion [...] in a measure of moral latitude, is vicious because it is truly without a cause."[34] The absence of a real cause[35] can be explained by a peculiarity of financial markets, which is the confusion between the interests of sellers and buyers that prevents the natural and necessary opposition between the two to achieve, if not an equilibrium – a notion not yet employed by economic writers[36] –, at least some moderation in price formation: "[Nature] tempers things so much, through the confrontation of two opposing in-

33 De la Vega, *Confusion de confusiones*, 14. This argument often is used to characterize financial markets. For example, see "Share" in Malachy Postlethwayt's *The Universal Dictionary of Trade and Commerce*, vol. 1, 3rd ed. (1766) where he contrasts the trading of shares in 1720 London and especially in Paris, which are marked by an excessive attention to the "uncertain rumor," with trading in Amsterdam, which was much more regular.

34 D'Aguesseau, "Mémoire sur le commerce," 179.

35 Adam Smith also questions the absence of a visible cause: "How then comes it that stocks are thus every day fluctuating without any visible cause?" Adam Smith, *Lectures on Jurisprudence*, ed. Ronald L. Meek et al. (Oxford: Clarendon Press, 1978), 536.

36 About the emergence of the concept of equilibrium in political economy, see Jean-Claude Perrot, "Histoire des sciences, histoire concrète de l'abstraction," in *Des sciences et des techniques: Un débat*, ed. Roger Guesnerie and François Hartog (Paris: Edition de l'Ecole des Hautes Etudes en Sciences Sociales, 1998), 25–37.

terests, that it gives rise to a price almost proportionate to the needs of sellers and buyers."[37]

The legitimate profit – inherent in all reasonable commercial transactions – therefore becomes an illegitimate profit. For d'Aguesseau, the share price is thus an artifice since it is not the result of a legitimate cause. His legal and moral perspectives were not isolated. Rather, they were shared by those authors writing about finance, often financiers themselves, who recognized and analyzed this artificiality specific to asset markets: what Isaac de Pinto called the reversal between cause and effect. In his *Tableau ou Exposé de ce qu'on appelle le commerce, ou plutôt le Jeu d'actions en Hollande*,[38] Pinto explained this mechanism in the context of equity trading in 1720 as well as trading in English public debt after the end of the Seven Years' War (1763). At first, trading – both in shares or government bonds – fueled a financial market boom; then, it fueled the financial market itself through its own speculative mechanisms, stimulating almost without limits the purchase and sale of assets. Pinto argued that, after 1763 and as the equity market became too narrow, finance turned towards public credit and triggered a market boom, which, in turn, led the state to intensify its recourse to finance: "Speculation in annuities has become essential and necessary as soon as the government, instead of borrowing three million sterling, firstly borrowed six, then eight, then finally twelve: the consequence became the cause and speculation came to the rescue of the mass [of government bonds] that gave birth to it."[39]

The Fundamental Value: Early and Modern Perspectives

The causes of disorder on the financial markets, therefore, were numerous and clearly identified by early authors. One way of proving that this disorder was only apparent was to highlight the fundamental value of the assets. It was this approach, as we have seen, that was at the heart of the revolution in the theory of finance during the 1960s since, following the works of Samuelson and Fama, fundamental value was defined as the discounted value of the expected dividends of the asset, recalculated at each moment by economic actors in light of new information. Hence market price is generally the best estimate of

---

37 D'Aguesseau, "Mémoire sur le commerce," 191.

38 Isaac de Pinto, *Traité de la circulation et du crédit* (Amsterdam, 1771), the "Tableau" is on pages 291–312.

39 De Pinto, *Traité de la circulation*, 310.

fundamental value.[40] The concept of fundamental value also presented itself in early financial literature – extending from de la Vega, who argued that the price of shares is partly explainable because it relates to the fundamentals of the companies that issue them, up to Pinto, who referred to the "intrinsic value" of shares or extensions (*reports*) on the futures markets.[41] The implicit idea in these early economic representations was that things have a value for themselves, potentially different from their market price and partly independent from trade. This value was interpreted in different ways. In the scholastic perspective, the fair price referred to a collective consensus with specific properties, such as reflections on the rarity of the commodity in relation to demand or the generation of an income distribution that allows all individuals to live according to the status that God assigned to them. In the perspective of the corporative economy, the intrinsic quality required in the production of goods (as described and required by manufacturing regulations) leads to the formation of a benchmark price independent from the market. By contrast, for economists such as William Petty and Richard Cantillon, it was the quantity of land and labor used to produce a commodity which defines its value. In all of these cases, price is distinct from value, and there is no mechanism guiding the first to the second. It was precisely in this gap that the pre-liberal political economy situated a large part of its analyses.

The same distinction can be found in the writings of the authors who analyzed the financial market. According to them, market prices differ – sometimes quite substantially – from fundamental value. For equities, fundamental value is commonly defined as the expected amount of dividends. Jean-Pierre Richard, in his well-known manual about trade and the Amsterdam stock exchange, for instance, wrote that shares of the Company of the Indies "may be bought and sold spot or forward, sometimes at a high and sometimes at a low price, depending on the dividends that may be approximately expected from the Company."[42] The

40 "In an efficient market at any point in time the actual price of a security will be a good estimate of its intrinsic value," Eugene Fama, "Random Walks in Stock Market Prices," *Financial Analysts Journal* 21 (1965), 55–59, here 56.

41 De Pinto, *Traité de la circulation*, 295. Mortimer, *Every man*, speaks of "intrinsic value" (11), a notion also employed on several occasions by Defoe ("instrinsick value," *The Anatomy of Exchange-Alley*, 63 or "intrinsick worth," *The Villainy of Stock-Jobbers Detected* (London, 1701), 37). D'Aguesseau refers to "fair value" as the value of an asset whose price corresponds with its "intrinsic goodness" (200). In June 1720, an anonymous author proposed "An estimate of the intrinsik value of South-Sea stock," which he evaluated as much less than the recently acquired "imaginary value."

42 Jean-Pierre Ricard, *Le négoce d'Amsterdam, contenant tout ce que doivent savoir les marchands & banquiers, tant ceux qui sont établis à Amsterdam que ceux des pays étrangers* (Rouen,

fundamental value is often disrupted and, to quote d'Aguesseau, this is why "paper [i.e. assets] is found on the stock market above or below the fair value that it should have had given its intrinsic goodness."[43] Disruptions stem from the constant flow of new information (a "combination of fortuitous causes" according to d'Aguesseau), which obfuscate, or even makes entirely invisible, fundamental value. This is because only part of the available information helps to better estimate future dividends, whereas other parts generates confusion. In today's terms, we would say that the markets do not confirm the informational efficiency hypothesis. Joseph de la Vega, whose book mainly focuses on the causes of market-price deviations in relation to fundamental value, proposed a subtle analysis of the use of available information by highlighting two contradictions. First, if information has real value, it cannot be public knowledge since, he reckoned, only private correspondence provides reliable information. Second, each actor has a different interpretation, particularly concerning the relative importance attributed to each new piece of information: "one portion of the speculators would buy on the strength of the Indian news, while another sells on the basis of the unclear European situation."[44] This plurality of interpretations means that actors form different forecasts about the evolution of prices. There is a striking difference here from the standard neo-classical model, since it is the very mechanism of production and exploitation of information that prevents the fundamental value from being realized or, in other words, that prevents market price from being an expression of fundamental value.

Self-referentiality in Markets

There is therefore a strong instability in price formation, which leaves room for multiple forms of speculation. Contemporaries described these at length under the name *agiotage* or *stockjobbing* – most of the time to criticize, although

1723), 397. A similar observation can be found three decades earlier, concerning the Amsterdam stock exchange, in Le Moine de l'Espine, *Le négoce d'Amsterdam ou traité de sa banque* (Amsterdam, 1694), 87–88. Neil De Marchi and Paul Harrison, "Trading 'in the Wind' and with Guile," 53, underline that, from the beginning of the seventeenth century it was "self-evident wisdom among contemporaries that share prices should reflect company performance." By contrast, there also was a group of authors who insisted on the arbitrary nature of fixing dividends. This was one of the arguments used by Father André Morellet in his criticism of the Company of the Indies, *Mémoire sur la Compagnie des Indes* (1769), 117 sq.

43 D'Aguesseau, "Mémoire sur le commerce," 200.

44 De la Vega, *Confusion de confusiones*, 9–10.

also to explain, them. Early thinkers on finance thus were more focused on the question of exchange and market compared to the issue of value; they recognized speculation as the very principle producing bubbles and regarded it as central to the formation of asset prices. D'Aguesseau, who wrote while the Mississippi Bubble still was raging, argued that those buying shares of the Mississippi Company were much less interested in the increase of the dividend than in the upsurge of the selling price.[45] For him, the profit generated by this upsurge was only accidental and momentary and thus unacceptable, since "it does not arise from the thing itself" or, in other words, because it was not connected to the fundamental value. The resulting bubble, he predicted, was destined to burst, both for moral and economic reasons – just as the System itself was destined to disappear – because price must return to its fair value: "It is morally certain that [the shares] will one day return to their initial value because we return sooner or later to nature and so it will be proved by the event [the coming crash] that these shares were brought to an excessive and insane price."[46]

How then do we explain these continual price increases and then decreases, given that the fundamentals are not involved? The answer that runs through all the texts refers to mechanisms of self-referentiality, a notion that early authors placed at the heart of their reflections. The first reference for the market, therefore, is not the intrinsic value or the fundamentals of the company or the economy, but the market itself, that is to say the behavior of investors who constantly watch each other.[47] Imitation is at the heart of the functioning of the financial market. Witness to and actor in Law's System, Cantillon described in his *Essai* the herd behavior of market participants, explaining it by the ignorance of many of them.[48] Half a century earlier, de la Vega depicted the same general behavior: "As there are so many people who cannot wait to follow the prevailing trend of opinion, I am not surprised that a small group becomes an army. [Most people] think only of doing what the others do and of following their examples."[49] This self-referentiality was expressed, in the texts, through the omni-

---

45 It is noteworthy that this is precisely Joseph Stiglitz's definition of speculation and financial bubble: "If the reason that the price is high today is *only* because investors believe that the selling price will be high tomorrow [...] then a bubble exists" (Joseph E. Stiglitz, "Symposium on Bubbles," *Journal of Economic Perspectives* 4 (1990): 13–18).

46 D'Aguesseau, "Mémoire sur le commerce," 251–261.

47 "The fact that investors agree to hold securities on condition of being able to resell them at an acceptable price produces a self-referential situation in which market actors train their attention on the market itself," Orléan, *The Empire of Value*, 234.

48 Cantillon, *Essai sur la nature*, 172–173.

49 De la Vega, *Confusion de confusiones*, 30.

presence of the vague notion of "opinion on the stock exchange itself"[50] (as de la Vega called it), that is to say a dominant trend that forms on the market under changing circumstances – sometimes objective, sometimes less so – and which serves as a benchmark for the decisions made by a large number of actors. Depending on the magnitude of this dominant opinion, polarization of behaviors is more or less intense. Most authors considered these spontaneous consensuses as momentary, highly volatile, and therefore susceptible to manipulation (from the dissemination of false information to the simulation of purchases, or sales to drive bullish or bearish operations). Once established, these consensuses are powerful, demonstrating, as such, the superiority of the collective over the individual on financial markets, because one alone cannot be right against the whole market. This is explained well by de la Vega, in a passage that is not without anticipating the famous metaphor of the beauty contest presented by Keynes in *The General Theory:*

> If [...] there arrives a piece of news which would induce a speculator to buy, while the atmosphere prevailing at the stock-exchange forces him to sell, his reasoning fights his own good reasons. At one moment his reasoning drives him to buy, because of the information that has just arrived; at the other it induces him to sell because of the trend at the Exchange.[51]

Much attention thus was given to self-referentiality in price formation in contrast to today's financial theories, which refuse or only reluctantly accept this explanation of the formation of agents' beliefs and thus struggle to explain phenomena such as the appearance of bubbles. Early writers instead well understood that this self-referentiality is consubstantial to the stock markets, because it is connected to the very nature of the trade of financial assets (unregulated confrontation between supply and demand; information asymmetries). These authors also attached great importance to the physical dimension of the financial market as something that reinforces self-referentiality. They described it as a set of spaces where, in addition to official places, information (both true and false) is invented and the opinion on the stock exchange formed. For de la Vega, this world of confusion has no common language, no shared civility and no collective rationality, all of which reinforces uncertainty and, as a consequence, the influence of imitation, since each individual has to make his or her own choices. He wrote: "I really thought that I was at the construction of the Tower of Babel,

50 De la Vega, *Confusion de confusiones*, 9.
51 De la Vega, *Confusion de confusiones*, 22.

when I heard the confusion of tongues and the mixture of languages on the stock exchange."[52]

The *loci* of finance – *rue Quincampoix*, the gardens of *Hôtel de Soissons* or Exchange-Alley – therefore were considered places without order. This view was expressed, for instance, in legislation introduced in France, starting in 1720, which aimed to prevent a repetition of the abuses generated by the System. A 25 October 1720 *arrêt* (royal decree) thus called for the need to put an end to "the tumultuous meeting which takes place at the stock exchange."[53] To this end, a regulated Paris *Bourse* was instituted by law in 1724. It is noteworthy how much this legislation was influenced by the regulations that had long been in force in the kingdom of France to control another speculative market, namely the grain trade. The monarchy, since the Middle Ages, feared speculation on the political product represented by wheat; it became similarly worried about speculation on public debt securities after 1720, which it also viewed as a political product. The 1724 *arrêt* thus sought to limit information asymmetries at the newly established *Bourse* by implementing a series of measures influenced by the police of public grain supplies. These included the spatial centralization of trade, the imposition of legal operating hours, and limitations on the number of authorized stockbrokers (*agents de change*). In much the same way as the grain trade, the aim was to transform a deregulated space into a regulated place. It was a vain attempt repeated a hundred times since, *ad nauseam*.

Conclusion

Financial markets, as we have seen, present specific analytical difficulties. These difficulties are related to the existence of two different types of assets valuations – expected dividends and asset price anticipation – and to mechanisms peculiar to these markets, such as the joint-evolution of prices and demand. For reasons specific to neoclassical theory – particularly its insistence on defining fundamental value as external to the market – the standard model defined by Samuelson and Fama (which became mainstream from the 1970s) only has focused on expected dividends as the main factor determining price formation.

It is noteworthy that early economists, who wrote about finance between 1680 and 1780, tried instead to take into account both types of asset valuation.

52 De la Vega, *Confusion de confusiones*, 14.

53 Many French legal texts on financial markets from 1720 to 1820 are published in A.S.G. Coffinières, *De la Bourse et des spéculations sur les effets publics* (Paris, 1824), here 12.

As a consequence, they faced problems raised by the anticipation both of dividends (such as the quality and asymmetry of information) and of prices (various forms of self-referentiality). The major reason for their innovativeness was probably that their intellectual framework (i. e. the early political economy) was very open: no concept of equilibrium, a pragmatic approach towards the notion of information, a willingness to consider the role of chance, etc. The paradox is that the recent exhaustion of the Samuelson-Fama paradigm, which is structured around informational efficiency, has led financial theory to rediscover and reconsider some ideas formed in the eighteenth century. This only can lead to a better understanding of financial markets, both ancient and modern.

Christine Zabel

From Bubble to Speculation – Eighteenth-Century Readings of the 1720s

In July 1789, the self-declared French National Assembly decided to take on the Old Regime's debts as a holy obligation.[1] With this announcement, the new regime endorsed the political and economic value of property, but it also bound the revolutionary events in a quite peculiar way to the fiscal administration of the passing regime. This had to do with the nature of French debts, since most French loans had been taken out in form of life annuities.[2] In such a scheme, the creditor sold the promise of future annual income (*rentes*) in exchange for a lump-sum payment to the creditor (here, the French state). Because the longevity of the contract was contingent upon a nominee's survival, the members of the National Assembly could not, with their declaration of property as an unalienable right, put an abrupt end to Old Regime practices such as life annuities if they did not want to dispossess subscribers and beneficiaries.[3] With their oath to never pronounce "bankruptcy" and to still take on the Old Regime's debts, the self-declared National Assembly thus lodged, as Rebecca Spang has pointed out, "the fiscal past in the revolutionary present and made the desire for a transcendent future all the more pressing."[4]

---

1 Rebecca Spang, *Stuff and Money in the Time of the French Revolution* (Cambridge, Mass.: Harvard University Press, 2015), 15.

2 See David Weir, "Tontines, Public Finance, and Revolution in France and England, 1688–1789," *The Journal of Economic History* 49 (1989): 95–124, especially 97.

3 Spang, *Stuff*, 72.

4 Spang, *Stuff*, 72. The debate over the achievements of the Revolution are as old as the Revolution itself. The question of the "old" in the New Regime was then prominently raised by Alexis de Tocqueville in his seminal work on the French Revolution, *L'Ancien Régime et la Révolution* (Paris: Lévy, 1865) and has since engaged scholars of the Old and New Regime. It also, in the twentieth century, has culminated in the debate between "Marxist" and "revisionist" interpretations of the Revolution. See, for an overview of these debates, for example: Gail Bossenga, "Origins of the French Revolution," *History Compass* 5 (2007): 1294–1337; Robert Foster and Timothy Tackett, "The Origins of the French Revolution: A Debate," *French Historical Studies* 16 (1990): 741–765; Michel Vovelle, "L'historiographie de la Révolution française à la veille du bicentenaire," *Annales historique de la Revolution Français* 272 (1988): 113–126; Lynn Hunt, *Politics, Culture and Class in the French Revolution* (Berkeley: University of California Press, 1984); Thomas Doyle, *Origins of the French Revolution* (Oxford: Oxford University Press, 1980); or more recently Thomas Kaiser and Dale Van Kley, eds., *From Deficit to Deluge: The Origins of the French Revolution* (Stanford: Stanford University Press, 2011).

https://doi.org/10.1515/9783110592139-015

In order to cope with this indebtedness to the past, the new *Comité de mendicité* decided in 1789/90, and in addition to creating a *Caisse d'épargne*, to transform ecclesiastical property into national property and to introduce a new currency, the *assignats* that would be backed by those disappropriated lands.[5] The new currency, however, was not uncontested in the National Assembly. In their search for arguments, both opponents and defenders looked back to the more recent French history, especially to the years of John Law's "System" but came to appreciate different aspects of Law's legacy. Both camps, however, began to strongly condemn *speculation* as an immoral form of money-making and traced it back to the years around 1720, but they approached it with slightly different emphases.

This focus on speculation in the late eighteenth century is surprising, because contemporaries had rarely used speculation in this context before. While they applied the term *bubble*, *windhandel*, *Système* or *stock-jobbing*, or the more pejorative notion of *agiotage*, to identify the stock market, or the Mississippi and South Sea schemes as early as the 1720s[6] and while they already referred to the *rue Quincampoix* (the bourse) as a temple for the money-devil, French, Dutch or English sources scarcely apply the term *speculation* to the stock market or to the events of the 1720s before the early years of the New Re-

---

5 Spang, *Stuff*, 30–31. See, for the *Caisse d'épargne*, also Guy Thuillier, *Une ténébreuse affaire: La Caisse Lafarge. 1787–1892* (Paris: Comité d'Histoire de la Sécurité Sociale, 1999); Jean-Marie Thiveaud, "Aux origines de la notion d'épargne en France: Ou du Peuple-prévoyance à l'État-providence (1750–1830)," *Revue d'économie financière* 42 (1997): 179–213; William Roberds and François Velde, "Early Public Banks," *Federal Reserve Bank of Chicago Working Paper Series* 7 (2014): 1–92; See, for the financial politics of the Revolution, also Michael Sonenscher, "The Nation's Debt and the Birth of the Modern Republic: The French Fiscal Deficit and the Politics of the Revolution of 1789," *History of Political Thought* 2 (1997): 267–325; See also Gail Bossenga, "Financial Origins of the French Revolution," in *From Deficit to Deluge: The Origins of the French Revolution,* ed. Thomas Kaiser and Dale Van Kley (Stanford: Stanford University Press, 2011), 37–66. For a study of property during the French Revolution, see Rafe Blaufarb, *The Great Demarcation: The French Revolution and the Invention of Modern Property* (Oxford: Oxford University Press, 2016).

6 For the reception of the South Sea Bubble and the conception of "Wagnis", see Helen J. Paul, "The Concept of *Wagnis* and the South Sea Bubble of 1720," in *Wagnisse: Risiken eingehen, Risiken analysieren, von Risiken erzählen*, ed. Stefan Brakensiek, Christoph Marx, and Benjamin Scheller (Frankfurt and New York: Campus Verlag, 2017), 111–126. See also William Deringer, "For What It's Worth: Historical Financial Bubbles and the Boundaries of Economic Rationality," *Isis* 106 (2015): 646–656; Richard Dale, *The First Crash: Lessons From the South Sea Bubble* (Princeton: Princeton University Press, 2004).

gime.[7] In other words, whereas for historians John Law's undertaking or the Mississippi and the South Sea bubbles are the quintessence of speculation gone wrong, contemporaries did not necessarily recognize them as such.

This raises important historiographical as well as epistemological questions: why would contemporaries talk about *bubble*, *agiotage*, *Système* or *windhandel* as soon as the 1720s, but less of *speculation?* What did eighteenth century Europeans imply when they referred to the events with one term or another? Furthermore, we need to inquire about the epistemological changes in eighteenth-century political economy that made it possible for contemporaries to eventually use *speculation* synonymously with *agiotage* and to identify it as passionate and self-interested gambling with the public good. This will help us to understand that later references to *speculation* were quite different from earlier ones, which pointed to a commercial epistemology that trusted the reasonable and self-interested calculations of the individual trader.[8]

Narrating the Crash

Stock trading was familiar to Europeans at least since the beginning of the seventeenth century, when the Dutch *Vereendigde Oostindische Compagnie* began to sell shares in 1602. From then on, English, French, and Dutch contemporaries described their trade with *stocks*, *actions*, *acties* or *effekten* as *stock-jobbing*, *com-*

7 This is contrasted by our own usage of speculation in historical research, see: Ernst Heinrich Krelage, *Bloemenspeculatie in Nederland: De Tulpomanie van 1636–'37 end de Hyacintenhandel 1700–36* (Amsterdam: P.N. van Kampen en Zoon, 1942); Lodewijk Petram, *The World's First Stock Exchange* (New York: Columbia Business School Publishing, 2014), 184–201; Louis Bachelier, *Theory of Speculation: The Origins of Modern Finance* (Princeton and Oxford: Princeton University Press, 2006); Urs Stäheli, *Spectacular Speculation: Thrills, the Economy, and Popular Discourse* (Stanford: Stanford University Press, 2013); Kim Christian Priemel, "Spekulation als Gegenstand historischer Forschung," *Jahrbuch für Wirtschaftsgeschichte* (2013): 9–26. Since Charles Mackay's interpretations of speculation, immorality, irrationality, and even demonic energy have been topoi in the languages of the historiography on speculation. Charles Kindleberger reflected this heuristic problem in: Charles Kindleberger and Robert Z. Aliber, *Manias, Panics and Crashes: A History of Financial Crisis*, 6th ed. (Basingstoke: Palgrave Macmillan, 2011). A study worth mentioning that reflects on contemporary uses of "speculation" is Will Slauter, "Forward-Looking Statements: News and Speculation in the Age of the American Revolution," *The Journal of Modern History* 81 (2009): 759–792.

8 Lynn Hunt points to the fact that revolutionaries used "service to the public good" instead of politics/being a politician, since the latter notion was seen as narrowness, or as a sign of "*partie prise*" and so denounced "all these perversions of the ancient ideal of *homo politicus*." See Hunt, *Politics*, 3.

merce d'actions, or with a pejorative meaning as *agiotage*, *effektenhandel* or *windhandel* (the last notion was only used in the eighteenth century).[9]

The collapse of the Mississippi and the South Sea companies in 1720 proved a fateful year, often discussed as the first international financial crises.[10] Despite the international character of the 1720 financial collapses, we can locate national emphases in narrations of the events.[11] Contemporary British writers and pamphleteers predominantly interpreted the crash of the South Sea Company, and its scheme of transforming public debt into circulating paper credit, as the bursting of a bubble caused by an emotional and irrational craze for stocks that had infested the majority of the British people. We find the bubble-metaphor as early as 1720 in various media, e.g. satirical texts, pamphlets, plays, as well as cartoons and poems. Edward Ward's *South-Sea Song Upon the Late Bubbles*,[12] published in 1720, provides a prominent example. In referring to the Bubble, the poem emphasizes the emotional character of the stock-trade, displaying its frenzy as an addiction (quite similar to that to wine) or as madness. In the sixth stanza, the poem also alludes to the meteorological metaphors of clouds and air:

> Our South-Sea Ships have golden Shrouds,
> They bring us Wealth, 'tis granted,
> But lodge their Treasure in the Clouds,
> To hide it till its wanted.

The following stanza explicitly connects this meteorological metaphor with the bubble, which Ward suggests also consisted, like clouds, of water and air:

> O Britain bless thy present state,
> Thou only happy Nation,
> So odly [sic] Rich, so madly Great,
> Since Bubbles came in fashion.

---

9 Inger Leemans (Vrije Universiteit Amsterdam) currently is preparing an important paper that historicizes for the first time the usage of *windhandel* in the Netherlands. For further readings on the representations of wind, see also Alessandro Nova, *The Book of the Wind: Representations of the Invisible* (Montréal: McGill-Queen's University, 2011).

10 Peter M. Garber, "Famous First Bubbles," *The Journal of Economic Perspectives* 4 (1990): 35–54.

11 See Inger Leemans' ongoing work on the history of wind-trade, but also Lina Weber's dissertational work (working title): *Bound by Debt. Political Arguments Concerning State Finance in Great Britain and the Dutch Republic 1694–1795.*

12 Edward Ward, *The Delights of the Bottle: or, the Compleat Vintner. With the Humours of Bubble Upstarts* [...]. *A Merry-Poem. To Which is Added, A South-Sea Song Upon the Late Bubbles* (London, 1720), 57–58.

Successful Rakes exert their Pride,
And count their airy Millions,
Whilst homely Drabs in Coaches ride,
Brought up to Town on Pillions.

The eighth stanza continues to contrast the irrationality of the many ("young Rattles and unthinking Fools") with the rational, self-interested scheme of the "Few Men, who follow Reason's Rules," thus referring to the directors of the South Sea Company, whom the British public held accountable for the crash and who Ward described as "grow[ing] fat with South-Sea Diet". The tenth stanza then shows how the Bubble evaporated into air, leaving nothing more than worthless paper:

Five hundred Millions, Notes and Bonds,
Our Stocks are worth in Value,
But neither lie in Goods or Lands,
Or Money, let me tell ye.
Yet tho' our Foreign Trade is lost,
Of mighty Wealth we vapour,
When all the Riches that we boast
Consist in scraps of Paper.[13]

In a similar vein, William Rufus Chetwood, the author of the play *Exchange-alley; or, The Stock-Jobber Turn'd Gentleman*[14] held that "Projectors successfully Bubble the Publick in all their Schemes".[15] In the skit, Mr. Bubble represents those projectors who cheat subscribers of their savings for the sake of their own self-interest. In a conversation with Mr. Cheat-all, Mr. Bubble enumerates his new fabulous projects such as joint-stock insurances for flying (wind)ships that travel to the moon.[16] Chetwood thus again connected the bubble metaphor, recalling the seductive power of nonsensical projects (that necessarily disappoint), with the metaphoric elements of air or wind. Wind also appeared in William Hogarth's emblematical print *The South Sea Scheme*, published in 1721. In the engraving the Devil, who himself indulges in the craze, sends his winds to push the merry-go-round of stock-jobbing to rotate.

Besides talking about bubbles, Chetwood's play and Hogarth's engraving also referenced newly emerging wind-metaphors that gained momentum in

13 Ward, *A South-Sea Song*, 57–58.
14 William Rufus Chetwood, *Exchange-Alley; or, The Stock-Jobber Turn'd Gentleman; with the Humours of Our Modern Projectors* (London, 1720).
15 Chetwood, *Exchange-Alley*, The Preface.
16 Chetwood, *Exchange-Alley*, 14.

Image 1: William Hogarth, *The South Sea Scheme* (London 1721).
(Courtesy of the British Museum)

the Low Countries in 1720.[17] Similarly in the Netherlands, contemporary plays such as the famous *Quinquampoix, of the windhandelaars*[18] by Pieter Langendijk began to merge the British bubble-metaphor with that of wind – the latter was indeed vital for successful maritime trade and hence for the joint-stock companies – as did various cartoons, published in *Het Groote Tafereel der Dwaasheid.*[19] The latter was a compilation of caricatures focusing on the stock market crashes of the 1720s and on the person of John Law (image 2).

One of the engravings entitled *Kermis wind-kraamer* (image 3) shows various metaphoric elements of wind-trade, while portraying Law in three different mo-

17 See Inger Leeman's ongoing work on wind trade.

18 Pieter Langendijk, *Quinquampoix, of the windhandelaars* (Amsterdam, 1720). See also Joyce Goggin, "Crise et comédie: Le Système de John Law dans le théâtre néerlandais," in *'Gagnons sans savoir comment': Représentations du Système de Law au XVIIIe siècle à nos jours*, ed. Florence Magnot-Ogilvy (Rennes: Presses Universitaires de Rennes, 2017), 163–182.

19 *Het Groote Tafereel der Dwaasheid*, republished in the *Great Mirror of Folly: Finance, Culture, and the Crash of 1720*, ed. William N. Goetzmann et al. (New Haven: Yale University Press, 2013).

Image 2: "De inventeur der windnegotie, op zyn zeege-karn," in *Het Groote Tafereel der Dwaasheid* (Amsterdam, 1720). (Courtesy of Yale University)

ments of his scheme: sitting on a cloud, producing steam, and finally filling balloons with wind. Another anonymous engraving published in the *Het Groote Tafereel* entitled *John Law en anderen torsen hun schulden op hun schouders* (image 4) similarly depicts Law with wind-filled balloons that seem too heavy for him to control. In the scene, Hercules offers his assistance so as to prevent dropping the load. "Petit Tems [sic]", or little *Chronos*, who is at the center ground of the engraving, holds a skittles ball and prepares to roll it towards the human bowling pins – with John Law at their center. The engraving suggests that it was only a matter of time until Law's scheme would fall. In the scene, dark times are foreshadowed by the night sky as well as by an allusion to Ovid's account of Medusa from Book 4 of his *Metamorphosis* (upper right corner). The animals strolling

Image 3: "Kermis wind-kraamer en grossier," in *Het Groote Tafereel der Dwasheid* (Amsterdam, 1720). (Courtesy of Yale University)

around recall the first analysis of the Amsterdam stock market by José de la Vega. In his *Confusión de confusiones*, published as early as 1688, the Spanish-Jewish merchant explained the role emotions played in the stock market by comparing human passions to different animals.[20] The skittles further admonish that

20 José de la Vega, *Confusión de confusiones* (Amsterdam, 1688).

the human bowling pins were part of a grand play that even Law was not able to control. The caricature thus suggests that Law's supporters only followed their irrational instincts and passions like animals, without actually understanding what they were doing.

Image 4: "John Law en anderen torsen hun schulden op hun schouders," in *Het Groote Tafereel der Dwasheid* (Amsterdam, 1720). (Courtesy of Yale University)

Similarly, another caricature in *Het Groote Tafereel* invokes *Chronos*. In the *Eere-Titel* (image 5) we see a moment before a great showdown (we see a curtain which suggests a backstage scene); the god of chronological time, now grown and of old age, holds a mirror in order to show John Law his reflection and effect that time would reveal. Another engraving shows the perishing *Bubble heer* (image 6), which lies dying on Madame Compagnie's lap, the latter of whom also resembles a corpse.

These caricatures from *Het Groote Tafereel* portray the Scotsman as a selfish projector who, fooled by his vanity, was not in control of his own scheme. Further contemporary artistic representations of bubbles seem to confirm these interpretations. We have numerous examples of bubbles depicted as *vanitas*, re-

Image 5: "Eere-Titel, of Gordyn voor het Schouburg," in *Het Groote Tafereel der Dwaasheid* (Amsterdam, 1720). (Courtesy of Yale University)

calling the fleetingness of life, the brevity and fragility of beauty and success, and the fugacity of occasion that comes and goes (image 7). Bubbles in the context of children's games, in turn, evoke juvenile passions untamed by reason or by a sense of responsibility (image 8). In this light, the *bubble heer* Law resembles a child, which does not yet understand the consequences of its actions.

With the caricatures of *Het Groote Tafereel* that, in various instances, depicted wind-trade as trade with wind-filled bubbles or balloons – just as Homer had done in his *Odyssee* – the Dutch concentrated on the contingencies of the stock market that stock-jobbers neglected to acknowledge. This narration implies that one could not fully understand the market that resembles wind and that is only

Image 6: Romeyn de Hooghe, "De stervende bubbelheer John Law," in *Het Groote Tafereel der Dwaasheid* (Amsterdam, 1720). (Courtesy of Yale University)

perceivable from its effects. Much as the speed of wind is unpredictable, this account of the 1720s suggests that the stock market could neither be forecasted nor controlled, similar to human bowel movements and the excrements of stock-jobbers, as shown in *De verwarde actionisten* (image 9). As the wind comes and goes, wind-traders are subject to chance and, indeed, *Fortuna* figures in many of the engravings of *Het Groote Tafereel*, as shown in image 9.

In his *Lettres Persanes*, Charles de Secondat, Baron de Montesquieu similarly depicted Law as the son of the wind-god Aeolos and a nymph from Caledonia and interpreted him as a systematic, yet immature wind-broker, who travelled with the blind god of chance. At the epicenter of the broker's seductive scheme

Image 7: Gerard Valck, *Vanitas stilleven* (Amsterdam, 1652). (Courtesy of the Rijskmuseum Amsterdam)

is Law's invitation to join the "Empire of Imagination", which promises all those who dared to dream surprising, unknown and yet un-imagined riches.[21] In order to join the "Empire of Imagination", commercial expertise, intelligence or specific skills were not required, nor did clients need to know how to observe the market. The only necessary prerequisite was trust in the man who promised a new and better future. The reference to *Fortuna* (*Het Groote Tafereel*) or the "blind

21 Charles de Secondat, Baron de Montesquieu, *Lettres persanes* (Paris: Garnier, 1956), letter CVLII, 255.

Image 8: Cornelis Hubert van Meurs, *Bellenblazende jongen en een meisje* (Amsterdam, 1720–30). (Courtesy of the Rijksmuseum Amsterdam)

god of chance", who accompanies Montesquieu's mythological Law, suggests an epistemological lack of understanding as to why Law's regime went down the way it did. Those representations of *Fortuna* insinuate that the events might not be fully comprehensible at all, neither for John Law nor for anybody else.

Other French mid-century commentators, however, had stronger verdicts on Law's legacy than Montesquieu. Denis Diderot, Voltaire, the Abbé Raynal, François Véron Duverger de Forbonnais, and Jean-François Melon all interpreted the years between 1715 and 1720 even more disapprovingly as the years of the *Système Law.* The pejorative notion of a *Système* "became a chronological mark-

Image 9: "De verwarde actionisten Torenbouw tot Babel," in *Het Groote Tafereel der Dwaasheid* (Amsterdam, 1720). (Courtesy of Yale University)

er"[22] for the era of Law's influence and referred to ideas that, although coherent, were not compatible with the empirical world and thus were destined to lead to utter chaos. According to these views, which emphasized the systematic character of the Mississippi scheme, Law had set out, with devilish self-interest, to rip the French of their savings.[23]

22 Rebecca Spang, "The Ghost of Law: Speculation on Money, Memory and Mississippi in the French Constituent Assembly," *Historical Reflections/Réfléxions Historique* 31 (2005): 3–25, here 8.

23 Spang, "The Ghost of Law," 8, 10–11. See, for the various Old Regime interpretations of the *Système Law*, especially 10–14 of the same article. See also the edited volume by Florence Magnot-Ogilvy, ed., *'Gagnons sans savoir comment': Représentations du Système de Law du XVIIIe à nos jours* (Rennes: Presses universitaires de Rennes, 2017).

A New Epistemology of Speculation

While blind *Fortuna* figured in the majority of the engravings of *Het Groote Tafereel*, and while the mythological Law of Montesquieu's account travelled in conjunction with the blind god of chance, mid-century French economic thinkers and practitioners who argued for the liberalization of the grain trade began to depart from such a fatalistic account. Their theories and ideas mirrored a deep wish to understand the structures of the market and of what we would call the economy, while also acknowledging that commercial or financial rules needed constant updates based on empirical observation and could not be learnt all at once. Armed with their new commercial epistemology which they called "speculation", these economic thinkers and practitioners not only departed from a moralizing, older Christian language, but they also attempted to distance their project from all former commercial endeavors linked to the *Système.*

In his 1753 *Essai sur la police générale des grains*,[24] a commodity-trader named Claude Jacques Herbert vindicated the liberalization of the grain trade, criticizing the interventionist administrations of Louis XV and his predecessors. For him, the current prohibitive regime was a concession to the irrational passions of the people, who, blinded by a short-sighted self-love, could not see beyond immediate needs.[25] In order to counteract the people's passions and destructive self-love, Herbert now placed not a single actor, neither a financial genius like Law, nor the French state, but traders at the center of such a new, free and speculative market. Because a trader's profit-making was, in his view, based on reason and not passion, self-interest was the best guarantee of a sufficient supply of grain. Reasonable speculations, however, were impossible to undertake, if traders did not have the liberty to follow their self-interest and pursue their own benefit:

> The man who intends to devote himself to the commerce of grain, cannot undertake any speculation, if he has not the entire liberty to dispose of his merchandise at his pleasure, & at all times. Because everybody, who is sensible and calculates, cannot buy a thing, &

24 Claude Jacques Herbert, *Essai sur la police générale de grains, sur leurs prix, sur les effets de l'agriculture* (Berlin, 1755).

25 Herbert, *Essai*, 94–95. For more details, see Christine Zabel, "Challenges of Food Security: Free Trade, Distribution and Political (In)Stability in Mid 18th Century France," *European Journal of Security Research* 3 (2018): 35–50; see, for the economic context Herbert was writing in Steve Kaplan, *Bread, Politics and Political Economy in the Reign of Louis XV*, 2nd ed. (New York: Anthem Press, 2015), esp. 47–49; see furthermore Philippe Minard, "Économie de marché et État en France: Mythes et legends du colbertisme," *L'Économie politique* 37 (2008): 77–94.

> conserve a merchandise that is subject to so many accidents, if he does not envisage that all his expenses will pay off, & that he will even profit from them.[26]

Three years later, in his *Discours sur les vignes*, he similarly held that self-interested profit-making was the best means to establish order.[27] With this concept of professional commercial speculation, Herbert made a profound impression on his readers. Soon after Herbert's explanations, also the Inspector General of Coinage, François Véron Duverger de Forbonnais explained in his *Elemens du Commerce* of 1754 that prices could only be balanced in a speculative market.[28] Forbonnais held elsewhere that the French state was risking its very subsistence, because it did not allow traders to decide when or how to keep or sell their goods. French traders, in short, did not yet have the liberty to speculate– a fact that, according to Forbonnais, led to a dangerous increase of commodity prices and so assembled money in the wrong pockets:

> We do not have any traders yet in the proper sense of the word in this branch of interior commerce. Many small merchants [...] intervene in the transport from one market to another; but the circle of their traffic embraces only a very small number of markets in their neighborhoods. Their speculations on the overhaul of grain are almost inexistent; their agency, far from stretching out to interior circulation, exerts itself, for lack of capital, in such a narrow circle, that it has no other effect than to overcharge to the profit of multiple intermediaries, and their agency is limited and stretches only slowly step by step.[29]

A few years later the physician Claude-Humbert Piarron de Chamousset agreed with Herbert's analysis and similarly held that the French needed to endorse the

26 "Celui qui aura dessein de s'adonner au commerce des grains, ne peut faire aucune spéculation, s'il n'a la liberté entière de disposer de sa merchandise à son gré, & en tout tems. Car tout homme sensé qui calcule, ne peut acheter des bleds, & conserver une marchandise sujette à beaucoup d'accidens, s'il n'envisage qu'il en pourra tirer tous ses frais, & même du benefice." See Herbert, *Essai*, 179–180.

27 Claude Jacques Herbert, *Discours sur les vignes* (Dijon, 1756), 64–65.

28 François Véron Duverger de Forbonnais, *Elemens du Commerce*, 2nd ed. (Leiden, 1754), 1:152. See also, Zabel, "Challenges," 40–41.

29 "Nous n'avons point encore de Négocians proprement dits dans cette branche de Commerce intérieure. Beaucoup de petits Marchands [...] s'entremettent du transport d'un marché dans un autre; mais le cercle de leur trafic, embrasse un très-petit nombre de marchés dans leur voisinage. Leurs spéculation sur la garde des Grains, est presque nulle; leur agence, loin d'étendre la circulation intérieure, s'exerce, faute de capitaux, dans un cercle si borné, qu'elle ne fait que surcharger de profits intermédiaires multipliés, celle qui se fait lentement de proche en proche." See François Véron Duverger de Forbonnais, *Examen du livre intitulé Principes sur la liberté du commerce des grains, Supplément au Journal d'août 1768* (Paris, 1768), 19.

new value of self-interest, if they wanted to avoid further food shortages.[30] Even Herbert's critic, Jean-Gabriel Montaudouin de La Touche, acknowledged the new epistemology and its emphasis on observational and speculative skills when he maintained that "The content of this controversy is very important since it concerns the public good".[31]

A central claim of this "political economy of speculation" was that traders should be able to pursue their self-interest in order to serve the whole nation. Yet, it also held that they could only do so if they acquired a new form of knowledge that helped them to better address the ever-changing and unstable structure and contingencies of the market-cosmos. This had to be superior to the older concept of experiential commercial knowledge in the vein of Jacques Savary's *Parfait Négociant.*[32] In contrast to Savary's concept, the new epistemology was not based on continuity of action; instead, it helped to adapt and change plans, if necessary, and to create a price *equilibrium* through market competition. Therefore, traders needed the liberty to speculate, a liberty that those individuals dealing with grain did not yet have.[33] Hence, the speculation that Herbert and his followers argued for included a constantly updated calculation of possibilities as well as the continuous observation of changes. According to this new epistemology, speculation implied practical know-how, but it went far beyond empirical reflection. Speculators now needed to make a wager on the *time* and *place* of their present and future commercial engagements. This wager, in turn, required continuous updates and was thus relatively unreliant upon former trading practices. For these economic thinkers and practitioners, speculation was the best epistemological tool to establish the new economic science as Chamousset ob-

---

30 See Claude-Humbert Piarron de Chamousset, *Observations sur la liberté du commerce des grains* (Amsterdam, 1759), 54–55. Often falsly ascribed to Herbert.

31 "Le fond de cette controverse est très-important, puisqu'il intéresse le bien public." See Jean-Gabriel Montaudouin de La Touche, *Supplément à l'Essai sur la policé générale des grains* (La Haye, 1757), 3.

32 Jacques Savary, *Le parfait Négociant ou Instruction generale pour ce qui regarde le commerce de toute sorte de marchandises, tant de France que des pays estrangers* (Paris, 1675). See, for the subject of France as a commercial Republic also James Livesey, *The Making of Democracy* (Cambridge, Mass.: Harvard University Press, 2001); Kaplan, *Bread*, 97–111, 52–96. See, for the conception of commerce and its changing perception, Amalia Kessler, *A Revolution in Commerce: The Parisian Merchant Court and the Rise of Commercial Society in Eighteenth-Century France* (New Haven: Yale University Press, 2007), 16–56.

33 Herbert, *Discours*, 33.

served: "This diligence & this economy make the merchants' science & revenues. It is the surest means to overthrow monopolizers".[34]

Within a decade, or by the 1760s, the new commercial epistemology of speculation obtained substantial attention. Most prominently, this epistemology of commercial speculation was disseminated by the later Inspector General of Manufacture and Commerce, Louis-Paul Abeille, in his *Lettre d'un Négociant*[35] of October 1763. He wrote this letter in order to defend Louis XV's reform project, which created the desired free national market and, even more importantly, allowed all citizens to freely partake in commerce.[36] As for Herbert, Abeille understood speculation as the best means to follow one's own interest and to identify the best time and location to engage in an enterprise according to consumer-demand and competition.[37] Abeille repeated these arguments in his *Reflexions sur la police de grains*,[38] written in February 1764 and published the following month, which impressed his readers much as Herbert's ideas had done a decade before. Not only was the Physiocrats' leading figure, François Quesnay, taken with Abeille's arguments; the physiocratic *Gazette du Commerce* also maintained a very similar point-of-view, in that speculation was necessary for a free grain market.[39] Correspondingly, the financial expert Emmanuel-Étienne Duvillard, who was the son of a Huguenot family from Geneva and who worked at the French finance ministry in the 1770s, adapted this conception of commodity-speculation and began to apply it to the financial realm. Having now looked at the emergence of the commercial epistemology of speculation in the 1750s and 1760s, we will shed light on the mathematization of this notion in order to explain its moralization and condemnation in the wake of the French Revolution.

34 "Cette diligence & cette économie font la science & les revenus des marchands. Le moyen le plus sûr de faire tomber les monopoleurs." See Chamousset, *Observations*, 55–56.

35 Louis-Paul Abeille, *Lettre d'un Négociant sur la nature du commerce de grain* (Marseilles, 1763); see also Zabel, "Challenges," 42–46.

36 See Kaplan, *Bread*, 91–92.

37 Abeille, *Lettre*, 10–11.

38 Louis-Paul Abeille, *Reflexions sur la police des grains en France et en Angleterre, mars 1764* (Paris, 1764).

39 *Lettre à l'Auteur de la Gazette du Commerce. Extrait de la Gazette du 3 Mars 1764. De Paris le 22 Février 1764* (Paris, 1764).

From Speculative Calculations to Egoistic Speculations

The Genevan mathematician Emmanuel-Étienne Duvillard had been confronted with the long-term consequences of life-contingent contracts early in his career, especially when he worked under the *Contrôleur general des finances*, Anne Robert Jacques Turgot, from January 1775 to May 1776, or exactly when annuities were converted into alternative credit systems. Inspired by this conversion, which still did not put an end to the Genevan bankers' disastrous annuity schemes,[40] Duvillard went back to his native city to study the annuity schemes and to work on what would ten years later become his *Recherches sur les rentes, les emprunts et les remboursemens.*[41] The publication would be approved by the Marquis de Condorcet, the *Académie des Sciences*, and the new *Contrôleur general des finances*, Charles Alexandre de Calonne.[42]

In his *Recherches*, finished in 1786, Duvillard explored how life annuities could be less onerous for the debtor (the French public treasury) while also attracting people with capital to invest. He proposed an improved annuity scheme and invented investment evaluation criteria that are comparable to the modern 'Modified Internal Rate of Return'. Duvillard then determined the "evolution of [the] rate of return (y)", the "optimal lending duration (t*), the optimal internal rate (y*) and the optimal lenders future value (m*)".[43] In his *Recherches*, Duvillard also provided the mathematical formula for the proposed three-layered speculation. He determined "the future value of the reinvested annuities (m), the compound rate of return (y)" and applied them to the "equivalent placement of the original capital (c)". The mathematician then concluded his computations by stating that the annuity placement, as he defined it, was "equivalent to an usual placement that lasts during the same term than the annuities (t), at the

---

40 Genevan bankers came up with a popular scheme "of the 30 virgins of Geneva." (30 Genevan girls were randomly picked as nominees for literally thousands of annuities to the effect that a French government official regularly came to Geneva to check on their continuing survival). The rates of return with a starting point of ten percent were thus variable and adapted to the numbers of survivors. See Spang, *Stuff*, 23.

41 Emmanuel-Étienne Duvillard, *Recherches sur les rentes, les emprunts et les remboursemens* (Paris, 1787).

42 Guy Thuiller, ed., *Le premier actuaire de France: Duvillard (1755–1832)* (Paris: Association pour l'Étude de l'Histoire de la Sécurité Sociale, 1997), 1.

43 See Yuri Biondi, "The Double Emergence of the Modified Internal Rate of Return: The Neglected Work of Duvillard (1755–1832) in a Comparative Perspective," *European Journal of the History of Economic Thought* 13 (2006): 311–335, here 311–312, 314, 318.

same compound rate [y] as [... shown] above".[44] By means of this *spéculation*, as Duvillard called his calculations, he identified the optimal value of a *rente*.[45]

Armed with this mathematized concept of speculation that combined political economy and actuarial mathematics,[46] Duvillard harshly criticized his contemporaries' treatment of the *rentes* and their proposed remedies for the financial problems of the French state. He pointed out that, instead of calculating the development of compound interest of lent capital,[47] French political arithmeticians mainly discussed the usefulness of different mortality tables. According to Duvillard's conceptualization of 1786, such an approach only could offer very limited remedies for the financial problems of the French state.[48] Yet, Duvillard not only criticized these political arithmeticians; he also came up with new re-financing strategies and claimed that he would have been able to save the government several million *livres* with his method of speculation.[49] Speculation was for him, and this is important to note, not gambling but a mathematized process of weighing possibilities and chances and of mitigating the risks of unwanted and indeed avoidable losses by means of various calculations of contingent factors and compound interests.[50]

When the National Assembly came together in the summer of 1789, it also made use of Duvillard's mathematized notion of speculation when discussing the state's finances and the possibilities of discounting the *rentes* without disowning French proprietors. In the parliamentary session of 7 August 1789, the Minister of Finances, Jacques Necker, however, urged the Assembly to act quickly, if they wanted to avoid the suspension of payments. He made clear that 30 million *livres* were needed immediately (more money would be required later), which in his opinion only could be acquired through further credits. Quite aware that France could not attract foreign money in its current unstable political situation, he claimed that private investors would only grant the necessary loans if they felt a "patriotic sentiment". In the plenary session, Necker explicitly opposed a detailed and time-consuming calculation, which he called *spécula-*

---

44 See, for explanation and translations, Biondi, "The Double Emergence," 315–316.
45 Biondi, "The Double Emergence," 316.
46 Duvillard, *Recherches*, Avertissement.
47 Duvillard, *Recherches*, 2.
48 Duvillard, *Recherches*, 119. The French political arithmetician Duvillard was referring to was Antoine Deparcieux and his *Essai sur les probabilités de la durée de la vie humaine: d'où l'on déduit la manière de déterminer les rentes* [...] (Paris, 1746). See, for Deparcieux's arithmetic, also Cem Behar and Yves Ducel, "L'arithmétique politique d'Antoine Deparcieux," in *Arithmétique Politique dans la France du XVIIIe siècle*, ed. Thierry Martin (Paris: INED, 2003), 147–161.
49 See also Biondi, "The Double Emergence," 318.
50 Thuiller, *Le premier actuaire*, 12–13.

tion, and so insisted on acting without delay and on giving out annuities with a five percent-interest rate.[51]

On 12 September 1789, the *Comité féodale de l'Assemblée Nationale* gave its report on the present financial situation. In it, the committee reflected on the possibility of liquidating life-contingent contracts such as the *rentes*. But it made clear that it strongly opposed this course of action, arguing that this would take away the compound returns and destroy the subscribers' future options that they were promised when they purchased annuity-contracts. If the state was to rebuy the *rentes*, so the report advised, it would have to found such a redemption upon one of two possible speculations that both included a detailed evaluation and calculation of future compound interest rates. In September 1789, the *Comité* thus committed the new regime to Duvillard's speculative finance in the sense that it urged the Assembly to take time to reasonably calculate all possibilities in order to find an offer that would not unjustly disown French citizens by taking away their future compound interests. The report declared:

> As regards the debtor, the buy-back cannot but be founded on one or the other of these two speculations: either the debtor who undertakes it [the buy-back] finds more advantages in spending a sum of which the interest is superior to the load by which it is burdened, or he wants to sacrifice a sum in order to deliver his cause as well as his successors from the chance of events and from a higher or lower frequency of possible mutations: but nobody can be forced to subscribe to one or the other of these two speculations; each must remain master to manage his own property as he considers suitable.
>
> It is thus impossible to force all owners to liquidate the buy-out under this term or another, and to pay a [stable] interest until the payment: therefore the interest rate must remain variable and must follow the evolution that the funds' price will undergo.[52]

---

51 *Archives parlementaires de 1787 à 1860. Recueil complet des débats législatifs et politiques des chambres françaises. Imprimé par ordre du Sénat et de la Chambre des Députés*, Fondé par MM. Madival et E. Laurent. Première Série (1787 à 1799), 8:361–362.

52 "Le rachat à l'égard du débiteur ne peut être fondé que sur l'une ou l'autre de ces deux spéculations: ou le débiteur qui le fait trouve plus d'avantage à débourser une somme dont l'intérêt est supérieur à la charge dont il est grevé, ou il veut bien sacrifier une somme pour délivrer sa chose, et ses successeurs du hasard des événements et d'une plus ou moins grande fréquences des mutations éventuelles: mais aucun ne peut être forcé de souscrire à l'une ni à l'autre de ces deux spéculations; chacun doit rester maître d'administrer sa propriété comme il juge à propos.

Il est donc impossible d'assujettir tous les possesseurs à faire liquider dans un terme quelconque le rachat, et à en payer l'intérêt jusqu'au payement: dès lors il faut que le taux de rachat demeure variable, et suive les révolutions que le prix des fonds éprouvera lui-même." See *Archives Parlementaires*, 8:630.

While, in 1789, the Committee advocated a detailed speculation that aimed to avoid disowning French citizens and to defend private interests, the Convention took a different position in the year II of the New Regime. The president of the Committee of Finance, Pierre-Joseph Cambon, in particular, reported to the Convention in 1793 that the annuity system was the main cause of France's financial disaster and that the revolutionaries had not to the present day been able to get rid of it. His committee was mandated to come up with a plan to demonetarize the annuity system. It reported: "You ordered a long time ago that your committee of finances gives you a report on life annuities. The *agioteurs* await this report with impatience and hopelessness; the egoists, usurers and vampires of the Old Regime are alarmed by it".[53] Although Cambon began his report with references to *agiotage* and *agioteurs*, it is clear that the "vampires" he mentioned were those speculators he referred to on plenty of other occasions.[54] With life annuities now seen as speculative schemes, invented by egoistic and monopolizing bankers and denounced by the Convention in 1793, speculation was betokened as *agiotage*, which only served selfish passions detrimental to the nation's good. How did this change in the usage of the term speculation, from a detailed mathematical calculation to an immoral and condemned money-making scheme, happen within only a few years?

To understand this shift, we must look into the ongoing debate about the *assignats*, which brought about a renewed concern with John Law's legacy and which, in turn, had deep repercussions on the notion of speculation. For defenders of the *assignats* (in April 1790, these were transformed from state bonds into legal tender), the new currency was the best means to solve the disastrous financial situation and to thus avoid the state's bankruptcy. When, in late summer 1790, the National Assembly discussed whether to issue further *assignats* without any interest (the first *assignats* had been given out with an interest rate of five per cent), defenders of the idea repudiated any comparison of the *assignats* with John Law's paper-money. This included Parisian deputy of the third estate, Pierre-Hubert Anson:[55]

53 "Vous avez ordonné depuis long-temps à votre comité des finances de vous faire un rapport sur les rentes viagères. Les agioteurs l'attendent avec impatience et désespoir; les égoïstes, les usuriers et les vampires de l'ancien régime en sont alarmés." See Pierre-Joseph, *Cambon, Rapport et projet de décret sur la dette publique viagère, présentés à la Convention nationale* [...] (Paris, 1793), 1.

54 See, for ex. Cambon, *Rapport*, 4–7.

55 See, for the reception of John Law's system, Arnaud Orain's new monograph: *La politique du merveilleux: Une autre histoire du Système de Law (1695–1795)* (Paris: Fayard, 2018), here especially 308–309. Others, who made similar points as Anson, were Pierre-Louis Roederer, Jérôme

> I am always surprised to hear somebody say that an *assignat-monnoie*, without interest, effectively substituted to the bearer, will not diminish *agiotage*. [...] when speaking of *agiotage* that took place at the times of Law, one forgets that it [*agiotage*] began when the Scotsman exchanged [hard] money for shares in his bank, which were very different from his notes [*billets*]; at that time the possibility of benefits provoked hope, bred crazy speculations, & from this strange operation followed a terrible decline. In truth, I reproach myself for speaking to you about this when this [the *assignat-monnoie*] is such a different kind of paper-money whose solidity cannot be contested any longer.[56]

Anson made clear, when reflecting on the French experience of 1720, that it was not the introduction of paper-money itself that was at the origin of the system's degeneration – or of *agiotage*, for that matter. Rather, John Law's mistake, according to the Parisian deputy, was to connect his paper-money to the stocks of his bank. Consequently, *agiotage* and speculation lay not in the nature of paper-money but was provoked by a connection of paper-money and the stock market. It is interesting to note that Anson employs a vision of the year 1720 that he betokens as "emotional craze of speculation" – a classification that, though not new in its moral condemnation, would have been rather unfamiliar to Law's contemporaries. That he used the term "speculation", which had been reserved for a commercial and financial epistemology that put a trader's intelligence at its center, suggests a reading of the events of the 1720s that did not leave any ambiguity about whether people understood the ways in which they risked the nation's well-being. The reference to speculation indicates that those responsible for the system willingly endangered the nation, because they put their ego-

---

Pétion de Villeneuve, La Rochefoucauld. See Orain, *La politique*, 309. See also, Antoine E. Murphy, "John Law and the Assignats," in *La Pensée économique pendant la Révolution française*, ed. Philippe Steiner and Gilber Faccarello (Grenoble: Presses Universitaires, 1990), 431–448. See, for the understanding of Law's Système, Edgare Faure's seminal work, *La banqueroute de Law, 17 juillet 1720* (Paris: Gallimard, 1977); but also more recently John Shovlin's article, "Jealousy of Credit: John Law's 'System' and the Geopolitics of Financial Revolution," *Journal of Modern History* 88 (2016): 275–305.

56 "Je suis toujours étonné d'entendre dire qu'un assignat monnoie, sans intérêt, substitué aux effets au porteur, ne diminuera point l'agiotage. [...] lorsqu'on parle de l'agiotage qui eut lieu du temps de Law, on perd de vue, qu'il commença lorsque cet Écossois fit donner valeur de monnoie aux actions de sa banque, bien différentes de ses billets; alors des bénéfices éventuels firent concevoir des espérances, engendrèrent des spéculations folles, & de là la terrible décadence qui suivit cette étrange opération. En vérité, je reproche à moi-même de vous en entretenir, lorsqu'il s'agit d'une monnoie si différente, dont on ne conteste plus la solidité." See Pierre-Hubert Ansons, *Opinion de M. Anson, député de Paris, sur la liquidation de la dette publique* [...] (Paris, 1790), 7.

istic passions first. This, however, should not happen in a new regime founded on a republican spirit – for in Anson's view, 1790 was nothing like 1720.

Yet, those like Dupont de Nemours, who strongly opposed the *assignats* (and, even more so, their new iteraction), did not avoid linking 1720 and 1790. The deputy of Lyon, Nicolas Bergasse, went a step further and not only compared the two moments in French history, but, as Arnaud Orain has recently shown, he gave preference to Law's System. In his *Lettre de M. Bergasse*[57] (1790) he demonstrated similarities between Law's System and the *assignats*, while favoring the former despite its terrible effects:[58]

> First, I hold that if there is a difference between the present notes & those of Law, the difference is maybe all to the advantage of Law's notes. It is wrong that Law's notes were lacking mortgage as some dare to suggest. By contrast, it is easy to show that they were backed by a mortgage that was more solid than what is presented to us for the *assignats-monnoie.*[59]

Although Bergasse did not refrain from denunciating the Scotsman's System,[60] he thought a new emission of *assignats* would have similar, if not worse, consequences for France. According to the deputy, such measures would give way to *agiotage* and speculation, instead of putting an end to the old credit and annuity system.[61] To strengthen his arguments, Bergasse annexed a table of comparison to his letter, wherein he confronted the "système de la caisse d'escompte des assignats-monnoie" with the "système Law".[62] For Bergasse, such a comparison

57 Nicolas Bergasse, *Lettre de M. Bergasse, député de la sénéchaussé de Lyon, à ses commettans, au sujet de sa Protestation contre les assignats-monnoie: accompagnée d'un tableau comparative du système de Law avec le système de la caisse d'escompte, des assignats-monnoie* [...] (Paris, 1790).

58 See, for this strategy of comparison between the System Law and the system of the *assignats* that the opponents of the *assignats* employed, as well as for the reference to Dupont de Nemours, Nicolas Bergasse, Jean Sifrein Maury, Jean-André Périsse-Duluc, Abbé Maury, Antoine-François Delandine and François Louis la Grand Boislandry; Orain, *La politique*, 310–313.

59 "Et d'abord je soutiens, que s'il y a une différence entre les billets actuels & ceux de Law, elle est peut-être toute à l'avantage des billets de Law. Il est faux que les billets de Law fussent dénués d'hypothèque comme on ose l'avancer. Il est au contraire aisé de démontrer qu'ils étoient garantis par une hypothèque tout autrement solide que celle qu'on nous présente pour les assignats-monnoie. Le produit de la ferme Générale, de la ferme du tabac, du commerce de l'Inde, du commerce d'Afrique, du commerce des Indes occidentales, toutes les recettes du Royaume, le privilège de fabrication des espèces, voilà l'hypothèque des billets des Law." See Bergasse, *Lettre*, 5.

60 Bergasse, *Lettre*, 10.

61 Bergasse, *Lettre*, 26 and 46.

62 See, for the table of comparison, Bergasse, *Lettre*, 41–55.

showed that if Law and the Regent, who were better situated to avoid a worst-case-scenario than the people in his own days, could not prevent a situation that gave way to egoistic interests – or to *agiotage* and speculation – then far less was France prepared to avoid such calamities in the early 1790s:

> In Law's times they went bankrupt with bursting safes & in our times we will go bankrupt with empty safes.
>
> And the French nation & its prosperities are sacrificed to whom? To those interested in the savings bank, to *agioteurs*, to speculators of all classes, & to those numerous bribers who declare themselves their partisans.[63]

This interpretation, employing a comparison between the paper-money of 1720 and that of 1790, sought, as Orain rightly has emphasized, to defend the interests of landowners vis-à-vis the interests of the *rentiers*. This was a reading of events that pleased Englishman and observer of the French Revolution Edmund Burke, who similarly disliked speculations, which, in his opinion, were provoked by the introduction of the *assignats*. Burke thus was one of the proponents who used a similar notion of speculation as the opponents of the revolutionary currency. With his account of the revolutionary events, he also transported these ideas to his native country.[64]

Defenders of the *assignats*, in turn, held that the new Legislative Assembly (*Convention*) as the sovereign body had the right to interfere with individual property rights.[65] In this context, radical defenders and staunch republicans began to reinterpret 1720 not only as a reminder of its calamities, but also as a valuable moment in French economic and financial history. Such an interpretation was already present in Louis-Sébastien Mercier's *De J.-J. Rousseau considéré.*[66] In a footnote, Mercier explained that Rousseau, though one of the most illustrious authors of the Revolution, was much mistaken in his judgement of

---

63 "On verra dans l'histoire du systême, que le Régent & Law étoient des hommes tout autrement habiles que les faiseurs d'affaires d'aujourd'hui [...] Au tems de Law on fit la banqueroute les coffres pleins; & de notre tems on la fera les coffres vuides.

Et la Nation Françoise & ses prospérités se trouveront sacrifiées; à qui? Aux intéressés de la caisse d'escompte, aux agioteurs, aux spéculateurs de toutes les classes, & aux nombreux soudoyés qui se déclarent leurs partisans." See Bergasse, *Lettre*, 54–55.

64 Edmund Burke, *Reflections on the Revolution in France, and on the Proceeding in Certain Societies in London Relative to that Event*, 4th ed. (London, 1790), 281–283. See, for the defense of landowner interests and the reception of these ideas by Edmund Burke, Orain, *La politique*, 310–311.

65 Orain, *La politique*, 312–313.

66 Louis-Sébastien Mercier, *De J.-J. Rousseau considéré comme l'un des premiers auteurs de la Révolution* (Paris, 1791).

paper-money. Yet, in his opinion, not only Rousseau but also the Minister of Finance, Jacques Necker, had limited knowledge about finance. Hence, for Mercier, John Law would have been the better fit to solve the present crisis:

> One will forever remember that M. Necker fought against this salutary means [the introduction of the *assignats-monnoies*] without offering anything else in its place; his entire genius consisted of borrowing, borrowing, borrowing, and then of niggling, niggling, niggling [...] If you'd resuscitated Law at Necker's place, you would have seen this grand man correcting his plans, putting himself suddenly at the height of the revolution, and marching majestically towards immortality in embracing the constitution and the French regeneration with an imposing firmness as worthy of her [the constitution] as of him.[67]

In contrast to the ideas of the Finance Minister, who suggested continuing to borrow money (which mostly meant selling more annuities), Law's legacy (here: the introduction of paper-money) pointed to a more viable solution for the republic. Correspondingly, the radical Jacques Roux demanded showing no mercy towards monopolizers and *agioteurs*, or anybody who discredited the republican currency.[68] If such republican principles had been honored before, he wrote,

> You would not be famished, ruined, hopeless, and poisoned by venomous reptiles, by parasitical speculators, by vampires, who, due to a deadly fusion with monopoly, take hold of comestible commerce, devouring the proprietors, the manufacturers, and liberty, which leads us, due to such usurious traffic, to the harbor of the counter-revolution.[69]

According to the view of radical republicans and radical defenders of the *assignats*, Law's paper-money did not introduce a false spirit of speculation that caused the current financial misery. Rather, it was people like Necker, who

---

67 "On se souviendra éternellement que M. Necker a combattu ce moyen de salut [introduction des assignats-monnoies] sans savoir rien mettre à sa place; tout son génie avoit consisté à emprunter, à emprunter, à emprunter, et puis à pédantiser, à pédantiser, à pédantiser; [...] Ressuscitez Law à la place de Necker, vous auriez vu le grand homme corriger ses plans, se mettre tout-à-coup au niveau de la révolution, et marcher majestueusement à l'immortalité, en embrassant la constitution et la régéneration Françoise avec une fermeté imposante digne d'elle et de lui." See Mercier, *De J.-J. Rousseau*, 80–81, fn. 1; see also Orain, *La politique*, 314.

68 Jacques Roux, *Disours sur le jugement de Louis-le-dernier, sur la poursuite des agioteurs des accapareurs et des traîtres* [...] (Paris, 1792), 8.

69 "Vous ne series pas affamé, ruiné, désespéré, empoisonné par des reptiles venimeux, de spéculateurs parasites, par des vampires, qui, par une combinaison meurtrière du monopole, s'emparent du commerces des comestibles, dévorent les propriétés, les manufactures, la liberté, et nous font arriver, par des traffics usuraires, au port de la contre-révolution." See Roux, *Disours*, 7. See also *Archives Parlementaires*, 67:458, and Maurice Dommaget, *Jacques Roux (le curé rouge) et la Manifeste des 'Enragés'* (Paris: R. Lefeuvre, 1948).

sought refuge in more loans and in more, increasingly onerous annuity schemes. If there was fault in Law's System, they continued, it was that it was not radical enough,[70] that it did not succeed in what it promised (no debts) and so eventually succumbed to speculation or, in other words, to more loans and to more annuities. We thus can identify a conjunction between radical republicanism, a radical defense of the *assignats* (which led to the *terreur économique*), a re-evaluation of Law's legacy, and a radical condemnation of speculation.[71]

Cambon also connected these four pillars. More precisely, for the President of the Financial Committee, *agiotage* was committed by those who did not necessarily know the extent of their detrimental behavior for the state when they bought annuities. Speculation, however, was an even worse deed, because it was committed by those who understood the consequences of their actions. The vampires and speculators cited before were those bankers who came up with annuity schemes like the Genevan one, which offered contracts with several heads and with eight to ten per cent interest. Their omnipresent seductions not only ensnared all those who bought their annuities but also tricked the ministers to agree to their schemes:

> The speculators surrounded the ministers, they monopolized almost the entire borrowings in annuities. They were more or less their merchants; they were granted a commission of one per cent [...] those monopolizers of borrowings in annuities held the government in their hands; they fabricated political news to accredit their operations. They had emissaries in the corners of every street, in the cafés and in the salons [...] they called all their colleagues at the bourse of Paris to raise or lower the public credit as they wished.[72]

It is interesting to note the ways that Cambon's notion of speculation echoed previous epistemologies – speculators were those who had the *savoir faire*, who had the kind of special expertise to play the entire nation, including ministers like

---

70 See, for the radicalism in Jacobin thought, Patrice Higonnet, *Goodness Beyond Virtue: Jacobins During the French Revolution* (Cambridge, Mass.: Harvard University Press, 1998), 2.

71 See, for the so-called *térreur économique*, François Hincker, "Comment sortir de la terreur économique?," in *Le Tournant de l'an III: Reaction et terreur blanche*, ed. Comité des travaux historiques et scientifiques (Paris: Éditions du CTHS, 1997), 149–158. See, for the politics of terror, e. g. Patrice Gueniffey, *La politique de la terreur: Essai sur la violence révolutionnaire, 1789–1794* (Paris: Fayard, 2000).

72 "Les spéculateurs environnaient les ministres, ils accaparaient presque l'entier emprunt en viager. Ils en étaient les marchands en gros; on leur accordaient une commission d'un pour cent [...] ces accapareurs des emprunts viagers maîtrisent le gouvernement; ils fabriquaient des Nouvelles politiques pour accréditer leurs opérations. Ils avaient des émissaires au coin de toutes les rues, dans les cafés et dans les salons [...] ils appelaient tous leurs collègues à la bourse de Paris, pour faire hausser et baisser à leur gré le credit public." Cambon, *Rapport*, 4–5.

Jacques Necker. However, the epistemological meaning of speculation that was familiar from those economic thinkers who wrote in the 1750s and 1760s and who argued for the liberalization of the grain trade was now accompanied by a strong moral judgment. Cambon's report offered a table of *rentes viagères* sold between 1702 and 1787, which demonstrated the financial problems caused by such speculations. The table showed that, between 1720 and 1724, 100,000,000 *livres* were invested in annuities per year (contrasted by 500,000 *livres* invested in 1705). Indeed, there were similarly high capital-investments in the 1770s, but they were sold with much higher interest rates (four per cent in the 1720s compared to eight to ten per cent in the 1770s). The table thus makes it clear: the problem with Law's system was not the introduction of paper-money but that its collapse provoked a new wave of investments in annuities. The real problem was introduced only later by these "speculators" and "vampires", who came up with annuity schemes at over eight per cent and on several heads.[73]

In the context of contemporary economic and political pressure, those radical republicans and fierce defenders of the *assignats* like Cambon and Roux, who were confronted with their inability to dispose of the Old Regime's debts, began to identify the old credit-practice of private annuities as the main cause of France's financial disaster, which gave them an useful explanation for the problems of the new fiscal regime without questioning the introduction of the *assignats*. In their view, the bankers' private self-interest to make money out of money (speculation) had knowingly ruined the French state. The partisans of the *assignats* now firmly abnegated any continuity of old fiscal practices in the new regime, condemning every such practice as an act against the nation and against the public good. This condemnation of any form of speculative enterprise was taken very seriously. Even when Maximilien de Robespierre argued in favor of the annuity-subscribers and defended their good intentions as ordinary citizens, he was opposed by the president of the Committee of Finance, Pierre-Joseph Cambon.[74]

73 See Cambon, *Rapport*, 17.
74 Weir, "Tontines," 124.

Conclusions

Although we can trace an ongoing interest in Law's legacy back to the Old Regime,[75] both opponents and defenders of the *assignats* between 1791 and 1793, although too young to have experienced John Law's scheme themselves,[76] developed a distinct interest in Law's *Système*, while also employing new arguments condemning or appreciating those years under Law's influence. The preoccupation with the *assignats* and with John Law had deep repercussions on the notion of speculation. For the opponents of the *assignats*, the introduction of paper-money had given way to an immoral form of money-making, which they called *agiotage*, or – and this was rather new in the eighteenth-century – which they also betokened as *speculation*. Speculation now implied strong moral connotations, because it called to mind the traders' or bankers' *savoir le faire*. For opponents of the *assignats*, the gaze back to Law's *Système* demonstrated that the introduction of paper-money could have the same or even worse effects than in 1720. The years of Law's *Système* thus were years of financial speculation that they wanted to avoid in the present state.

By contrast, the defenders of the *assignats* applauded Law's idea to introduce paper-money that was backed by mortgage. They still found 1720 problematic, however, because the *Système* did not triumph over the older annuity system and eventually gave way to increased investment in this credit market. Those who engaged in this practice by buying annuities, they called – quite familiarly – *agioteurs*. Yet, all those bankers who knew what they were doing and who came up with new, and more onerous annuity schemes, they began to call *spéculateurs*. In this sense, speculation still echoed the older, epistemological implications. The personalized form of *speculator*, however, points to newer, yet powerful moral implications.

Such interpretations of speculation contrasted the commercial epistemology of speculation disseminated by mid-eighteenth century economic and financial thinkers like Herbert, Forbonnais, Abeille or Duvillard. For them, speculation not only took into account empirical knowledge but also anticipated the unseen, such as changes that might happen in the future. Speculation thus enhanced an actor's perspective on the market and so helped to broaden the scope of actions that was necessary if one wanted to contribute to the public good (e. g. subsistence or the reform of the annuity market). Hence, the partisans of this commercial epistemology sought to liberate self-interest from moral judgment.

---

75 See footnote 56.

76 Spang, "The Ghost of Law," 10 – 11.

The republicans, who liked to evoke the sacred character of the nation, however, went back to an older, Christian-infused condemnation of self-interest – updating the older Christian language of usury with the notion of speculation. Their interpretation of speculation as an egoistic and passion-driven, yet skillful risking of the nation's good was (and still is) easily transferred back to all kinds of economic and financial calamities, and it was soon disseminated in other European languages. We find such a reading of speculation within a few years in French, Dutch and English.[77] Such a definition of speculation, still powerful today, made it thus harder for us to appreciate the different contemporary readings of the 1720's crashes as *stock-jobbing*, *bubbles*, *windhandel*, or *Système*.

---

77 Data bases like the *English Short Title Catalogue* or the *Burney Collection* give a first impression. See also my ongoing work, tentatively entitled *Augmenting Reality: Speculation in Early Modern Europe*.

Daniel Menning

Selected Bibliography

Aldridge, David D., *Admiral Sir John Norris and the British Expeditions to the Baltic Sea 1715–1727* (Lund: Nordic Academic Press, 2009).

Altorfer, Stefan, "Bulle oder Bär? Der bernische Staat und die 'South Sea Bubble' von 1720," in *Globalisierung – Chancen und Risiken: Die Schweiz in der Weltwirtschaft 18.–20. Jahrhundert*, ed. Hans-Jörg Gilomen, Margrit Müller, and Béatrice Veyrassat (Zürich: Chronos, 2003), 61–86.

Åmark, Karl, *Sveriges statsfinanser 1719–1809* (Stockholm: Norstedts, 1961).

Amsinck, Caesar, "Die Ersten Hamburgischen Assecuranz-Compagnien und der Actienhandel im Jahre 1720," *Zeitschrift des Vereins für Hamburgische Geschichte* 9 (1894): 465–494.

Ashton, Thomas S., *Economic Fluctuations in England 1700–1800* (Oxford: Clarendon Press, 1959).

Attack, Jeremy/Neal, Larry, eds., *The Origins and Development of Financial Markets and Institutions: From the Seventeenth Century to the Present* (Cambridge and New York: Cambridge University Press, 2009).

Bachelier, Louis, *Theory of Speculation: The Origins of Modern Finance* (1900; Princeton and Oxford: Princeton University Press, 2006).

Balen, Malcolm, *A Very English Deceit: The Secret History of the South Sea Bubble and the First Great Financial Scandal* (London: Fourth Estate, 2003).

Banallec, Yves/Le Lan, Jean Yves, "La Compagnie des Indes et la traite des noirs," *Bulletin et mémoires de la Société polymathique du Morbihan* 132 (2006): 95–120.

Barber, Brad M./Odean, Terrance, "Boys Will Be Boys: Gender, Overconfidence and Common Stock Investment," *Quarterly Journal of Economics* 116, no. 1 (2001): 261–292.

Beckert, Jens, *Imagined Futures: Fictional Expectations and Capitalist Dynamics* (Cambridge, Mass.: Harvard University Press, 2016).

Beckett, J.V., "Cumbrians and the South Sea Bubble, 1720," *Transactions of the Cumberland & Westmorland Antiquarian & Archaeological Society* 82 (1982): 141–150.

Bell, Stuart, "A Masterpiece of Knavery? The Activities of the Sword Blade Company in London's Early Financial Markets," *Business History* 54 (2012): 623–638.

Bernstein, Peter L., *Capital Ideas: The Improbable Origins of Modern Wall Street* (New York: The Free Press, 1992).

Black, Jeremy, *Continental Commitment: Britain, Hanover and Interventionism 1714–1793* (London and New York: Routledge 2005).

Blackburn, Robin, *The Making of New World Slavery: From the Baroque to the Modern, 1492–1800* (London: Verso, 1997).

Bonney, Richard, "France and the First European Paper Money Experiment," *French History* 15 (2001): 254–272.

Bossenga, Gail, "Financial Origins of the French Revolution," in *From Deficit to Deluge: The Origins of the French Revolution*, ed. Thomas Kaiser and Dale Van Kley (Stanford: Stanford University Press, 2011), 37–66.

Brantlinger, P., *Fictions of State: Culture and Credit in Britain, 1694–1994* (Ithaca: Cornell University Press, 1996).

https://doi.org/10.1515/9783110592139-016

Brealey, Peter, "The Charitable Corporation for the Relief of Industrious Poor: Philanthropy, Profit and Sleaze in London, 1707–1733," *History* 98 (2013): 708–729.
Brunnermeier, Markus K., "Bubbles," in *The New Palgrave Dictionary of Economics*, ed. Garett Jones, 3rd ed. (London: Palgrave Macmillan, 2018).
Buat, Nicolas, *John Law: La dette ou comment s'en débarrasser* (Paris: Belles lettres, 2015).
Busteed, John, "Irish private banks," *Journal of the Cork Historical and Archaeological Society* 53 (1948): 32–38.
Cardoso, José Luis, "*Confusion de confusiones:* Ethics and Options on Seventeenth-Century Stock Exchange Markets," *Financial History Review* 9 (2002): 109–123.
Carlos, Ann M./Neal, Larry, "Women Investors in Early Capital Markets, 1720–1725," *Financial History Review* 11 (2004): 197–224.
Carlos, Ann M./Neal, Larry, "The Micro-Foundations of the Early London Capital Market: Bank of England Shareholders During and After the South Sea Bubble, 1720–25," *Economic History Review* 59 (2006): 498–538.
Carlos, Ann M./Maguire, Karen/Neal, Larry, "Women in the City: Financial Acumen, Women Speculators, and the Royal African Company During the South Sea Bubble," *Accounting, Business and Financial History* 16 (2006): 219–243.
Carlos, Ann M./Maguire, Karen/Neal, Larry, "'A Knavish People ...': London Jewry and the Stock Market During the South Sea Bubble," *Business History* 50 (2008), 728–748.
Carlos, Ann M./Maguire, Karen/Neal, Larry, "Women in the City: Financial Acumen During the South Sea Bubble," in *Women and Their Money 1700–1950: Essays on Women and Finance*, ed. Anne Laurence, Josephine Maltby, and Janette Rutterford (London and New York: Routledge, 2009), 33–45.
Carretta, Vincent, "Pope's *Epistle to Bathurst* and the South Sea Bubble," *Journal of English and German Philology* 77 (1978): 212–231.
Carruthers, Bruce, "Homo Economicus and Homo Politicus: Non-Economic Rationality in the Early 18th Century London Stock Market," *Acta Sociologica* 37 (1994): 165–194.
Carruthers, *City of Capital: Politics and Markets in the English Financial Revolution* (Princeton: Princeton University Press, 1996).
Carswell, John, *The South Sea Bubble* (London: Cresset Press, 1960; rev. ed. Washington, DC: Alan Sutton, 1993).
Cavaciocchi, Simonetta, ed., *Fiscal Systems in the European Economy from the 13th to the 18th Centuries* (Firenze: Firenze University Press, 2008).
Chancellor, Edward, *Devil Take the Hindmost: A History of Financial Speculation* (London: Macmillan, 1999).
Chaussinand-Nogaret, Guy, *Les financiers de Languedoc au XVIIIe siècle* (Paris: S.E.V.P.E.N., 1970).
Claeys, Thierry, *Dictionnaire biographique des financiers en France au XVIIIe siècle*, 2 vols. (Paris: SPM, 2011).
Clegg, John J., "Capitalism and Slavery," *Critical Historical Studies* 2 (2015): 281–304.
Coates, J.M./Herbert, J., "Endogenous Steroids and Financial Risk Taking on a London Trading Floor," PNAS 105 (2008): 6167–6172.
Coffman, D'Maris/ Leonard, Adrian/Neal, Larry, eds., *Questioning Credible Commitment: Perspectives on the Rise of Financial Capitalism* (Cambridge: Cambridge University Press, 2013).

Cole, Charles Woolsey, *French Mercantilism, 1683–1700* (New York: Columbia University Press, 1943).

Colley, Linda, *In Defiance of Oligarchy: The Tory Party, 1714–60* (Cambridge: Cambridge University Press, 1982).

Condorelli, Stefano, *The 1719–20 Stock Euphoria: A Pan-European Perspective, MPRA Paper* (2014).

Condorelli, Stefano, "La presse étrangère et le Système de Law (1716–20)," in *'Gagnons sans savoir comment': Représentations du Système de Law du XVIIIe à nos jours*, ed. Florence Magnot-Ogilvy (Rennes: Presses Universitaires de Rennes, 2017), 183–206.

Condorelli, Stefano, *Price Momentum and the 1719–20 Bubbles: A Method to Compare and Interpret Booms and Crashes in Asset Markets, MPRA Paper* (2018).

Condorelli, Stefano/Menning, Daniel, "Wirtschaftspolitik in Zeiten der europäischen Börseneuphorie: Die Gründung der Leyh- und Commercien-Compagnie und die Reform der Tuchproduktion in Hessen-Kassel 1721," *Hessisches Jahrbuch für Landesgeschichte* 68 (2018): 99–114.

Courbet, André, "Voltaire en Lorraine: Les séjours de 1720 et 1735," *Cahiers Voltaire* 13 (2014): 51–68.

Cowles, Alfred, "Can Stock Market Forecasters Forecast?," *Econometrica* 1 (1933): 309–324.

Cruickshanks, Eveline/Erskine-Hill, Howard, *The Atterbury Plot* (New York: Palgrave Macmillan, 2004).

Cummings, A.J.G., *The York Buildings Company: A Case Study in Eighteenth-Century Corporation Mismanagement*, unpublished Ph.D. dissertation (Strathclyde, 1980).

Cummings, A.J.G., "The Harburgh Company and Its Lottery 1716–1723," in *Business in the Age of Reason*, ed. R.P.T. Davenport-Hines (London: Routledge, 1987), 1–18.

Dale, Richard, *The First Crash: Lessons from First Crash* (Princeton: Princeton University Press, 2004).

Dale, Richard/Johnson, Johnnie E.V./Tang, Leilei, "Financial Markets Can Go Mad: Evidence of Irrational Behaviour During the South Sea Bubble," *Economic History Review* 58 (2005): 233–271.

Davies, K.G., "Joint-stock Investment in the Later Seventeenth Century," *Economic History Review* 4 (1952): 283–301.

De Bruyn, Frans, "Satire in Text and Image: Bubble Publications in England and the Netherlands Compared," in *The Great Mirror of Folly: Finance, Culture, and the Crash of 1720*, ed. William N. Goetzmann et al. (New Haven: Yale University Press, 2013), 159–174.

De Goede, Marieke, *Virtue, Fortune, and Faith: A Genealogy of Finance* (Minneapolis: University of Minnesota Press, 2005).

De Krey, Gary S., *A Fractured Society: The Politics of London in the First Age of Party, 1688–1715* (Oxford: Clarendon Press, 1985).

Delafosse, Marcel, "Planteurs de Saint-Domingue et négociants rochelais au temps de Law," *Revue d'histoire des colonies* 142 (1954): 1–21.

De Marchi, Neil/Harrison, Paul, "Trading 'in the Wind' and With Guile: The Troublesome Matter of the Short Selling of Share in Seventeenth-Century Holland," in *Higgling: Transactors and Their Markets in the History of Economics*, ed. N. de Marchi and M. Morgan, Annual supplement to *History of Political Economy* 26 (1994), 47–65.

Deringer, William, "For What It's Worth: Historical Financial Bubbles and the Boundaries of Economic Rationality," *ISIS* 106 (2015): 646–656.
Deringer, William, *Calculated Values: Finance, Politics, and the Quantitative Age* (Cambridge: Cambridge University Press, 2018).
Dickinson, H.T., *Walpole and the Whig Supremacy* (Aylesbury: The English Universities Press, 1973).
Dickson, Peter G.M., *The Financial Revolution in England: A Study in the Development of Public Credit, 1688–1756* (London: MacMillan, 1967).
Donnan, Elizabeth, "The Early Days of the South Sea Company, 1711–1718," *Journal of Economic and Business History* 2 (1930): 419–450.
Douthwaite, Julia V., "How Bad Economic Memories Are Made: John Law's System in *Les lettres persanes, Manon Lescaut*, and 'The Great Mirror of Folly'," *L'Esprit Créateur* 55 (2015): 43–58.
Dullinger, Josef, "Die Handelskompagnien Österreichs nach dem Oriente und nach Ostindien in der ersten Hälfte des 18. Jahrhunderts," *Zeitschrift für Social- und Wirthschaftsgeschichte* 7 (1900): 44–83.
Dumont, Georges-Henri, *L'Épopée de la compagnie d'Ostende* (Brussels: Le cri, 2000).
Duranton, Henri, "La ficelle de Law," in '*Gagnons sans savoir comment* ': *Représentations du Système de Law du XVIIIe à nos jours*, ed. Florence Magnot-Ogilvy (Rennes: Presses universitaires de Rennes, 2017), 111–126.
Eckel, Catherine C./Grossman, Philip J., "Men, Women and Risk-Aversion: Experimental Evidence," in *Handbook of Experimental Economics*, ed. Charles Plott and Vernon Smith (Princeton: Princeton University Press, 2008), 1061–1073.
Ericsson, Peter, "Corporative Privileges Undermined: The Meaning of Extra-Ordinary Taxation in Sweden in the 17th and 18th Centuries," in *Fiscal Systems in the European Economy from the 13th to the 18th Centuries*, ed. Simonetta Cavaciocchi (Firenze: Firenze University Press, 2008), 757–769.
Ermer, Elsa/Cosmides, Leda/Tooby, John, "Relative Status Regulates Risky Decision-Making About Resources in Men: Evidence for the Co-Evolution of Motivation and Cognition," Evolution and Human Behaviour 29 (2008): 106–118.
Fama, Eugene F., "Random Walks in Stock Market Prices," *Financial Analysts Journal* 21 (1965): 55–59.
Fama, Eugene F., "Efficient Capital Markets: A Review of Theory and Empirical Work," *Journal of Finance* 25 (1970): 383–417.
Faure, Edgar, *La banqueroute de Law, 17 juillet 1720* (Paris: Gallimard, 1977).
Félix, Joël, "The Most Difficult Financial Matter That Has Ever Presented Itself. Paper Money and the Financing of Warfare under Louis XIV," *Financial History Review* 25 (2018): 43–70.
Finucane, Adrian, *The Temptations of Trade: Britain, Spain, and the Struggle for Empire* (Philadelphia: University of Pennsylvania Press, 2016).
Freeman, Mark/Pearson, Robin/Taylor, James, "'A Doe in the City': Women Shareholders in Eighteenth- and Early Nineteenth-Century Britain," *Accounting, Business and Financial History* 16 (2006): 265–291.
Freeman, Mark/Pearson, Robin/Taylor, James, "Law, politics and the Governance of English and Scottish Joint-stock Companies, 1600–1850," *Business History* 55 (2013): 633–649.

Frehen, Rik G.P./Goetzmann, William N./Rouwenhorst, K. Geert, "New Evidence on the First Financial Bubble," *Journal of Financial Economics* 108 (2013): 585–607.

Frehen, Rik G.P./Goetzmann, William N./Rouwenhorst, K. Geert, "Finance in the Great Mirror of Folly," in *The Great Mirror of Folly: Finance, Culture, and the Crash of 1720*, ed. William N. Goetzmann et al. (New Haven: Yale University Press, 2013), 63–87.

Froide, Amy, *Silent Partners: Women as Public Investors During Britain's Financial Revolution, 1690–1750* (Oxford: Oxford University Press, 2017).

Frostin, Charles, *Les révoltes blanches à Saint-Domingue aux XVIIe et XVIIIe siècles* (Paris: L'École, 1975; Rennes: Presses Universitaires de Rennes, 2008).

Garber, Peter M., "Famous First Bubbles," *The Journal of Economic Perspectives* 4 (1990): 35–54.

Garber, Peter M., *Famous First Bubbles: The Fundamentals of Early Manias* (Cambridge, Mass.: MIT Press, 2000).

Gauci, Perry, ed., *Regulating the British Economy 1660–1850* (Oxford: Oxford University Press, 2011).

Gelderblom, Oscar/Jonker, Joost, "Mirroring Different Follies: The Character of the 1720 Bubble in the Dutch Republic," in *The Great Mirror of Folly: Finance, Culture, and the Crash of 1720*, ed. William N. Goetzmann et al. (New Haven: Yale University Press, 2013), 121–139.

Ghachem, Malick W., "'No Body to Be Kicked?' Monopoly, Financial Crisis, and Popular Revolt in 18th-Century Haiti and America," *Law & Literature* (2016), 403–431.

Girard, Albert, "La réorganisation de la Compagnie des Indes (1719–1723), I: L'oeuvre de John Law (1719–1721)," *Revue d'histoire moderne et contemporaine* 11 (1908–1909): 5–34.

Giraud, Marcel, *Histoire de la Louisiane française*, vol. 3: *L'époque de John Law, 1717–1720* (Paris: Presses universitaires de France, 1966).

Glaisyer, Natasha, *The Culture of Commerce in England, 1660–1720* (London: Boydell Press, 2006).

Glete, Jan, "The Swedish Fiscal-Military State in Transition and Decline, 1650–1815," in *War, State and Development: Fiscal-Military States in the Eighteenth Century*, ed. Rafael Torres Sánchez (Pamplona: Ediciones Universidad de Navarra, 2007), 87–108.

Go, Sabine, *Marine Insurance in the Netherlands 1600–1780: A Comparative Institutional Approach* (Amsterdam: Amsterdam University Press, 2009).

Goetzmann, William N./Rouwenhorst, K. Geert, *The Origins of Value: The Financial Innovations That Created Modern Capital Markets* (New York: Oxford University Press, 2005).

Goetzmann, William N. et al., eds., *The Great Mirror of Folly: Finance, Culture, and the Crash of 1720* (New Haven: Yale University Press, 2013).

Goggin, Joyce, "Crise et comédie: Le Système de John Law dans le théâtre néerlandais," in *'Gagnons sans savoir comment:' Représentations du Système de Law au XVIIIe siècle à nos jours*, ed. Florence Magnot-Ogilvy (Rennes: Presses Universitaires de Rennes, 2017), 163–182.

Grauers, Sven, "De politiska relationerna mellan Arvid Bernhard Horn och Georg Heinrich von Görtz åren 1707–1719," *Karolinska förbundets årsbok* (1963): 159–208.

Grenier, Jean-Yves, "Ordre et désordre: Échange et marchés dans le mercantilisme anglais et français (XVIIe–XVIIIe siècle)," *Vierteljahrsschrift für Sozial- und Wirtschaftsgeschichte*, Beiheft 228 (2013), 83–111.

Groeneveld, Frederikus P., *De economische crisis van het jaar 1720* (Amsterdam: Universiteit van Amsterdam, 1949).

Harris, Ron, *Industrializing English Law: Entrepreneurship and Business Organization, 1720–1844* (Cambridge: Cambridge University Press, 2000).

Harsin, Paul, *Les doctrines monétaires et financières en France du XVIe au XVIIIe siècle* (Paris: F. Alcan, 1928).

Harsin, Paul, *Crédit public et banque d'Etat en France du XVIe au XVIIIe siècle* (Paris: Dros, 1933).

Harsin, Paul, "La création de la Compagnie d'Occident (1717): Contribution à l'histoire du système de Law," *Revue d'Histoire économique et sociale* 34 (1956): 9–41.

Hatton, Ragnhild M., *Charles XII of Sweden* (London: Weidenfeld and Nicolson, 1968).

Haudrère, Philippe, *La Compagnie française des Indes au XVIIIe siècle: 1719–1795*, rev. ed., 2 vols. (Paris: Les Indes Savantes Editions, 2005).

Hayden, Judy, "Of Windmills and Bubbles: Harlequin Faustus on the Eighteenth-Century State," *Huntington Library Quarterly* 77 (2014): 1–16.

Hayek, F.A., "Richard Cantillon," *Journal of Libertarian Studies* 7 (1985): 217–247.

Heckscher, Eli F., *Sveriges Ekonomiska Historia från Gustav Vasa. Första delen. Före frihetstiden*, 2 vols. (Stockholm: Bonniers, 1936).

Hémardinquer, Jean-Jacques, "Law, Liège et la reconstruction industrielle d'Arcis-sur-Aube en 1720," in *Actes du 95e congrès national des sociétés savantes, hist. mod., Reims, 1970*, 2 vols. (Paris: Bibliothèque nationale, 1974).

Herring, William R., "Neither Pistols nor Sugar-Plumbs: The Rhetoric of Finance and the 1720 Bubbles," *Advances in the History of Rhetoric* 21 (2018): 147–162.

Hersant, Marc, "Saint-Simon et Law: Poésie des finances, poésies du financier," in *'Gagnons sans savoir comment': Représentations du Système de Law du XVIIIe à nos jours*, ed. Florence Magnot-Ogilvy (Rennes: Presses universitaires de Rennes, 2017), 279–288.

Hill, B.W., "The Change of Government and the 'Loss of the City'," *Economic History Review* 24 (1971): 395–413.

Hoffman, P./ Postel-Vinay, G./Rosenthal, J., *Des marchés sans prix: Une économie politique du crédit à Paris, 1660–1870* (Paris: Ed. de l'Ecole des hautes études en sciences sociales, 2001).

Hoppit, Julian, *A Land of Liberty? England 1689–1727* (Oxford: Clarendon Press, 2000).

Hoppit, Julian, "The Myths of the South Sea Bubble," *Transactions of the Royal Historical Society* 12 (2002): 141–165.

Hoppit, Julian, *Britain's Political Economies: Parliament and Economic Life, 1660–1800* (Cambridge: Cambridge University Press, 2017).

Hunt, Lynn, "The Global Financial Origins of 1789," in *The French Revolution in Global Perspective*, ed. Suzanne Desan, Lynn Hunt, and William Max Nelson (Ithaca: Cornell University Press, 2013), 32–43.

Ingrassia, Catherine, Authorship, Commerce, and Gender in Early Eighteenth-Century England: A Culture of Paper Credit (Cambridge: Cambridge University Press, 1998).

John, A.H., "The London Assurance Company and the Marine Insurance Market of the Eighteenth Century," Economica 25 (1958): 126–141.

Julén, Jonatan, Om Sveriges statsskuld 1718 och betalningen av densamma (Gothenburg: Göteborgs Kungl. vetenskaps- och vitterhets-samhälle, 1916).

Kaiser, Thomas E., "Money, Despotism, and Public Opinion in Early Eighteenth-Century France: John Law and the Debate on Royal Credit," The Journal of Modern History 63 (1991): 1–28.

Kaiser, Thomas E./Van Kley, Dale, eds., From Deficit to Deluge: The Origins of the French Revolution (Stanford: Stanford University Press, 2011).

Kavanagh, Thomas M., *Enlightenment and the Shadows of Chance: The Novel and the Culture of Gambling in Eighteenth-Century France* (Baltimore and London: Johns Hopkins University Press, 1993).

Keynes, John M., *The General Theory of Employment Interest and Money* (1936; London: Macmillan, 1973).

Kindleberger, Charles P., *Manias, Panics and Crashes: A History of Financial Crises* (London: MacMillan Press, 1978).

Kindleberger, Charles P./Aliber, Robert Z., *Manias, Panics and Crashes: A History of Financial Crises*, 6th ed. (London: Palgrave Macmillan, 2011).

Kingston, Christopher, "Marine Insurance in Britain and America, 1720–1844," *Journal of Economic History* 67 (2007): 379–409.

Kleer, Richard, "'The Folly of Particulars': The Political Economy of the South Sea Bubble," *Financial History Review* 19 (2012): 175–197.

Kleer, Richard, "Riding a Wave: The Company's Role in the South Sea Bubble," *Economic History Review* 68 (2015): 264–285.

Kleer, Richard, *Money, Politics and Power: Banking and Public Finance in Wartime England, 1694–96* (London: Routledge, 2017).

Krelage, Ernst Heinrich, *Bloemenspeculatie in Nederland: De Tulpomanie van 1636–'37 end de Hyacintenhandel 1700–36* (Amsterdam: P.N. van Kampen en Zoon, 1942).

Lacombe, Robert, "Histoire monétaire de Saint-Domingue et de la République d'Haïti, des Origines à 1874," *Revue d'histoire des colonies* 152 (1956): 273–337.

Lamy, Céline, "Le carnaval des agioteurs: Critiques du pouvoir dans les récits de la banqueroute de Law," in *Fantaisie poétique et dérision des puissants: Études transversales*, ed. Élisabeth Gavoille (Tours: Université François Rabelais, 2011), 89–103.

Laurence, Anne, "Lady Betty Hastings, Her Half-Sisters, and the South Sea Bubble: Family Fortunes and Strategies," *Women's History Review* 15 (2006): 533–540.

Laurence, Anne, "Women Investors, 'That Nasty South Sea Affair' and the Rage to Speculate in Early Eighteenth-Century England," *Accounting, Business and Financial History* 16 (2006): 245–264.

Laurence, Anne, "Women, Banks and the Securities Market in Early Eighteenth-Century England," in *Women and Their Money 1700–1950: Essays on Women and Finance*, ed. Anne Laurence, Josephine Maltby, and Janette Rutterford (London and New York: Routledge, 2009), 46–58.

Laurence, Anne/Maltby, Josephine/Rutterford, Janette, ed., *Women and Their Money 1700–1950: Essays on Women and Finance* (London and New York: Routledge, 2009).

Levasseur, Émile, *Recherches historiques sur le Système de Law* (Paris: Guillaumin et Cie., 1854).

Lindeberg, Gösta, *Svensk ekonomisk politik under den Görtzka perioden* (Lund: Gleerup, 1941).

Lindegren, Jan, "Krig och skuld. Den svenska statsskuldens historia ca. 1600–1800," *Kungl. Vetenskapssamhällets i Uppsala Årsbok* (2007–2008): 81–110.
Linder, Nikolaus, "'Diess Jahr hat das grosse Unglück so allerorten in Franckreich, Engelland, Holland, Genf um sich gegriffen ...': Zu den Gründen für den Bankrott der ersten Berner Bank 1720," in *Globalisierung – Chancen und Risiken: Die Schweiz in der Weltwirtschaft 18.–20. Jahrhundert*, ed. Hans-Jörg Gilomen, Margrit Müller, and Béatrice Veyrassat (Zürich: Chronos, 2003), 87–98.
Linder, Nikolaus, *Die Berner Bankenkrise von 1720 und das Recht: Eine Studie zur Rechts-, Banken- und Finanzgeschichte der Alten Schweiz* (Zürich: Chronos, 2004).
Lüthy, Herbert, *La Banque protestante en France de la révocation de l'Edit de Nantes à la Révolution*, 2 vols. (Paris: S.E.V.P.E.N., 1959/1961).
MacDonald, James, "The Importance of Not Defaulting: The Significance of the Election of 1710," in *Questioning Credible Commitment: Perspectives on the Rise of Financial Capitalism*, ed. D'Maris Coffman, Adrian Leonard, and Larry Neal (Cambridge: Cambridge University Press, 2013), 125–146.
Magnot-Ogilvy, Florence, ed., *'Gagnons sans savoir comment': Représentations du système de Law du XVIIIe à nos jours* (Rennes: Presses Universitaires de Rennes, 2017).
Marion, Marcel, *Les impôts directs sous l'ancien régime principalement au 18:e siècle* (Paris: Cornély, 1910).
Martin, Thierry, ed., *Arithmétique Politique dans la France du XVIIIe siècle* (Paris: INED, 2003).
Mayer, Franz Martin, *Die Anfänge des Handels und der Industrie in Österreich und die orientalische Compagnie* (Innsbruck: Verlag der Wagner'schen Universitätsbuchhandlung, 1882).
McCloskey, Deirdre N., *Bourgeois Equality: How Ideas, Not Capital or Institutions, Enriched the World* (Chicago and London: University of Chicago Press, 2016).
McCollim, Gary B., *Louis XIV's Assault on Privilege: Nicolas Desmaretz and the Tax on Wealth* (Rochester: Rochester University Press, 2012).
Melville, Lewis, *The South Sea Bubble* (New York: Franklin, 1968).
Mitchell, Matthew David, "'Legitimate commerce' in the Eighteenth Century: The Royal African Company of England Under the Duke of Chandos 1720–1726," *Enterprise and Society* 14 (2013): 544–578.
Moulton, James R., *Peter the Great and the Russian Military Campaigns During the Final Years of the Great Northern War, 1719–1721* (Lanham: University Press of America, 2005).
Mulcaire, T., "Public Credit: Or the Feminization of Virtue in the Marketplace," *PMLA* 114 (1999): 1029–1042.
Murphy, Anne L., *The Origins of English Financial Markets: Investment and Speculation before the South Sea Bubble* (Cambridge: Cambridge University Press, 2009).
Murphy, Anne L., "Demanding 'Credible Commitment': Public Reactions to the Failures of the Early Financial Revolution," *Economic History Review* 66 (2013): 178–197.
Murphy, Anne L., "Financial Markets: The Limits of Economic Regulation in Early Modern England," in *Mercantilism Reimagined: Political Economy in Early Modern Britain and Its Empire*, ed. Philip J. Stern and Carl Wennerlind (Oxford: Oxford University Press, 2013), 263–281.
Murphy, Antoin E., *Richard Cantillon: Entrepreneur and Economist* (Oxford: Clarendon Press, 1986).

Murphy, Antoin E., "John Law and the Assignats," in *La Pensée économique pendant la Révolution Française*, ed. Philippe Steiner and Gilber Faccarello (Grenoble: Presses Universitaires, 1990), 431–448.

Murphy, Antoin E., *John Law: Economic Theorist and Policy-maker* (Oxford and New York: Clarendon Press, 1997).

Neal, Larry, *The Rise of Financial Capitalism: International Capital Markets in the Age of Reason* (Cambridge and New York: Cambridge University Press, 1990).

Neal, Larry, "'For God's Sake, Remitt Me': The Adventures of George Middleton, John Law's London Goldsmith-Banker, 1712–1729," *Business and Economic History* 23 (1994): 27–60.

Neal, Larry, "The Monetary, Financial and Political Architecture of Europe, 1648–1815," in *Exceptionalism and Industrialisation: Britain and Its European Rivals, 1688–1815*, ed. L. Prados de la Escosura (Cambridge: Cambridge University Press, 2004), 173–189.

Neal, Larry, *'I Am Not Master of Events': The Speculations of John Law and Lord Londonderry in the Mississippi and South Sea Bubbles* (New Haven and London: Yale University Press, 2012).

Neal, Larry/Quinn, Stephen, "Networks of Information, Markets, and Institutions in the Rise of London as a Financial Centre, 1660–1720," *Financial History Review* 8 (2001): 7–26.

Newman, Jennifer, "Anglo-Dutch Commercial Cooperation and the Russia Trade in the Eighteenth Century," in *The Interactions of Amsterdam and Antwerp with the Baltic Region, 1400–1800*, ed. Johanna Maria van Winter (Leiden: Nijhoff, 1983), 95–103.

Nova, Alessandro, *The Book of the Wind: Representations of the Invisible* (Montréal: McGill-Queen's University, 2011).

O'Brien, Patrick K., "The Political Economy of British Taxation, 1660–1815," *Economic History Review* 41 (1988): 1–32.

O'Brien, Patrick K., "The Rise of a Fiscal State in England, 1485–1815," *Historical Research* 66 (1993): 129–176.

O'Day, Rosemary, *Women's Agency in Early Modern Britain and the American Colonies* (London: Pearson and Longman, 2007).

Odlyzko, Andrew, "Newton's Financial Misadventures in the South Sea Bubble," Working Paper (2018)

O'Malley, Gregory E., *Final Passages: The Intercolonial Slave Trade of British America* (Chapel Hill: The University of North Carolina Press, 2014).

Orain, Arnaud, *La politique du merveilleux: Une autre histoire du Système de Law (1695–1795)* (Paris: Fayard, 2018).

Orain, Arnaud/Thézé, Laurent, "Publicité, contre-publicité et représentations économiques du système de Law: Le motif alchimique dans les poésies et chansons de la Régence," in *'Gagnons sans savoir comment' Représentations du système de Law du XVIIIe à nos jours*, ed. Florence Magnot-Ogilvy (Rennes: Presses Universitaires de Rennes, 2017), 129–148.

Orléan, André, *De l'euphorie à la panique: Penser la crise financière* (Paris: Ed. Rue d'Ulm, 2009).

Orléan, André, *The Empire of Value* (Cambridge, Mass.: MIT Press, 2014).

Ormrod, David, *The Rise of Commercial Empires: England and the Netherlands In the Age of Mercantilism, 1650–1770* (Cambridge: Cambridge University Press, 2003).

Parrish, David, "A Party Contagion: Party Politics and the Inoculation Controversy in the British Atlantic World, c. 1721–1723," *Journal for Eighteenth-Century Studies* 39 (2016): 41–58.
Perrot, Jean-Claude, *Une histoire intellectuelle de l'économie politique (XVIIe–XVIIIe siècle)* (Paris: Editions de l'EHESS, 1992).
Paul, Helen J., *The South Sea Bubble: An Economic History of Its Origins and Consequences* (London and New York: Routledge, 2011).
Paul, Helen J., "The Concept of *Wagnis* and the South Sea Bubble of 1720," in *Wagnisse: Risiken eingehen, Risiken analysieren, von Risiken erzählen*, ed. Stefan Brakensiek, Christoph Marx, and Benjamin Scheller (Frankfurt and New York: Campus Verlag, 2017), 111–126.
Petram, Lodewijk, *The World's First Stock Exchange* (New York: Columbia Business School Publishing, 2014).
Pettegree, Andrew, *The Invention of News: How the World Came to Know About Itself* (New Haven: Yale University Press, 2014).
Pettigrew, William A., *Freedom's Debt: The Royal African Company and the Politics of the Atlantic Slave Trade, 1675–1752* (Chapel Hill: Omohundro Institute of Early American History and Culture and University of North Carolina Press, 2013).
Phillips, Nicola, *Women in Business, 1700–1850* (Woodbridge: The Boydell Press, 2006).
Pincus, Steve, "Rethinking Mercantilism: Political Economy, the British Empire, and the Atlantic World in the Seventeenth and Eighteenth Centuries," *William & Mary Quarterly* 69 (2012): 3–34.
Piola Caselli, Fausto, ed., *Government Debts and Financial Markets in Europe* (London: Pickering & Chatto, 2008).
Platt, Virginia B., "The East India Company and the Madagascar Slave Trade," *William and Mary Quarterly* 26 (1969): 548–577.
Plumb, J.H., *The Growth of Political Stability in England, 1675–1725* (Atlantic Highlands: Humanities Press, 1967).
Poitras, Geoffrey, *The Early History of Financial Economics, 1478–1776: From Commercial Arithmetic to Life Annuities and Joint Stocks* (Cheltenham and Northampton: E. Elgar, 2000).
Prados de la Escosura, L., ed., *Exceptionalism and Industrialisation: Britain and Its European Rivals, 1688–1815* (Cambridge: Cambridge University Press, 2004).
Priemel, Kim Christian, "Spekulation als Gegenstand historischer Forschung," *Jahrbuch für Wirtschaftsgeschichte* (2013): 9–26.
Pritchard, James S., *In Search of Empire: The French in the Americas, 1670–1730* (New York: Cambridge University Press, 2004).
Prügl, Elisabeth, "'If Lehman Brothers Had Been Lehman Sisters …': Gender and Myth in the Aftermath of the Financial Crisis," *International Political Sociology* 6 (2012): 21–35.
Puning, Ernst, "Transnationality and the Brazilian Slave Trade: The Case of the Corisco Company (1715–1730)," in *La Guinée Équatoriale aux Archives Nationales (XVIIIe – Début XXe Siècles)*, ed. Valérie Wulf (Paris: L'Harmattan, 2015), 71–94.
Randall, Adrian, *Riotous Assemblies: Popular Protest in Hanoverian England* (Oxford: Oxford University Press, 2006).
Reinert, Erik S. et al., *80 Economic Bestsellers before 1850: A Fresh Look at the History of Economic Thought*, Research Paper (2017).

Reinert, Sophus A., *Translating Empire. Emulation and the Origins of Political Economy* (Cambridge, Mass.: Harvard University Press, 2011).
Reinert, Sophus A., "Rivalry: Greatness in Early Modern Political Economy," in *Mercantilism Reimagined: Political Economy in Early Modern Britain and Its Empire*, ed. Philip J. Stern and Carl Wennerlind (Oxford: Oxford University Press, 2013), 384–370.
Ring, Victor, *Asiatische Handlungscompagnien Friedrichs des Großen: Ein Beitrag zur Geschichte des preußischen Seehandels und Aktienwesens* (Berlin: Carl Heymanns Verlag, 1890).
Roberds, William/Velde, François, "Early Public Banks," *Federal Reserve Bank of Chicago Working Paper Series* 7 (2014): 1–92.
Rogers, Nicholas, *Crowds, Culture, and Politics in Georgian Britain* (Oxford: Clarendon Press, 1998).
Rosenhaft, Eve, "Women and Financial Knowledge in Eighteenth-Century Germany," in *Women and Their Money: Essays on Women and Finance 1700–1950*, ed. Anne Laurence, Josephine Maltby, and Janette Rutterford (London: Routledge, 2008), 59–72.
Rosenhaft, Eve, "'All That Glitters is not Gold, but …': German Responses to the Financial Bubbles of 1720," in *Money in the German-Speaking Lands*, ed. Mary Lindemann and Jared Poley (Oxford and Providence: Berghahn, 2017), 74–95.
Rothschild, Emma, "An Alarming Commercial Crisis in Eighteenth-Century Angoulême: Sentiments in Economic History," *Economic History Review* 51 (1998): 268–293.
Rowlands, Guy, *The Financial Decline of a Great Power: War, Influence, and Money in Louis XIV's France* (Oxford: Oxford University Press, 2012).
Ryder, Michael, "The Bank of Ireland, 1721: Land, Credit and Dependency," *Historical Journal* 25 (1982): 557–582.
Samuelson, Paul, "Proof that Properly Anticipated Prices Fluctuate Randomly," *Industrial Management Review* 6 (1965): 41–49.
Sayous, André.-E., "L'affaire de Law et les Genevois," *Revue d'Histoire Suisse* 17 (1937): 310–340.
Schmidt, Karl-Heinz, "Geldwirtschaft, Banken und Finanzen," in *Im Auftrag der Krone: Friedrich Karl von Hardenberg und das Leben in Hannover um 1750*, ed. Wilken von Bothmer and Marcus Köhler (Rostock: Hinstorff, 2011), 93–99.
Schubert, E., *The Ties That Bound: Eighteenth Century Market Behavior in Foreign Exchange, International Goods, and Financial Assets*, unpublished Ph.D. dissertation (Urbana-Champaign, 1986).
Schulte Beerbühl, Margrit, *The Forgotten Majority: German Merchants in London, Naturalization, and Global Trade 1660–1815* (New York and Oxford: Berghahn, 2007).
Schumpeter, Joseph, *History of Economic Analysis* (London, G. Allen and Unwin, 1955).
Scott, William R., *The Constitution and Finance of English, Scottish, and Irish Joint-stock Companies to 1720*, 3 vols. (Cambridge: Cambridge University Press, 1912).
Shea, Gary S., "Financial Market Analysis Can Go Mad (in the Search for Irrational Behaviour During the South Sea Bubble)," *Economic History Review* 60 (2007): 742–765.
Shea, Gary S., *(Re)financing the Slave Trade with the Royal African Company in the Boom Markets of 1720*, CDMA Working Paper Series 201114, Centre for Dynamic Macroeconomic Analysis (St. Andrews, 2011).
Sheehan, Jonathan/Wahrman, Dror, *Invisible Hands: Self-Organization and the Eighteenth Century* (Chicago: The University of Chicago Press, 2015).

Sherman, Sandra, "Credit, Simulation, and the Ideology of Contract in the Early Eighteenth Century," *Eighteenth-Century Life* 19 (1995): 86–102.

Sherman, Sandra, *Finance and Fictionality in the Early Eighteenth Century, Accounting for Defoe* (Cambridge: Cambridge University Press, 1996).

Shovlin, John, "Jealousy of Credit: John Law's 'System' and the Geopolitics of Financial Revolution," *Journal of Modern History* 88 (2016): 275–305.

Slauter, Will, "Forward-Looking Statements: News and Speculation in the Age of the American Revolution," *The Journal of Modern History* 81 (2009): 759–792.

Slechte, C.H., "De Maatschappij van Assurantie, Disonteering en Beleening der stad Rotterdam van 1720, bekeken naar haar produktiefactoren over de periode 1720–1874," *Rotterdams Jaarboekje* 7 (1970): 252–310.

Slechte, C.H., *Een Noodlottig Jaar voor veel Zotte en Wijze: De Rotterdamse Windhandel van 1720* (The Hague: Martinus Nijhoff, 1982).

Sonenscher, Michael, "The Nation's Debt and the Birth of the Modern Republic: The French Fiscal Deficit and the Politics of the Revolution of 1789," *History of Political Thought* 2 (1997): 267–325.

Spang, Rebecca, "The Ghost of Law: Speculating on Money, Memory and Mississippi in the French Constituent Assembly," *Historical Reflections* 31 (2005): 3–25.

Spang, Rebecca, *Stuff and Money in the Time of the French Revolution* (Cambridge, Mass.: Harvard University Press, 2015).

Sprinchorn, C.K.S., "Madagaskar och dess sjöröfvare i Karl XII:s historia," *Karolinska förbundets årsbok* (1921): 241–276.

Stäheli, Urs, *Spectacular Speculation: Thrills, the Economy, and Popular Discourse* (Stanford: Stanford University Press, 2013).

Stasavage, David, "Partisan Politics and Public Debt: The Importance of the 'Whig Supremacy' for Britain's Financial Revolution," *European Review of Economic History* 11 (2007): 123–153.

Staves, Susan, *Married Women's Separate Property in England, 1660–1833* (Cambridge, Mass.: Harvard University Press, 1990).

Steensgaard, Niels, "The Companies as a Specific Institution in the History of European Expansion," in *Companies and Trade: Essays on Overseas Trading Companies During the Ancien Régime*, ed. Leonard Blussé and Femme Gaastra (Leiden: Leiden University Press, 1981), 245–264.

Stern, Philip J./Wennerlind, Carl, eds., *Mercantilism Reimagined: Political Economy in Early Modern Britain and Its Empire* (Oxford: Oxford University Press, 2013).

Stiglitz, Joseph E., "Symposium on Bubbles," *Journal of Economic Perspectives* 4 (1990): 13–18.

Stratmann, Silke, *Myths of Speculation: The South Sea Bubble and 18th-Century English Literature* (Munich: Wilhelm Fink, 2000).

Supple, Barry, *The Royal Exchange Assurance: A History of British Insurance 1720–1970* (Cambridge: Cambridge University Press, 1970).

Swingen, Abigail L., *Competing Visions of Empire: Labor, Slavery, and the Origins of the British Atlantic Empire* (New Haven: Yale University Press, 2015).

Temin, Peter/Voth, Hans-Joachim, "Riding the South Sea Bubble," *American Economic Review* 94 (2004): 1654–1668.

Temin, Peter/Voth, Hans-Joachim, *Prometheus Shackled: Goldsmith Banks and England's Financial Revolution After 1700* (Oxford: Oxford University Press, 2013).

Torres Sánchez, Rafael, ed., *War, State and Development: Fiscal-Military States in the Eighteenth Century* (Pamplona: Ediciones Universidad de Navarra, 2007).

Troickij, S.M., "Le Système de John Law et ses continuateurs russes," in *La Russie et l'Europe, XVIe–Xxe siècles*, ed. Fernand Braudel et al. (Paris: S.E.V.P.E.N., 1970), 31–69.

Ullmann, Hans-Peter, *Der Staat, die Spieler und das Glück: Lotterien im Deutschland des 18. und 19. Jahrhunderts* (Berlin: de Gruyter, 1991).

Van Rijn, G., *De Aktiehandel in 1720 te Rotterdam en de Maatschappij van Assurantie, Discontering en Beleening dezer Stad* (Rotterdam, 1899).

Velde, François R., "Government Equity and Money: John Law's System in 1720 France," (2004), http://www.heraldica.org/econ/law.pdf, last visit 22.04.2019.

Velde, François R., "John Law's System," *The American Economic Review* 97 (2007): 276–279.

Velde, François R., "French Public Finance between 1683 and 1726," in *Government Debts and Financial Markets in Europe*, ed. Fausto Piola Caselli (London: Pickering & Chatto, 2008), 135–165.

Velde, François R., "Was John Law's System a Bubble? The Mississippi Bubble Revisited," in *The Origins and Development of Financial Markets and Institutions: From the Seventeenth Century to the Present*, ed. Jeremy Attack and Larry Neal (Cambridge and New York: Cambridge University Press, 2009), 99–120.

Velde, François R., "Introduction," in *Lettres sur le Visa des dettes de l'État ordonné en 1721*, ed. François-Michel Chrétien-Deschamps and François R. Velde (Paris: Classiques Garnier, 2015), ix–lxiv.

Villain, Jean, "Le rôle de la capitation extraordinaire de 1722," *Revue historique de droit français et étranger* 32 (1954): 108–116.

Voth, Hans-Joachim, "Blowing Early Bubbles: Rational Exuberance in the South Sea and Mississippi Bubbles," in *The Great Mirror of Folly: Finance, Culture, and the Crash of 1720*, ed. William N. Goetzmann et al. (New Haven: Yale University Press, 2013), 89–97.

Walsh, Patrick, "The Bubble on the Periphery: Scotland and the South Sea Bubble," *Scottish Historical Review* 91 (2012): 106–124.

Walsh, Patrick, *The South Sea Bubble and Ireland: Money, Banking and Investment, 1690–1721* (Woodbridge: The Boydell Press, 2014).

Weir, David, "Tontines, Public Finance, and Revolution in France and England, 1688–1789," *The Journal of Economic History* 49 (1989): 95–124.

Wells, John/Wills, Douglas, "Revolution, Restoration, and Debt Repudiation: The Jacobite Threat to England's Institutions and Economic Growth," *Journal of Economic History* 60 (2000): 418–441.

Wennerlind, Carl, *Casualties of Credit: The English Financial Revolution, 1620–1720* (Cambridge, Mass.: Harvard University Press, 2011).

Yamamoto, Koji, "Piety, Profit and Public Service in the Financial Revolution," *English Historical Review* 126 (2011): 806–834.

Yamamoto, Koji, "Beyond Rational vs Irrational Bubbles: James Brydges the First Duke of Chandos During the South Sea Bubble," in *Le crisi finanziarie: Gestione, implicazioni sociali e conseguenze nell'età preindustriale. Selezione di ricerche*, ed. Giampiero Nigro (Firenze: Firenze University Press, 2016), 327–357.

Yamamoto, Koji, *Taming Capitalism Before Its Triumph: Public Service, Distrust, & Projecting in Early Modern England* (Oxford: Oxford University Press, 2018).
Zabel, Christine, "Challenges of Food Security: Free Trade, Distribution and Political (In) Stability in Mid 18th Century France," *European Journal of Security Research* 3 (2018): 35–50.

Index

https://doi.org/10.1515/9783110592139-017